How Sondheim Found His Sound

How Sondheim Found His Sound

Steve Swayne

UNIVERSITY OF MICHIGAN PRESS
Ann Arbor

Published in the United States of America by
The University of Michigan Press
Manufactured in the United States of America
♾ Printed on acid-free paper

2008 2007 2006 2005 4 3 2 1

A CIP catalog record for this book is available from the British Library.

Library of Congress Cataloging-in-Publication Data

Swayne, Steve, 1957–
How Sondheim found his sound / Steve Swayne.
p. cm.
Includes bibliographical references (p.) and index.
ISBN 0-472-11497-2 (cloth : alk. paper) 1. Sondheim, Stephen—
Criticism and interpretation. I. Title.
ML410.S6872S93 2005
782.1'4'092—dc22 2005002481

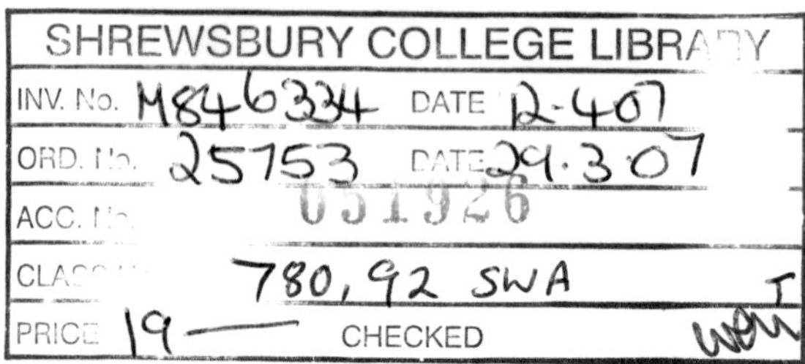

to my parents

Louis Swayne, Jr. and
Lelia Catherine Swayne

for their high expectations,
great sacrifices
and boundless love

Acknowledgments

This book represents the culmination of work that began more than fifteen years ago in a classroom at the University of Washington. I had no idea that a term paper on *Merrily We Roll Along* would lead to graduate study at the University of California at Berkeley, a serendipitous lunch with an outgoing professor there, and a stimulating apprenticeship with an incoming one. Neither did I think that a letter from Sondheim—the first of many, as it happened—would lead me to abandon my plan to mine my doctoral thesis for this book and choose instead to prospect another, more challenging claim.

There have been many who have assisted me thus far, and if I fail to name them all in these pages, it is one more of the errors this book undoubtedly contains. I take full responsibility for these errors, even as I take pleasure in thanking those who have helped me get a few things right.

Among my academic colleagues, pride of place must go to Larry Starr, who taught that class in Seattle. His curious spirit and unorthodox views gave me courage to begin down this path. Thanks also to Stephen Rumph, a former Berkeley colleague who, as of this writing, is Larry's colleague. He invited me to return to Seattle and share a little of what I've learned over the years. Thank you both.

The list of Berkeley supporters is necessarily longer. Joseph Kerman counseled me over lunch, and he occasionally still follows up on me. Wye Jamison Allanbrook and I talked about the importance of Jane Powell and Doris Day in our lives. Katherine Bergeron endured more than any advisor should be called upon to endure. And my student colleagues at Berkeley gave me courage to continue. Thanks to all of you, especially Danielle Fosler-Lussier and David Schneider. You two helped me stay on track in so many ways.

My colleagues at Dartmouth College are also numerous and supportive. Sondheim is not Bill Summers's thing, but Bill has never flagged in encouraging me to become the best scholar I could. Ted Levin critiqued my early work and sketched out a trail for me to blaze. Jon Appleton, Larry Polansky, and Melinda O'Neal offered perspectives and incentives that I needed. Jennifer Matsue Milioto gave me permission to write this book and not a different one. Mark Williams, Lynn Higgins, and Mary Desjardins opened my mind to discoveries in their fields. Sydney Stowe and Bill Pence were gracious with their time and resources. Jane Carroll was always eager to talk Broadway with me and find funding for me. Jamshed Bharucha and Lenore Grenoble gave me confidence to keep on working. And Jean Callahan helped me to arrange the tasks of life in their correct order. Thank you all.

I am grateful to the Dartmouth students who have looked over my work and have wrestled with me on some of the issues presented in these pages. Jason, Daniel, Lisa, Greg, Carl, John B., Nathan, Tyler, Kamil, Oliver, Justin G., Jamie, Laura, Bill, Clinton, Craig, Amanda, Alison, Amish, Shayne, Andrea, Justin M., Eric, Emily, Wendy, Lauren, Derek, Christena: you all helped me more than you will know. Tom: thanks for the good research and probing questions you provided. And Brian: "as iron sharpens iron . . ."

Other people in other places also have made this book possible. Geoffrey Block, John Breglio, Patricia Chute, Mark Dinham, Wayne Dynes, Lara Housez, Michael H. Hutchins, Nancy Kieffer, Gregory King and Peter Sultan, Linda Kirland, Ray Knapp, Kim Kowalke, Jim Leve, Ralph Locke, Cathy Loeb, James Lovensheimer, Stephen Murray, Gregory Nigosian, Richard Rosendall, Paul Salsini, Caldwell Titcomb, Paul Varnell, John and Lynn Wadhams, Scott Warfield: there are traces of all of you in these pages. Thank you.

Then there are the institutions that have made this book possible. A grant from the Woodrow Wilson National Fellowship Foundation gave me time to write this book, and the other fellows gave me motivation to extend my reach. The staff at the Wisconsin Center for Film and Theater Research at the University of Wisconsin made research there a pleasure. Special thanks go to the members of the AMS Publications Committee for their subvention from the Lloyd Hibberd Publication Endowment Fund of the American Musicological Society. Other colleagues in the AMS (especially the New England chapter) and the Society for American Music have helped me refine some of my ideas over the years. The newsletters and news from the Sondheim Society (United Kingdom) have broadened my understanding and appreciation for Sondheim. And the good people of Opera North (Lebanon, New Hampshire) have always been kind and encouraging.

The world of publishing creates its own list of those who aid and comfort. Thanks to Mary Francis at the University of California Press, Gayle Sherwood and Jeffrey Magee at Indiana University Press, and Michael Flamini at Palgrave, all of whom, in various ways, helped this book arrive safely in Ann Arbor. The same goes for Rosemary Gawelko, Hope Chirino, Juliet Perez, Arminda Trevino, Victoria Traube, Robin Walton, Frank Korach, Marie Carter, Melinda Mondrala, and Clemens Morgenroth, who provided permissions for copyrighted material. Myrna Katz Frommer and Harvey Frommer, whose last-minute gift was an unexpected delight, are angels. Chris Hebert at the University of Michigan Press has been a remarkable editor, and my indebtedness to him will continue long after I finish writing this. And I thank him especially for inviting Polly Fallows to serve as my text editor. Both Chris and I can avouch that you have been a joy to work with.

Four other colleagues helped in unexpected ways. Linda Hall at Williams College has answered my every query with the thoroughness that her job demands and an amiability that transcends it. Stephen Banfield at the University of Bristol has cheered and challenged me as I followed him in an enterprise that he has already treated in impressive detail. Mark Eden Horowitz at the Library of Congress lent both his professional skills and his personal interest to advise and direct me. And Charles Hamm in Norwich, Vermont, offered guidance that was as invaluable as it was timely. I thank you all for making this book stronger, and I apologize for those passages where I failed to heed your counsel.

Words hardly suffice to thank those who remain. Paul McKibbins (Rilting Music): I will always remember our first meeting, your question about Sondheads, and your kind words and gentle interventions on my behalf. Maxyne Lang (Williamson Music): I have yet to meet you in person, and yet already I owe you so much. Steven Clar: How you manage to do all the things you do, I will never know. Stephen Sondheim: I will always marvel at how generous you have been in making your work and your thoughts available to me. Thank you.

And Mike Backman: For the birthday gift twelve years ago of every Sondheim Broadway score, for the daily gift of your love, and for so much more: thank you.

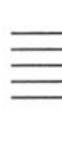

Contents

A Chronology of Sondheim's Creative Career

1946 *By George* (musical; book, music, and lyrics by Miriam Dubin, James Lincoln, and Steve Sondheim; George School)

1948 *Phinney's Rainbow* (musical; book and lyrics by Stephen Sondheim and Josiah T. S. Horton; Williams College)

1949 *All That Glitters* (musical; book by Stephen Sondheim; Williams College)
(ca.) *Bequest* (novel; abandoned)
Variations on a Theme (Katie Malone) for Piano

1950 Sonata for Piano in C major
"No Sad Songs for Me" (song in revue, *Where To From Here*, Williams College)
Mary Poppins (musical; abandoned)

1951 *High Tor* (musical; abandoned)
I Know My Love (play by S. N. Berman; song, a Christmas carol)
Sonata in G minor for Violin Solo ("A Very Short Violin Sonata")

1952 (ca.) Concertino for Two Pianos (three out of a projected four movements)

1953 *Topper* (screenplays for television series [with George Oppenheimer])
Climb High (musical; unproduced)
The Man with the Squeaky Shoes (television show; unproduced)

1954 *The Lady or the Tiger?* (television musical [with Mary Rodgers]; song, "I Wonder Why"; unproduced)

Saturday Night (musical, first version; book by Julius J. Epstein)

1955 *A Mighty Man Is He* (play by George Oppenheimer and Arthur Kober; song, "Rag Me That Mendelssohn March")
The Madwoman of Chaillot (musical treatment; based on play by Jean Giraudoux; abandoned)

1956 *The Girls of Summer* (play by N. Richard Nash; song, "The Girls of Summer")
I Believe in You (television play; song, "They Ask Me Why I Believe in You"; unproduced)
The Last Resorts (musical; song, "Pour le sport"; abandoned)

1957 *West Side Story* (musical; lyrics; music by Leonard Bernstein; book by Arthur Laurents)
Ring Round the Moon (musical; abandoned)

1958 *The Jet-Propelled Couch* (television musical; abandoned)

1959 *Gypsy* (musical; lyrics; music by Jule Styne; book by Arthur Laurents)
Happily Ever After (television musical; abandoned)

1960 *Invitation to a March* (play by Arthur Laurents; incidental music)

1962 *A Funny Thing Happened on the Way to the Forum* (musical; book by Burt Shevelove and Larry Gelbart)
The World According to Jules Feiffer (revue by Jules Feiffer; song, "Truly Content," and incidental music for *Passionella;* incidental music for monologue, *George's Moon*)

1963 *Hot Spot* (musical; music [with Mary Rodgers]; lyrics [with Martin Charnin]; book by Jack Weinstock and Willie Gilbert; two songs: "Don't Laugh" and "That's Good, That's Bad")

1964 *Anyone Can Whistle* (musical; book by Arthur Laurents)

1965 *Do I Hear a Waltz?* (musical; lyrics; music by Richard Rodgers; book by Arthur Laurents)

1966 *Evening Primrose* (television musical; screenplay by James Goldman)
The Mad Show (revue; book by Larry Siegel and Stan Hart; song: "The Boy From. . . ," lyrics by "Estaban Ria Nido")

1968 *The Exception and the Rule* (alternately, *The Race to Urga* and *A Pray by Blecht*) (musical; lyrics; music by Leonard Bernstein; book by John Guare; abandoned)
crossword puzzles for *New York* magazine

1969 *The Thing of It Is* (film; screenplay by William Goldman; song, "No, Mary Ann"; unproduced)

1970 *Company* (musical; book by George Furth)

1971 *Follies* (musical; book by James Goldman)
Twigs (one-act plays by George Furth; incidental music)

1973 *A Little Night Music* (musical; book by Hugh Wheeler)
The Last of Sheila (film; coauthor with Anthony Perkins)
The Enclave (play by Arthur Laurents; incidental music)

1974 *Candide* (musical; additional lyrics; music by Leonard Bernstein; book by Hugh Wheeler)
Stavisky . . . (film score; Alain Resnais, director)
The Frogs (musical; book by Burt Shevelove)

1976 *Pacific Overtures* (musical; book by John Weidman; additional material by Hugh Wheeler)
Side by Side by Sondheim (musical revue)
The Seven Per Cent Solution (film; song: "I Never Do Anything Twice")

1979 *Sweeney Todd* (musical; book by Hugh Wheeler)
Madwoman of Central Park West (play; book by Phyllis Newman and Arthur Laurents; two songs [see *Hot Spot*, 1963])

1980 *Marry Me a Little* (musical revue; book by Craig Lucas)

1981 *Merrily We Roll Along* (musical; book by George Furth)
Reds (portion of film score; Warren Beatty, director; song: "Goodbye for Now")

1984 *Sunday in the Park with George* (musical; James Lapine, director)

1985 *Merrily We Roll Along* (La Jolla production; additional material by James Lapine)

1987 *Follies* (revised for London production)
Into the Woods (musical; book by James Lapine)

1990 *Dick Tracy* (film; Warren Beatty, director; five songs: "Sooner or Later (I Always Get My Man)," "More," "Live Alone and Like It," "Back in Business," and "What Can You Lose?")

1991 *Assassins* (musical; book by John Weidman)

1992 *Putting It Together* (musical revue)
Singing Out Loud (film musical; screenplay by William Goldman; songs: "Dawn," "Sand," "Water Under the Bridge," others; unproduced)

1994 *Passion* (musical; book by James Lapine)

1995 *The Doctor Is Out* (play, coauthor with George Furth; San Diego)

1996 *Getting Away with Murder* (new name for *The Doctor Is Out;* New York)
The Birdcage (film; two songs: "Little Dream" and "It Takes All Kinds" [cut])

1997 *Saturday Night* (premiere in London)

1999 *Saturday Night* (premiere in Chicago)
Wise Guys (workshop production; book by John Weidman; later, *Gold!*, then *Bounce*)

2000 *Moving On* (musical revue)

2003 *Bounce* (musical; Chicago and Washington, D.C., productions)

2004 *The Frogs* (revised by Nathan Lane; Broadway premiere)
Opening Doors (musical revue; revision of *Moving On*)

Introduction

As he and Mark Eden Horowitz wound up their discussion on the musical *Assassins,* Stephen Sondheim offered a description of himself and of his working method.

> I've discovered over a period of years that essentially I'm a playwright who writes with song, and that playwrights are actors. And what I do is I act. So what I'll do [later today] is: I'll go upstairs, and I'll get back into the character of Wilson Mizner, and I'll start singing to myself. It'll take me a while to make that transition, because it's been a couple of days since I've been Wilson, but I'll get upstairs, and I'll be Wilson.[1]

Upstairs, of course, refers to the brownstone in Turtle Bay, not far from the United Nations headquarters in Manhattan. When Sondheim moved in, Katharine Hepburn, who lived next door, complained about the duration and volume of his piano playing. Sondheim began his creative life as a pianist. Of his own volition, he composed; he wrote lyrics out of necessity. And acting for him, in a traditional sense, was more or less limited to college.

Acting for Sondheim also included a fair amount of vicarious projection, given his well-documented love of film. "I think cinematically when I'm writing songs, and I stage them . . . in my head. And I realize that I stage them like a movie."[2] Not only does Sondheim act when he composes, but he also directs the action.

Sondheim's comments to Horowitz about *Passion,* the character of Fosca, and the actress who played her further expand what Sondheim meant about being a playwright, composer, and director.

> When Donna Murphy auditioned for us, we gave her ["Fosca's Entrance"]. Her audition performance could have gone on stage that night. She's intelligent. There's something in her that identified with the character right away, and I write careful scenes. I say this with no

> modesty at all: When I'm writing dramatic stuff, I'm a playwright. This is a worked-out scene, and I can instruct the actress how to play this scene, and the music is part of the dialogue. I can tell her why the music gets quick *here*, why it gets slow *here*, why there's a ritard *there*, why there's a so-called key change *here*, why it suddenly goes up and down—all of that—because I have reasons. Now the actress may choose to ignore them, but Donna, who was just auditioning, did not have a chance to ask me, but she understood it. And this piece is psychologically very well laid out, and all it takes is a good actress to understand it exactly. It's one of the reasons why actors like to sing my stuff, because I'm essentially a playwright in song, and I'm not asking them to sing songs, I'm asking them to play scenes. It doesn't matter whether they're in 32 bars or 33 bars or 109 bars or six minutes. One of the reasons it convinces you is because psychologically it's true.[3]

Marni Nixon, the voice behind so many sopranos in Hollywood musicals, made a similar observation about the psychological truth in a Sondheim song. After comparing his music to modern art, where context helps to determine meaning, she spoke of how "his melodies and his lyrics are so wed together. It's almost like they have to be done the way they're set up on the page. That doesn't mean that you have to do them personality-less or anything. But you find the essence of the song like Mozart: what is musically correct becomes dramatically correct. You find the character through the song."[4] Such a discovery of character through song is possible because Sondheim has set himself the task of "do[ing] things musically to . . . make the character."[5]

So what does Sondheim draw upon when he goes upstairs to make a character? His training as a pianist, theorist, and composer; his knowledge of classical music and of Tin Pan Alley, Broadway, and Hollywood song; his life in the theater, onstage, backstage, and in the pit; his love of film, which gave him two of the happiest moments of his creative career:[6] all of these influences factor into his creation of a character through song. And all of these influences can be seen in Sondheim's development as a creative artist from his adolescence up to his breakthrough musical, *Company* (1970), and beyond.

This book attempts to show that many of these elements were solidly in place long before *Company*. Sondheim himself said that he gradually discovered that he was a playwright to his core. Just as this self-awareness dawned slowly upon Sondheim, so too did time slowly give him the creative ingredients that he mixes together as a playwright in song. And while Sondheim has continued to grow and change post-*Company*, these creative ingredients filled his cupboard even before *A Funny Thing Hap-*

pened on the Way to the Forum (1962), his first commercial success as composer-lyricist. Combining the ingredients in novel ways would occupy Sondheim for his entire creative life, but most of the ingredients—the musical language, the theatrical and cinematic sensibilities—were already coming into his possession by the time he graduated from Williams College in 1950. This book provides an early inventory of the cupboard, an early account of how Sondheim found his sound.

And as should be clear from the outset, "sound," in Sondheim's case, means much more than music. If the actions and thoughts of a character affect changes of tempo and key, then an analysis of how a character comes to act or think is just as important in exploring Sondheim's sound as is a melodic or harmonic analysis. Thus, we cannot understand his sound by considering the music alone. We must go upstairs and try to be Sondheim. We must draw upon music, theater, and film to begin to enter Sondheim's sound world.

His remarks over the years and his predilections for certain eras of artistic exploration help to direct us. Thus, a question naturally arises: Can we trust Sondheim to be honest with us about his own thoughts and actions? The question is raised not in disrespect but as a caution. Sondheim, after all, is human, and like all humans, he can tell the truth, misremember the truth, embellish the truth, or reinvent the truth. (Stravinsky was especially good at the latter two.) All indications suggest that Sondheim has never been one deliberately to gild the lily or mislead his pursuers. It is unlikely that he has taken up duplicity late in life.

Taking Sondheim's remarks and songs as a starting point, then, this book offers a biography of his style. Its aims are modest, adhering to the fields of "biographical" inquiry as Sondheim has discussed them and eschewing theoretical approaches that ride madly off in all directions (to borrow a favorite quotation of Sondheim's).[7] It seeks to discover his creative universe, to look at his influences and at how he has incorporated them.

One last prolegomenon, therefore, is needed: the question and place of influence, especially since the idea of influence has been problematized in recent years. Joseph Straus succinctly summarized three major strands of influence theory: (1) "influence as immaturity," where "capable artists . . . are less and less susceptible to influence as they mature, until they eventually attain a unique and personal voice"; (2) "influence as generosity," where "susceptibility to influence . . . is a sign not of incapacity but of value—the more fully the tradition is assimilated, the better the artist," a strand of which the best-known proponent is T. S. Eliot; and (3) "influence as anxiety," where the artist is engaged in a creative Oedi-

pal struggle that "seeks artistic freedom by symbolically killing the precursor-parent," a view most famously promoted by Harold Bloom.[8] Indeed, the notion of the "anxiety of influence" has by now taken on the air of an inexorable truth. According to this third view, every modern artist wrestles mightily with the art and artists of the past, eager to overcome the anxiety the past induces.

Sondheim feels no such anxiety. As this book will demonstrate more fully, Sondheim has spoken often and freely about the music, theater, and films he likes, and on occasion has made explicit references to how past works crop up in his own work. He has also freely acknowledged his own eclecticism, seeing in it neither a curse nor a blessing but a fact of his creative life. Addressing these influences and unraveling the eclecticism becomes a project that, in many ways, Sondheim assuredly invites the acute viewer-listener to undertake. A scholar whose métier is critical theory might impute anxiety to Sondheim's influences, but such an imputation lies outside the scope of the project at hand.

Of the three options Straus offers, then, Sondheim would seem to fit best into the second category, that of generous assimilation of a given tradition. This presumes, though, a certain degree of artistic freedom that, truth be told, does not exist fully within the for-profit theater. Eliot may have been free to be generous in acknowledging his predecessors, but in musical theater, one is obliged to abide by the conventions and not to rock too many boats if one expects to draw an audience. For all of Sondheim's pioneering accomplishments, he remains a man bound by the traditions of his genre—and bound by choice, not out of anxiety or immaturity or even generosity. One might call it an influence of necessity, as Sondheim not only internalizes the influences of his youth but externalizes them regularly to remind himself and the larger community of musical theater practitioners and aficionados of his place within that community. The traces of the past are as clear in Sondheim's art as are the breaks with that past, and both already begin to appear in Sondheim's supposed immaturity.

Let us, then, begin to explore these traces and breaks, these influences. Let us begin the kaleidoscopic journey into Sondheim's sound. And let us begin where Sondheim begins whenever he speaks of his musical influences: with classical music.

I

Sondheim the Classicist

The American musical theater is filled with composers who wrote, performed, knew, and loved classical music. Herbert, Romberg, Friml, Weill, Blitzstein, Loewe, Bernstein, Coleman, Kander: Sondheim is hardly unique. Each of these composers would favor different composers, sounds, and techniques from the classical realm and would combine them in unique ways. Add to this Sondheim's early inclination toward drama—perhaps abetted by a childhood filled with drama—and we begin to understand how his sound differs from those of his predecessors and peers, as he crafted a distinctive musical amalgam wed to character and situation in a way that few other composers would rival.

Sondheim's emergence as an aficionado of classical music was in no way assured. His love of music certainly goes back to his early years—at least to the age of five—and was driven from the start by his love of innovation and technology. The adult collector of games is foreshadowed in the child's fascination with his parents' Capehart phonograph player, with its arm that could turn discs over automatically. He soon became fascinated by the music the phonograph played, mostly "pop records and whatever show tunes there were,"[1] in keeping with the music that was made in the Sondheim household. His dressmaker father Herbert was a self-taught pianist who regaled guests and clients alike with his renditions of Broadway favorites. Herbert's oldest son began classical piano lessons at age seven, though he stopped two years later. After 1940, Sondheim no longer had his father around to play piano; his parents divorced in that year. And Herbert's technique was not developed enough to play classical music anyway. Even so, at the New York Military Academy, the eleven-year-old Sondheim entertained himself by playing MacDowell's "To a Wild Rose" and other classical chestnuts on the chapel's pipe organ.[2]

His musical development after military school is less clear, but some of his tastes were soon established. According to his own recollection, he served as Hammerstein's musical mentor from his teenage years forward, well before Hammerstein would take him on as a dramatic apprentice.

> Early on in our acquaintance . . . [Hammerstein] confessed to being baffled by "modern" music that wasn't tuneful in the traditional sense. Because he was curious, I gave him for his birthday a recording of the Ravel trio (I wanted to start him off as tunefully as possible), and I followed it each year with slightly more contemporary-sounding pieces. I never got him quite as far as *Wozzeck*, but by the time he died seventeen years later, I'd led him through the marshes of Prokofiev and into the thickets of Stravinsky.[3]

One does the math and comes up with July 1943 as the month and year of that gift of the Ravel. Given that Sondheim would date his penchant for collecting records to his later teen years, perhaps 1943 is a bit early. Whatever the precise date was, how did he move from Broadway show tunes to American parlor music to European art music in such a short period of time, let alone to something as arcane as the Ravel trio? By the same means through which the five-year-old was exposed to music: the phonograph.

Sondheim the classical collector

Sondheim was an inveterate record collector, with a zest for expanding his collection. In 1987, he said: "I have a very large record collection, 25–30,000 records, which consist mostly of instrumental music of the nineteenth and twentieth century. I have been collecting since I was seventeen years old."[4] The Library of Congress received most of this collection, which was estimated to be between eleven thousand and thirteen thousand records.[5] Whichever number is correct, it was a considerable private collection.

The Library of Congress also received the record catalog, a typed inventory of four-by-six index cards that show signs of having survived the February 1995 fire that damaged Sondheim's office. Nearly all of the cards are singed at the top and slightly damaged by water; the information on a few has been partially destroyed. And the catalog is not complete. Some cards are missing, and Sondheim remarked that some recordings were not cataloged.

But a picture emerges of his collection. Every composer represented is given a separate card, on which several works are listed. The cards are arranged in alphabetical order by last name. In many cases, a composer's works take up more than one card. (See figures 1a and b.) Rarely is there any mention of performers, and explicit references to labels or other identifying features of individual records are nonexistent. Instead, the cards list the works that appear on the recordings. Multiple copies of a work (which occur usually among the multiple-card composers) are sometimes indicated with a number in parentheses; more often the repeated work is listed later in the inventory. And as Sondheim remarked in 1987, the recordings are mostly of instrumental—that is, classical—music, and mostly from 1850 to 1950 or so. For example, there are more cards for Kodály (twelve) than there are for Beethoven (ten) or Mozart (eleven). Thus the record collection does offer a way of confirming Sondheim's musical tastes and classical influences.[6]

In an interview with David Savran, Sondheim provided a window into how records added to his musical education. He pulled no punches about his general dislike of opera, a dislike highlighted by most commentators. But these remarks also reveal how Sondheim became acquainted with opera and, presumably, with a wider classical repertory.

> I've never liked opera and I've never understood it. Most opera doesn't make theatrical sense to me. Things go on forever. I'm not a huge fan of the human voice. I like song, dramatic song. I like music and lyrics together, telling a story. . . . When I studied with Milton Babbitt he said I had to get into opera. Knowing that I was a Strauss fan, he first sent me to *Rosenkavalier* and I left after one act. I thought it was endlessly boring. I'd heard a lot of opera on record and I liked some of Puccini's music, so I then went to the Met to see *Bohème*.[7]

Sondheim's comment about "hear[ing] a lot of opera on record" finds support in a photograph taken in 1986 with the composer seated in what appears to be his study. On the wall behind him stands a sizable record collection, consisting mostly of boxed sets, some commercially packaged, others repackaged in special boxes that Sondheim acquired in order to preserve space. (He put the record jackets into storage, which provides a window into his habits, that is, he generally listened without liner notes "contaminating" his experience.) While most of the labels are unreadable, several Puccini operas are identifiable, including *Madama Butterfly*, *La Bohème*, *Manon Lescaut*, *Turandot*, *La Fanciulla del West*, and *La Rondine*.[8] Sondheim's record catalog also shows that he owned a recording of every Puccini opera and of five Richard Strauss operas; of Wagner—opera where conceivably "things go on forever"—the catalog mentions only *Tristan* and *Meistersinger*.

HINDEMITH, Paul (1895-1963)

The 4 Temperaments (with Shostakovich: Concerto for Piano, Trumpet & Strings)

Symphonic Dances

Mathis der Maler

Nobillissima Visione; Symphonic Metamorphosis on Themes by Weber

Sonata in D for Violin & Piano (with Copland: Sonata)

(2) Symphony in E-flat

Concert music for Brass & Strings: Concertino for Horn & Orchestra

Concert Music for Piano, Brass & 2Harps; Concerto for Orchestra; Cupid & Psyche

String Quartet #1

Symphony - "Die Harmonie der Welt"

FIG. 1a. A sample card from Sondheim's record catalog (24)

FIG. 1b. Composers in Sondheim's record collection represented with multiple cards

Bach, J.S. (14)
Balakirev (4)
Bartók (16)
Beethoven (10)
Bloch (6)
Brahms (15)
Bridge (4)
Britten (13)
Cage (4)
Chopin (18)
Copland (10)
Davies (3)
Debussy (16)
Delius (6)
Dello Joio (3; first missing)
Diamond (2)
Dohnányi (3)
Dowland (3)
Dukas (3)
Dvořák (9)
Elgar (8)
Enesco (4)
Falla (6)
Farkas (2)
Fauré (8)
Feldman (2)
Field (2)
Fine, I. (3)
Finzi (2)
Flagello (2)
Flanagan, W. (2)
Foote (2)
Foss (2)
Foster (2)
Françaix (4; 1 missing)
Franck (6)
Frumerie, Gunnar de (2)
Gabrieli, G. (2)
Gade (2)
Gershwin (4)
Gideon (2)
Ginastera (3)
Glass, P. (2)
Glazunov (8)
Gliere (2)
Glinka (3)
Goehr (2)
Goossens (2)
Górecki (2)
Gottschalk (3)
Gould (4)
Gounod (3)
Grainger (3)
Granados (8)
Grieg (7)
Griffes (3)
Guarnieri (2; first missing)
Haba (2)
Halffter, R. (2)
Hamilton, Iain (2)
Handel (4)
Hanson (3)
Harris, Roy (3)
Harrison, Lou (2)
Haydn (5)
Henze (3)
Herrmann (4)
Hiller, L. (2)
Hindemith (17)
Hoddinott (3)
Holmboe (2)
Holst (8)

Honegger (8)
Hovhaness (7)
Howells (3)
Husa (2)
Ibert (5)
Imbrie (2)
d'Indy (3)
Ireland (8)
Ivanov (2)
Ives (14)
Jacob, G. (2)
Janáček (8)
Jolivet (4)
Jongen, J. (2)
Joplin (2)
Kabalevsky (4)
Kennan (four recordings of *Night Soliloquy*)
Khrennikov (2; first missing)
Kodály (12)
Koechlin (3)
Kokkonen (2)
Korngold (4)
Kraft, W. (2)
Kreisler (2)
Krenek (4)
Kupferman, Meyer (2)
Lalo (2)
Lambert (2)
Landowski, Marcel (2)
Langlais (2)
Larsson, Lars-Erik (3)
LeClair (2)
Legley (2)
Lekeu (2)
Lesur (2)
Liadov (3)
Ligeti (2)
Linde, Bo (2)
Liszt (13)
Luening (2)
Lyapunov (3)
Lyatoshinsky (2, half full)
Mahler (4)
Malipiero (2)
Martin, Frank (6)
Martino (2)
Martinů (10)
Massenet (2)
Mathias, W. (2)
McCabe (2)
Medtner (4)
Mendelssohn (10)
Mennin (2)
Menotti (2)
Messiaen (4)
Miaskovsky (2)
Mignone (2)
Milhaud (15)
Mompou (3)
Moniuszko (2)
Montsalvatge (2)
Moore, Douglas (2)
Moszkowski (2)
Mozart (11)
Muczynski (2)
Muller, Karl Franz (2)
Musgrave (2)
Musorgsky (5)
Nielsen (6)
Paganini (4)
Persichetti (3)
Peterson-Berger (2)
Piston (5)
Ponce (4)
Porter, Q. (2)
Poulenc (13)
Prokofiev (18)
Puccini (2; all the operas)
Purcell (4)
Quilter (2)
Rachmaninoff (18)
Rameau (2)
Rangström (1, but full)
Rautavaara (2)
Ravel (13)
Rawsthorne (3)
Reger (3)
Reich (1, but with numerous and unusual check marks)
Respighi (4)
Revueltas (2)
Riegger (3)
Rieti (3)
Rochberg (3)
Rodrigo (5)
Rorem (3)
Rosenberg, Hilding (3)
Rossini (3) (no complete operas)
Rózsa (3)
Roussel (9)
Rubbra (3)
Saeverud (2)
Saint-Saëns (11)
Sarasate (3)
Satie (7)
Sauguet (2)
Scarlatti, D. (2)
Schat, Peter (2)
Schibler, Armin (2)
Schickele (3)
Schmidt, F. (2)
Schmitt (3)
Schoenberg (8)
Schubert (12)
Schuller (3)
Schuman (4)
Schumann, R. (10)
Scriabin (4)
Serocki, Kazimierz (2)
Sessions (3)
Shchedrin (2)
Shostakovich (14)
Sibelius (7)
Siegmeister (2)
Sinding (2)
Siqueira (2)
Skalkottas (2)
Strauss, J. (2)
Strauss, R. (10)
Stravinsky (17)
Szymanowski (5)
Tchaikovsky (12)
Tcherepnin (4)
Vaughan Williams (13)
Verdi (2)
Wagner (3, barely)
Webern (4)

As for Strauss, Sondheim began studying with Babbitt in 1950, by which time he had supposedly become "a Strauss fan," but one obviously unfamiliar with *Rosenkavalier*. One can only guess what Strauss he knew: the swaggering *Don Juan* of the composer's youth, perhaps, or the other hypertheatrical tone poems, or the valedictory oboe concerto of 1945, which was released on recording in 1947, the time that Sondheim studied at Williams College and the year he began collecting records. But the chief route by which he came to know Strauss shows the interpenetration of music, theater, and film in Sondheim's development.

> I was such a movie fan that I think I got into Romantic and tonal music first as opposed to classical—you know, pre-Beethoven—and as opposed to contemporary because of movies. All the movie scores were Strauss-influenced and influenced by late nineteenth-century Romanticism. I got into that kind of symphonic music, I think, unconsciously through listening to [Erich von] Korngold and [Max] Steiner and [Franz] Waxman.[9]

One could linger long over Sondheim's record collection, noting the names of composers and pieces that are virtually unknown to the most assiduous music historian. But what quickly becomes apparent in looking at this catalog is its classical bent. And Sondheim came to appreciate classical music pretty much on his own. His parents did not whet his appetite for such music, nor could their record collection rival that of their son, given that Sondheim was a member of the first generation that grew up with the phonograph. But most members of that generation did not buy thousands of records. Sondheim was a collector from the start, with his well-known and extensive game collection being simply one expression of his acquisitiveness. And when it came to recordings, Sondheim collected mostly classical recordings and, if his remarks to Savran are to be believed, listened to them as well.[10]

Ravel

It seems appropriate to refer to Ravel as Sondheim's childhood musical sweetheart, considering how well Sondheim's love of Ravel is documented and how far back that love goes. And like one who sings the praises of a first crush, Sondheim has made claims for Ravel that are enormous if not downright oversized. "The particular influences [on me] are Ravel, who, I think, apart from influencing me, is essentially responsible for most popular music that has been written in the twentieth century. That is to say, his harmonic influence, all the secondary sevenths, is what pop music has existed on even into the age of rock. But certainly he is a huge influence on me."[11]

Most scholars would disagree with Sondheim about Ravel's influence on pop music. Much of American popular music derives both its harmonic and its rhythmic contours from African and African-American roots. The seventh chords that make up the basic 12-bar blues form, coupled with the harmonic substitutions—the secondary sevenths—that every competent jazz player knows, have far greater resonance in pop harmony than does the sonic world created by Ravel.

But Ravel was in fact influenced by African-American music. The slow movement of his Sonata for Violin and Piano (1927) is marked "Blues" and represents an attempt by a white Frenchman to inject some black soul into his music. And it wasn't the first such attempt in France, as is shown by Debussy's numerous black-inspired piano pieces ("Le petit negre," "Golliwogg's Cakewalk," "Minstrels," "General Lavine—*eccentric*") and the rags that Stravinsky wrote while he lived in Paris early in the century.

The confluence of Ravel's indebtedness to black music and Sondheim's indebtedness to Ravel finds a natural focal point in one of Sondheim's favorite pieces by Ravel, the Concerto for the Left Hand for Piano and Orchestra of 1930. In two appearances on the British Broadcasting Corporation's *Desert Island Discs* radio program, separated by some twenty years, Sondheim selected the Ravel as one of his must-have discs. His decision was based in part on his familiarity with a particular recording: "My idea of the ideal way to play the Ravel Left Hand Concerto is the way Cortot played it, because it was the first I heard. As far as I was concerned, everybody else is wrong. If I had heard somebody else play it—Feltsman play it—then that would be my ideal."[12] Another factor was his academic connections with the piece: "One of the reasons I would take it to the island is not only that I love it, but it's also the subject of my senior thesis in college. So it's something I spent a lot of time on and got to love as much as maybe Ravel loved it himself."[13]

But a large part of the work's appeal must be its dark beauties, some of which are clearly influenced by the blues. All serious students of Sondheim must familiarize themselves with this work, written by Ravel for Paul Wittgenstein, a concert pianist who lost his right arm in World War I. (Wittgenstein commissioned works from several composers, including Prokofiev, who also wrote a left-hand concerto for him.) Wittgenstein's tragic loss already resonates with many of Sondheim's dramatic characters—the one-armed pianist as outsider—and Ravel wrote music of stunning drama and depth for Wittgenstein. The opening (example 1) is shrouded in murkiness and uncertainty; its echoes can be heard in some of the brooding music from *Sweeney Todd* (the opening of "The Ballad of Sweeney Todd" and Sweeney's "There was a barber and his wife" readily come to mind). When a melody emerges (m. 3), it is tentative and somewhat reluctant to open itself up, not unlike "Send In the Clowns." The motivic, almost fragmentary nature of the melody also finds an echo in Sondheim's music (for example, "What Can You Lose?" from *Dick Tracy;* see chap. 3). The prolonged climax on the dominant chord, ending on the suspended dominant chord as a launching pad for the piano's entrance (example 2), resembles similar prolongations in Sondheim, such as on the word "love" in "Company." (Indeed, "Company" resembles a dramatic reconception of the concerto.) And the jaunty 6/8 march of the second main section of the concerto (rehearsal no. 17) is in the same league as the 6/8 "A Weekend in the Country" *(A Little Night Music)*, "The Ballad of Sweeny Todd," and "How I Saved Roosevelt" *(Assassins)*.

While much of the concerto may be tinted by black music, it is in the second theme of the Allegro section that the blues coloration comes through loudest and clearest. This theme was actually sounded near the opening of the concerto, as it appears in tandem with the initial tentative melody (horns at rehearsal no. 1). Its full flowering, however, does not occur until the Allegro. Against the unyielding rhythm of a marchlike vamp, the bassoon intones a syncopated version of the melody, bending it rhythmically and pitch-wise in a way that is reminiscent of a blues singer (at rehearsal no. 28; example 3). And Ravel plied this melody again and again in different orchestral combinations, including a lush string section that sounds as much like Duke Ellington's orchestra as a classical musician's score (beginning at rehearsal no. 35).

Sondheim himself was not as susceptible to the charms of black music as was Ravel. Yet when he acclaimed another composer he admired greatly, Harold Arlen, Sondheim focused on the "kind of Southern blues" that Arlen's music managed to express (or, perhaps more accurately, on how Arlen's music fit Sondheim's image of southern blues). "His harmonic structures and his harmonies are, to me, endlessly rich, inventive and fascinating, and I never tire of his music."[14] Chapter 2 will explore Sondheim's sonic relationship with Arlen. But here it is worth noting the connections between Ravel and Arlen, namely, their "endless rich, inventive and fascinating" harmonies and their affinity with the blues.

Example 1. Ravel, Concerto for the Left Hand for Piano and Orchestra, opening

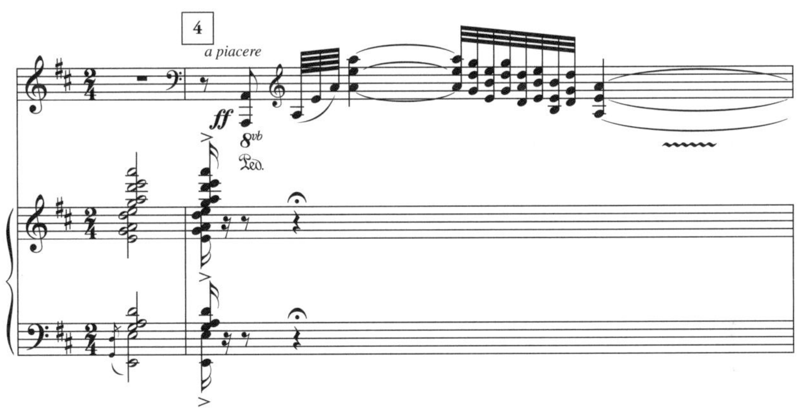

Example 2. Ravel, Concerto for the Left Hand for Piano and Orchestra, rehearsal no. 4

Sondheim volunteered to Stephen Banfield that "the preponderance of the two specific colors ('dark' versus 'romantic') of the waltzes . . . [from *A Little Night Music*] is the pervasive influence in my writing of Ravel, particularly *La Valse* (dark) and the *Valses nobles et sentimentales* (romantic)."[15] And while this identification comes when Sondheim was in his sixties, one can see evidence of this Ravelian pervasiveness throughout his creative life. Two unpublished waltzes for piano from around 1950 show a clear debt to Ravel. And the waltzes "Next to You" and "Alaska" from *Bounce* (the latter was cut after the Goodman Theatre production and folded into "The Best Thing That Ever Has Happened")

EXAMPLE 3. Ravel, Concerto for the Left Hand for Piano and Orchestra, rehearsal no. 28

similarly contain a dramatic sweep and utilize a harmonic palette that together confirm Sondheim's primary focus on Ravel, and not the Viennese masters, when he created his waltzes.

This distinction may appear unimportant at first, seeing how Ravel himself looked to Vienna in his waltzes. "The title *Valses nobles et sentimentales* sufficiently indicates my intention of composing a series of waltzes in imitation of Schubert. . . . I conceived of [*La valse* (1919–20)] as a sort of apotheosis of the Viennese waltz, mingled with, in my mind, the impression of a fantastic, fatal whirling."[16] Fourteen years before the completion of *La valse,* Ravel indicated that he wanted to pay "homage to the memory of the great Strauss—not Richard, the other one, Johann."[17] Ravel placed *La valse* in an imperial court, about 1855, which would put it just ahead of the successes of Johann Strauss II, and Schubert clearly predates both *La valse*'s scenario and the great Strauss for the *Valses nobles* (1911). Ravel's Vienna was an early one that was saturated with the waltz.

But Ravel's view of the waltz differed from that of the great Strauss. While the passion of the Viennese models is invoked, in *La valse* that passion turns frenetic and leads to collapse. "It is a dancing, whirling, almost hallucinatory ecstasy, an increasingly passionate and exhausting whirlwind of dancers, who are overcome and exhilarated by nothing but 'the waltz.'" "*La valse* is tragic, but in the Greek sense: it is a fatal spinning around, the expression of vertigo and of the voluptuousness of the dance to the point of paroxysm."[18] As one critic noted, "Ravel's apotheosis elevates Viennese dance-band music to the status of orchestral high-art music and amateur dancing couples to professional ballet-dancers. Most importantly, he elevates musical materials to their breaking-point."[19] One's mind quickly embraces the waltz "Last Midnight" (from *Into the Woods*), where the harmonies hark back to Ravel and the dramatic trajectory of the song compares with the paroxysms of *La valse*. And while fatigue rather than frenzy marks the final waltz of the *Valses nobles*—marked "Epilogue," where the music slowly atomizes all the preceding waltzes into sonic ephemera—this, too, has a parallel in the epilogue of *Passion*, where the slow musical trance in 12/8 (i.e., four groupings of three, akin to four bars of a waltz) finds melodies as well as characters dissolving into nothingness.

One can only imagine the reasons why Sondheim was drawn so strongly to Ravel. There is an eerie similarity, though, between the approach these two composers took to composing and how their music has been received. In the 1980 edition of the *New Grove Dictionary of Music and Musicians*, G. W. Hopkins wrote the following of Ravel—

> As a final precaution against insecurity, Ravel adopted a detached attitude to his art: it was for him an "act," possibly of imitation, possibly of reportage. . . . The decisive charge against Ravel would seem to be that of coolness . . . and it is possible in this light to view the irony, parody, imitation and other "second-order creation" of Ravel as a facet of that fatally aimless cleverness which is a symptom of cultural decadence.[20]

—yet how these words sound as though they could have been written of Sondheim. There is extensive documentation on why Sondheim may have had cause to be insecure, especially given his relationship with his mother, Foxy.[21] In terms of his art, Sondheim said that his college composition teacher, Robert Barrow, taught "that music is a matter of craft and technique like, as it turns out, all art, and the fact that art is work and not inspiration, that invention comes with craft."[22] "Before Barrow, I waited for all the tunes to come into my head. *But he took all the romance out of the music*. 'You learn the technique,' he said, 'and then you put the notes down on paper and that's what music is!' I adored it."[23] And the damning descriptions of "coolness" and "cleverness" would dog Sondheim from the 1960s through the 1970s and beyond.

About *La valse*, one critic wrote that it "plots the birth, decay and destruction of a musical genre: the waltz."[24] In a similar fashion, Sondheim deconstructed the waltz in the way he deployed it in *A Little Night Music*, by rescandalizing a previously scandalous dance through making

it the sonic sign of decoupling instead of coupling.[25] What one must always keep in mind is that Sondheim learned to waltz courtesy of Ravel more than Rodgers (or the Viennese waltz circle) and that Ravel's influence is felt in Sondheim's waltzes beyond the resemblance in musical vocabulary.

The Variations on a Theme (Katie Malone) for Piano Solo (1949) also gives ample proof to the connection between Sondheim, the waltz, and Ravel.[26] The romantic idiom of the variations suggests that Sondheim had not fully fallen under the Hindemithian sway of Barrow; indeed, the variations, for most of their duration, conjure up the world of the MacDowell salon piece. But the waltzlike ending of the work, with its right-hand arabesques and thirteenth-chord harmonies, clearly spins into a Ravelian sound world.

The musical resemblance between Ravel and Sondheim is even clearer in Sondheim's Williams thesis of the following year, the Piano Sonata in C major. As of this writing, the sonata is unpublished, and few scholars have seen the work, let alone commented on it at any length.[27] But it is a repository of Sondheim's classical mentors, with Ravel standing tall among them.

A comparison of Ravel's Quartet in F Major (1903) and Trio in A Minor (1908) with Sondheim's sonata shows how close was the attention Sondheim paid to Ravel. The first movements of all three works are cast in sonata form; all immediately begin with the first theme. There appears to be little echo of Ravel in Sondheim's first theme. But in the second theme, Sondheim not only looked to Ravel: he stole from him. Ravel's second themes in both works are uncommon in that they return, untransposed but reharmonized, in the recapitulation. Similarly, Sondheim's second theme appears in his recapitulation in precisely the same way, with an untransposed theme and a transposed accompaniment. Moreover, just as Sondheim ingeniously interwove the first and second themes of his sonata's first movement in the development section (mm. 106–12), so did Ravel in the first movement of the trio (mm. 77–81; six before rehearsal no. 10).[28]

Certainly Sondheim's most extended remarks about Ravel are found in his paper written in the fall of 1949 for Music 19, the first semester of "Music and Musicians of the Twentieth Century." The sixteen-page paper, "Two Piano Concertos from the Pen of Maurice Ravel," earned Sondheim an A–, mostly because his instructor, Joaquín Nin-Culmell, wanted more information about "its [i.e., the D major concerto's] roots & flowering; its relation to the concerto in the XIXth c.; its relation to French music in general, etc." (note on p. 8). Sondheim's analyses are fairly straightforward, blow-by-blow accounts of the various musical events in each of the concertos. Still, Nin-Culmell wrote, "[T]he music has been listened to with understanding & sympathy. The musical observations are, for the most part, justified & interesting" (note on p. 16).

But Sondheim moved beyond musical observations. He voiced his opinions as well. He did not listen uncritically. Concerning the second movement of the G major concerto, he wrote about the "very long 'cantilena' sung in the piano against a slow waltz vamp (also in the piano) which persists throughout the movement" (12). If there is any reluctance to pass judgment here, he sheds it at the end: "though I may be one in a million, I find the 2nd movement too simple—simple to the point of dullness and verbosity" (16).

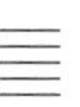

The very next sentence—the paper's penultimate sentence, in fact—once again shows how important the D major concerto was to Sondheim even then. "But in the Concerto for the Left Hand, in its complex and complete economy, unity, and clean structure, I find nothing left out, nothing to be desired." And in his final sentence, he offered a confession. "Guess I'm just a Romantic at heart." For Sondheim back then, the G major concerto was less pleasing in terms of its structure, was too brittle, and employed orchestral effects less integrally. For the D major concerto, no amount of praise was sufficient. "The Concerto is remarkable in its qualities both as a *tour de force* and as a unified work of art. At times savage, ironic, song-like, harshly rhythmic, it emerges as a clear- and clean-cut construction, formally complex in its simplicity (pardon my paradox). That is, it is easy to analyze, but difficult to compose. In short, I like it" (8). And over a half-century later, he still liked it.

Sondheim made other observations that return the reader to the idea that Ravel and popular music are somehow interconnected. In the second paragraph of the paper, he used a long quotation by David Hall. He provided no bibliography, but clearly Nin-Culmell was familiar with Hall's work, since he underlined Hall's name and wrote next to it: "Poor source." Sondheim seemed drawn to the Romantic imagery in which Hall enveloped the left-hand concerto. But note the parallels both to black music and to popular theater music (and recall Sondheim's comments, quoted earlier, about Arlen).

> As Ravel worked at this concerto [i.e., the G major concerto] for his own use, he was haunted by memories of the jazz that had so fascinated him in the nightclubs of New York's Harlem and Greenwich Village. These recollections inspired jazzlike themes of his own, but

> they seemed unsuitable for incorporation in the two-handed concerto which was following traditional design and was not at all in the Broadway idiom. Rather than throw away the new ideas inspired by jazz however, Ravel decided to make use of them in the one-handed Wittgenstein concerto. This gave him the impetus to begin the commissioned work, while at the same time he continued the writing of the concerto he intended for himself (1).[29]

Sondheim returned on several occasions in the paper to talk about the influence of jazz on the left-hand concerto, even if he seems less than totally convinced of its presence. "Jazz elements are slightly noticeable in the B section [of the concerto], in its strong rhythmic treatment (the vamp) and in the syncopated statements of the [second Allegro] theme" (7). Twice he quoted Ravel's remarks about the concertos. "From a certain viewpoint my [G major] Concerto has some resemblance to the Violin Sonata. It includes some elements borrowed from jazz, but only in moderation" (9). Compare this remark of modest jazz elements with Ravel's estimation of the left-hand concerto: "It is of a different character [than the Concerto in G]. . . . [It has] many jazz effects, but the writing is not so simple. . . ." (14; ellipses and editorial remarks in Sondheim's paper). Of the two concertos, then, the one that Sondheim preferred is the one that is more heavily infused with jazz and gets closer, to use Hall's terms, to the Broadway idiom.

That idiom uses vamps in its musical accompaniments, and here is yet another observation by Sondheim that not only ties Ravel to popular music but also illustrates how he has influenced Sondheim, himself a master of the vamp. Sondheim first used the term to talk about the accompaniment in the allegro marchlike section of the left-hand concerto. "Throughout this section, the following orchestral 'vamp' (if you will excuse the expression), or basic rhythmic accompaniment predominates" (4, followed by a musical figure of the vamp in question). Over the next few pages, Sondheim traced the comings and goings of the vamp in the concerto, using the term without apology after introducing it. And his description of the slow movement of the G major concerto as a slow waltz vamp has already been mentioned. In using this term, Sondheim drew a connection between the accompaniment figures in classical music and those in popular music, especially theater music, where accompanists are often told to "vamp until ready." Sondheim's focus on accompaniment, at this early stage in his career, underscores why the accompaniments in his own music, like those in Ravel, are often harmonically and rhythmically complex.

When one looks at the record collection, there are other composers who take up more space than does Ravel. At thirteen cards, Ravel barely pulls ahead of Kodály. But his output, when compared to other major composers who interested Sondheim, is rather small. Thus it is striking how many duplications there are in Sondheim's Ravel collection. He may have idolized Cortot's performance of the left-hand concerto, but that did not keep him from owning no fewer than eight different recordings of the piece. And of the seminal (for Sondheim) Trio in A Minor, he owned seven recordings, compared to the seminal (for Ravel) Quartet in F Major, of which he owned three.[30]

Given that it was Ravel's harmony that so influenced Sondheim, it is fitting to close this section on Ravel by recalling Sondheim's description of that harmony as found in the left-hand concerto.

> The harmony is what I would call "typically Ravelian." Lots of ninths and elevenths . . . open and parallel fifths and sevenths, modulation by enharmonics, etc. Perhaps the most interesting of his harmonic ideas in this work is the climactic treatment of the [bluesy] theme in the [Allegro] section. It is stated in major parallel sevenths over successive pedals. (7)

This is the string-heavy Ellington moment alluded to earlier, and it is worth noting that Sondheim's analysis omits a crucial detail. The "major parallel sevenths" are actually blues-inflected dominant seventh chords, as the music starts with a C^7 (rehearsal no. 28) and moves downward to an A^7 (rehearsal no. 31), repeating the theme untransposed but harmonizing it a minor third lower. The music then repeats the untransposed theme a third time, this time harmonizing the first half with an F♯^{7} (rehearsal no. 33) and the second half with an E♭^{7} (one measure after rehearsal no. 34). Ravel thus not only utilized the same compositional trick that appeared in the quartet and the trio—reharmonizing an untransposed melody (here, the C^7 and A^7 appearances), which Sondheim emulated in his sonata—but he also employed the standard jazz technique of tritone substitution for an untransposed melody (here, F♯^{7} and E♭^{7} substituting for C^7 and A^7, respectively).

This reharmonization of an untransposed melody is a feature that Sondheim uses on numerous occasions. The undulation between $\hat{6}$ and $\hat{5}$ that marks the opening of "I'm Still Here" (*Follies*, 1971), harmonized originally by the tonic (in the score, E♭, at "Good times and bum times"), is later harmonized by the supertonic (F, at "In the depression . . ." and elsewhere), the mediant (G, at "Strummed ukuleles" and elsewhere), and the dominant (B♭, at "Beebe's Bathysphere" and elsewhere). In the song "Finishing the Hat" (*Sunday in the Park with George*, 1984), Sondheim incorporated the falling-third bass line that features prominently in all of the Ravel examples mentioned above.

Always standing by (E♭ minor)
Reaching for the sky (C♭ major)
Coming from the hat (G♭ major)

Here, as in the Ravel examples, the melody remains untransposed, while the accompaniment employs seventh harmonies and the pedal moves at the end of each line. This same type of reharmonized melody occurs in the opening of "You" *(Bounce)*, where the bass line movement is nearly identical with that in the left-hand concerto—here, I-vi-IV-ii—but the chords are not dominant sevenths. The changes in melody may seem to invalidate a comparison with Ravel, but a similar reharmonization at the end of "What's Your Rush?" (also from *Bounce*) adheres more closely to the Ravel and earlier Sondheim examples. Here, an ascending melodic figure of $\hat{6}$-$\hat{2}$-$\hat{3}$ (C-F-G) is harmonized as follows: C-suspended that resolves to C^9; F^{13}; $B\flat^{9}$ add 6 over an F bass; E♭ (tonic), but delayed, with a nagging A in the alto that eventually yields to a ninth chord.

It is understandable that Sondheim would revere Ravel as a master craftsman. More than this, though, techniques Sondheim discovered in Ravel's music routinely appear in his own. Ravelian reharmonization becomes a compositional staple. Nearly every time a waltz appears in Sondheim's work, the ghost of Ravel is not far away. And while Sondheim's claims for Ravel's harmonic importance may be overblown for popular music, they accurately reflect its importance for Sondheim, as will be seen when we return to Ravel and examine how his musical ethos intersects with those of other composers.

Satie (and other Frenchmen)

While the French composers of the early twentieth century may be interchangeable in some people's minds, they are distinct in Sondheim's. When told by an admirer that his music sounded as though influenced by Debussy, Sondheim responded, "It's Ravel more than Debussy."[31] And indeed the cooler, more analytical Ravel does suit Sondheim more than does the warmer, more impressionistic Debussy (though he owned more

Debussy than Ravel, in part because Debussy wrote more than Ravel).

As for other twentieth-century Frenchmen who may lurk in Sondheim's sonic background, Banfield suggested that there are correspondences between, among others, Sondheim and Ibert, Milhaud, and Poulenc on different occasions.[32] Sondheim did own recordings of these composers, especially Milhaud and Poulenc (fifteen and thirteen inventory cards, respectively), so he knew their music well. "I love Milhaud's French suites. The Provençale Suite I love. I love some of his small tuneful stuff. What I like about that whole group of composers—Milhaud, Françaix, all those people, and Poulenc (although he is far superior)—is the kind of bubble and joy and—there must be some fabulous French word for it—*joie de vivre*."[33] Banfield also suggested that Fauré appears from time to time as a sonic hue in Sondheim, and even though "Sondheim says he has largely bypassed Fauré in his love affair with French music,"[34] he owned a substantial amount of Fauré (eight inventory cards).

But the one other French composer who seems to have a fairly regular representation in Sondheim is Erik Satie. And here it is a fairly specific representation of Satie: that found in his *Trois gymnopédies* of 1888. Satie himself revivified the term, deriving it from the ancient Greek *gymnopaidikē,* a choral dance sung and performed by three age-graded choruses of naked boys and men.[35] Satie's pieces have a severity of line and rhythm that could be heard as "classical," in the sense of Greek classicism, and compared to other music being written in 1888—Wagner was all the rage in France at the time—Satie's music is spare to the point of being nude. Given that Satie often named his pieces somewhat whimsically, there is no reason to try to plumb the pieces for clues as to why he unearthed a long-forgotten name for his three piano pieces.

The style of these pieces is identical and fairly self-contained, which has led commentators to use the term *gymnopédie* to describe the manner in which a piece is written. Satie's pieces have the following features: the basic pulse is three slow beats per unit of music (i.e., measure); the accompaniment consists of a bass note sounded on beat 1 and a chord in the tenor register on beat 2, with nothing sounded in the accompaniment on beat 3; the melody is slow-moving yet long-breathed; the rhythm of the accompaniment continues for the entire piece; the harmony owes more to ancient modes than to the more familiar major and minor modes; the chords use sevenths and ninths. To restate the style of the *gymnopédie* in words that Sondheim used for Ravel, the music consists of complex harmonies, a vamp as accompaniment, and a singable melody.

And the classicism of the *gymnopédies* makes them a natural extension of Sondheim's love of Ravel, where a similar kind of reserve and severity often appear.

Banfield identifies several moments in Sondheim as being indebted to the sound world of the Satie *gymnopédie:* the slow waltz, "Someone Is Waiting," from *Company;* the discarded "All Things Bright and Beautiful" from *Follies;* the slow opening section of "The Miller's Son" from *A Little Night Music;* an unused accompaniment figure among the sketches for *Pacific Overtures;* and the discarded "Boom! Crunch!" replaced by "Last Midnight," from *Into the Woods*.[36] In the case of *Night Music*, Banfield also revealed that, in a list of possible musical patterns to copy for the show, Sondheim named Satie, among others.[37] (In addition to the *Gymnopédies*, Satie wrote waltzes and sarabandes, which are also in triple meter.) These Satie-like moments (and others, such as the Dinner Table Music in *Night Music*, a slowed-down rendition of the "Night Waltz II") come from Sondheim's maturity, but Sondheim also looked to Satie as a younger man. The incomplete slow movement of his piano sonata, in fact, may be Sondheim's purest expression of *gymnopédisme*. While Sondheim's melody is more active than those that Satie used, the movement is in a slow three, is harmonically modal, and employs the broken bass-chord accompaniment so characteristic of Satie's *Gymnopédies*.

Yet this identification of *gymnopédisme* in Sondheim has an important musical moment that serves as a counterbalance. Though he found it dull and verbose, the slow movement of the G major Ravel concerto also has a *gymnopédie*-like cast to it. Perhaps Sondheim's use of this style of writing invokes both composers, as Sondheim tried to improve upon Ravel by using the tools that Satie had developed.

Rachmaninoff (and other Russians)

Next to Ravel, Rachmaninoff would seem to be Sondheim's favorite composer. In the two interviews where he attributes pop harmony to Ravel, he also sings the praises of Rachmaninoff and his affection for the music. "So it's Ravel, Rachmaninoff—another wonderful harmonist . . ."[38] "[Ravel] is a huge influence on me and a lot of the more angular tonal composers like Bartók, Stravinsky, Prokofiev, a lot of Rachmaninoff—I'm very much into Russian Romantic."[39] Sondheim's love of Rachmaninoff influenced more than just his music. He was nicknamed the "George School's own Rachmaninoff" in the school yearbook, probably because he was playing the first movement of Rachmaninoff's Second Concerto at the time. (He also played Chopin's Polonaise-Fantasy and Ravel's *Valses nobles et sentimentales*, the latter "entirely for my own pleasure.")[40] In his unfinished novel, *Bequest*, written while he was at Williams, Sondheim's protagonist, pianist-composer Edward Gold, is referred to as "Mr. Rachmaninoff."[41] And as recently as 1998, Sondheim referred to Rachmaninoff as "one of my favorites."[42]

But this lifelong love of Rachmaninoff seems to find little outlet in Sondheim's music, in which one rarely hears either the long-breathed melodies that are a Rachmaninoff trademark or anything resembling his sumptuous harmonies. Thus it is all the more curious to find Sondheim saying of Rachmaninoff that "the way the tune sticks in your head has less to do with melodic line than what [he does] harmonically underneath."[43]

Yet for all the emphasis on his melodic and harmonic skills, Rachmaninoff was also a master contrapuntalist whose works are overrun with complex inner voices that play with and against the melody and harmony. While the melodies routinely draw comment, very often they are accompanied by extended countermelodies, with the result that Rachmaninoff's harmonies are often arrived at through linear means. The Piano Concerto no. 2 in C Minor, op. 18, for example, is melodically and harmonically resplendent, but it also is filled with shorter melodic lines in the inner voices (example 4). The activity of these inner voices give Rachmaninoff's music its rich texture; they are the "harmonically underneath" musical matter that Sondheim so readily imitates in his own work, which nevertheless manages to sound nothing like Rachmaninoff.[44]

EXAMPLE 4. Rachmaninoff, Concerto no. 2 in C Minor, op. 18, second theme from first movement

This link between Rachmaninoff and counterpoint is strengthened when one considers Sondheim's education at Williams. While his principal composition teacher, Robert Barrow, would later amass his lecture

notes to create a veritable textbook on harmony, for much of his career he relied on C. H. Kitson's *Counterpoint for Beginners* (1927) to teach the basics of species counterpoint.[45] A look at Sondheim's piano sonata and other sketches from his college days further demonstrates his acute interest in counterpoint at this time in his life. The combination of Barrow's rigor, the emphasis on counterpoint, and Sondheim's own predilection for Rachmaninoff likely gave Sondheim cause to appreciate the contrapuntal complexity in Rachmaninoff's music.

This music remains popular among the general public, so it should come as no surprise that Sondheim's most popular song to date owes some allegiance to the Russian. When asked about the musical form of "Send In the Clowns," Sondheim responded: "There isn't any; it's a rhapsody. That's a Rachmaninoff piano prelude and, as such, has the kind of wandering, liquid quality, it seems to me, that Rachmaninoff has. It's a very deliberate Rachmaninoff imitation."[46] Sondheim's remarks suggest that the model for the song would most assuredly be among the twenty-four preludes, opp. 23 and 32, that Rachmaninoff wrote for piano and that Sondheim owned in recorded form. The undulating character of the D major prelude, op. 23, no. 4, readily comes to mind; it is in 3/4 and has an accompaniment figure that unfolds in triplets, not unlike the accompaniment of Sondheim's song. However, before Sondheim called the song a Rachmaninoff prelude, he referred to it as a rhapsody, and this designation inevitably leads to comparisons between the song and the *Rhapsody on a Theme of Paganini*.

The *Rhapsody* occupies an unusual (for Sondheim) position in his record collection. Relatively few items are represented in it more than once, but there are four different recordings of the *Rhapsody*. No other Rachmaninoff composition is as well represented, and Sondheim was unequivocal about its place in his affections. "I guess my favorite piece of [Rachmaninoff's] is the *Rhapsody on a Theme of Paganini*."[47]

Upon closer study, "Send In the Clowns" appears to be a very deliberate imitation of the famous eighteenth variation of the *Rhapsody*. The song and the variation share the same repetitiveness and relentlessness of their main tunes. The melodies seem as if they were spun out effortlessly, a characteristic that, while common to Rachmaninoff, is somewhat unusual for Sondheim. Though the variation is in 3/4, the incessant triplets give the sensation of compound meter, thus making a comparison with the song more secure (given that it is mainly in 12/8, or quadruple compound meter). Both the variation and the song take on a "kind of wandering, liquid quality," to repeat Sondheim's words. And the release in particular gives evidence that the *Rhapsody* is in the background. There, both the descending line in the inner voice—a typically Rachmaninovian touch—as well as the unusual harmonic shift on the word "sure" (compare the end of Rachmaninoff's tune)—seem to spring from the *Rhapsody*. In the printed version, "Send In the Clowns" serendipitously shares the same key as the variation. And bearing in mind that the Rachmaninoff variation is built on an inversion of the Paganini melody, the ascending three notes that begin "Send In the Clowns" are a near inversion of the descending three-note figure that permeates the "Night Waltz I" (at the words "eight o'clock" and elsewhere throughout the song). Assuming that Sondheim told the truth when he spoke of "a very deliberate Rachmaninoff imitation," one must search hard for a better exemplar than this variation.

Sondheim's one true Russian musical pastiche, one that draws as much from Russian folk music as from Russian art music, is the Cossack's dance that the Russian ambassador sings in "Please Hello" *(Pacific Overtures)*. (Similarly, the music for the French ambassador borrows from the French music hall tradition of the nineteenth century and not from Ravel.) But in his lyrics for *Merrily We Roll Along*, Sondheim makes witty reference to another of his Russian loves, in a scene where producer Joe Josephson warns the songwriting team of Franklin Shepard and Charley Kringas that Frank's score is unapproachable. While freely admitting that he doesn't see a score so strong every day, Joe criticizes the (fictitious) score for being avant-garde and devoid of plain old melodies. As producer, he is interested in making a return on the backers' investment, and Frank's score, however accomplished it may be, sounds to him like death at the box office. He reminds Frank of the bottom line with the remark: "I'll let you know when Stravinsky has a hit." Stravinsky may be a great composer, Joe concedes, but his music won't sell tickets on Broadway, as *The Seven Lively Arts* revealed.[48]

Elsewhere Sondheim has remarked that "Opening Doors"—the song in which this exchange between Frank, Charley, and Joe occurs—is semiautobiographical, which makes the reference to Stravinsky even more amusing.[49] When speaking on BBC's *Desert Island Discs* in 2000 about his choice of Stravinsky's *Symphony of Psalms* (1930), Sondheim offered up a recollection that further confirms the autobiographical elements in *Merrily*.

> The "Alleluia" [in the third movement] has a chord progression I'm so jealous of, I wish I had thought of it. And I used to stand on street corners in my college days with a girl I knew and a married couple—a guy I went to college [with] and his wife—and we would stand on

street corners and sing just the little chord progression of "Alleluia," which is in four-part harmony. [See example 5.] It's the only time I've ever indulged in such silliness. But the whole piece is wonderful.[50]

EXAMPLE 5. Stravinsky, *Symphony of Psalms,* opening of third movement.

Silly though this stunt may have been, it obviously seared that chord progression—and Stravinsky's music—into Sondheim's mind. (He sang the bass part.) Though the chord progression is not the same, the three highly dissonant chords in the song "Sunday" *(Sunday in the Park with George)*—the three that occur before the painter Georges Seurat says the word "harmony," whereupon they resolve in harmonious fashion—sound as though they were lifted out of *Les noces* or the Symphonies of Wind Instruments. Closer to the "Alleluia" are the three chords that close the "Hymnos" from *The Frogs* (1974), and much of the music in that score finds Sondheim mixing contemporary rhythms with almost neoclassical sonorities. Stravinsky may have never had a Broadway hit, but that was no bar to Sondheim's enthusiasm for his music, as evidenced by the seventeen cards devoted to recordings of it that Sondheim owned.

Sondheim named at least two other Russians as being among his favorites, two who stand at different ends of the Romantic/neoclassical continuum. Of Tchaikovsky, Sondheim said little more than that he was among the first classical composers to whom Sondheim was exposed. "The first music I heard was mid-nineteenth century Brahms and then going on through Tchaikovsky [and] Rachmaninoff. And so my heart responds, as one always does, to the first love."[51] Which Tchaikovsky appealed to Sondheim is a matter of conjecture, given that his record collection includes all of the symphonies, ballets, concertos, piano and chamber music and most of the songs and symphonic poems. (Predictably, there is only one opera; surprisingly, it is the atypical *Mazeppa*, not the more popular *Yevgeny Onegin*.)

The antithesis of Tchaikovsky is Prokofiev, or at least the music Prokofiev wrote prior to his return to the Soviet Union in 1935, at which point his language became more Romantic (though within a twentieth-century idiom). In addition to sharing with Chopin and Rachmaninoff the distinction of having the most inventory space devoted to his music (eighteen cards each), Prokofiev is further distinguished by virtue of his place in Sondheim's performing repertory. When asked if he knew the Prokofiev sonatas while he was at Williams, Sondheim said he didn't. "I have a memory of the *Visions fugitives* but that, I think, outside of the *Love for Three Oranges* 'March,' which I played on the piano, too, are the only Prokofiev I think I ever came into immediate contact with."[52] One can almost envision Sondheim playing the march, with its angularities and odd harmonies accentuated rather than smoothed over, its sudden change of dynamics thundered out or softly articulated. And although it is an overtly American sound, the March from the Treaty House and the Lion Dance at the end of act 1 of *Pacific Overtures* owe a small debt to the world of Prokofiev and the Prokofiev march that Sondheim had under his fingertips.

Connections between Sondheim and Prokofiev remain virtually uncharted. Banfield wrote about the "Prokofiev-like polytonality" of "There's Something about a War" (cut from *A Funny Thing Happened on the Way to the Forum*) and the "uncharacteristically discursive" harmonic scheme of "Green Finch and Linnet Bird" from *Sweeney Todd*, which "could almost have been written by Prokofiev or Berkeley."[53] But the links between Sondheim and Prokofiev clearly run deeper than a harmonic similarity here or there. The contrapuntal writing in the Prokofiev sonatas would have intrigued Sondheim, whose penchant for ostinati and vamps finds a cognate in Prokofiev's motoric rhythms.

As far as other Russians, Sondheim's record collection contains records by many of the composers so brilliantly ticked off in Ira Gershwin's song "Tschaikowsky [and Other Russians]" (*Lady in the Dark*, 1941, music by Kurt Weill), and more. Shostakovich alone merits fourteen cards in Sondheim's inventory; Glazunov has eight. If Sondheim's love for French music was mostly concentrated in the direction of Ravel, his love for Russian music was more catholic, even as Rachmaninoff remained at the center of that affection.

The "Hindemith phase"

In his review of Sondheim's youthful Concertino for Two Pianos (arranged by Jonathan Sheffer for orchestra with piano obbligato), Anthony Tommasini, music critic for the *New York Times,* suggested that

> Stephen Sondheim surely could have become a composer of serious concert works. His acclaimed theater scores make clear that he had the talent and then some. But Mr. Sondheim, who composed books and scores for four shows before he was 21, knew he was a "Broadway Baby," to quote a song title from his landmark 1971 musical *Follies.* . . . Still, what would Sondheim concert works have sounded like?[54]

To help him answer his own question, Tommasini asked Sondheim what he might have been listening to when he was writing the concertino. "I don't recall. But when I listen to it now, I'd say I was in my Hindemith phase, especially 'The Four Temperaments.' "[55] Banfield had earlier surmised, note unheard, that the sonata (which predates the concertino) would show traces of Hindemith, anticipating that Barrow's own study with Hindemith would rub off on his advisee's honors project. And indeed, after he heard a private recording of the sonata in 2001, Sondheim remarked that he was surprisingly unembarrassed by his student effort, even though "warmed-over Hindemith it may be."[56]

It is tempting to limit Sondheim's self-described Hindemith phase to 1950, given the way Hindemith fell out of favor among American composers after World War II.[57] But beyond questions of respectability lay questions of influence. Is it likely that Sondheim's love of Hindemith was simply a phase he outgrew? Or did the Hindemith phase last beyond his contact with Barrow?

Before looking at the Hindemith in Sondheim, one needs to retrace Barrow's contact with Hindemith. According to his file in the Williams College Archive, Robert George Barrow (1911–87) earned three degrees from Yale—a bachelor of arts in 1932, a bachelors in music in 1933, and a masters in music in 1934—and was the recipient of the Ditson Fellowship for Foreign Study in 1934. The award enabled him to study conducting with Sir Henry Wood and composition with (in his own words) "the distinguished composers Ralph Vaughan Williams and Paul Hindemith."

But beyond this statement, there is no evidence that Barrow actually studied with Hindemith. There is no record of Barrow in the archives of the Berlin Hochschule für Musik, where Hindemith was teaching in 1934, nor is there any correspondence between Barrow and Hindemith among the papers of the Hindemith-Institut of Frankfurt. In fact, for the years 1934–35, there is no correspondence between Hindemith and *any* American students.[58] Whatever study Barrow may have had with Hindemith, it occurred at a time when Hindemith was under a great deal of personal and professional duress as the Nazis sought to punish him for the musical sins of his youth. And although Hindemith would later come to the United States and teach at Yale, there is no correspondence between Barrow and Hindemith among the papers of the Paul Hindemith Institute at Yale. If Barrow's time with Hindemith was significant to the young American composer, it appears to have been less significant to the German one.

Ironically, at the time Barrow said he studied with Hindemith, Hindemith was drafting *Komposition und Kompositionsunterricht*, which, according to one scholar, "might loosely but suitably be translated as *How to Teach Prospective Composers*." In it, Hindemith warns composition teachers to ground students in the technical standards and ethical responsibilities of composition.

> A student trained in this way will not capitalize on the name of his teacher in order to enhance his own reputation, as sadly happens so often nowadays. He will realize that striving to perfect one's art is the only thing that matters and that the less he exploits his personal contacts to get ahead the more surely he will make his own way.[59]

Barrow made his way somewhat narrowly within the confines of the Berkshire Mountains of western Massachusetts and its environs. His published compositions are mostly designed for church use; his unpublished works were performed by local groups. He founded the Berkshire Choral Society, a large civic chorus that drew from nearby New York state as well as Massachusetts, and also was the editor of the "Williams Series" of music for male voices, published by E. C. Schirmer. His musical vocabulary is best summed up in the note (authored by Barrow?) on his "Quartet for Six" of 1969: his language "is definitely contemporary in style, although not atonal."

One interesting feature of Barrow's teaching style reported by Sondheim is that he used no text.

> He taught rigidly out of a little black book compiled over the years into which he had compressed a lot of texts. He had a completely anti-romantic approach to music. I had always imagined that writing music was all about sitting in your penthouse or your studio until this lady muse twitters around your head and sits on your shoulders and goes, "Da-da-da dum, da-da-da-dum." Instead, Robert Barrow was talking about leading tones and diatonic scales, and I fell in love. He took all the mystery out of music and taught craft. Within a year I was majoring in music. He changed my life by making me aware that art is craft, not inspiration.[60]

This emphasis on craft suggests that Sondheim may have known Hindemith's *Unterweisung im Tonsatz* (1937), whose English translation, *The Craft of Musical Composition*, came out in 1942. But more recently Sondheim said that he never read Hindemith's book. "As far as I know, I never read any formal book on composition or harmony or counterpoint, except for a tiny little blue book on the principles of counterpoint" (Kitson's *Counterpoint for Beginners*).[61] Barrow apparently was enamored not only with counterpoint but with Hindemith's manner of contrapuntal manipulation; a former student remembers taking a course, "Dissonant Counterpoint," in which they wrote what Barrow called "Hindemith chorales."[62] Barrow's focus on counterpoint provides a link between Sondheim's early work and Hindemith, especially in the piano sonata Sondheim wrote under Barrow's tutelage, with its fugato standing as the central episode of the third movement.

The linear counterpoint that suffuses the sonata informs later Sondheim as well. Take, for example, the song "Our Time" (from *Merrily We Roll Along*). Between the lyric "We're the shapers" and "up to us, man, to show 'em," a descending line, one note to the bar, appears in the alto voice of the accompaniment, and flowers into its own melodic gesture right before the song heads to its refrain, "It's our time . . ." Because of contrapuntal lines like this one, Sondheim's songs cannot be reduced to lead sheets, the musical shorthand of reproducing the melody and reducing the harmony to chord abbreviations. Nearly all of his songs employ linear counterpoint in some form or fashion.

And beyond the songs, Sondheim's contrapuntal ensembles are legendary. The contrapuntal texture in the title song of *Company* is not nearly as dense as one would find in a fugue. But in 1970, this number, made up of soloists who have to nail their lines rhythmically and melodically, was revolutionary in its reach. Fritz Holt, the production stage manager for the show, said that "the 'Company' number took longer to stage than any number I've ever been involved with. We had everyone sit in chairs, like in a classroom. Each person was assigned his 'Bobbys' and 'Babys' and 'Bubis.' It took the first morning of rehearsals—four hours—to do the first page. Everyone was scared."[63] The image of the classroom, with its overtones of didacticism and sterility, plays into the image of Sondheim the intellectual Broadway composer. In his next show, the 1971 *Follies,* he wrote a contrapuntal ensemble—the montage of "Rain on the Roof," "Ah, Paris!" and "Broadway Baby"—that never seemed to work and was cut during its Boston tryout.[64] As if to make up for this slight, Sondheim composed yet another contrapuntal montage for the next musical, *Night Music,* bringing together "Now," "Later," and "Soon" in a deliberately unexpected way. "In those days," Sondheim said, "I was just getting into contrapuntal vocal and choral writing . . . a little in *Company* and a lot in *The Frogs.*"[65] But the vocal canon in the title song of *Saturday Night* shows an interest in applying contrapuntal techniques to vocal writing that, by the time of *The Frogs,* was already twenty years old. To trace all this contrapuntal interest to Hindemith and to him alone is next to impossible. But given that Hindemith, of all the composers identified thus far, was the one most interested in counterpoint, Sondheim's "Hindemith phase" seems to have lasted well beyond 1950.

Another Hindemithian device that appears early in Sondheim is the use of the suspended dominant. The harmony of the suspended dominant is by no means unique to Hindemith or Sondheim, as may be seen in the Ravel left-hand concerto. But it also points in the direction of Hindemith. In Sondheim's sonata, the lack of traditional dominants and the preponderance of suspended dominants are both noteworthy, given that the harmonic language throughout aims to emulate Hindemith, who also often approached the tonic in nontraditional ways. (The "Alleluia" from the *Symphony of Psalms* also contains a suspended dominant of sorts in its penultimate chord, and in view of Sondheim's anecdote about his fondness for this moment, the Stravinsky provides another locus for this sonority.)

The warmed-over Hindemith of the sonata may represent Sondheim's first extended use of the suspended dominant, but its recurrence in his later work shows its fundamental importance as a part of Sondheim's sound world. In the title number from *Company,* the suspended

dominant saturates the texture, and in its historical context it sounds of a piece with some of the popular "art" songs from the late 1960s (e.g., the work of Jimmy Webb and Burt Bacharach). But because much of the rest of the score also employs this device, and not for reasons of contemporary currency, its use in "Company" is emblematic of Sondheim's core sound world, which was forged through his exposure to Hindemith. The title numbers of *Merrily We Roll Along* (1981) and *Into the Woods* (1987) also use the suspended dominant extensively, and "My Friends" (*Sweeney Todd*, 1979) is, with the exception of one chord, exclusively built around this sonority. And "sonority" is the proper designation for this suspended dominant, as Sondheim used it coloristically (as in "My Friends") and not as a chord that precedes the tonic. (Compare also the "Parabasis" from *The Frogs* [1974], which sounds like a study for "My Friends," and "Ariadne," written for the show's 2004 revisal, which also has a chain of suspended dominants.) Sondheim unabashedly dubbed this sonority "my favorite chord," calling it "sort of a jazz chord."[66] Perhaps the chord emerges in his music from a confluence of Ravel and Hindemith, both of whom turned to jazz in the 1920s. At a minimum, the omnipresence of this sonority in Sondheim suggests a far greater reach for the musical language contained in the sonata—and Hindemith, who in part lay behind this language—than has heretofore been proposed.

Beyond the linking of the suspended dominant with Hindemith, there are moments in Sondheim that simply sound as though lifted out of a Hindemith score. The central sections of "I Know Things Now" and "On the Steps of the Palace," from *Into the Woods* (1987), have sonic traces of Hindemith, and the opening of the "Witch's Lament," also from *Into the Woods,* bears a distant relationship with the opening of the third movement of Hindemith's Third Piano Sonata. In other words, Hindemith was more than a phase for Sondheim; his musical language became a part of Sondheim's musical language.

And this is reflected in the record collection, where Hindemith occupies seventeen cards (the same number as Stravinsky), making him one of Sondheim's largest holdings. Certainly most of these recordings would have been purchased after 1950, the time of the "Hindemith phase." And in a way, it is appropriate for Sondheim to be a musical grandson to Hindemith, for he is a dramatic one. One might imagine that Hindemith, who wrote an opera about the painter Matthias Grünewald, would have respected *Sunday in the Park with George,* and that the composer of *Cardillac,* with its homicidal title character, would have nodded approvingly in the direction of *Sweeney Todd.*

We know that Copland did nod approvingly in the direction of Sondheim. In his biography, *Aaron Copland: The Life and Work of an Uncommon Man*, Howard Pollack told the story of a visitor to Copland's Rock Hill residence in the 1980s. During the visit, "Bernstein telephoned and, upon hearing Copland in the background merrily singing 'A Weekend in the Country' . . . protested, 'He never sings any of my songs!'"[67] Sondheim, then, had a salubrious effect on Copland.

But what kind of effect did Copland have on Sondheim? This question has largely gone unasked because most commentators presume to know the answer, in no small part because of Sondheim's work at Williams. In the spring of 1950, Sondheim wrote another paper for Nin-Culmell, this time for Music 20, the second semester of "Music and Musicians of the Twentieth Century." His twenty-five-page essay, "Notes and Comment on Aaron Copland with Special Reference to His Suite, *Music for the Theatre*," profited from his earlier effort on Ravel; this time, Nin-Culmell gave him an A with nary a comment on the paper.

Ever since Sondheim wrote these two papers, commentators have linked Ravel and Copland as his principal influences. And the manner in which they have done so begins to look like a game of telephone, where an original message gets distorted after it has been passed from person to person. Milton Babbitt spoke of Ravel and Copland, although he did not suggest resonance of either composer in Sondheim's music. "[Sondheim's] only interests in recent music to speak of [around 1950] were Ravel and Copland, although they were neither near nor dear to my heart. We mostly got deep into Mozart sonatas and Beethoven symphonies from esoteric, detailed points of view."[68] At that time, Sondheim wrote his Concertino for Two Pianos, whose first movement, according to Meryle Secrest, was provocatively named "Letters from Aaron Copland to Maurice Ravel."[69] In fact, although Sondheim later gave a rationale for this suggestive subtitle, there is no certainty that the movement ever was so named.

> [A]bout Aaron Copland [and] Maurice Ravel. I was just very self-conscious about stealing aspects of their music from them and [the first movement] did have that title at one time. In fact, I was surprised to look at the manuscript and not see it there anymore. . . . Maybe I never officially called it [this], maybe it was a joke I made. I don't really know.[70]

(Perhaps part of the rationale is found in that Sondheim and John Ryan, his friend for whom he wrote the concertino, enjoyed playing a two-piano version of Copland's *El Salón México*.)[71] Still, Secrest construed Babbitt's comments thus: "Sondheim wanted to study Copland and Ravel, his major interests in college, and made exhaustive analyses of Beethoven symphonies and Mozart sonatas."[72] Prior to Secrest's biography, Banfield asserted that Copland was one of Sondheim's primary mentors. He would repeat that assertion in the most recent version of the major English-language music reference, *The New Grove Dictionary of Music and Musicians*, where he wrote that "Sondheim's musical language, in which melody and harmony are closely argued, retains strong affinities with Ravel and Copland."[73] And in his brochure notes for the New York Philharmonic's live recording of *Sweeney Todd*, James M. Keller returns to Sondheim's lessons with Babbitt and states unequivocally that "Mozart, Beethoven, Copland and Ravel became the subjects of their joint analyses."[74]

It seems clear that Sondheim and Babbitt did *not* study Ravel and Copland. It also is clear that Ravel is a major influence on Sondheim. But how much of Copland can be located in Sondheim? Sondheim's own remarks provide a pathway.

In one interview, he volunteered that "you can't be an American without being influenced by Copland." His next sentence, though, tempered this statement. "I'm also influenced by Leonard Bernstein, who was influenced by Copland; we all eat from the same cake."[75] In his research for his biography of Copland, Pollack asked Sondheim about Copland's influence. Sondheim wrote in reply: "Copland's general harmonic language (when it was tonal) colored my general musical thinking, just as it did almost every other subsequent American composer of tonal music." Pollack concludes that "Sondheim . . . who met the composer only once, partly grounded his style—as *A Funny Thing Happened on the Way to the Forum* (1962) makes patent—in the work of Copland, along with Ravel, one of his favorite composers."[76] The disclaimers here—only one meeting; a partial grounding—resonate with Sondheim's rather bland attribution of Copland's influence, and Pollack's formulation allows for Sondheim to like Copland without being influenced by him.

In fact, there are moments in Sondheim's music that clearly sound like Copland. It is a happy accident that Pollack and Banfield light on the same music from *Forum;* Pollack has remarked on the opening of the overture, and Banfield has analyzed "Free," the song from which the overture's musical fragment derives. "This song is close to Milhaud's style, itself only a few steps away from that of one of Sondheim's primary mentors, Copland."[77] Like Pollack and Banfield, I too hear the sound world of Copland in this song, or, more precisely, Copland as filtered through Leonard Bernstein, one of Copland's foremost champions in the 1950s, the same decade when Bernstein and Sondheim collaborated on *West Side Story*. "Free" especially shows some indebtedness to the music of *West Side Story* (particularly with the song's repeated emphasis on the tritone in the refrain), but in the verses of the song Copland's voice comes to the surface. The avoidance of conjunct melodic intervals, the two-part counterpoint landing on dissonant intervals at the strong beats, and the rhythmic variation in the last measure as the melody spans the interval of the ninth all sound like Copland's wide open spaces, an appropriate musical metaphor for the freedom the slave Pseudolus is seeking.

But when the Copland question was put directly to Sondheim, his answer was unequivocal.

> Copland hasn't particularly influenced me. He's influenced every American writer. But the only time I'm aware of having been influenced by Copland is in *Assassins* where I was trying to recreate a certain expanse of Americana. It occurs mostly in the harmonies of "Hail to the Chief," at the beginning. But no, Copland doesn't influence me particularly.[78]

This more recent disclaimer of Copland's influence resonates with Sondheim's earlier statements about Copland's place in his music. Every American composer owes a musical debt to Copland; Sondheim's particular debt to Copland comes through Bernstein; and though the indebtedness is real, it should not be made out to be more pervasive than the music suggests.

Indeed, Copland's influence fails to appear when one would most expect to see it, namely, in the sonata that was written concurrently with Sondheim's paper on *Music for the Theatre*. The metrical cast of the movements does not resemble the metrical shifts so often found in Copland's music. The thickness of Sondheim's harmonies runs counter to the leanness of texture usually associated with Copland. Even the employing of traditional forms as scaffolding—a sonata form for the first movement, a modified rondo for the third, and a likely ABA form for the incomplete slow movement—differs from Copland's characteristic slow-fast-slow alternation in large-scale compositions. Elsewhere I have written about Sondheim's motivic development as the most apt connec-

tion that exists between his writing and Copland's,[79] and indeed the sonata bests Copland in generating reams of musical material from the humblest of motives. One would expect that this early work would clearly show the springs from which Sondheim imbibed to create his own musical language. Copland's spring, Appalachian or otherwise, is notably dry in the sonata.

Copland's influence on American composers is due in large part to his success in so many different genres of music. While he is best known in the public mind as a composer of populist works—*Fanfare for the Common Man* and the ballets *Billy the Kid*, *Rodeo*, and *Appalachian Spring*—his body of compositions runs the gamut from symphonies and symphonic music to film music, from chamber and solo piano works to opera and songs. With a musical vocabulary that ranged from French neoclassicism through an American vernacular to high modernist serialism, Copland achieved successes in every musical language he adopted. It is easy to look at his protean abilities and suggest that Sondheim profited from the older composer's example. It is also easy to see how Copland as filtered through Bernstein made its way into Sondheim's consciousness.[80] Copland as pasticheur of American folk music is of a piece with Sondheim as pasticheur of American musical theater. These are easy connections to draw.

But it is more difficult to suggest that Sondheim misrepresented either himself or his music when he asserted that Copland's influence upon him was muted at best. Perhaps someone will augment Banfield's assertions and show more conclusively than has heretofore been shown that Sondheim borrowed extensively from Copland's musical vocabulary.[81] Until that time, it is best to accept that Copland remained a lifelong love of Sondheim's—witnessed as recently as 2000 with his choice of *Music for the Theatre* as one of his desert island discs[82] and evident in the ten inventory cards devoted to the composer—but that Copland's impact on Sondheim's musical language was minimal.

Other classical composers

Beyond the influences of the composers so far mentioned, Sondheim has named a number of composers and pieces that appeal to him. After talking in an interview about his dislike of opera, Sondheim named those operas he did like.

> I saw *Bohème* in a 700-seat theatre and cried for two-and-a-half hours straight. That's my idea of opera. I still think *Bohème* is long-winded

> but it attempts to tell a story and to characterize musically. I like *Carmen*, I like *Bohème*, I like some of *Tosca*. Puccini generally I like best, and the first act of *Peter Grimes*, and *Porgy and Bess*, and *Wozzeck*. That about does it.[83]

His choices fit squarely within his delimited preferences; *Carmen* (1875) is the earliest piece on this list, and *Peter Grimes* (1945) is the latest. And it is instructive to note that *Porgy and Bess*—the only stage work other than his own that Sondheim elected to take with him to a desert island—is listed as an opera in league with Britten and Berg.

Sondheim's other desert island discs are, with the exception of the Stravinsky *Symphony of Psalms* and the stage works, purely instrumental. In the 2000 BBC program, Sondheim named Brahms's Piano Concerto no. 2, op. 83 (1881), as his favorite classical piece. Twenty years earlier, he included Ravel's *Valses nobles et sentimentales* and Bartók's Concerto for Orchestra; these were supplanted by the Copland and *Sunday in the Park with George*.[84] And elsewhere, in talking about his extensive record collection, he identified a mail-order record catalog to which he subscribed. "There are certain Norwegian and South American composers whom I like a lot and when they have new pieces out I send for them and I listen to them over and over again and see if I like them."[85] Expanding his comment to encompass all of Scandinavia and not just Norway, Sondheim has indicated that those composers include Nystroem and Montsalvatge as well as others.[86]

To trace evidences of musical influence from each of these composers would be an impossible task. Yet Sondheim has helpfully identified two instances where he borrowed from other composers. In his list "Songs I Wish I'd Have Written (At Least in Part)," he named Montsalvatge's "Canción de cuna para dormir a un negrito" (Cradle Song for a Little Black Boy). Anyone who listens to this will quickly recognize how Sondheim reinterpreted it in "Wait" *(Sweeney Todd)* and how vestiges of it appear in "Don't Look at Me" *(Follies)*. Similarly, in the third movement of Nystroem's *Sinfonia del mare* (1947–48), there is an undulating figure that sounds immediately Sondheimesque even as its location (the accompaniment for "Too Many Mornings" from *Follies* and "Boca Raton" from *Bounce*) may be at first difficult to place: "the Montsalvatge and the Nystroem are the two conscious things that I've [borrowed from], one the chord progression, the other the vamp. Everything else is merely an imitation of style."[87]

Sondheim's disclaimer overlooks an example of homage paid to one of the operas that pleased him. In the theater, the end of "Epiphany"

(*Sweeney Todd,* 1979) often gets lost in the applause that follows Todd's high note and the triumphant chord that comes from the pit. (In the live recording at the New York Philharmonic, the last three measures are cut.) But in the original cast recording one hears a shadow sound that follows the triumphant one. The triumphant chord is repeated, only for the number to end with the dissonant shadow sound. In the dramatic context of the musical, this is more than a sonic echo. It signals that Todd's triumphalism has its dark side, that his "epiphany" has an unsettling dis-ease about it. And this unsettled quality is revealed not in the staging but in the music; our ears, not our eyes, tell us that something is not all right with Todd's discovery. The corollary to this musical gesture is found in Benjamin Britten's *Peter Grimes,* albeit the third act, not the first, which Sondheim professed to like. There, after the townspeople have gathered and determined to mete out vigilante justice on Peter Grimes, they roar out his name in anger. Their enraged cry at first is met by silence. When they cry out a second time, a single muted horn answers, tentative and scarcely audible. A third cry is answered by two muted horns, again barely audible but suggestive of some uncertainty yet to unfold. The shadow sound here, as in *Sweeney Todd,* heightens the tension.

And then there's Berg. In 1977, in his introduction to Fordin's Hammerstein biography, Sondheim mentioned *Wozzeck;* ten years later, he named *Wozzeck* again and elevated it to the rank of one of his favorite operas. It is not difficult to understand why this score appealed to Sondheim. In addition to the expressionist representation of Büchner's story in Berg's hands—it plays almost as melodramatically as does *Sweeney Todd*—the music is overtly symphonic: Act 1 is cast as a five-movement suite; act 2 is a five-movement symphony; and act 3 is a set of five musical inventions (with an orchestral interlude that serves as a sixth invention on a key). As representational drama and as absolute music, *Wozzeck* succeeds as do few operas after Wagner. And Berg—unlike Wagner—managed to express his vision in a compact ninety-minute work.

It is worth dwelling on *Wozzeck* in greater detail, as its structural complexity has often obscured its dramatic efficacy. When asked about *Wozzeck,* Berg showed a clear understanding of what he had created.

> What I do consider my particular accomplishment is this. No one in the audience, no matter how aware he may be of the musical forms contained in the framework of the opera, of the precision and logic with which it has been worked out, no one, from the moment the curtain parts until it closes for the last time, pays any attention to the var-

ious fugues, inventions, suites, sonata movements, variations, and passacaglias about which so much has been written. No one gives heed to anything but the vast social implications of the work, which by far transcend the personal destiny of Wozzeck. This, I believe, is my achievement.[88]

If Berg had difficulty getting his critics to move away from the analysis of the music to an appreciation of his drama, Sondheim has suffered from the opposite oversight, as his drama is often praised while his music (especially in terms of its structure) goes un(der)examined. Sondheim's admiration of *Wozzeck* must principally reside where Berg suggested it must, namely, with the impact of the story abetted by a powerful score. And yet Sondheim could hardly be unaware of "the precision and logic with which [that score] has been worked out," for his own scores show a similar attention to precision and logic. Nearly every classical musician who knows twentieth-century music well would name *Wozzeck* as a musical masterpiece as well as a dramatic one. That Sondheim should mention *Wozzeck* twice over the course of a decade as an opera he likes shows his appreciation not only of good drama but also of one of the high-water marks of classical music.[89]

And once again: classical music within a circumscribed time frame. He knew earlier music; he talked about analyzing Mozart's G minor symphony with Babbitt. But he prefers the middle to late Romantics, like Brahms and Bizet and Rachmaninoff and Puccini, the early moderns, like Ravel and Prokofiev and Stravinsky, the "pre-post-moderns," like Gershwin and Britten, and even a high modernist like Berg. At the time when Sondheim heard Hindemith's "Four Temperaments," the piece was barely ten years old (and the recording he likely heard was freshly minted).[90] And his desert island musical companions are—with the exception of his own works—classical pieces. No Rodgers. No Kern. No Porter or Berlin or Arlen. Nothing from his peers; nothing from the generations that followed him (though, on a different occasion, he confessed to a partiality for Adam Guettel's *Floyd Collins* (1996),[91] a beautifully acerbic musical that makes Sondheim sound like Schubert). Babbitt remarked that Sondheim "wanted his music to be as sophisticated and as knowing with the obvious restraints of a Broadway musical. After all, very few Broadway composers were all that educated. Richard Rodgers, who was considered the smartest of that gang, had no real connection with the world of serious music, and he was so self-centered I don't think he thought there was much for him to learn."[92] If Rodgers wasn't interested in classical music, Sondheim certainly was.

Thus Sondheim could poke fun at himself in "Opening Doors." There are very few tunes in Stravinsky that go "bum-bum-bum-di-dum," at least to the proverbial tired businessman who wants to tap his toes a bit. Even the tune that this producer sings is remarkably angular and unsympathetic to the voice. Here it is a chiseled melody instead of a liquid one, and in the original version of *Merrily*, we watch as Frank, the one-tune composer in the musical, moves from his teenage highbrow (even Coplandesque) aspirations ("The Hills of Tomorrow") to the compromise of commercial musical commodity. The melody gets ironed out, turned to pabulum, if you like, right before our ears.

Thus the quotation of "Some Enchanted Evening"—which is really a misquotation, as Joe Josephson half-remembers the melody—is Sondheim's way of concurring with Babbitt. Sondheim could—and occasionally did—write a melody as lyrical as any by Rodgers, as the homogenized version of Frank's melody in "Good Thing Going" demonstrates. But that type of domestication and commodification interested him little. The unusual harmonic turns, the countermelodies and contrapuntal connivances, the motivically generated melodies that populate Sondheim's canon: such are more the concerns of a classically trained composer, not a commercially oriented one. Of course, Sondheim was both, but in pitching his sound in a classical direction he all but guaranteed the limited commercial appeal of his music (though the music, I should hasten to add, is not the sum total of his shows).

Still, this classical orientation comes from Sondheim's earliest years. It predates his work with Bernstein on *West Side Story* in 1957, though the organization of that score would give Sondheim a better grasp on handling ensembles. It predates his lessons with Babbitt from 1950 to 1952, though he learned from Babbitt how composers control musical flow over long stretches of time. It even predates his studies at Williams, although the sonata he wrote there shows him consolidating his classical knowledge in an amalgam that begins to point to his own distinctive compositional voice. As a teenager, Sondheim was already a connoisseur of modern music, and even if he partook of its more tonal streams, it was more modern than his forebears knew.

It comes as no surprise, then, that Sondheim was also enthralled by the music of Bernard Herrmann. Herrmann came into Hollywood shortly after the high Romanticism of Korngold, Steiner, and Waxman, and while he could write a Romantic tune, he developed a musical palette that edged past Puccini toward the Richard Strauss of *Salome* and *Elektra*. He wrote the music for *Hangover Square*, a 1945 movie that tells the story of a young composer torn between the worlds of commercial and art music. The composer also experiences psychotic episodes that lead him to commit mayhem, murder, and arson. (It all sounds very Sondheimesque.) These episodes are triggered by sharp, shrill dissonance, thus putting the composer's own music into relief as more palliative, more respectful. A harmonic analysis reveals that the opening of the composer's concerto is firmly in the key of D minor, although our ears tell us that the music (Herrmann's) resides somewhere between the lush late Romanticism of Rachmaninoff and the stentorian early Modernism of the enfant terrible Prokofiev. And what does all this have to do with the then fifteen-year-old Sondheim? Simply that he stayed to watch the movie a second time in order to memorize the opening of the concerto and later wrote Herrmann a fan letter[93]—and all this before Herrmann came into greater prominence through his collaboration with Alfred Hitchcock and while scores like those of Korngold, Steiner, and Waxman were still the norm.

So the decade that witnessed the start of the Rodgers and Hammerstein revolution—*Oklahoma!*, *State Fair*, *Carousel*, *Allegro*, and *South Pacific*—as well as Berlin's *Annie Get Your Gun* and Porter's *Kiss Me, Kate*, and that would end with Frank Loesser's *Guys and Dolls*, found Sondheim listening to Ravel and memorizing Herrmann, writing a term paper about Copland and imitating Hindemith. For someone who wanted to write Broadway shows, Sondheim's musical palette seemed to be developing at cross purposes to the audience he would have to reach.

Parenthetically, this seriousness of musical background and its dumbing down for mass consumption provide a point of comparison between Sondheim and Kurt Weill. While musicologists have tried to show continuities across Weill's career, the scholarly community has tended to talk about "the two Weills": the classical, serious Weill of Europe and the popular, commercial Weill of America.[94] Another way to read this supposed schizophrenia is to argue that the American Weill was never completely successful (relative to the European) because of his training in and vestigial allegiance to classical music. The parallel to Sondheim draws itself.[95] While Sondheim has never made a conscious attempt to write concert music beyond his early works—and recently indicated that he has no desire to start doing so—his classical training informs his craft in a way that the mass market finds less than appealing. Sondheim stands alongside Weill in the way they drew upon classical music in a sustained manner throughout their careers. (Frank Loesser's *The Most Happy Fella* stands out as a notable foray into classical music; Bernstein's body of musicals is relatively small.) Tellingly, Sondheim

greatly preferred the classical Weill to the commercial one, finding much of the Broadway music "anathema" but liking the acerbity of *The Threepenny Opera*.[96]

Bernstein criticized Sondheim early on for the studious complexity he heard in *A Funny Thing Happened on the Way to the Forum*, from 1962.[97] But Sondheim did not deliberately render his Broadway music complex in comparison with other composers, as Bernstein accused. Instead, it appears that Sondheim may have circumscribed his own adventurous language in order to make his Broadway music more readily accessible. Because of his classical exemplars, Sondheim's complex writing has been a part of his musical vocabulary from his Williams days forward.[98]

Sondheim the classicist at work

All of this helps to account for the rudiments of Sondheim's sound from a musical point of hearing. But tracing his music back to classical exemplars doesn't explain how Sondheim turns his musical language to dramatic ends. It is in this dramatic use of musical language that Sondheim moved away from Rodgers and Porter and Berlin and on through Puccini to Verdi and Wagner. While American musical theater before Sondheim witnessed a growing integration of its various parts, it was atypical for Broadway composers to do more than capture the general mood of the lyrics in their music. Rare was the song whose music sought to comment on the lyrics, to question or contradict them, or to reinforce them with a musical logic that owes more to classical music and opera than to popular song. The goal generally was to write a hit tune, not to engage in musical drama. But musical drama is fundamental for Sondheim.

"Not While I'm Around" from *Sweeney Todd* offers an example of the wedding of classicism and drama in music. To begin with, it refutes the idea that Sondheim could not write a hummable melody; this song is achingly beautiful and quite memorable. Coupled to the relative simplicity of the melody is its uncomplicated abab′ formal structure (which together forms the first part—A—of a larger ternary structure). All of this is in keeping with the character who introduces the song, Tobias (Toby), a sweet-hearted but dim-witted fellow who knows no guile. His song, in other words, is as straightforward as he is. But in the central part of the song (B), which contrasts sharply with the opening section, Toby's agitation and inability to order his thoughts are reflected in a change of melody, vocal range, harmony, and form. Next, Mrs. Lovett, the person he seeks to protect, answers him (A′). By this time, we know that she turns dead people into meat pies, but in singing his song back to him, she aims to convince Toby that she is a fellow innocent. However, the wandering dissonant countermelody that accompanies her belies her words. This contrary countermelody disappears when Toby breaks away and reasserts his unimpeachable character. Mrs. Lovett is left to watch and listen and scheme against him. And this "dialogue" between guilelessness and duplicity occurs in the music, not in the lyrics or the staging. (The song is also remarkable for its subtle use of suspended dominants and contrapuntal devices other than the countermelody.)

The fact that we so clearly hear what Sondheim is doing—and some may not hear at first how Sondheim sets Mrs. Lovett up by creating such a simple song to begin with—shows at a minimum how Sondheim's approach to musical language has become the lingua franca of Broadway. Popular songs use techniques that were once reserved for film scoring or opera, communicating aurally what is happening dramatically. But one hardly thinks of listening to most Gershwin or Porter or Rodgers songs for such encoded information; yet one can *not* listen to Sondheim any other way. This is certainly one reason why the concert hall and the opera house have been quick to embrace him. His musical values reward the audience that pays attention to the musical argument he advances.

Kim Kowalke, noted Weill scholar, rightly observed that the term *songwriter* is "inadequate for Sondheim, who arguably has engaged diverse musico-dramatic and melopoetic problems more consistently and imaginatively than any composer since Richard Wagner."[99] As apt as the comparison between Wagner and Sondheim may be, one situates these composers side by side with a discomfort that goes beyond Sondheim's implicit distaste for Wagner. Though he himself has confessed to a loathing for Verdi, Sondheim is surely America's answer to the Italian composer.[100] From the early, more traditional musicals *(Saturday Night, Forum)* to the trailblazing musicals of his middle years to the retrospective works of his late years, Sondheim's dramatic works have traced a trajectory not unlike Verdi's works. Indeed, it is tempting to call *Passion* Sondheim's *Otello* and *Bounce* his *Falstaff*. But more than the shape of the works themselves is the shape of the music within the works. For just as Verdi invested his music with more dramatic force than had his predecessors, so Sondheim brought to the Broadway musical more musico-dramatic heft than had those who came before him. Like Verdi, and unlike Wagner, Sondheim treasured the song. And like Verdi, whose works are performed over a century after their composition, it is safe to state that Sondheim's musicals will continue to generate interest well into the future, and for primarily the same reason as do Verdi's operas: they present compellingly dramatic music.

Coda

This chapter opened with a reference to Richard Strauss and closes with a nod to his last opera. In *Capriccio*, Strauss tried to give music and words an even hand. In the end, though, the glorious music won. (*Capriccio* wasn't one of the five operas in Sondheim's collection, but he did own a recording of the instrumental sextet that opens the opera.)

Sondheim the lyricist deserves all the praise he has received. Sondheim the composer has received far less praise. Could it be because he tends more toward the classical than most lovers of musical theater enjoy?

> My period is from Brahms through 1930s Stravinsky. I like music before and I like music after, but that's where I live. Britten shows up a lot in the stuff I write. *Sunday in the Park with George* is a Britten score, I think. I'm very fond of English music. As far as American music goes, I was brought up on show tunes from the so-called Golden Era, a phrase I deplore, but there it is. You know, Kern and Gershwin. Those are influences, too. So it's Ravel, Rachmaninoff—another wonderful harmonist—Britten, Stravinsky, Kern, Gershwin, Arlen. A *lot* of Arlen.[101]

In chapter 2, I explore Sondheim in relationship with the golden era of Broadway and Tin Pan Alley. But since Sondheim highlighted classical composers first among his influences, it is right for those who want to talk seriously about his music to go to these classical composers first.

It may be too much to call Sondheim a classical composer, as he does not fit the twentieth-century conception of one. But he is like an earlier composer—Rossini—in the manner in which he applies the tools of his trade to the exigencies that he faced. It is likely that Rossini rarely wrote his operas with an eye to posterity; he was more interested in scoring a commercial success than insuring that his name would be in the history books. And in Rossini's day, the notion of "classical composer" did not yet exist. He was a professional musician who practiced his compositional craft adeptly and to great public acclaim.

So it is with Sondheim, who not only was brought up on show tunes but also brought show tunes up to the level of classical music. Given his musical influences, such an elevation was as inevitable as it was likely unintentional. But as he himself said, "There it is." It remains to those who respect Sondheim the composer to treat his music with the same depth of understanding and respect that he brought to the music he loved, music that echoes in his own music.

2

Sondheim the Tunesmith

The Big Six and Broadway

As was revealed in the previous chapter, Sondheim named George Gershwin and Harold Arlen as significant influences on his musical development. Together with Jerome Kern, Irving Berlin, Richard Rodgers, and Cole Porter, Gershwin and Arlen make up what many writers consider the Big Six of American songwriters who created the golden era, if not of Tin Pan Alley, then certainly of Broadway and Hollywood.[1] Sondheim arguably chose the best-known and the least-known members of the Big Six, and it happens that he, Gershwin, and Arlen share some unusual traits, including a few "possibles" (Arlen's word) for future stage works. Sondheim's choice also raises questions about the differences among the three, differences that, upon examination, may not separate them as much as first glance would suggest.

I cannot hope to talk about all of the show, film, and independent songs that the Big Six introduced to the world. Instead, I will steer my remarks toward some of the Broadway shows and revivals that appeared from Sondheim's youth to his first professional Broadway shows in the late 1950s. (See table 1.) Such a focus serves a number of purposes.

First, it shows that the Big Six ruled Broadway during this time when Sondheim was developing his creative skills. Even though one of them, Gershwin, died in 1937 and another, Kern, died in 1945, every year between 1935 and 1959, save for 1956, has at least one show that was composed by a member of the Big Six. Other older composers occasionally emerged from the shadows of time and newer composers began to assert themselves, but the Big Six remained unrivaled.

Second, a narrower swath of time—1944 to 1948—witnessed the premieres of some of the finest Broadway scores of the living members of the Big Six. Berlin's *Annie Get Your Gun* and Porter's *Kiss Me, Kate* are universally held to represent the pinnacles of these two men's Broadway efforts, and Rodgers considered *Carousel* his favorite, with its score

TABLE 1. A Selective List of Broadway Shows, 1935–59

Year	Show	Composer/Lyricist
1935	*Porgy and Bess*	George Gershwin/DuBose Heyward and Ira Gershwin
	Jubilee	Cole Porter/Porter
	Jumbo	Richard Rodgers/Lorenz Hart
1936	*On Your Toes*	Rodgers/Hart
	The White Horse Inn	Ralph Benatzky/Benatzky
	Red, Hot and Blue!	Porter/Porter
1937	*Babes in Arms*	Rodgers/Hart
	I'd Rather Be Right	Rodgers/Hart
	Pins and Needles	Harold Rome/Rome
	Hooray for What!	Harold Arlen/E. Y. Harburg
1938	*The Cradle Will Rock*	Marc Blitzstein/Blitzstein
	I Married an Angel	Rodgers/Hart
	You Never Know	Porter/Porter
	Knickerbocker Holiday	Kurt Weill/Maxwell Anderson
	Leave It to Me	Porter/Porter
	The Boys from Syracuse	Rodgers/Hart
1939	*Too Many Girls*	Rodgers/Hart
	Very Warm for May	Jerome Kern/Oscar Hammerstein II
	DuBarry Was a Lady	Porter/Porter
1940	*Higher and Higher*	Rodgers/Hart
	Louisiana Purchase	Irving Berlin/Berlin
	Hold on to Your Hats	Burton Lane/Harburg
	Cabin in the Sky	Vernon Duke/John LaTouche
	Panama Hattie	Porter/Porter
	Pal Joey	Rodgers/Hart
1941	*Lady in the Dark*	Weill/I. Gershwin
	Best Foot Forward	Hugh Martin/Ralph Blane
	Let's Face It	Porter/Porter
1942	*Porgy and Bess* (revival)	G. Gershwin/Heyward and I. Gershwin
	By Jupiter	Rodgers/Hart
	This Is the Army	Berlin/Berlin
1943	*Something for the Boys*	Porter/Porter
	Oklahoma!	Rodgers/Hammerstein
	One Touch of Venus	Weill/Ogden Nash
	A Connecticut Yankee (revival)	Rodgers/Hart
	Carmen Jones	Georges Bizet/Hammerstein
1944	*Mexican Hayride*	Porter/Porter
	Follow the Girls	Phil Charig/Dan Shapiro and Milton Pascal
	Song of Norway	Edvard Grieg/Robert Wright and George Forrest
	Bloomer Girl	Arlen/Harburg
	The Seven Lively Arts	Porter (incl. Stravinsky's *Scènes de Ballet*)/Porter
	On the Town	Leonard Bernstein/Betty Comden and Adolph Green
1945	*Up in Central Park*	Sigmund Romberg/Herbert Fields and Dorothy Fields

Table 1. *Continued*

Year	Show	Composer/Lyricist
	Carousel	Rodgers/Hammerstein
	The Red Mill (revival)	Victor Herbert/Henry Blossom
	The Day before Spring	Frederick Loewe/Alan Jay Lerner
	Billion Dollar Baby	Morton Gould/Comden and Green
1946	*Show Boat* (revival)	Kern/Hammerstein
	St. Louis Woman	Arlen/Johnny Mercer
	Call Me Mister	Rome/Rome
	Annie Get Your Gun	Berlin/Berlin
	Around the World	Porter/Porter
	Beggar's Holiday	Duke Ellington/LaTouche
1947	*Street Scene*	Weill/Langston Hughes
	Finian's Rainbow	Lane/Harburg and Fred Saidy
	Brigadoon	Loewe/Lerner
	The Telephone and *The Medium*	Gian Carlo Menotti/Menotti
	High Button Shoes	Jule Styne/Sammy Cahn
	Allegro	Rodgers/Hammerstein
1948	*Look, Ma, I'm Dancin'*	Martin/Martin
	Magdalena	Heitor Villa-Lobos/Wright and Forrest
	Love Life	Weill/Lerner
	Where's Charley?	Frank Loesser/Loesser
	The Rape of Lucretia	Benjamin Britten/Ronald Duncan
	Kiss Me, Kate	Porter/Porter
1949	*South Pacific*	Rodgers/Hammerstein
	Miss Liberty	Berlin/Berlin
	Lost in the Stars	Weill/Anderson
	Gentlemen Prefer Blondes	Styne/Leo Robin
1950	*The Consul*	Menotti/Menotti
	Call Me Madam	Berlin/Berlin
	Guys and Dolls	Loesser/Loesser
	Out of This World	Porter/Porter
1951	*The King and I*	Rodgers/Hammerstein
	Make a Wish	Martin/Martin
	A Tree Grows in Brooklyn	Arthur Schwartz/D. Fields
1952	*Pal Joey* (revival)	Rodgers/Hart
	Wish You Were Here	Rome/Rome
	My Darlin' Aida	Giuseppe Verdi/Charles Friedman
1953	*Porgy and Bess* (revival)	Gershwin/Heyward and I. Gershwin
	Wonderful Town	Bernstein/Comden and Green
	Can-Can	Porter/Porter
	Me and Juliet	Rodgers/Hammerstein
	Kismet	Alexander Borodin/Wright and Forrest
1954	*The Pajama Game*	Jerry Ross/Richard Adler
	Peter Pan	Various
	Fanny	Rome/Rome
	House of Flowers	Arlen/Truman Capote
1955	*Plain and Fancy*	Albert Hague/Arnold B. Horwitt

TABLE 1. *Continued*

Year	Show	Composer/Lyricist
	Silk Stockings	Porter/Porter
	Damn Yankees	Ross/Adler
	Pipe Dream	Rodgers/Hammerstein
1956	*My Fair Lady*	Loewe/Lerner
	The Most Happy Fella	Loesser/Loesser
	Bells Are Ringing	Styne/Comden and Green
	Candide	Bernstein/LaTouche, Richard Wilbur, and Dorothy Parker (later, Sondheim)
1957	*West Side Story*	Bernstein/Sondheim
	Jamaica	Arlen/Harburg
	The Music Man	Meredith Willson/Willson
1958	*Flower Drum Song*	Rodgers/Hammerstein
1959	*Once Upon a Mattress*	Mary Rodgers/Marshall Barer
	Gypsy	Styne/Sondheim
	The Sound of Music	R. Rodgers/Hammerstein
	Fiorello!	Jerry Bock/Sheldon Harnick
	Saratoga	Arlen/Mercer

being "more satisfying than any I've ever written."[2] And though some aficionados believe that *House of Flowers* (1954) is Arlen's best Broadway score, both *Bloomer Girl* and *St. Louis Woman* have beauties that time has not obscured. Add to this the return of *Show Boat* to Broadway, and Sondheim's early teens were awash with some of Broadway's best.

Third, this was an era when composers and producers felt emboldened to take musical and dramatic risks that did not poison the box office. While the original production of *Porgy and Bess* wasn't an audience smash, the truncated 1942 and "full-length" 1953 revivals were, vindicating Gershwin's vision of a more complex musical language on Broadway.[3] The prevalence of serious ballet—begun in *On Your Toes* (1936) and embedded in musicals from *Oklahoma!* (1943) forward—reshaped the expectations of Broadway audiences, eventually giving way to the razzle-dazzle dance-driven musicals of Bob Fosse and Michael Bennett. The hegemony of 32-bar song form began to weaken, as composers and lyricists created extended ensembles and scenes not unlike those found in opera. And opera and Western concert-hall music played regularly on Broadway, most notably in the works of Menotti but also in the dramatic hodgepodges made of the music of Grieg, Verdi, and Borodin. Works like *Street Scene* (music by Kurt Weill), *Billion Dollar Baby* (Morton Gould), and *Magdalena* (Heitor Villa-Lobos) overtly straddled the line between art and commerce, while Hammerstein, in *Carmen Jones*, ignored the line altogether. Even Stravinsky was on Broadway, courtesy of *The Seven Lively Arts,* whose poor reception Sondheim hinted at in his lyric for "Opening Doors" *(Merrily).*

Sondheim came of age in the midst of this golden age of Broadway, an era rivaled only by the heyday of Tin Pan Alley in the first two decades of the century. While Sondheim came to know the music of his own generation and the generation that followed, his personal favorites are heavily weighted in favor of the Big Six. No doubt he found a particular richness in these composers, but his choices also stem in part from his own activity in the theater and from a certain detachment from and apathy toward the work of those around him.

When questioned about the presence of Broadway shows in his record collection, Sondheim responded, "I did, indeed, regularly purchase all the Broadway shows, I'd say up through the mid-sixties, and then I sort of lost interest." Then, in the answer to a question about his favorite musicals, the pre-1966 orientation becomes even more pronounced.

> The musicals I like, besides the ones I've been connected with: certainly *Show Boat* and *Porgy and Bess* and *Carousel* are my three favorites. *Allegro* I like because of my personal association with it. *My Fair Lady* was the most entertaining show I ever saw, I think, but not a score I particularly like, except for one song, "Why Can't a Woman be More Like a Man?" [*sic:* the title is "A Hymn for Him"]. Some other musicals I like—I like *She Loves Me*. I like the scores of *Chicago* and *Cabaret,* not so much the shows. Although that could easily be said of lots of shows by Kern, Gershwin, Porter, so forth, and Arlen's score for *St Louis Woman* is a particular score I love, but the show is unwieldy. So, no, there aren't very many shows I think are really good.[4]

Sondheim's list of favorite scores beyond Kander and Bock—a list that pointedly excludes Frederick Loewe's *My Fair Lady*—includes the work of five of the Big Six, with four of them represented by specific works.

Sondheim and Broadway in the 1940s

In looking to the Big Six, Sondheim was not looking to the past. Instead, this was the same decade—the 1940s—when his tastes for classical music were being developed. It is likely that from 1943 forward Sondheim saw most of the shows listed in table 1.

The Rodgers-Hammerstein shows are especially easy to chronicle, as each of the early ones has a tale attached to it. Sondheim took his baby-sitter to see *Oklahoma!* by getting standing-room tickets for himself and his friend Jimmy through Jimmy's dad, "Ockie" Hammerstein. At the end of act 1 of *Carousel*, he cried so profusely on Dorothy Hammerstein's fur wrap that he permanently stained it. He worked as a gofer on *Allegro*. Mary Rodgers introduced him to Harold Prince on the opening night of *South Pacific*—at least, according to Prince's recollection, which differs from Sondheim's as to the time of their meeting but not on whether either one of them attended the premiere.[5]

As for other shows from this period, Sondheim recollected that his first live musical was Benatzky's *The White Horse Inn* (1936), a work definitely situated in the Romberg-Herbert school.[6] He also recalled seeing *The Boys from Syracuse*, which opened in November 1938 and ran for seven months, and *Very Warm for May*, which opened almost exactly a year later but was fated to run a dismal fifty-nine performances.[7] He himself has talked about *The Medium* and *The Telephone* on Broadway and has compared *Passion* to "a chamber opera, like *Rape of Lucretia*."[8] His Williams instructor, Irwin Shainman, recalled conversations with Sondheim in which they "talked about *Allegro* a lot, *Me and Juliet*, and shows that didn't appeal to a lot of other people: *Billion Dollar Baby*, *Beggar's Holiday*, and *The Day Before Spring*."[9] And given Sondheim's explicit identification of *St. Louis Woman* and *Show Boat*, it seems likely that he saw both in 1946, the latter of which was directed by Hammerstein, Kern's collaborator on *Show Boat* and Sondheim's mentor at the time.

Kern

Hammerstein would have likely served as the link between Sondheim and Kern if the two had had any contact with each other before Kern's death in November 1945. With only the boarding school show *By George* to his credit, Sondheim would have been at best a curiosity to Kern. But Kern would later come to figure prominently in Sondheim's life, albeit from a more academic standpoint: his songs formed an important part of Sondheim's post-Williams studies with Milton Babbitt.[10] Sondheim's name for his musical holding company—Burthen Music—is derived in part from the name Kern gave to the refrains of his songs. And it is clear from the number of uncredited Hammerstein remarks that appear in Sondheim's liner notes for an album of Kern songs that Hammerstein continued to steer Sondheim in the direction of Kern even after his extensive studies with Babbitt.

These notes "show [Sondheim's] concern with the details of Kern's technique at every turn and allow us to judge which of them have rubbed off on his own music."[11] Chief among those similarities between Kern and Sondheim is their propensity toward frugality of musical means. "All of [Kern's] best songs," wrote Sondheim, "have that economy indigenous to the best art: the maximum development of the minimum of material."[12] While Sondheim attributed his mastery in making a lot out of a little to his lessons with Babbitt, his piano sonata already showed a concern for and facility in maximizing his musical material, and his senior-year paper on Copland found him praising Copland for this same developmental trait. Thus, Kern, like Richard Strauss, approached music in a way that appealed to the motivically oriented Sondheim.

Kern's hold on Sondheim's musical imagination seems strongest in the works of Sondheim's youth. In the title song from *Phinney's Rainbow*, harmonies carom through chord changes faster than in "All the Things You Are." The bridges to "When I See You" and "Let's Not Fall In Love" *(All That Glitters)* use the same harmonic scheme (moving through the circle of fifths) as the Kern song, and the first song has the operetta-like melodic shape associated with Kern. While the chorus of "I Love You, Etcetera" *(Glitters)* sounds contemporary, the verse could easily introduce a Kern song. And in "I Must Be Dreaming" *(Glitters)* one finds Sondheim's best Kern pastiche, a purer amalgamation of Kern's melodic and harmonic language than the earlier Kern-flavored "Still Got My Heart" *(Phinney's Rainbow)*. Given that nothing in the documentary record suggests that Sondheim was trying to write Kern pastiche at this time, the voice of Kern in six of the eight songs published from the Williams musicals underlines the importance of *Show Boat*'s score to Sondheim, and this at a time when he had seen three Rodgers and Hammerstein shows (and worked on one of them).

But these Kern-like musical gestures from the late 1940s find less of a home in the mature Sondheim. Kern's modulations and harmonic wanderings—often occurring to and from the bridge ("Smoke Gets in Your Eyes," "The Way You Look Tonight," "The Song Is You") but also appearing in the main section of a song ("Long Ago and Far Away," "She Didn't Say Yes," "All the Things You Are")—are distinctive in that they usually occur within the bounds of standard song form and return to the key from which the wanderings began. Sondheim's mature modulatory excursions, in contrast, often occur in songs where standard song form is exploded or abandoned altogether ("Another Hundred

People," *Company;* "The Right Girl," *Follies;* "I Know Things Now" and "Agony," *Into the Woods*) or where the final cadence is in a different key from the beginning of the song ("Too Many Mornings," *Follies;* "Soon," *A Little Night Music;* "Like It Was" and "Not a Day Goes By," *Merrily We Roll Along*). The verses of "You're Gonna Love Tomorrow" and "Love Will See Us Through" (both from *Follies*) giddily move from key to key—and the latter ends in the same key in which it began—which is surely one reason why Sondheim identified the two songs as being in the spirit of Kern,[13] as is "Little White House/Who Could Be Blue?," the song that the other two songs from *Follies* replaced. But in general, the mature Sondheim treated modulation and harmony differently than Kern did.

Similarly, the long-breathed, rangy melodic lines that populate Kern's songs find few companions in Sondheim's mature songs. The principal reason for this disparity is that Sondheim was far more interested in making the melody and lyrics work together than was Kern. For example, "Good Thing Going" (from *Merrily*) employs the motivic development and wide-ranging intervals that figure prominently in Kern, but it is far wordier than a similar Kern song would be (e.g., "The Way You Look Tonight"). Seldom in Sondheim is a song granted the melodic lyricism that Kern would grant, where a measure of music may have only one or two long notes. "Loveland" *(Follies)*, identified by Sondheim as indebted to Kern, employs this sustained-note feature.[14] In "There Is No Other Way" *(Pacific Overtures)*, especially in its middle section, the melody unfolds as would a Kern melody, as does "Goodbye for Now" (from the 1981 film *Reds*; the affinity to Kern is also chronologically accurate, considering the movie's setting after the Bolshevik revolution of 1917). And "Lovely," from *Forum*, is possibly one of the most Kern-like songs Sondheim has written, with its two-notes-to-a-bar opening, the turning motif that soon follows, its harmonically more daring bridge, reminiscent of Kern's "Yesterdays," and its final tag, introduced by a deceptive harmony.

Sondheim's choice of *Show Boat* as one of his favorite musicals thus seems to say more about his belief in the musical's theatrical potency and less about Kern's long-term influence on his musical language. Certainly the score contains a wealth of brilliant music, and some commentators have suggested that Kern engaged in pastiche through the musical evocation of bygone eras, thus making a comparison to Sondheim particularly apt. ("After the Ball," *Show Boat*'s main period song, truly was from a bygone era, having been written by Charles K. Harris in 1892 and made famous through its interpolation in *A Trip to Chinatown.*)[15] But in addition to containing Kern's evergreen songs, *Show Boat* tells the story of three generations of a single family, covers five decades of their lives, and comments on such issues as racism, miscegenation, alcoholism, gambling, and abandonment. *Show Boat* is good theater, and Sondheim's comments about musicals indicate a preference for music and drama to work together to create good theater.

One could hardly expect Sondheim to emulate Kern too closely. As the oldest member of the Big Six, Kern tended to be the most old-fashioned as well, with melodies that looked to the Old World more than did those of the other five. But Kern's consummate artistry—the result in part of his training at the New York College of Music—as well as his reinterpretation of European operetta for American sensibilities made him worthy of study for Babbitt. And Sondheim clearly mastered these lessons; nearly forty years later, he analyzed, à la Babbitt, "All the Things You Are" for his students at Oxford University.[16] He learned from Kern, even while most of his mature music sounds nothing like Kern.

> It's been received wisdom for so many years that Kern is a songwriter's songwriter. But the Princess Theater musicals! Ninety percent of it is *pitti, pitti, pitti*—vamps—and those very wordy Wodehouse lyrics. A lot of that stuff is *no good at all.* On the other hand, you listen to "They Didn't Believe Me" [lyrics by Herbert Reynolds, from *The Girl from Utah* (1914), immediately before the Princess Theater musicals] and you never want to write a song again.[17]

Sondheim placed two later Kern songs on the list "Songs I Wish I'd Have Written (At Least in Part)": "I Am So Eager" and "The Song Is You," both from the 1932 musical *Music in the Air.* Hammerstein wrote the lyrics for both. The rangy, operetta-like *valse lente* of the former, with its unexpected harmonic turns and dramatic appoggiaturas in its first strain, make Sondheim's identification of "One More Kiss" as a Romberg pastiche open to question, although Hammerstein's dovetailing lyrics (Bruno's "Each moment is dear" elides with Frieda's "Dear, ev'ry moment we're here . . .") make up much of the delight in this song. As for the latter, Sondheim's notes for the Columbia recording say it all.

> I think it the best ballad Kern wrote, and perhaps the best anyone has written. It is long, rich and brilliantly constructed. The slow but relentless build at the end of the release, bursting into the restatement of the main theme with its last note shooting up an octave over its previous positions, is as glorious a climax as has ever been reached in a

> thirty-two bar chorus (which, despite its seeming length, this song is). It deserves that word which is anathema to critics but which describes Kern's music in such songs as this one: inspired.[18]

Berlin

In his notes on Kern songs, Sondheim gave one-sentence descriptions of three other songwriters from the Big Six.

> The most striking characteristic of Gershwin's songs is their harmonic decoration and (in the faster ones) their rhythmic drive. In Rodgers's music, "deceptive simplicity" (in *Time* magazine's phrase) is the trademark—sudden shifts of spare block harmonies under essentially diatonic, often repeated-note melodies with occasional unexpected chromatic leaps. The impressive feature of Porter's songs is their "sophistication"—the frequent use of Latin-American rhythms, the lush chromatic harmony, and the lengthy extensions of standard chorus forms (as in *Night and Day* and *Begin the Beguine*, the two longest and most famous examples).[19]

Considering what Sondheim felt about Arlen's music, Arlen's absence here is somewhat surprising, even as it gives yet another indication of his stature in comparison with the other members of the Big Six. The failure to mention Berlin, by way of contrast, almost seems deliberate. Forty years later, Sondheim summed up Berlin's style and its impact on him by calling Berlin a "very good character actor" whose brilliance lies more in his gifts as a lyricist than as a composer. "I will admire Berlin more than love him."[20]

Berlin was far less schooled musically than was Kern (or Sondheim), but he was the most popular songwriter of the first half of the twentieth century. He had three successful careers, one after the other: as the consummate Tin Pan Alley composer in the first decades of the century, then the Hollywood composer of the 1930s, and lastly as the Broadway musical composer of the 1940s. Berlin had unquestionably been directly involved in Broadway before the forties, but as a songwriter more for revues than for book musicals (however flimsy early books were). Thus, in *Annie Get Your Gun* (1946), Berlin showed his skills not only as a songwriter but also as a dramatist, even as he composed the entire score with remarkable speed. (Kern was supposed to write the music, but he died in November of the preceding year.)

In his list of songs he wished he had written, Sondheim named two songs from *Annie Get Your Gun:* the well-known "You Can't Get a Man with a Gun" and the less well known "I Got Lost in His Arms." (He also named "Let's Face the Music and Dance" from the film *Follow the Fleet.*) And in citing models for songs in *Follies,* Berlin stands behind "Beautiful Girls" (in the guise of "A Pretty Girl Is Like a Melody"). But although Berlin lived until 1989, Sondheim never met him, save possibly at Hammerstein's farm when *Annie Get Your Gun* was in development.[21] And in offhandedly naming composers whose scores are better than the shows in which those scores appear, Berlin, to the extent that he is acknowledged, is subsumed (as is Rodgers) by the words "so forth." While it would clearly overstate the case to suggest that Berlin's omission was deliberate, it is not an overstatement to note that he was not as influential as was Kern or Rodgers. By the time Sondheim's sun was rising on Broadway, Berlin's was setting. Indeed, Berlin's last Broadway show, *Mr. President* (1962), ran for only eight months and was bounded on either side by the two-year run of *Forum.*

Three Berlin songs offer a glimpse into those qualities of Berlin's writing that Sondheim particularly liked. Commenting on the lyric of "You Can't Get a Man with a Gun," he said, "[M]ost people . . . don't appreciate how brilliant Irving Berlin was as a comic lyric writer. . . . He was right up there with Cole Porter, or any of the rest of them."[22] "Let's Face the Music and Dance" has the kind of motivic concentration that Sondheim so admired in Kern. And "I Got Lost in His Arms" is shot through with descending countermelodies that complement the insistent repeated-figure of the main melody (and ends with a suspended dominant). Skillful wordplay, motivic focus, and the "harmonically underneath" link these three songs firmly with Sondheim's language.

And there are other places where Berlin and Sondheim intersected, albeit not musically speaking. Early in the 1950s, Sondheim was thwarted in his attempt to write a musical based on Alva Johnston's book *The Legendary Mizners,* because producer David Merrick had taken out an option on it in the hopes that Berlin would write the score.[23] Nearly fifty years later, *Bounce* arrived.[24] Also in the fifties, Arthur Laurents proposed to Merrick that Sondheim write the music and lyrics for what would become *Gypsy.* By that time, Sondheim was the fourth composer Merrick would approach. Berlin and Porter, both of whom had had mammoth successes with Ethel Merman before, turned Merrick down, and Cy Coleman and Carolyn Leigh wrote four songs on spec for Merrick, none of which suited him.[25] Of course, Merman turned Sondheim down as well. Lastly, according to Jonathan Tunick, Sondheim's longtime orchestrator, *Merrily We Roll Along* in Hal Prince's hands was supposed to be "this happy, upbeat, accessible show . . . like a Jule Styne or an Irving Berlin musical."[26] Next to *Anyone Can Whistle* (1962), *Merrily* was Sondheim's biggest musical flop.

While the lyrics to *Gypsy* have made Sondheim proud, and while the musical on the Mizner brothers may yet prove to be a hit, these stories make the mere mention of Berlin's name seem like a jinx on Sondheim's aspirations.[27] Sondheim's relative silence about Berlin is unlikely to be superstitious. But beyond his appreciation of a handful of songs, and given the distance in age between the two men, it is understandable that there are few connections to draw between Berlin and Sondheim.

Porter

More connections naturally and actually exist between Sondheim and Porter. Sondheim's meetings with Porter give in turn an amusing and wistful glimpse into the life of the one member of the Big Six who, in many ways, is Sondheim's closest kindred spirit. Porter was born to parents of means, as was Sondheim. His music lessons date from his early days. He headed to Yale ostensibly to become a lawyer, but while there, he busily composed music for the collegiate shows as well as for other ensembles and occasions. Against his family's wishes, he chose music as a career, sharing with Berlin and Sondheim the distinction of being the lyricist for his songs. But unlike Berlin, whose lyrics trafficked in the sentimental and the commonplace, Porter excelled at writing cynical and catty words about the ways of the upper crust, in whose company he traveled. If Sondheim wasn't a poseur like his first fully sketched professional character, Gene (in *Saturday Night*), neither was he at the zenith of the social register, as was Porter. And lastly, the open secret of their homosexuality links the two men, although the way each dealt with being gay merits a study all its own.

With the possible exception of Rodgers, Porter was the first of the Big Six to hear Sondheim's music when he was still in college. Linda Porter, Cole's wife, owned an estate in Williamstown,[28] and it was there, shortly after Porter's success with *Kiss Me, Kate*, that Sondheim played for Porter songs from *All That Glitters*, his collegiate show for the spring of 1949. As Secrest tells it, the audition was very encouraging, with Porter making numerous suggestions to Sondheim on how to improve the music. Sondheim also played for Porter "The Bordelaise," a parody of "Begin the Beguine." "'Poor thing, he knew exactly what I was doing,' Sondheim said, but Porter's only comment was 'You should extend the ending more.' He added, 'I extend endings a lot.'"[29]

A second encounter with Porter was more propitious for Sondheim. The ten years between "The Bordelaise" and *Gypsy* witnessed a sharpening of Sondheim's skills as a lyricist, and he related how Porter's delight in Sondheim's quadruple rhyme "he goes," "she goes," "egos," and "amigos" was almost sexual.[30] And like Porter, Sondheim excelled at the "list song," a genre he would continue to explore in his mature shows.[31]

Porter's influence on Sondheim, in fact, seems best located in the lyrics rather than the music. For Sondheim, "Lucy and Jessie," sung by the character Phyllis, is his Porter pastiche for *Follies*.[32] The song shares some features with Porter's "It's All Right with Me": its opening minor key; the descending chromatic line in the refrain (heard on the syllables "*Lu*-cy is *jui*-cy" and continuing in the orchestra); the small leaps of fourths and thirds (the pitch intervals traversed in the syllables mentioned above), downward in Sondheim but upward in Porter; and the final cadence in the relative major key. The Porter lyric, unlike the Sondheim lyric, does not describe a dualistic character, but the saga of a person trying to decide between two people—an absent former flame and a present and tempting potential fling. This dilemma resembles the struggle Phyllis faces in deciding whether she will be Lucy or Jessie.

Beyond this direct linkage to Porter's musical language, a propensity toward Latin beats and harmonies—a Porter trait—extends throughout Sondheim's work, from the early "Bordelaise" to the bossa nova "The Ladies Who Lunch" (*Company*, 1970) to the faster, salsa-like "Putting It Together" (*Sunday in the Park with George*, 1984). Although "The Bordelaise" from *All That Glitters* wasn't published, "I Love You, Etcetera" was, with its beguine-like accompaniment running throughout. Considering that all the members of the Big Six showed a predilection for Latin music at one time or another, connecting Sondheim's Latin flair solely to Porter is unnecessarily schematic, although Sondheim explicitly did so in his Kern notes.

As it happens, none of the three Porter songs Sondheim chose uses Latin beats and harmonies in its printed version. The lyrical facility that frames Porter's ability to make syllabic chains in songs and lengthen the refrains in songs is the principal feature of "Let's Not Talk about Love," a song that instantly conjures up the patter in "Getting Married Today" *(Company)*. "Let's Be Buddies" is a harder song to pin down, as its lack of complication belies Sondheim's claim that Porter is known for his sophistication. Here, Porter took a Kern-like approach and spun out a standard verse-and-chorus song from a minimum of motivic cells, accomplishing much within a narrow compass. In contrast, "Ev'ry Time We Say Goodbye" has many things to recommend it, among them its insistently repetitive melody (different from, yet reminiscent of, "I Got Lost in His Arms"); the variant of the second A section (the form is ABA′B′) that raises one note a half step; the unexpected melodic high point on the word "love"; and the skillful handling of the potentially mawkish phrase "how strange the change from major to minor." In fact, with this song's blue harmonies and repetitive melody, it begins to sound like an Arlen tune, which might be another reason Sondheim included it on his list.

Rodgers

Accounts about the collaboration between Rodgers and Sondheim make fascinating reading,[33] and it is tempting, for salacious reasons, to describe in full the debacle that attended *Do I Hear a Waltz?* in 1965. But by the time of the musical, Sondheim was thirty-five, with two Broadway shows behind him for which he had written both music and lyrics. Though his musical language would forever be open to influence—the Witch's rap *(Into the Woods)* points to this catholicity—Sondheim had been cool to Rodgers's charms before their collaboration. Rather, as has already been stated, the early songs show a marked melodic and harmonic debt to Kern.

On one level, it is counterintuitive to think that Sondheim would imitate least the composer with whom he had the most contact, both personally and musically. As table 1 shows, of all the members of the Big Six, Rodgers was the most widely represented in the years 1935–59, with nineteen original shows and two revivals. (Porter is next with fifteen shows; Arlen had six shows; Berlin, five; Kern had two shows, including the revival of *Show Boat;* and Gershwin had only *Porgy and Bess,* though it appeared three times during this period.) In terms of longevity of his career and the number of hits (both songs and shows), Rodgers remains the gold standard for the musical.

But Sondheim's allegiance was to Hammerstein, not to Rodgers. And in reading the biographical accounts of Rodgers, one can easily see why. In his autobiography, *Musical Stages,* Rodgers doesn't mention Sondheim at all until the events of *Do I Hear a Waltz?* Children and adolescents found little warmth and much diffidence in Rodgers.[34] His two daughters seemed to have had a particularly difficult time, especially the older, Mary, whose musical, *Once upon a Mattress,* made it to Broadway in 1959, three years before Sondheim had his first commercial success as a composer. In her introduction to a reprint of *Musical Stages,* Mary does the best she can to make lemonade out of her sour relationship with, and bitter memories of, her father.[35]

Sondheim's friendship with Mary began in the summer of 1945, as her father brought the whole family to Hammerstein's farm in Doylestown, Pennsylvania, for working weekends. "At her first meeting with Steve Sondheim, [Mary] thought he was the most brilliant, entrancing person she had ever met and they struck up a lasting friendship."[36] Mary was also one of the first people Sondheim confided in about his sexuality,[37] and the combination of her disclosures to him about her family's dysfunction, her thwarted love for him, and her parents' antipathy toward homosexuals may have also led Sondheim away from Rodgers.[38]

Beyond the personal diffidence, Sondheim never embraced Rodgers and his musical language the way he embraced Kern, Gershwin, and Arlen. On a technical level, this hardly makes sense, as Rodgers often made much out of little, using musical motives like seed from which whole melodies grew. For example, two well-known Rodgers songs use the same three-note lower-neighbor rocking idea—"THERE'S A SMALL hotel" and "this NEARLY WAS mine"—with dramatically different results. Like Kern and Copland (to name two disparate composers), Rodgers was a motivic composer, and on that level his music impressed Sondheim.

What seemed to surprise Sondheim was Rodgers's limited musical understanding. According to Mary Rodgers, Sondheim

> was about nineteen when he asked if I could get my father to give him an interview. I set it up. But Steve was disappointed. "It was awful," he said. "He couldn't tell me anything." My father was not an intellectual writer. He had gone to Juilliard, and he knew plenty. But he didn't sit down and figure out intellectually where a song should go or how it should be constructed.[39]

From Sondheim's vantage point, Rodgers's lack of thought affected their collaboration on *Do I Hear a Waltz?* Walter Kerr opined that

> the songs here were musical-comedy songs, generally of a high order. But will musical-comedy songs carry the evening when the evening isn't a musical comedy? The materials in this instance might have been abrasive even for light opera—certainly they did not seem to suggest

such treatment. What, then? I don't know the answer, short of intimate opera itself.[40]

And Sondheim similarly dismissed the musical-comedy approach that Rodgers imposed upon their collaboration (Rodgers was the producer of the musical as well as the composer). "You've got to do it as a semi-opera . . . And Dick thought in terms of song."[41] After the personal breakthrough Sondheim had achieved with *Anyone Can Whistle* the year before—a score built of motives that develop, extended musical scenes, portrayals of the characters using musical means—Rodgers's "old-school" approach on *Do I Hear a Waltz?* clashed with Sondheim's aesthetic.

Even when Sondheim turned to praise Rodgers's music, his words contain a grain of judgment. Frank Rich asked Sondheim to explain why he listed *Carousel* as one of his favorites. "Musically, it's my favorite score second to *Porgy and Bess*. . . . Its music is so rich. Those songs are so full of feeling. It's Rodgers absolutely at his flowering best."[42] One gets the sense from these last three words that Sondheim's infamous remark about Rodgers being a man of infinite talent and limited soul still represented his opinion of the man nearly thirty years later.[43] Rodgers, whose musical training was spotty and who took only minutes to write songs, may not have been disciplined and profound enough for Sondheim. Thus Sondheim's oft-repeated tale—that he has spent his creative life trying to fix *Allegro*[44]—speaks not only to the concept, book, and execution but also to a score that did not have the heft to propel Hammerstein's ideas.

Allegro, of course, looms large in understanding Sondheim. Almost as if in anticipation of the problems with *Do I Hear a Waltz?*, Cecil Smith commented that the score for *Allegro* "[was not] very good Broadway . . . nor does it satisfy the minimal requirements of the lyric theatre."[45] In his own descriptions of working as a gofer on the Rodgers and Hammerstein *Allegro* two years before *Glitters,* Sondheim is strangely silent about the music while being effusive about Hammerstein's vision.[46] But this, again, is an indication of his affinity with Hammerstein. As if it were an afterthought, Sondheim told a college newspaper reporter that he hoped "Hammerstein and the other half of the famed Hammerstein-Rodgers team, Richard Rodgers, will be able to see [*All That Glitters*] in Williamstown since they will be in Boston next weekend where their new production, *South Pacific,* is trying out."[47]

The clash between Rodgers and Sondheim also emerges in an interview Rodgers gave to Kenneth Leish around 1968. Rodgers identified the "unsympathetic" and "unpleasant" heroine of *Do I Hear a Waltz?* as the biggest flaw in the musical. He continued: "The lyrics were brittle, and not loving at all. I don't think that helps." When Leish responded, "That was what he [Sondheim, but perhaps Laurents] was aiming at, though it didn't work," Rodgers backed away slightly.

> Yes. Yes, surely, and the music has to reflect the content of the lyrics and the book. I'm not trying to cop out, as they say, and blame the fact that the score wasn't terribly good on somebody else. I know it wasn't very good. But it was preceded by a good score, perhaps a number of good scores.[48]

What Rodgers seemed loath to admit was that his style of music, as successful as it had been since the 1920s, might never mesh with Sondheim's vision of music and drama.

Rodgers's musical style left Sondheim wanting more. Kern is more lyrical, Gershwin more inventive, Porter more sparkling, Arlen more brooding. Rodgers, the man of unlimited talent, did not find it necessary regularly to push his lyricism or invention or brilliance or moodiness to the extremes. His "good" was better than the best of most of the songwriters around him. But for Sondheim, it seems that Rodgers's "flowering good" wasn't always good enough.

Thus the agreement between Sondheim and Rodgers on the strength of *Carousel* merits attention. When Rodgers was approached to turn Ferenc Molnár's *Liliom* into a musical, he and Hammerstein first addressed issues of location (from Budapest to New England) and conclusion (*Liliom* ends more darkly than does *Carousel*).

> But there was still a major problem: what kind of music to write and where should it go? How do you sing *Liliom*? Oscar and I kept reading and rereading the play, searching for clues. Suddenly we got the notion for a soliloquy in which, at the end of the first act, the leading character would reveal his varied emotions about impending fatherhood. That broke the ice. Once we could visualize the man singing, we felt that all the other problems would fall into place. And somehow they did.[49]

While Sondheim did not list "Soliloquy" among the songs he wished he had written (at least in part), one doesn't have to look far in his work to find soliloquies that resemble Billy Bigelow's in *Carousel*. The song Sondheim did choose is the bittersweet, "sorry-grateful" "What's the Use of Wond'rin'," where Julie Jordan confesses, in essence, that she can't help loving that man of hers even though their lives together seem doomed. And though Rodgers and Hammerstein added sunlight to Molnár's play, the musical's darker elements deeply affected Sondheim. "I remember how everyone goes off to the clambake at the end of Act One and Jigger [the hoodlum villain] just follows, and he was the only one walking on stage as the curtain came down. I was sobbing."[50]

It hardly seems possible that, though the musical *Carousel* shook the fifteen-year-old Sondheim to the core, its music has found little place in Sondheim's own writing. If there is any lasting legacy of Rodgers in Sondheim, perhaps it is located not in musical style but in meter, specifically in three-quarter time. While the waltz was popular before Rodgers came on the scene, he more than any other member of the Big Six kept it alive throughout his career. The notion of a "hit waltz" may seem oxymoronic today, but a cursory survey of Rodgers's songbook turns up countless waltzes that have become standards (e.g., "Falling in Love with Love," "Lover," "Oh, What a Beautiful Mornin'," "This Nearly Was Mine," "My Favorite Things"). While Porter was exploring Latin music and Arlen the blues, Rodgers mined the waltz.

And Sondheim followed his footsteps. Although the musical language of Sondheim's waltzes owes more to Ravel and Satie than to Broadway, still the example of Rodgers's waltzes could not have escaped Sondheim. Consider *Carousel*'s opening.

> For the overture to *Carousel* I decided not to have an overture. . . . [We opened] on a pantomime scene, with the orchestra playing a single piece, the "Carousel Waltz," rather than the usual medley. In this way we also gave the audience an emotional feeling for the characters in the story and helped to establish the mood for the entire play.[51]

In Rodgers's description the "emotional feeling" seems to reside more in the pantomime than in the music. Wherever its locus, compare the opening of *Carousel* with that of *Follies*, with its opening waltz and pantomime, and echoes of Rodgers will be found in Sondheim's music even when it sounds nothing like Rodgers's.

These echoes, though, seem accidental and perhaps even coincidental rather than demonstrative of influence. The one published waltz from Sondheim's Williams shows, "How Do I Know?" *(Phinney's Rainbow)*, has a Kern-like verse, after which the main waltz chorus sounds more like Burton Lane or Frederick Loewe than Rodgers. Both Lane and Loewe had hit shows in 1948, just months before Sondheim premiered *Phinney's Rainbow*. Moreover, their musicals produced hit waltzes, and

Sondheim's song sounds like a conflation of "Look to the Rainbow" *(Finian's Rainbow)* and "Come to Me, Bend to Me" (*Brigadoon*, 1947). ("The Q-Ladies Waltz," also from *Phinney's Rainbow*, has not been published, but in its concept and execution this song sounds as though it prefigured the waltz "Cora's Chase" in *Anyone Can Whistle*.) And in the two instrumental waltzes that come from the Williams years (found in the Wisconsin archives), the sound world is indebted to Ravel. From the beginning, Sondheim moved away from Rodgers's musical and dramatic conception of the waltz.

The suite of waltzes in *Company* illustrates Sondheim's dramatic use of the waltz. The married men, all would-be insurgents in the sexual revolution, regale Robert with erotic possibilities in an au courant jazz waltz ("Have I Got a Girl for You"). Next, they lampoon Robert's quest for domesticity by indirectly impugning their own marriages, to the tune of a 1930s comic waltz that resembles the Arlen-Harburg song "Lydia, the Tattooed Lady" ("Whaddya Want to Get Married For?"). Lastly, an undeterred Robert pines for the perfect companion in his 1890s *valse lente* ("Someone Is Waiting"). The music metaphorically accompanies Robert as both recede farther and farther from present-day realities into fantasy. The suite of waltzes that opens *Carousel* can claim no similar musical or dramatic journey.

Milton Babbitt's comments on Rodgers provide a fitting conclusion. Undoubtedly Sondheim and Babbitt discussed Rodgers's music in the early 1950s. Babbitt's remarks, then, likely reflect not only his own opinions but also his conversations with Sondheim. "Dick was always a problem, always a thorn in Steve's side. I think Steve admired him and wanted to please him but Dick made that very difficult."[52]

Sondheim would forever be ambivalent toward Rodgers. And while Rodgers may have made the relationship difficult, it is clear that Sondheim was no saint when it came to Rodgers. One understands Rodgers's summation of the relationship: The less said, the better.

Jacob and Hyman and Steve! Oh, my!

On more than one occasion Sondheim has been asked to name his musical parents. The answers have all been fairly close to each other, with two songwriters invariably heading the list. One could view the consistency as the result of rote repetition, that is, Sondheim's having learned his lines and recited them when the question was posed. But an analysis of his music affirms his hierarchy of influences, which makes all the more

enlightening his unrehearsed response in 1998 to a question not ostensibly about broad influences.

> SWAYNE: You have talked a lot about how much Arlen's music means to you. What is it about that music you like?
>
> SONDHEIM: I love Arlen's harmony. I just think his harmonic language is wonderful. Also, his freedom of structure, but particularly the harmonic language. Yeah. He's much more influential on me than Copland.
>
> In fact, I'd say of all the songwriters—theater songwriters, movie songwriters . . . I'd say he's the most influential. Much more than Rodgers, Porter, Berlin, Gershwin. Gershwin also, with Arlen. They're not dissimilar in those kinds of very rich, quite complex chordal structures.[53]

When, four years later, Frank Rich interviewed Sondheim for the Kennedy Center's Sondheim Celebration, Sondheim reaffirmed the pairing and the reasons for it.

> RICH: Correct me if I'm wrong, but it seems to me that of the great songwriters in the theatre that came before you, the two composers you seem to most admire are George Gershwin and Harold Arlen. Why?
>
> SONDHEIM: Oh, boy, it's hard to talk about music and say specifically what you like about it. I can tell you that in both cases it's about harmonic richness. Harmony is, of the three elements of music, the one that gets me; it's not melody or rhythm, it's harmony. The way one recognizes composers—not just Gershwin, Arlen, Kern, Rodgers, Porter, but Beethoven, Brahms and Stravinsky—is by their harmonic language. And the richest and most inventive harmonies in show music, I think, are those of Gershwin and Arlen. I could wallow in *Porgy and Bess,* the chords alone. And any song by Arlen is just, you know . . .[54]

Jacob Gershovitz and Hyman Arluck: unlike his two most influential tunesmiths, Sondheim elected not to change his name. One died when Sondheim was seven and thus never heard a Sondheim tune; the other, his health failing, took special pleasure in seeing and hearing *Pacific Overtures*.[55] Yet these two songwriters had been yoked together—and had yoked themselves together—long before Sondheim recognized them as his major forebears.

According to Carl Van Vechten, after Arlen's "Stormy Weather" became a hit song in 1933, "George said to me, 'Harold is the most original of all of us.' "[56] And Arlen similarly held Gershwin in the highest esteem, going so far as to elevate him over Copland in terms of individuality and greatness.[57] In February 1955, two months after the premiere of *House of Flowers*, columnist Robert Coleman set Arlen's love of Gershwin in an intriguing context. Robert Breen, the impresario who from 1952 to 1956 managed a successful international tour of *Porgy and Bess*, had wanted to put at least one, and perhaps two, other shows in repertory with Gershwin's opera in the hopes of smoothing out his problems with cash flow.[58]

> While composing the *House of Flowers* score, Arlen started work on what he considers to be his most ambitious and distinguished project, *Blues Opera*. This will have a book by Mr. and Mrs. Robert Breen, based on *St. Louis Woman*.
>
> *Blues Opera* is to be included on the agenda of Blevins Davis and Breen's American Musical Repertory Theatre. It will have a cast recruited from *Porgy and Bess*. . . . Arlen's favorite composer is George Gershwin, so it is fitting that *Blues Opera* should command the attention of Breen and Davis.[59]

Others tell the story of *Blues Opera* (renamed *Free and Easy*), with its five-year delay, its unsuccessful European premiere, and its present obscurity.[60] What is intriguing, beyond the yoking of Gershwin and Arlen, is how Sondheim is similarly tied to these works. *Porgy and Bess* is his favorite work, and he saw the Breen production when it was in New York (March–November 1953). He may have attended an audition for *House of Flowers* where he heard Arlen sing and play.[61] He singled out *St. Louis Woman*—the music that lay behind *Free and Easy*—as "a particular score I love," although that love may have come late in life.[62] In his choice of Gershwin and Arlen, Sondheim brings together the only two members of the Big Six who wrote not only songs and musicals but also what is, by every reasonable definition, opera (Arlen composed recitatives for *Blues Opera*). "A troubled modern songwriter with a classic pedigree" is how Banfield described Sondheim, but it could also fit Gershwin quite well, if Arlen less so.[63] The harmonic sophistication of the two composers provides an outward sign of an inner quality Sondheim admired in both: a seriousness of musical intention to which he himself aspired. How, then, do Gershwin and Arlen peep out from Sondheim's music?

Rachmaninoff's second concerto wasn't the only piece of concert music Sondheim navigated in his teens. Mary Rodgers Guettel remembered an early encounter with Sondheim when the latter was about fifteen years old.

> [S]omehow he made his way to the piano, and I had either never heard *Rhapsody in Blue* or *An American in Paris*, or something. And he sat down and played a great hunk of it. I was just done in by this, not only by what I was listening to, because I'm still a huge Gershwin fan, but by the ability of this guy to do that. . . . I just knew that this was an incredibly talented person with an incredible musical sensitivity and was the smartest person I had ever met in my whole life.[64]

Sondheim has affirmed that he was able to play the Gershwin *Rhapsody*.

And he knew *Porgy and Bess* before Breen's production had become a fixture on Broadway. The musical values of the score resonated with Sondheim as a youth and have continued to do so throughout his life. When he appeared on the BBC's program *Desert Island Discs* in December 2000, Sondheim led off his choices with the Gershwin. "I think it's the finest American musical. I always find *Porgy* moving, and I always find it surprising and inventive, and I'm always jealous of it. I've always wished that I had written it."[65] And when asked, at the close of the show, to choose only one of the pieces he named, he answered without hesitation: *Porgy and Bess*.

Thus the presence of only one Gershwin song on Sondheim's list of those he wished he had written is not all that surprising. Along with Berlin, Gershwin created a catalog of songs that are extremely well known, so his work does not need to be rediscovered to the extent that other tunesmiths' work does. Similarly, "My Man's Gone Now"—the song Sondheim chose—serves as a partial placeholder for all of *Porgy and Bess*, which (unlike the other songs on his list) was part of a work he wished he had written in full.[66]

The song itself is remarkable not only for its many unusual features—the "unbalanced" five-bar introduction, the wailing that seems to come straight from a grieving soul, the sliding chromatic chords that accompany the vocal glissandi—but also for its treatment of a characteristic Gershwin feature: the 32-bar song (AABA′). Table 2 provides an outline of how "My Man's Gone Now" both adheres to and explodes this standard song form. The table also analyzes another song on Sondheim's

Table 2. A Comparison of Song Forms

	Intro/Verse	A	A(′)	B	A(″)	tag
"My Man's Gone Now," *Porgy and Bess* (Gershwin)	5 mm. instrumental introduction	"My man's gone now . . .": 9 mm. (8 + 1 in echo of intro), plus 4-m. "keening" tag; 13 mm.	"Ole Man Sorrow's come . . .": same music as A, but with an additional 2-m. "fill" between A′ and B; 15 mm.	Two 8-mm. phrases ("Ain' dat I min' workin' . . ." and "But Ole Man Sorrow's marchin' . . .": music in each phrase same for first five mm.; first phrase has a 1-m. "ending"; second phrase echoes last 2 mm. twice; concludes with 4-m. "keening" tag; 25 mm.	"Ole Man Sorrow sittin' . . .": though accompanied by chorus, same 8-m. phrase as A; continues with a second phrase (9 mm.); concluded by 5-m. wail; 22 mm.	Orchestral peroration, followed by a communal (and very chromatic) wail; 14 mm.
"What's the Use of Wond'rin'," *Carousel* (Rodgers)		"What's the use of wond'rin'": 10 mm. (4 + 6)	"Common sense may tell you": same as A, save for last half of last measure	Two 4-m. phrases ("Somethin' made him . . ." and "And somethin' gave him . . .": music in each phrase same for all but last note; second phrase has a pickup	"So when he wants your kisses": same as A, save for last two measures, which uses a plagal cadence (similar to an "Amen")	

Table 2. *Continued*

	Intro/Verse	A	A(′)	B	A(″)	tag
"Finishing the Hat," *Sunday in the Park with George* (Sondheim)	27 mm. verse: mm. 1–10 reprise earlier songs; mm. 12–15 reprise yearning motive; mm. 16–27 set up material that will reappear	A1 — "Finishing the hat": 8 mm. (4 + 4)	A′1 — "Mapping out a sky": 10 mm.; 2-m. tag at end	B1 — "And how you're always turning back . . ." 14 mm.; two 4-m. phrases, followed by three iterations of main A motive (2 mm. each)	A3/tag — "Finishing a hat": 14 mm.; a combination of a return to an A section and a final tag; vocal line is a repetition of main A motive (thus, the reason why the elision occurs; see B1)	
		A2 — "Studying the hat": 8 mm. (4 + 4); same as A1	A′2 — "Studying a face": 10 mm.; same length as above, but goes in new directions from A′1 at third m.	B2 — "And when the woman . . .": 14 mm.; last two mm. are instrumental instead of vocal, effecting an elision with what follows		

list from the Big Six that nods in the direction of the 32-bar song as well as a song by Sondheim that does the same.

The harmonies of Gershwin's song have a special relationship to Sondheim. Many of the chords in "My Man's Gone Now" are built not from thirds but from fourths. The second harmony of the introduction, for example, features a stacking up of fourths. That particular chord forms the basis of the chord progression that begins on the words "gone now," as that measure and the next three measures all have chords that, while analyzable using harmonic language based on the triad, employ fourths in creative ways. The "echo" of the introduction that follows each phrase (the last measure in example 1) likewise is built from fourths.

Example 1. Gershwin, "My Man's Gone Now" *(Porgy and Bess)*, opening phrase

The significance of this fourth-saturated harmony becomes clearer when one looks at Sondheim's early "classical" music that will later filter into his Broadway scores. Moments in songs like "Company" (the long held notes in the refrain), "The Right Girl" (*Follies:* the instrumental fills between sections), "It Would Have Been Wonderful" (*Night Music:*

the bridge, "the woman was perfection"), and on through to the more recent shows use fourth-saturated harmony in a manner similar to Gershwin. The instances of fourth-saturated harmony in *Pacific Overtures,* from "The Advantages of Floating in the Middle of the Sea" to its concluding number, "Next," are legion. In other words, Sondheim's desire to write *Porgy and Bess* is matched by a musical language that could have naturally allowed him to write "My Man's Gone Now" and much of Gershwin's score.

"My Man's Gone Now" exhibits another aspect of writing that distinguishes it from many of the songs Sondheim listed and that places it closer to classical music—and Sondheim's songs. The amount of counterpoint in the song, of multiple musical lines spinning a web of harmony arrived at in a linear fashion, is quintessentially Sondheim. A careful listen to the Gershwin will reveal that, in addition to the "melody" sung by Serena, the orchestra has countermelodies that accompany the main melody. These appear in the middle of the orchestral fabric, moving by step and emerging briefly before returning to the larger sound world of the song. A fine example occurs when Serena vocalizes on "Ah." The orchestral bass voice resembles the emphatic statements first heard in the introduction to the song, and the orchestral soprano voice remains almost static until Serena comes to rest on her final note. The inner voices of the orchestra, in contrast, fill out the harmony by moving, usually by step, in each measure. One thinks of Sondheim's comments about Rachmaninoff and the other composers, whose music is controlled by the "harmonically underneath" material.

Sondheim's songs routinely exhibit a similar devotion to contrapuntal details. An easily recognizable countermelody appears in "Send In the Clowns," beginning at the first bridge ("Just when I stopped . . ."), and the countermelody in "Our Time" *(Merrily)* was mentioned in chapter 1. But Sondheim's use of counterpoint is typically less visible than these examples and is brought about in the same way as the inner voices in "My Man's Gone Now." In "Losing My Mind" *(Follies),* the first four measures of the song use four different chords generated by a chromatic countermelody in the accompaniment. That chromatic figure is inverted in the main section of the very next song "Lucy and Jessie" (thus neatly showing how different are Sally and Phyllis, the two women who sing these songs). In the former case, the countermelody makes consummate sense, since the song represents a Gershwin pastiche (of "The Man I Love").[67] Given that the four songs mentioned above represent Sondheim both as a deliberate pasticheur and as a composer writing in his own distinctive voice, they collectively demonstrate that counterpoint holds a particular place in Sondheim's compositional aesthetic.

As it happens, *Porgy and Bess* also is a compendium of counterpoint of different kinds. In addition to the linearly derived harmonies of "My Man's Gone Now," Gershwin wrote a moving chorus for the end of act 2, as six different characters utter six different prayers (and melody lines) simultaneously. The "constructedness" of the prayers shows Gershwin taking care to ensure that his "independent melodies" would work together. Similarities between this chorus and Sondheim's ensembles can be heard in, for example, "A Weekend in the Country" *(Night Music)*, "Please Hello" *(Pacific Overtures)*, "God, That's Good!" *(Sweeney Todd)*, "It's a Hit" *(Merrily)*, and the first-act finale to *Into the Woods*. And echoes of Gershwin's contrapuntal technique are present even in the "cacophonous choruses" in the interrogation scene that closes act 1 of *Anyone Can Whistle*. (One also hears shades of Bernstein's quintet from *West Side Story*, a comparison I shall address below.)

In addition to this style of counterpoint in *Porgy and Bess*, Gershwin engaged in more traditional forms of contrapuntal writing, such as in the crap-game fugue of act 1 (where Crown kills Robbins; the music returns in act 3 when Porgy kills Crown). Others have written about the construction of Gershwin's fugue and about his contrapuntal exertions in it, including inverting and retrograding the fugue subject.[68] While none of Sondheim's musicals contains a complete fugue, some of the ensembles mentioned above feature the staggered entries of musical material that are characteristic of fugal writing. Sondheim had been interested in contrapuntal writing since his days at Williams, evidenced not only by his lessons with Barrow but also in surviving sketches and a fugato passage in his 1950 piano sonata.[69] As for contrapuntal tricks, such as inversion and retrograde, not much has been explored in this area beyond the inversions in "No One Is Alone" (from *Into the Woods:* of the "magic beans" motif, at "People make mistakes") and "What Can You Lose?" (from *Dick Tracy:* of the opening four-note motif, at "closes the door" and "friend, nothing more"). These examples hint that there may be more contrapuntal devices in Sondheim than have heretofore been explored. It is worth noting that, in the latter example, the musical inversion serves a dramatic point, as the optimism and risk posited at the beginning of the song are reversed by the likelihood of the risk-taker experiencing disappointment. In this way, Sondheim's use of counterpoint parallels Gershwin's use in the crap-game fugue, where the musical form creates a tension that emulates the actions on stage.

Gershwin's musical education wasn't as formalized as that of Kern or Porter (or Sondheim), but he did study throughout his life. His teachers included Charles Hambitzer, Rubin Goldmark, Wallingford Riegger, Joseph Schillinger, and Henry Cowell. He also wrote to Maurice Ravel and Arnold Schoenberg, asking them for lessons. Both composers turned Gershwin down, stating that, at the time he approached them, he had all the musical instruction he needed. The shared connection with Ravel makes Sondheim's selection of Gershwin's masterpiece propitious.

In choosing "late Gershwin" instead of the Gershwin of the Tin Pan Alley songs, Sondheim was favoring the more classical composer over the more popular one. Near the end of his life, according to Steven Gilbert, "Gershwin tended to think in terms of counterpoint rather than the normal vernacular of 'chords.'"[70] Such a manner of "thinking" finds resonance in Sondheim, whose music rarely appears in lead-sheet form but rather as a song with a fully realized accompaniment. Earlier, Gilbert had written: "Gershwin's last songs are indeed different, and in ways other than phrasing and structure. Carefully written accompaniments, contrapuntal bias, the thoughtful selection of key, a flirtation with quartal harmony, and the influence of Gershwin's studies with Joseph Schillinger mark the late songs in special ways."[71] Change "Joseph Schillinger" to "Robert Barrow and Milton Babbitt," and the same could be written about Sondheim's songs and studies. But these musical characteristics in Sondheim owe as much if not more to Sondheim's prolonged exposure to classical music, where accompaniments are always written out, where counterpoint and key are given careful consideration, and where quartal harmony serves as a modern answer to traditional triadic harmony. The late Gershwin sound, in Gilbert's formulation, resembles much continental music from the 1920s and 1930s. Thus Sondheim's assessment of Gershwin's harmonic richness and the influence that richness has on Sondheim makes perfect sense, in that Gershwin, in *Porgy and Bess*, competed most directly with the modernist composers whom Sondheim also admired in his teens and twenties.

Sondheim also recognized the variegated pedigree of *Porgy and Bess*. When asked which operas (if any) appealed to him, he mentioned Gershwin's work after *Peter Grimes* and before *Wozzeck*.[72] On the *Desert Island Discs* program, he referred to Gershwin's work as a musical. When asked by the host of that program if he distinguished between opera, operetta, and musical theater, Sondheim answered: "No. Those [distinctions] are for critics and scholars."[73] Perhaps *Porgy and Bess* influenced him because of its musical and dramatic transgressions: the former being its intricate score and its deviation from standard Broadway musical practices (e.g., the abandonment of clear 32-bar song form and the use of extended recitative), and the latter being its comparative lack of caricature in its portrayal of black characters—a feature that has been obscured by time but was not lost on its original audience and performers—and the violent and unsavory nature of the denizens of Catfish Row. Gershwin paid for these transgressions at the box office; *Porgy and Bess* ran for 124 performances, a coup for an opera but unimpressive for a Broadway show in the 1930s.

The critical opinion of *Porgy and Bess* at its premiere sounds strangely like a pre-echo of the reception given to a Sondheim show. According to chronicler Gerald Bordman, "[T]he major New York newspapers sent both their drama and music critics to the opening. The drama critics were far more enthusiastic than the music commentators."[74] Similarly, critics would praise a Sondheim show for its dramatic ingenuity and the felicity of Sondheim's lyrics while wishing that someone else—someone more *tuneful*—had provided the score.[75] When *Porgy and Bess* is placed in its historical context, one appreciates more easily why Sondheim chose it above all others as the work that he wished he had written.

Comparisons of Sondheim to Gershwin will be complete when the Metropolitan Opera balks at doing a Sondheim show and takes half a century to mount one. In *Opera News*, the house magazine for the Metropolitan Opera and the flagship opera magazine for the United States, there was no mention of the 2002 Sondheim Celebration at the Kennedy Center, neither in any feature articles nor in its "Dateline" calendar listing productions throughout the world. Given the magazine's desire to cover "crossover" phenomena, the omission is odd. The August 2002 issue, for example, has a cover photo in which "Broadway's Patti LuPone poses as Jenny in *Mahagonny*, while opera's Stephanie Blythe wields the rolling pin of Mrs. Lovett in *Sweeney Todd*." This, at a time when the Sondheim work was being performed in Washington, D.C., albeit not by performers from the world of opera. Nevertheless, *Opera News* covered the Chicago Lyric Opera's production of *Sweeney Todd*, which starred baritone Bryn Terfel in the title role and featured longtime Sondheim collaborator Paul Gemignani in the pit.[76]

Just as it took time for the highbrow musical establishment to pay Gershwin his due, so the major musical institutions of New York are slowly warming to Sondheim. Gershwin seemed to court the approval of those institutions, and the various public opinion brokers of his day vacillated between elevating Gershwin to the rank of serious composer and demoting him to the level of a common tunesmith.[77] Sondheim has appeared less concerned about his standing among "serious" musicians, and for the most part, classical music critics and traditional musicologists have left his music alone. This has not stopped other critics from trying to make Sondheim into a modern Gershwin, however. In reviewing the 1983 Radio City Music Hall production of *Porgy and Bess,* Clive Barnes sketched a musical continuum that unabashedly placed Gershwin at one end and Sondheim at the other.

> The full grandeur of Gershwin's original concept is here completed. What a sensational opera this is. It has always been regarded—quite wrongly—as simply a Broadway musical. It was always something much more, and indeed a pointer to the future of both the Broadway musical and opera itself.
>
> It suggested that the living future of opera—or serious musical theater if you balk at the word opera—was to be in the hands of men like Kurt Weill, Leonard Bernstein and Stephen Sondheim.

Barnes continued: "Opera, as created by purely classically oriented composers, was deader than a dodo," the "final classical gyrations" of Britten and Stravinsky notwithstanding. "Classic opera was to become a superb fossilized art—the preserve of interpreters rather than creative artists. In this new staging of *Porgy* . . . it emerges as grand opera and grand popular entertainment."[78]

Barnes wrote these words four years after the premiere of *Sweeney Todd,* Sondheim's "virtual opera." Sondheim: "I first started *Sweeney Todd* as an out-and-out opera. I started to set Bond's text, and it's a compact play. It's short, but it is so jammed with material that I realized if I were to sing the whole it would turn out to be a nine-hour-and-a-half *Ring* cycle, and it didn't seem worth that kind of time or attention."[79] Like *Porgy and Bess,* which Gershwin called a "folk opera" (i.e., something other than a standard-issue opera), so Sondheim has created musical theater pieces that defy easy categorization. Michael John LaChiusa, in the crossover cover story in *Opera News,* quoted William Bolcom (a composer who crosses over from the classical side of the aisle). "It doesn't matter what a work calls itself, just as long as it's good music theater."[80] So it is with *Porgy and Bess* and, in LaChiusa's words, "the always-inventive works of Sondheim and his collaborators."[81] Sondheim, more than any other composer in America, is Gershwin's rightful theatrical heir. Thus one may reasonably expect that he will be ranked with Gershwin (and Ives and Copland) as one of America's musical titans. Indeed, with Terry Teachout's article "Sondheim's Operas," the canonization is well under way.[82]

Arlen

Edward Jablonski tells a humorous story about the contrast between the omnipresence of Arlen's music and his anonymity. A cabby who had picked up Arlen started, in the course of the drive, to whistle "Stormy Weather." Arlen asked the driver to name the composer. After three incorrect guesses (Berlin, Rodgers, and Porter), Arlen informed the cabby that he had written the tune. The driver asked his passenger to identify himself, and Arlen gave his name. "At this the cabby turned around in his seat and asked, 'Who?' "[83]

The reasons why Arlen remains the least well known member of the Big Six are fairly easy to enumerate. First, his personality was more retiring than those of his peers. Arlen did not assert himself in Hollywood and Broadway to the extent that the other members of the Six did.

Second, he did not have a steady collaborator. Ted Koehler, E. Y. "Yip" Harburg, Johnny Mercer, and Ira Gershwin were his main lyricists, but Arlen also set the words of (among others) Jack Yellen, Lew Brown, Leo Robin, Ralph Blane, Dorothy Fields, Truman Capote, and Martin Charnin. In addition, he occasionally assisted in the writing of lyrics, and for the unproduced 1973 teleplay *Clippety Clop and Clementine,* he is listed as sole lyricist. The sheer verbal variety contained in Arlen's songs makes it difficult to speak of them as a unified body of work, and the chronological overlapping of lyricists frustrates attempts to categorize his work into periods (as can be done with Rodgers). Only Kern among the Big Six exceeds Arlen in the number of collaborators.

Third, and unlike Kern, Arlen seemed to have what one writer called a Broadway curse.[84] His most successful show, *Bloomer Girl,* ran for 654 performances, a very respectable run. But in comparison with the shows of his peers that also appeared in the 1940s (see table 1), Arlen came up short on Broadway. While Hollywood paid composers well—and Arlen scored successes in *The Wizard of Oz* (1939) and *A Star Is Born* (1954)—films rarely turned songwriters into household names, and the broad popular exposure to his songs did not secure for Arlen instant recognition.

Fourth, recognition was bound to be limited for Arlen because of his association and identification with black musicians. His towering successes in the early 1930s came from his work in Harlem; "Between the Devil and the Deep Blue Sea," "I've Got the World on a String," "Stormy Weather," and "Ill Wind" all come from various editions of the *Cotton Club Parade*. He composed a song cycle, *Americanegro Suite*, in 1941. Two years later, when Vernon Duke was unable to come to Hollywood to add more songs to his Broadway success *Cabin in the Sky* (with its all-black cast), Arlen stepped in and provided "Happiness Is a Thing Called Joe." His three musicals after *Bloomer Girl—St. Louis Woman, House of Flowers,* and *Jamaica*—had predominantly black casts at a time when few black musicals played on Broadway. (Even *Bloomer Girl* had a subplot involving emancipation, in which Dooley Wilson sang "The Eagle and Me.") To many musicians of his day, black and white, Arlen seemed to have a unique affinity with the blues, with his "Blues in the Night" establishing for all time, rightly or wrongly, his association with black music and, with the music, the black experience.

Roger Edens's account of a rehearsal at the Cotton Club, with its insider-outsider language, makes for somewhat embarrassing reading today. "[Arlen] was really one of them. He had absorbed so much from them—their idioms, their tonalities, their phrasing, their rhythms—he was able to establish a warming rapport with them. . . . I was always amazed that they had completely accepted Harold and his super-minstrel-show antics."[85] Arlen had been granted access to a community that most of white America knew only fleetingly. He subsequently fell into a crease of American culture; he became neither Richard Rodgers nor Duke Ellington, neither Cole Porter nor Fats Waller. Gershwin is the best comparison, but unlike Gershwin, Arlen mounted no sustained attack on the world of "serious" music. Whereas Gershwin, in the popular imagination, escaped a primary identification with Negro music, that music overwhelmed Arlen, guaranteeing his relative obscurity in the wider world.

Anyone who heard Arlen sing, especially in the 1955 Walden sessions, can attest how deeply he immersed himself in the black musical world. Sondheim's comments illustrate that immersion.

> Arlen . . . was the son of a cantor, and I don't know where he got that kind of Southern blues from. I always assumed that Arlen was from the South. Little did I know he's from Troy, New York, or someplace like that. [Arlen was from Buffalo.] I mean, you listen to his music, you say—like Johnny Mercer—you say, "That boy was born in the South. Somebody who grew up with 'the blues.'" Wrong. Wrong. He was an urban, upstate New York boy. I don't get it. But cantorial singing has something to do with that. Anyway, his harmonic struc-

tures and his harmonies are, to me, endlessly rich, inventive and fascinating, and I never tire of his music.[86]

It may be impossible to disentangle fully Arlen's "endlessly rich, inventive and fascinating" harmonies from his "Southern blues." But putting aside issues of race for the moment, let me demonstrate how Arlen's sound world intersects with Sondheim's.

The injection of my personal voice at this point is deliberate, because the connections between Arlen and Sondheim emerged at a rather delicate moment in my first interview with Sondheim. After establishing some of the history behind the 1990 film *Dick Tracy*, I asked Sondheim about a particular song.

> SWAYNE: "What Can You Lose" from *Dick Tracy*? I think in an issue of the *Sondheim Review*, they say it is not a pastiche.
>
> SONDHEIM: Oh, who cares about labels? No, I didn't mean it to be a pastiche of anything in particular. Warren wanted a song for that character—for 88 Keys—and he was intrigued with a scene that preceded this moment, in which 88 Keys said, "What can you lose?" or "What can I lose?"—I can't remember—it's part of the plot. And Warren said, "I love that phrase." I said, "O.K., I'll write one called 'What Can You Lose?'" It's as simple as that. But it was not meant to be pastiche, or non-pastiche. I don't always think in those terms. But in that case, it was meant to be a song of the period that would serve as something that 88 Keys could play at the piano as if it were written at that time, but use it as a personal message about his feeling for Breathless.
>
> SWAYNE: As I have been thinking about that song, it strikes me that it comes close to Arlen's music somewhat.
>
> SONDHEIM: Yeah.[87]

I met Sondheim's exasperation with a convoluted hedge, in case the identification with Arlen was misplaced. Neither he nor I would call "What Can You Lose?" an Arlen pastiche, and the analysis of the song in the next chapter operates under the presumption that the song is representative of Sondheim and not Arlen. But the acknowledgment that Arlen might lie behind the song—despite Sondheim's earlier assertion that, in his mind, no one in particular did so—suggests that the connections between Arlen and Sondheim may be much deeper than one imagines at first hearing. Sondheim admitted, "I usually have one Arlen song in every show," not in the sense of writing an Arlen pastiche but in drawing from the spirit of Arlen.[88]

To begin where Sondheim begins, with Arlen's harmonies, reveals Arlen's predilection for thirteenth chords. "I Had Myself a True Love," one of the Arlen songs on Sondheim's list, provides an example of three such chords in a row, beginning on the word "time" (example 2). Notice the thirteenths in each chord: G to E♭; C to A; and F to D.

an' once up - on a time I had a true love.

EXAMPLE 2. Arlen, "I Had Myself a True Love," excerpt

Reduced to their bare essences, the chords are as follows:

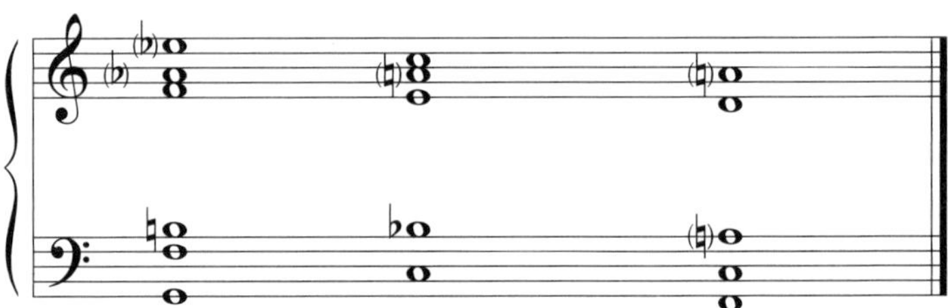

EXAMPLE 3

(A number of the accidentals appear in parentheses not because their presence is in doubt in this song but because similar chains of chords in other Arlen songs inflect these particular chordal elements differently.)

Two analytical observations need to be addressed. First, the thirteenth chords as used by Arlen here differ from the addition of the sixth degree that is a common practice in music of this period (most prominently in the songs of Kurt Weill, whose sixth-laden music Sondheim found unpleasing).[89] While clearly the sixth and thirteenth degrees are identical in terms of pitch, they are different in terms of deployment. As can be seen in the Arlen example, the pitches identified as thirteenths in the first two examples are added onto chords that already move beyond the simple triad (a ninth chord in the first example, a seventh chord in the second), whereas the final chord adds the sixth/thirteenth onto a major triad. This last chord could be interpreted as representative of the common practice use of the added sixth degree, but because the first two examples are clearly thirteenths and not added sixths, the final example can be heard as a continuation of the progression of thirteenth chords, as if the missing seventh (here, E♭) and ninth (G) were phantom notes (ones which, as often as not, would be added in jazz arrangements).

The second observation separates standard classical harmonic analysis from the harmonic language of Arlen and other songwriters. From a standard harmonic point of view, the first two thirteenth chords occur as the result of appoggiaturas that are immediately resolved, thus making the base chords a $V^{7\flat 9}/V$ followed by a V^7. While this analysis is technically correct (and would be completely appropriate for the use of appoggiaturas in the music of Brahms), it fails to consider the importance of the thirteenth in blue-note harmony, which is the language Arlen is using. It is not the resolution of the appoggiatura but the sounding of the thirteenth that is the main harmonic event in the passage. In the example above, these are not appoggiaturas but are chord tones that are followed by harmonically appropriate passing tones.

This second analytical point becomes even clearer when other examples from Arlen's songs are considered. As noted above, chains of thirteenth chords, subject to chromatic inflection, are a common feature in Arlen's music. For example, in "Blues in the Night," at the words "worrisome thing" and beyond, the progression above appears with what would be a flattened thirteenth (A♭) in the second chord. The chorus of "Buds Don't Bud" opens with a version of the first chord that substitutes naturals for the flattened notes. "The Eagle and Me" uses a simplified version of the thirteenth from the third measure of the chorus ("Eagle it like to fly") on throughout the rest of the song. And, to step outside of the songs Sondheim chose, a most delicious thirteenth chord occurs on the long-held syllable "-way" in the opening phrase from "The Man Who Got Away" *(A Star Is Born)*. This chord occurs neither as the result of adding a sixth nor because of the presence of an appoggiatura. It is a characteristically Arlenesque sound of a thirteenth chord.

Thus arises a third analytical observation. Talking about Arlen's thirteenth chords may seem unnecessarily esoteric, but Sondheim himself freely used this technical language.

I try to work away from the piano as much as possible, because if you work at the piano you get limited by your own technique. I have a fairly decent technique, but fingers tend to fall into favorite patterns, you know, and so maybe there's that thirteenth chord again. I didn't want any thirteenth chords in *Pacific Overtures*. That's what I like to play, so I wrote as much as I could away from the piano.[90]

One can easily see a connection between liking to play thirteenth chords and liking Arlen's songs, and all the more so since Sondheim said that it was Arlen's harmony that appealed to him.

Thirteenth chords were by no means the only unusual harmonic devices Arlen used, and the songs Sondheim identified are filled with extraordinary harmonic turns. (Arlen's harmonic language is "unusual" and "extraordinary" inasmuch as the other members of the Big Six, including Gershwin, rarely ventured as far as regularly as Arlen did.) As befits its lyric, "Blues in the Night" makes extensive use of "blue notes" (flattened thirds and sevenths). "I Wonder What Became of Me" sounds as though it opens in the key of B♭, establishes E♭ as the tonic, and ends in A♭, all the while utilizing an accompaniment figure reminiscent of Chopin's E minor prelude, op. 28, no. 4, and containing as many unexpected harmonic twists and turns as the Chopin. And in the release to "Buds Don't Bud," a chain of chords, beginning at the mention of moods that don't mood and ending in a heart beating in reverse, defy simple harmonic identification. (At this point in the score, while guitar chords and fingerings are provided, the indication *Guitar tacet* appears, revealing that the chords provided are not fully accurate distillations of Arlen's accompaniment.) Peter Matz's arrangement of this song for the 1955 Walden sessions and Harold Arlen's performance as vocalist together provide so many harmonic and melodic felicities that this version of the song deserves a much closer analysis than space allows. And though the focus here has been on the music, Harburg's witty lyrics for "Buds Don't Bud" make the song a standout.

Hearing Arlen sing "Buds Don't Bud" makes one appreciate more fully not only Sondheim's inclusion of the song on his list but also his lengthy comments about Arlen and about their encounter at the time Sondheim was working on *Saturday Night*.

SWAYNE: In his most recent book on Harold Arlen, Jablonski talks about how you played some of your music for Arlen in the '50s, that Arlen wasn't impressed then, but that he later changed his opinion about your work. Do you recall that meeting, as well as . . .

SONDHEIM: No, no. Jablonski is, as usual, making it up.[91] What happened was this. First of all, I had a social relationship with Arlen, which had to do with the fact that we were co-godfathers of the same child. He was a great friend of a couple named John and D.D. Ryan. D.D. Ryan was the costume designer for *Company;* John Ryan was a would-be producer who actually became a stockbroker. And they used to have sort of musical evenings at their house. I met Arlen once or twice up there. And, lo and behold, their first son was born, and they asked Harold and me to be co-godfathers. I thought they were hedging their bets, but that was all right.

My big encounter with Arlen—which was quite a vivid evening—was that I was invited (and I don't know why, or how) to E.Y. Harburg's apartment—"Yip" Harburg's—for a sort of party, which involved about, maybe, 15 or 20 people. And among them were Burton Lane and Harold Arlen. After a buffet dinner, everyone was sitting around and playing the piano. Now, I knew that I would be asked to play the piano. I don't know how I knew this, but I knew that, as a young composer, I would be asked to show off my wares, and I was 23 years old. I'd just written this score called *Saturday Night,* so I practiced all day. I decided if they asked me, I would be ready with three numbers: A fast, a slow and a fast.

SWAYNE: Which three?

SONDHEIM: Oh, the opening, "Saturday Night," and "This Is Nice, Isn't It?" and then one more, "One Wonderful Day." I could play and sing. I don't sing on pitch very accurately, but I'm enthusiastic and sort of charismatic at the piano, as most songwriters are. So sure enough, Burton Lane played some stuff, and Harold Arlen played some stuff. Then I got up, I was called on—I blushed—and Harburg or someone said, "This is the promising young composer." And I got up and played the opening, and everybody applauded very loudly. And I played "This Is Nice, Isn't It?," and they applauded even more loudly. And I ended with this screaming 2/4, "One Wonderful Day," and they all cheered.

And I sat down, very pleased with myself, on the couch next to Harold Arlen. And he turned to me and he said—devastating me—"You're afraid not to write a blockbuster, aren't you?" I wanted to go under the couch. And he did not say it meanly. What he was saying was: You don't have to knock the audience out each time. And it was a HUGE lesson. And you listen to songs like "A Sleepin' Bee," and I thought, "I get it, I get it, I get it!" "A Sleeping Bee" does not knock the audience out—it does when you think about it—[and all] it gets [is] a nice hand in the theater.

And there is room for charm, for understatement, and for all those other things. Arlen could write knockout numbers, as you well know, but he was saying to me: Take it easy.

Well, now, the message has a double edge, because I was 23 years old, and I was with my superiors—not my peers, my superiors—and I wanted to impress them. So it's excusable. But he was saying: Relax. And it meant a lot to me.

The only other thing I know about Arlen is I knew a playwright named Leonard Melfi. And Arlen, after his wife Anya had died, he went to *Pacific Overtures* three or four times, and Arlen wanted to see it again, he was so impressed; Melfi had to keep taking him back, because Arlen wouldn't go out alone, he had to go out with someone. I was very flattered by that.

But actually, I never talked to Harold again after those years. I just never ran into him. I went to an audition once, of *House of Flowers,* I think, and I heard him sing and play, and let me tell you: If you're into songwriting, they don't come any better than that. Hearing Harold Arlen play and sing makes me cry.[92] It was a thrill—thrilling.

So. That's my Harold Arlen story.[93]

If Arlen is, along with Gershwin, the most influential songwriter in Sondheim's life, then Sondheim's Harold Arlen story continues. In evaluating Sondheim's music for signs of Arlen, two general observations readily come to the surface. The first has already been discussed: harmony. While Sondheim does not show a predilection for thirteenth chords to the degree that Arlen did, the very fact of Arlen's harmonic complexity gave Sondheim license to explore nontraditional harmonies in his own songs. Moreover, the distance between Arlen's thirteenth chords and Sondheim's occasional forays into chords built on fourths is not far, as an example, a progression from "I Had Myself a True Love," demonstrates. As Example 4 shows, thirteenth chords (more so than triads) can be rearranged into collections of fourths, and the only "extraneous" note is the ninth (G) in the final measure. (In the two other cases, the "new" notes—D and G, respectively—appear as tones either in the song's melody line or in the accompaniment.)

Sondheim comes to his own complex harmonic language primarily through the door of classical music. (It is this interchangeability of thirteenth chords and collections of fourths, for example, that explains why the music from Skryabin's late period on occasion pre-echoes the world of the sophisticated Broadway song.) In Arlen, he finds a kindred spirit.

Arlen is also known for his "tapeworms," songs that go well beyond

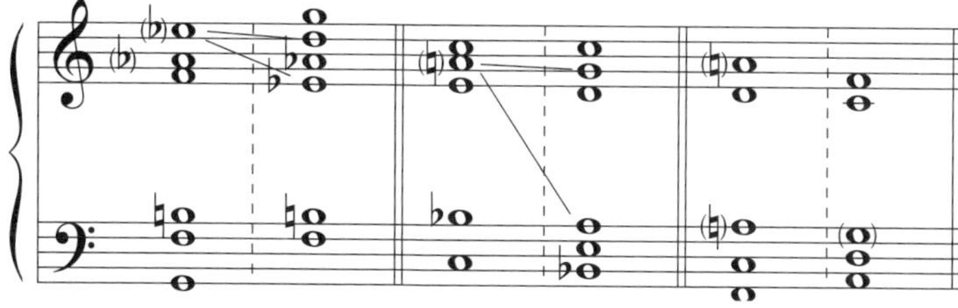

Example 4

the standard 32-bar formula. Of the five songs Sondheim picked, the refrains of "Buds Don't Bud" and "The Eagle and Me" come closest to fitting into standard song form, AA′BA″. In the former, the B section is 12 bars long, while the A sections are each the standard 8 bars in length, yet all contain irregular phrasing: the first phrase is three bars in length; the second, four; and a one-bar interlude concludes each A section. "Buds Don't Bud" is a "short" 36 bars long. In "The Eagle and Me," while A and B are each 8 bars long, A′ is 10 bars, as is A″, and the latter has a four-bar tag, making "The Eagle and Me" 40 bars long. "Blues in the Night" is 58 bars long, in part because the song's A sections are self-contained 12-bar blues. "I Wonder What Became of Me" and "I Had Myself a True Love" are 48 and 64 bars long, respectively.

Compare these expanded forms with Sondheim's more "traditional" Broadway songs. The main section of "Not While I'm Around" *(Sweeney)* is a thirty-two-bar song (ABAB′) that is sung a second time after a lengthy and irregular central section (a verse?). "Good Thing Going" *(Merrily)*, as the lyric proclaims, starts out like a song. It is cast in standard song form (AA′BA″), and the first three sections are each 8 bars long. Just as the lyric announces in the final section that "it could have kept on growing," the music takes the cue, and this final section expands to fill 14 bars (not including the three-bar bridge that joins the release to the final section). And then there are those songs, like "Send In the Clowns" *(Night Music)* and "Finishing the Hat" *(Sunday)*, that make a nod in the direction of standard song form as they unfold in their "tapewormy" way. (See table 2.) While Milton Babbitt may have shown Sondheim how to hold large expanses of music together,[94] Arlen gave Sondheim a model for the extended song.

Beyond harmony and form lie other similarities between Arlen's songs and Sondheim's, particularly in the realm of melody and accompaniment. Certain melodic gestures that are quintessentially Arlen—the octave jump, the repeated note[95]—find no regular place in Sondheim's melodies (although "The Best Thing That Ever Has Happened," from

Bounce, gives Arlen a run for his money in both the large-leap and repeated-note categories). In contrast, Arlen's habit of spinning longer melodies out of small kernels—the three notes of "Blues in the Night" or "Stormy Weather"; the two-note figure in the release of "Over the Rainbow"—prefigures Sondheim's habit of doing the same. Sondheim's kernels tend to be slightly larger than Arlen's, as has been said before, because of the greater density of the lyrics in Sondheim's songs. As for accompaniment, when one thinks of songs such as "Blues in the Night" and "The Man That Got Away," the relentless insistence of the rhythms helps to make these particular songs memorable. To call the accompaniment figures "vamps" may be too much, as the printed versions of the songs often differ greatly from the arrangements that made the songs popular. Even so, the driving repetitiveness of many of Arlen's accompaniments (including the "Chopin prelude" figure that appears not only in "I Wonder What Became of Me" but also in "I Had Myself a True Love") is mirrored in Sondheim's fondness for vamp-based accompaniments.

A structural matter also ties Sondheim to Arlen and back to Gershwin. Arlen did not write many waltzes, but those that he did write sound more like precursors to Sondheim's waltzes (both musically and lyrically) than do the more famous waltzes of Rodgers. "Lydia, the Tattooed Lady" foreshadows "Could I Leave You?" *(Follies)* in its faux innocence, and the dark humor in "Hallowe'en" and "Sunday in Cicero Falls" conjures up waltzes like "Cora's Chase" *(Whistle)* and "Last Midnight" *(Woods)*. Arlen's "Minuet," a solo piano number that he recorded for the Walden sessions, has too quick a tempo to be a true minuet and sounds, somewhat unsurprisingly, like a Ravelian waltz. Given that these waltzes play with the comic rather than the wistful or romantic elements of life and music, Arlen and Sondheim (especially outside of *Night Music*) share a similar approach to the waltz. And with Gershwin's doleful lament "My Man's Gone Now" also in three-quarter time, Sondheim had a far larger range of examples than the waltzes of Rodgers from which to choose when he set to writing his own pieces in three.

The Walden sessions contain another performance that is reminiscent of a particular Sondheim song. In "Can I Leave Off Wearin' My Shoes?" Harold Arlen sings a duet with June Ericson. With the numerous French words in the text, one thinks of "Come Play Wiz Me" *(Whistle)*, another duet *avec beaucoup de paroles françaises,* although Sondheim's appreciation of Kay Thompson's vocal arrangements in MGM movies also brings to mind "The French Lesson" from *Good News* (1947). And *Bloomer Girl*'s "T'Morra, T'Morra" echoes the Prince's sentiment in "Moments in the Woods" *(Into the Woods)*. The number of localized resemblances between Arlen and Sondheim no doubt could be multiplied and is likely to be uninformative, as the connections have little documentary corroboration. Yet they all require consideration in order to assess the degree to which Sondheim, the self-aware admirer of Arlen, also became the unconscious imitator of Arlen.

One unexpected connection between Arlen and Sondheim is the fact that they both were drawn to Jean Giraudoux's play of 1945, *The Madwoman of Chaillot*, at about the same time. An undated musical treatment of the play exists among Sondheim's papers and may have arisen shortly after *Saturday Night* was completed in early 1954.[96] Shortly before this, Arlen had returned from Hollywood to work in earnest on *House of Flowers*. In addition to working with Truman Capote (lyricist and librettist for the musical), Arlen met with Breen to discuss the latter's idea of a companion piece to *Porgy and Bess*. One of the suggestions was an adaptation of *Chaillot*.[97] Neither composer set the Giraudoux—that honor would go to Jerry Herman (*Dear World*, 1969)—but the proximity of their interest in the play may be more than coincidental. Undoubtedly the gathering at Harburg's apartment in 1954 entailed more than songwriters playing their songs for each other, and it is easy to imagine that Arlen and Sondheim discussed plays that might be turned into musicals. If this was the case, though, one cannot tell which man first suggested the Giraudoux. Given that nothing appears to survive from Arlen's contemplation of the play save for Jablonski's recollection, Sondheim seems to have taken this "possible" more seriously than did Arlen.

While the links between Arlen and Sondheim may remain somewhat murky, the links between Arlen and Gershwin are undeniable. "I Had Myself a True Love" and "I Wonder What Became of Me," the two "art songs" (Jablonski's description) from *St. Louis Woman*, sound as if they belong in *Porgy and Bess*, so much so that they could pass as Gershwin pastiches were it not for Arlen's blues pedigree and his rightful claim to this musical language. Small wonder, then, that Robert Breen saw in the songs for *St. Louis Woman* the seeds for his companion piece to *Porgy and Bess*.

And small wonder that Sondheim, in choosing Arlen, chose Gershwin also, and vice versa. Sondheim's music only fleetingly reflects the old-world attitudes of Kern, the protean accessibility of Berlin, or the cool professionalism of Rodgers, and when it does so, it is likely to be the result of imitating, rather than imbibing, their musical spirits. Sondheim's lyrics rival those of Porter, but his music heads in a direction different from Porter's. In his review of *Passion*, critic Nelson Pressley offered his assessment of Sondheim. "By placing six disparate shows cheek by jowl, the Sondheim Celebration is making a good case that despite his acclaim as a lyricist and brave storyteller, Sondheim's most lasting legacy will be for the unrivaled variety and penetrating depth of his music."[98] It would be difficult to argue against the assertion that Gershwin and Arlen plumbed the musical depths of popular song more deeply than did the other members of the Big Six. In staking his claim to these two men, Sondheim invites us to take his measure against them. As Pressley suggests, Sondheim is not found wanting.

Other songwriters

One could attempt, like Alec Wilder and Allen Forte, to account for the relative weight of other songwriters whose best work seems evergreen. Sondheim's list of songs he would like to have written, however, provides a personal map of the world of songwriting he values. The problem with his list remains its parenthetical subtitle ("At Least in Part"). In his remarks to a recital audience at the Library of Congress, Sondheim described how the program had been chosen from that list, and thus went some way toward explaining its rationale and purpose.

Sondheim gave among his reasons for including particular songs their power to move the emotions; their "enormous freshness and invention," "sheer skill and delight," tenderness, or joy; that they "contain favorite lyric lines" or "tell wonderful stories"; the brilliance of their comic lyric writing and their inventive rhyme; and, in the case of "My Man's Gone Now," that "it's the best song I ever heard, and it moves me. It's got a lyric by Dubose Heyward, whose lyrics for *Porgy and Bess* are, I think, the best lyrics in the musical theater."[99] The repeated emphasis on the words of the songs is striking, and one might begin to think that Sondheim takes his measure mostly against other lyricists and not composers. Yet it remains that he chose *Porgy and Bess* for the totality of its effect upon him, and he named songwriters and not lyricists as influential. Whether it is music or words that lay behind the selection of these 50 (instead of 150), three other songwriters in particular deserve mention.

Sondheim gave a reason for liking one of Cy Coleman's songs, "When in Rome," and five Coleman songs made it to Sondheim's list. As with the presence of songs from *St. Louis Woman*, it seems that a proximate event reminded Sondheim of Coleman's worth. *Little Me* was revived in 1998 and, like the Arlen score that was revived that same year, would have been relatively fresh in Sondheim's mind when he created his list. Considering the length of Coleman's career on Broadway, it is remarkable that Sondheim limited his choices to songs written before 1964. His predilection for early Coleman underscores his comments on losing interest in musical theater after the mid-1960s, for the list of Coleman's post-1964 triumphs is impressive: *Sweet Charity* opened in 1966; *Seesaw* (1973) premiered a month after *A Little Night Music; I Love My Wife* (1977) opened two days after the revue *Side by Side by Sondheim; Barnum* (1980) opened while *Sweeney Todd* was running and ran right over *Merrily*. On the strength of *I Love My Wife*, Coleman, according to Bordman, "was increasingly perceived as the most prolific and consistently successful Broadway composer of his day," an assessment in keeping with Bordman's coolness toward Sondheim.

If the database of Sondheim's CD collection is up to date, it is worth noting that the only post-1964 Coleman musicals Sondheim owns as CDs are *Sweet Charity*, *On the Twentieth Century* (1978), *The Will Rogers Follies* (1991), and *The Life* (1997). In contrast, he owns both the original cast recording and 1998 revival recording of *Little Me* as well as *Wildcat* (1960). Clearly, Sondheim admires Coleman and his work—he owned all of Coleman's shows on LPs—but as a contemporary Coleman (1929–2004) does not emerge as an influence on Sondheim's music. If anything, the influence appears to have gone in the opposite direction, if Stephen Holden's judgment of *Grace* (premiered in Amsterdam in October 2001) is accurate. "Who knew that Mr. Coleman could write music this lush? It is the closest he has come in his long career to a Sondheim-like elevation."[100]

With Hugh Martin (1914–), we have Sondheim's own word of Martin's presence in a Sondheim musical. "All the numbers Angie [Angela Lansbury] sang in [*Anyone Can Whistle*] were pastiche—her opening number ["Me and My Town"], for instance, was a Hugh Martin–Kay Thompson pastiche."[101] (To digress for a moment: Sondheim later disclosed that Lansbury's character, Cora, as musically conveyed, was based on Thompson, whose "highly sophisticated . . . arrangements show up in a number of MGM musicals. They have a heartlessness that I thought was very useful for Cora. They have also gaiety and pizzazz and a sophistication of harmonic language and imagination and invention—and [are] completely bloodless. And that seemed to me to be Cora.")[102] Sondheim's linkage of Martin and Thompson describes a genre of music rather than an actual working relationship; the extent of their collaboration was that they share vocal arrangements credits on *Broadway Rhythm*, and Martin's song "Pass the Peace Pipe" appears in *Good News* (Thompson arranged the music for both movies).

Martin makes an intriguing choice for Sondheim and again highlights the Gershwin-Arlen axis. "[Martin's] studies were oriented to guide him into a classical music career, but when [he] heard the music of George Gershwin, he made popular music his choice. In 1937, he sang in the Broadway show *Hooray for What* [composed by Arlen]."[103] Three of the four Martin songs Sondheim chose come from stage musicals, none of which was overly successful. The earliest of these songs (1941) credits Ralph Blane with the lyrics; Blane would serve as Martin's collaborator a few years later on *Meet Me in St. Louis,* from which Sondheim's fourth Martin song derives. The other two Broadway songs bring to mind Bordman's assessment. "Martin did the words and music for several later Broadway shows, but his clever way with words served him better than his facile melodic gifts."[104]

But one can easily see, in the best known of the Martin songs, just what Sondheim found so inventive about Martin's craft. "The Trolley Song" uses standard song form but, because of its alla breve tempo and various extensions, comes in at 86 bars. Wilder gives numerous reasons why the melody, harmony, and rhythm all conspire together to make the song so winning.[105] One feature he does not mention is its tight motivic construction. The last two phrases of the release, for example, are both a transposition and a subtle manipulation of its first two phrases, and each successive statement of the A section expands the "clang, clang, clang" figure more than the statement that preceded it (the first A spans a third; the second, a fifth; the last, an octave). Its infectiousness disguises its craft, and craft is Sondheim's métier. But with his relatively small output, Martin seems more likely a source for imitation than a font of influence. For all its resemblance to Romberg's waltzes, "One More Kiss" *(Follies)* also sounds like a pastiche of "The Boy Next Door" *(Meet Me in St. Louis),* especially with its use of accented dissonant melody notes throughout. And it is worth noting, in passing, that Sondheim's choice of "The Trolley Song," his conflation of Martin and Thompson, and his reference to MGM indicates that, Secrest's remarks notwithstanding, he did know something about film musicals.[106]

The third songwriter whose influence on Sondheim needs to be taken into account, if only to dismiss his importance, is Leonard Bernstein (1918–1990). Without question, Sondheim valued Bernstein's wisdom, professionally and musically, and Bernstein's Broadway successes (and failures) mostly preceded Sondheim's compositional debut with *Forum.* Bernstein was also a wordsmith, having provided additional lyrics for *On the Town* and having written all the lyrics for his *Peter Pan* (1950; not to be confused with the more successful one that premiered four years later). Sondheim found Bernstein's words on the purple side, which explains in part his disparagement of his own lyrics for "I Feel Pretty" (*West Side Story*, 1957): they were too close to Bernstein's style, at times sentimental, at times pompous.

The musically sophisticated nature of Bernstein's music could not help but appeal to Sondheim, who would have taken note of the intricacies in *West Side Story* (e.g., the "Tonight" quintet, the "Cool" fugue) and *Candide* before it ("Glitter and Be Gay" is the sole Bernstein choice on his list). But Bernstein wasn't the only musical sophisticate on Broadway whose music Sondheim had heard, and by the time he came to work alongside Bernstein, Sondheim had established many of the musical hallmarks of his style. In his pre-1955 work, he had written contrapuntal ensembles and fugues, albeit not as complex as Bernstein's, who was twelve years Sondheim's senior. The piano sonata of 1950 provides evidence of Sondheim's command of a complex musical language that shows little indebtedness to Bernstein. Sondheim's course had been set early and in a direction that Bernstein did not always find agreeable. Bernstein criticized the score for *Forum* "because of its having 'arbitrary' wrong notes, by which he meant (among other things) the tritones." Sondheim pointed out to Bernstein how tritone-heavy *West Side Story* is. "I made a jocular remark about 'I Feel Pretty' being the only song that didn't have a tritone in it, and Lenny was astonished. He had no idea of what he'd done."[107] To whatever degree the two composers' show music may sound alike, it may be because they had similar musical training in college and traveled in similar musical circles afterward, with Sondheim's inclining toward the theater and Bernstein's toward the concert hall.

West Side Story also has an instance where the young Sondheim guided the older Bernstein into the Broadway idiom of the day.

> The only music I had anything directly to do with . . . was "Something's Coming." . . . We needed something to give our hero some early strength in the piece. . . . So I said to Lenny, "What Larry Kert sings better than anybody but Judy Garland is a 2/4." "What is that?," said Lenny, knowing full well what 2/4 meant. I said songs like, "Hallelujah!," and then I explained what a showbiz 2/4 was. And he understood right away. . . . we wrote the song in about a day and a half. And it was during rehearsals, and I went to one end of his house and started to fiddle with the lyric, and he came up with the verse. And what I then did was take the verse and turn it into the 2/4. I said, "You gotta have a thumbline." And I showed him what a thumbline was. And he said, "Oh, you mean a cello line." . . . But the idea of [the 2/4 vamp around the legato thumbline] . . . was standard showbiz writing.

That's "One Wonderful Day" in *Saturday Night;* it was "Saturday Night," as a matter of fact. It was what we were all writing at that time. So what I did was: I took Lenny's tune from the verse and turned it into the chorus ["Could it be? Yes, it could."]. And that's my contribution to the music.[108]

(One could add that "The Trolley Song," which was also sung by Judy Garland, is a 2/4.)

Facile comparisons of the two composers overlook a profound difference between them. While Sondheim is a self-confessed harmony man, Bernstein is a rhythm man, and especially in his Broadway shows where dance is so important a component. In contrast, with the exception of *Follies,* no Sondheim show gives a prominent place to dance, comparatively few are the Sondheim rhythms that rivet themselves in the memory as do Bernstein's, and rare are the moments where meters change as mercurially in Sondheim's music as they do in Bernstein's. Tracing both composers back to Gershwin—as well as to Hindemith and Copland—more logically explains whatever similarities exist in their music than tracing Sondheim back to Bernstein.[109] Such a lineage also does justice to Bernstein's obvious interpolations of jazz, which find few expressions in Sondheim's songs. Bernstein and Sondheim took similar things from their compositional precursors, but their individual styles diverged significantly.

Nowhere is this clearer than in the "big finish." Many of the songs in Bernstein's musicals, both fast and slow ones, show a predilection for the theatrical flourish, as they build in rhythmic intensity and harmonic complexity to an apotheosis of sheer sound. Bernstein's choices of musical materials may have made this approach an easier task for him than it was for Sondheim, though knowledge of the two men's temperaments helps to explain the constant musical exuberance of Bernstein and the relative reticence of Sondheim. Certainly Sondheim knew how to build to a musical climax and has done so again and again. Yet, it is as if his chastisement by Arlen struck deeply. Sondheim's musical finishes are more succinct and less overwhelming than the almost Mahlerian endings that were Bernstein's wont. And those "big finishes" are affected by the choices of rhythms; while Sondheim, like Bernstein (and Copland before them), used Latin rhythms, Sondheim tended not to use the more exotic and hypnotic ones that Bernstein favored, instead preferring the tamer ones like the rumba and bossa nova, more in keeping with the way Porter used these rhythms (and recall Sondheim's identification of Latin American rhythms with Porter in his Kern liner notes).

In closing, connections can and must be drawn between Sondheim and songwriters other than those he has named. Weill scholars, for example, have expended a fair amount of ink on Sondheim's alleged indebtedness to Weill.[110] But the connections are clearest between the members of the Big Six in general, and Gershwin and Arlen in particular. It is possible that Sondheim, in naming his influences, has deliberately or unconsciously downplayed some significant musical stimuli. Given his candor about his models, however, such suppression seems unlikely. The following story provides yet another example of that candor and the improbability that Bernstein or Weill significantly influenced his music, for if they had, Sondheim would likely have said so.

The "Negro connection"

Frank Rizzo reported on "A Conversation with Stephen Sondheim" that took place on the campus of Trinity College (Hartford, Conn.) on March 9, 1997. "The issue of race—specifically the almost exclusively white world [Sondheim] creates on stage (as opposed to Hammerstein's exploration of race in *Show Boat*, *Carmen Jones* and *South Pacific*)—had Sondheim talking about nontraditional casting." Rizzo transcribed Sondheim's remarks.

> Nontraditional casting, which is happening now, is perfectly fine if an audience chooses not to see beyond the color of the people. In England, audiences do not see the color of the people they are looking at. American audiences do, and they bring with it all the weight and the baggage that comes with that. I think if you had presented *Oklahoma!* in 1943 [with nontraditional casting], it wouldn't have run a week. I think the audience would have been appalled. It's only in the last twenty years that Americans have begun to accept nontraditional casting, and even then, look at the big flap over *Miss Saigon*. The level of prejudice in this country is enormous. In London Bobby [in *Company*] was black [Adrian Lester]. Over here, it would *mean* something—"aaah, Bobby is the outsider, aaah."
>
> I write the stories that interest me. And if they're about "rich white guys" [referring to a criticism by another], then they're about rich white guys. If they're not, they're not . . . So it's sort of an irrelevant question, but an interesting one because it's about audiences rather than about writers.[111]

Sondheim is undeniably right that such questions tell us something about the questioner, and his answer to his unnamed critic sounds like his exasperation with those who insist that Robert (from *Company*) must be gay.[112] But there remains the curious situation that Sondheim named as his principal influences two songwriters who are closely associated with black music and chose two scores that have nearly all-black casts. Clearly, stories about "poor black women" also interest Sondheim. Why, then, save for one character in *Anyone Can Whistle* (and, obviously, all of *Pacific Overtures* as originally conceived), are his shows so white? And, more to the point, how could he have Gershwin and Arlen as musical influences and compose music that seems to have no connection to black music?

This latter question may overstate the case, for Banfield has helpfully cataloged references to ragtime, blues, gospel, and jazz inflections in Sondheim's music, from Dino's novelty piano solo that opens *Saturday Night* (1954) to the Wolf's apostrophes in "Hello, Little Girl" *(Into the Woods)*. Much of Cora's music in *Anyone Can Whistle* and "I'm Still Here" from *Follies* clearly draw from the wells of jazz and the blues. And "What's Your Rush?" from *Bounce* nods approvingly to the blues. But for someone who looked to Gershwin and Arlen for inspiration, Sondheim seems strangely uncomfortable using black-influenced musical styles as frequently as did his predecessors. "That Old Piano Roll" (cut from *Follies*) starts out like a rhythm-driven song, only to tumble into a torrent of words that vitiates the rhythm. And considering Sondheim's virtuosity with language, the Witch's "rap" (so designated) in *Into the Woods* is remarkably static. Could it be that Sondheim and his collaborators don't write black characters because they find it difficult to create them?

In Sondheim's case, he cannot be faulted for having an upbringing that kept him relatively isolated from African-Americans or from their music. Most of the jazz and blues Sondheim imbibed came in distilled form, either as "symphonic jazz" through classical composers (recall his comments on Ravel's left-hand concerto) or as "blackened Broadway" through the likes of Gershwin, Vernon Duke, and Arlen. In the 1940s and 1950s, he showed little interest in the trends in jazz springing up around him, and today one looks in vain among his recordings for Miles Davis, John Coltrane, Dizzy Gillespie, Max Roach, or (even) Dave Brubeck. To put it crassly: Sondheim liked black music far less than did Gershwin or Arlen.

Then again, America after World War II was quite different, musically and culturally speaking, from the Tin Pan Alley environment of

Gershwin's maturation or the Cotton Club "conservatory" where Arlen honed his skills. Had Sondheim been inclined to write "black music," he would have been the last of a dying breed. Arlen's "Broadway curse" may have less to do with his choice of collaborators than with their choice of vehicles; after 1945, the "sunny optimism" of white-created black musicals became less and less tenable.[113] Kurt Weill and Maxwell Anderson obliquely dealt with American race relations in *Lost in the Stars* (1950), and author Langston Hughes would write operas and musicals that featured blacks (primarily from 1949 to 1965), but the political tensions of the early civil rights era took their toll on the black entertainments of the day.[114] After the onslaught by Elvis Presley, Carl Perkins, Jerry Lee Lewis, and other whites in musical blackface, a predominantly white Broadway audience had little appetite for most black music and black musicals. It is no accident, for example, that Arlen's *Jamaica* (1957) emerges at the same time that record companies launch Harry Belafonte as an alternative to the rock-and-roll boom, given that producers found calypso less threatening and less overtly sexual than rhythm and blues.[115] By the time *Hallelujah, Baby!* came to Broadway in 1967—with its Jule Styne score and book by Arthur Laurents—the events of history had so outrun the events on Broadway that one critic complained that it was "a show that is 100 years too late."[116]

Sondheim's lack of engagement with black music thus became for him a blessing in disguise. His repeated identification with the harmony of Gershwin and Arlen gives him cover to deploy his own complex harmonies, at times indebted to Gershwin and Arlen but far less so than to the classical composers who fill his collection, and certainly little indebted to jazz and blues. Sondheim's "Negro connection," though tantalizing to suggest, falters on the musical evidence and the historical circumstances.

Yet, as the chapters on theater and film will explore, Sondheim may not be as "white" as some have made him out to be. No doubt he does not object to nontraditional casting, considering that the African-American actor Michael Benjamin Washington played Ted, one of the neighborhood fellows in the 2000 off-Broadway premiere of *Saturday Night*. (One could also cite Vanessa L. Williams's presence in the 2002 revival of *Into the Woods* as another example, although there is no requirement that all fairy-tale characters have to be white,[117] as well as Brian Stokes Mitchell's portrayal of Sweeney Todd in the Sondheim Celebration.) Beyond the suspension of disbelief, beyond the presence in *Anyone Can Whistle* of Martin (The Negro)—who imitates stereotypical black deportment by saying "cubber" instead of "cover," shows his progressive politics by having, as his occupation, "going to schools, riding in buses, eating in restaurants," and calls into question his ethnicity by identifying himself as Jewish[118]—there are places in Sondheim's oeuvre where he wrestles with race and class, albeit not in the terms of black and white. A slave hungering for freedom and a community shattered by the arrival of the sons of Europe: these are not the stories of rich white guys. (Nor is *Saturday Night*, arguably the closest Sondheim came to dealing with ethnicity.) One can wish that Sondheim had turned *Amistad* into a musical, but the politics of the second half of the twentieth century made such cultural work difficult. The musical *Ragtime* (1996), for example, reveals more about American race relations at the end of the twentieth century than does its fictional story about racial tensions at the beginning of that century, just as *South Pacific* (1949) served a similar purpose mid-century.[119] Sondheim's mentors and influences overtly trafficked in race-related stories and deployed their accompanying sounds. Sondheim's musical and dramatic travels stayed a polite distance from these worlds, but his familiarity with them nevertheless shows, and in unexpected ways.

The tag (in verse)

It's no sin that Berlin Sondheim only pastiches;
        Like Porter, his forte's in the words he unleashes.
A kernel of Kern'll appear, heart on sleeve,
        But Dick Rodgers's a stodgier composer to Steve.
He loves Gershwin's and Arlen's rich chocolaty hues,
        Yet his harmonic parlance owes less to the blues.
Add Rachmaninoff, Hindemith, Copland, Ravel,
        Britten, Berg, Montsalvatge, and Nystroem pell mell:
        Sondheim's music draws notes from a polyglot's well.

3

Pulling It Apart

Chapters 1 and 2 provided an overview of the musical aspects of Sondheim's sound. An analysis of a Sondheim song will demonstrate how these various aspects come together.

"*. . . now you have part . . .*"

By the time "What Can You Lose?" is sung in the movie *Dick Tracy*, quite a bit of Sondheim has already gone by.[1] The movie's sole love song, it is the fourth of five Sondheim songs in the movie. It begins under the dialogue, with a faintly heard string sound stealing in from the silence. A single high F♯ is held for some time before the piano continues with an introduction that is printed note-for-note in the published version of the song. (See example 1.) The wistful, descending lines of the opening include a glittering arpeggio high in the piano (mm. 1–4) that sets up the lyric, with its sentiment of love wilting before it has had a chance fully to blossom, a love weighed down with the anguish of having to make a decision: risk disclosure and possible rejection or remain both silent and unfulfilled. Two tempo indications rest on top of each other: the singer is told to sing a "lazy blues (quarter note = 108)," while the pianist is told to play "rubato."[2] The call simultaneously for metronomic precision and rhythmic flexibility illustrates the indecision that the song sets out to explore. The voice enters haltingly, only four syllables to a breath, as though the opening question is so difficult to utter that the singer finds it hard to move forward (mm. 4ff.). Not until he begins to reflect on the possibility that his intended may already see how he feels does the song take flight (mm. 12–16), only to stall because of another, more depressing possibility: that the object of his love knows how he feels and chooses not to acknowledge it (mm. 16–24). Twice as long as the flight of rapture, this sober realization leads the singer to start all over again, and the music signals this change of direction by returning to the

WHAT CAN YOU LOSE ?
Music and Lyrics by
STEPHEN SONDHEIM
Lazy Blues (♩ = 108)
Rubato
p
What can you lose?
On - ly the blues.
mp
p
Why keep con - ceal - ing ev - 'ry - thing you're
mp
feel - ing? Say it to her - - What can you lose?
May - be it shows,
p
She's had clues, which she chose to ig - nore.
poco cresc.
May - be, though, she knows, And just wants to go on as be - fore.
dim.
p
cresc.
mp
As a friend, noth - ing more.
p
mp

So she clos - es the door. Well, if she does, — you have part — of her. What if she had — to choose? Leave it a - lone.

Those are the dues. Hold it all in.

Once the words are spo - ken, Some - thing may be bro - ken. Still, you love her - - — Bet - ter a bone. Don't ev - en be - gin. With so — much to

What can you lose? But what if she goes? At least now, — win. There's too much to lose.

(ten.) *p* *mp* *sub. mf* *dim.* *sub. mp* *mp* *cresc.* *cresc. poco a poco* *mf* *poco dim* *p* *poco cresc.* *Rall.* *Rall...*

Example 1. Sondheim, "What Can You Lose?" *(Dick Tracy)*

music of the opening interrogative phrase (mm. 24ff.). This second time, however, when the song reaches its highest arc, the lyrics have a change of tone: before, they spoke of the possibility of love; now they speak of the likelihood of loss. Immediately the melodic line responds by sinking down to its lowest point, whereupon the singer resolves to be stoic in the face of unrequited affections: "With so much to win (love, companionship, completion, emotional fulfillment), there's too much to lose (friendship, affection, what emotional satisfaction already exists)." The chord that accompanies this final word shows the pain of the loss, with its harmonization of the melodic tonic with the flat supertonic; the dissonance of the major seventh helps to portray the sorrow brought on by the lack of a conclusive resolution of love. The upward turn of the melody for this final word also underscores the pain, as the vowel and pitch of the word "lose" approximate the involuntary sound one makes when experiencing discomfort. The final five notes of the piano affirm the singer's resignation, as they hark back to the arpeggio in the introduction, now slowed to near stasis. What was once wistful now sounds paralyzed. The song has indeed lost a lot, and its pathetic recollection of the opening of the song echoes the sentiment of the text—that indeed there is very much to lose.

The musical materials of "What Can You Lose?"—the melodic contrasts of flights of fancy and moments of despair, the way the song returns to the beginning midway through as if to make a second attempt at realizing its own potential, the second half's failure to achieve the climax reached in the first half, the valedictory melodic and harmonic gesture, the framing device of the wilted arpeggio—all these underscore the message of the lyrics—questioning, exploring radiant possibilities, admitting ultimate defeat. But the music contains other signals apart from the lyrics that inform the listener about the difficult choices these characters are facing in their relationship. For example, the web of motives and contrapuntal lines that weaves through "What Can You Lose?" provides a musical analogue to the dramatic entanglements we see on the screen. The descending third in the right hand of the piano's introduction mirrors the ascending four-note motive in the opening vocal line, whose compass is also a third. This opening motive (whose notes hereafter are referred to as [1]-[2]-[3]-[4]) generates all of the music for the voice; while the motive occasionally opens up to a fourth, the rocking back and forth between a step and a leap marks nearly every measure of the vocal line. In addition to the motive's intervallic consistency, it also appears in the same basic rhythmic guise (four eighth notes, with the final one tied across the bar or in midmeasure) no fewer than twenty-eight times. Because of the music's penchant to vary the motive's presentation often (step-leap, leap-step, leap-leap; notes [2] and [3] repeated at the same pitch; the leap of a third or a fourth; ascending vs. descending), the song becomes difficult to remember precisely; one must make a concentrated effort to commit its melodic nuances to memory. In many ways, the melody is as evanescent as the message of the lyric it carries.

Motivic melodies

Figure 1 provides a graphic reduction of the melody line of "What Can You Lose?" The graphic helps to reveal just how pervasive the four-note motive is in this song and how shrewdly Sondheim used it. (Vertical distances are by half steps; horizontal distances are by eighth notes; dots represent sung lyrics; arrows represent held notes; all iterations, regardless of pitch, begin on the same baseline.) To begin with, the upward direction of the motive corresponds to the interrogative nature of the lyric; just as a question ends with a rise of the voice at the end of the sentence, so the music reflects the question in the title. The opening iteration encompasses a minor third and is immediately answered by a repetition of the motive, which now spans a major third. Notice also how the interrogative nature of the opening is muted in that, in the second iteration, [4] is the same pitch as [2]; there is no rise at the end. The major third now takes over in this phrase until the repeat of the opening question, at which point the motive spans a perfect fourth and returns to the rise at [4]. The motive is slowly increasing its range. It is also acquiring accretions, as the third and fourth iterations in the first phrase add a tail to the motive, and experiencing compression, as the fifth iteration dispenses with the undulation that has been a feature of the motive in its first four iterations.

Before going on to talk about the motivic development in this song, it needs to be stressed that this type of motivic concentration is typical for Sondheim but less so for Tin Pan Alley, Broadway, and Hollywood composers. In the case of the latter, there typically is more than one idea within the first phrase of a standard song that was aimed to become a hit, even in those whose "hooks" are transparent. "Bewitched, Bothered and Bewildered," for example (from *Pal Joey*, 1940), is one of the most motivically oriented songs Rodgers ever wrote. It has an ascending three-note hook that has five iterations in the main part of the song and that is inverted in the bridge for three iterations. Similarly, the descend-

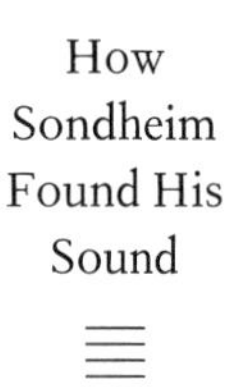

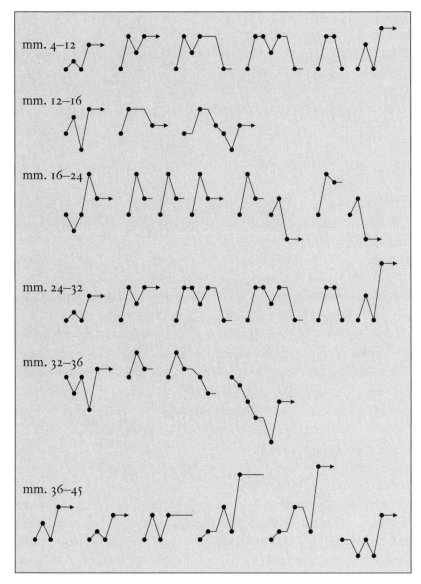

mm. 4–12
mm. 12–16
mm. 16–24
mm. 24–32
mm. 32–36
mm. 36–45

FIG. 1. A graphic representation of the melody of "What Can You Lose?"

ing line that appears at the title words will be reinterpreted as an ascending line in the bridge. As Sondheim remarked about the release of "People Will Say We're in Love" and Rodgers's lack of awareness of the musical sophistication he wove into that song,[3] it is likely that Rodgers came to these parallel constructions in "Bewitched, Bothered and Bewildered" by accident and not through careful planning. But the song contains two distinct ideas within its first phrase: the three-note hook and the scalar melody. Other songs from the classic American popular song composers—such as "Over the Rainbow," "They Say It's Wonderful," and "If I Loved You"—similarly have multiple ideas in their opening phrases.

Sondheim, in contrast, built the entire first phrase of "What Can You Lose?" out of versions of the opening four-note hook with no other ideas taking up melodic space. And this is a typical Sondheim practice in creating a melodic line. To borrow his own lyric, Sondheim's melodies often start out like songs, but whereas songs have motivic variety from the very beginning, Sondheim's songs exhibit a remarkable degree of motivic compression. In fact, as we shall see, the four-note motive of "What Can You Lose?" appears in other Sondheim songs, in each case becoming the generative kernel out of which the rest of the melody grows.

Such is the case in the *Dick Tracy* song, where the motive continues beyond the first phrase to control the melodic material. The first half of the second phrase (mm. 12–16) begins with a version of the four-note motive that continues to span a fourth, as it did at the end of the first phrase. Immediately after this, the motive is twice truncated into a three-note iteration that drops the final note of the motive. While its similarity to the motive and to the second through fourth iterations in the first phrase are clear upon close examination, Sondheim obscured the connections here by elongating certain notes to quarter notes and a dotted quarter note (instead of the eighth notes that are typical for the melody). Lastly, at measures 14–15, the motive circles back upon itself, as the six-note iteration uses [1]-[2]-[3]-[2]-[3]-[4]. The truncation, in other words, extends itself by attaching itself to another truncation.

The second part of this six-note iteration, in addition to being the last three notes of the four-note motive, can also be construed as the retrograde inversion of the first three notes of the motive, especially when one looks at these three notes in their various guises in the first phrase. I am not suggesting that Sondheim deliberately injected serial techniques into his compositional arsenal in such a straightforward song (although Len Cariou's comments on Sondheim's use of retrograde in "The Ballad of Sweeney Todd" do not put this possibility completely out of reach).[4] Rather, I am pointing out how the melody naturally unfolds from the original four-note motive. The connections are less deliberate than intuitive, but nevertheless they emerge because of Sondheim's proclivity toward motivic compression.

The notion of retrograde and inversion, however, becomes helpful in understanding how the melody conspires with the lyric to convey its

dramatic information. In the second half of the second phrase (mm. 16–24), the three-note truncation [1]-[2]-[3] becomes the central feature, turning around and around as the singer mulls over the thought that perhaps the beloved is not responding to the affectations of love because she wants to be "a friend, nothing more." At the realization of this possibility, the motive literally reverses itself, with the leap of the fourth that opened the truncation now becoming the drop of a fourth at the end. This also is an inversion of the question posed in the title words of the song. It is a musical as well as a textual deflation, and yet it comes directly from the opening motive.

The third phrase (mm. 24–32) is nearly identical with the first, except that the third and fourth iterations here are identical, whereas in the first phrase they were slightly different, and that the final leap is a perfect fifth, not a perfect fourth, thus further widening the intervallic space between notes, which will open even further in the final phrase. The first half of the fourth phrase (mm. 32–36) resembles the first half of the second phrase but also takes some striking departures. The pickup in the first iteration doesn't significantly alter its similarity to its companion in the second phrase, nor do the shortened note values change the parallels between the second and third iterations in both phrases. The third iteration, however, doesn't include the final note, which makes its descending scale seem somewhat untethered from the motive. What emerges instead is the scale as an important musical feature in its own right. Indeed, if the third iteration in the second phrase dovetailed two truncations, the third and fourth iterations in the fourth phrase turn on themselves even more thoroughly: [1]-[2]-[3]-[2]-[3] and [3]-[2]-[3]-[2]-[3]-[4]. The effective collapse of the motive similarly sketches the emotional collapse of the singer. The descent of a minor ninth here, which has no parallel in the song, mirrors the fall of the lover's hopes, that all might be lost if the beloved were forced to choose between friendship and love. Motive, melody, and text all work together at this moment.

The second half of the fourth phrase represents the toughening of the lover's resolve, and accordingly the motive returns in more recognizable forms. Still, the anguish of the journey has left its mark, as the fourth and fifth iterations here have upward leaps of, respectively, a perfect fifth and a minor sixth. They overreach the questions posed in the first and third phrases and echo the downward descent of a minor ninth (which, taking the fourth iteration, had a descent of a minor sixth). Even here, though, the contours of the opening four-note motive remain clear.

Sondheim molded the motive to abet dramatic ends through the music, but that does not discount the fact of a sophisticated motivic network at play here. And such motivic manipulations are a major factor in distinguishing a Sondheim melody from those of other songwriters. Kernels from as short as two notes (e.g., "Beautiful Girls") to as long as seven notes ("Good Thing Going") form the nub of most Sondheim melodies, with four- and five-note motives forming the backbone of his oeuvre. Even in patter-oriented songs (e.g., "Now" and "Getting Married Today"), the melodic skeletons are usually small motivic cells that are expanded through neighbor-note activity, note repetition, and/or cell repetition. For example, at first listen it is not obvious that the five-note phrase that opens the song "Sunday in the Park with George" ("A trickle of sweat") reappears in compressed form in the patter section of the song ("There are worse things than staring at the river on a Sunday"), or that the frantic middle section of "Side by Side by Side" ("What would we do without you?") uses a variant of the four-note motive that opened the song ("Isn't it warm?").

Concerning the latter, Steven Wilson argued that the pervasive appearance of $\hat{5}$-$\hat{3}$-$\hat{5}$-$\hat{4}$ in *Company* demonstrated a profound organic connection that weaves its way through the score.[5] Banfield, however, wondered whether this should be considered a *meaningful* procedure of unification, since Wilson's thesis proves "nothing other than that all music is based on a limited fount of serial intervals."[6] One could similarly posit that motivically constructed melodies are not all that unusual among songwriters. Yet, Sondheim's melodies take motivic construction to extremes.

A comparison between "Losing My Mind" *(Follies)* and the song on which it is putatively modeled, Gershwin's "The Man I Love," provides a useful example. Figures 2a and 2b provide graphic reductions of both songs. (Here, rhythm is not added to the reductions, in part because of the difficulty in rendering Gershwin's dotted eighth/sixteenth rhythms and in part because of the rubato-laden performance histories of both songs.) Unlike the A section for "The Man I Love," which is basically the outworking of one motive, "Losing My Mind" introduces two motives. The first motive is the same four-note idea that opened "What Can You Lose?," which is followed by a five-note idea notable mostly for the descent at its end. But note the last iterations in the first phrases of both songs. Whereas "The Man I Love" relaxes its motivic connections by introducing a scalar idea followed by repeated notes, "Losing My Mind" effectively inserts the second motive into the first one (especially given the change in the first motive seen in the fifth iteration). This motivic concentration is also found in the release of "Losing My Mind." Each of the iterations opens with a four-note figure, and the downward

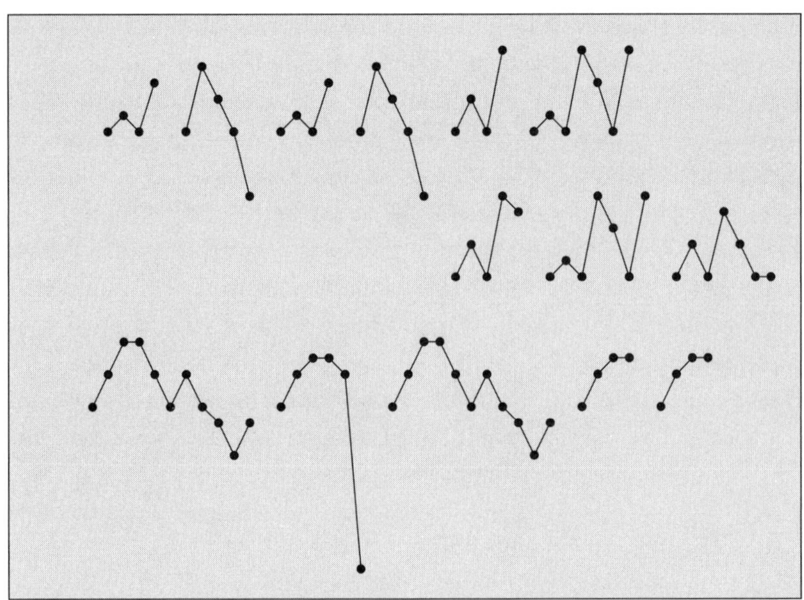

Fig. 2a. A graphic representation of the melody of "Losing My Mind"

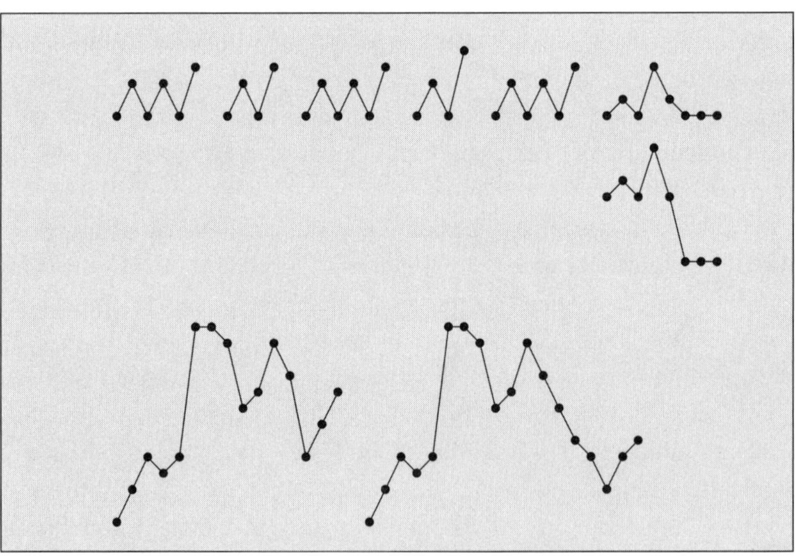

Fig. 2b. A graphic representation of the melody of "The Man I Love"

plunges bear a passing resemblance to the descent in the second motive. In contrast, the release of "The Man I Love" is a long, sinuous idea that, though built up of two interlocking motives (the three-note ascent that frames the melody and the two-note neighbor motion around which the center of the melody is constructed), emerges less as an outworking of motives and more as a tune that is pulled out of a skein of melody. Its second iteration, in fact, expands on the first, as the original fifteen notes become eighteen. The similar idea in "Losing My Mind" (i.e., the first and third iterations in the release) is less sinuous than frantic, as its eleven notes rush by. Could it be that their hurried feel is due in part to their having no obvious motivic connection to the rest of the song?

A look at one more song—"My Friends" *(Sweeney Todd)*—reveals again the same idea that opens "Losing My Mind" and "What Can You Lose?" and how Sondheim can deploy the same motive in different contexts (here, as an inversion of "Dies irae"). Figure 3 is a graphic reduction of this melody (here, with the graphics oriented around a fixed-pitch baseline), and it is clear at a glance how the melody literally emerges from the opening four-note motive. The second iteration inverts the first, and the subsequent iteration piles on repetition after repetition of the opening motive. Only the final iteration of this phrase is motivically independent from what precedes it, and it will be taken up in due course as its own motivic idea, capable of generating more melody.

These examples do not suggest that Sondheim lacked the skills or gifts to write an "old-fashioned" melody. The title song from *Anyone Can Whistle* defies distillation to a single musical motive, and the Arlen-like ballad "The Best Thing That Ever Has Happened" *(Bounce)* is a riot of motives, beginning with its ten notes all insistently on the same pitch. (The family resemblance between this song and "Come Rain or Come Shine" is clear.) But in what is likely his most traditionally melodic score ever—*Bounce*—Sondheim composed tunes built out of motives as if by instinct, from the emphasis of the motive $\hat{5}$-$\hat{5}$-$\sharp\hat{4}$-$\hat{5}$-$\hat{6}$ in the title song to its reinterpretation as $\hat{3}$-$\hat{6}$-$\sharp\hat{5}$-$\hat{6}$-$\hat{7}$ in the opening of the second-act song "Talent," and from the $\hat{2}$-$\hat{3}$-$\hat{5}$ figure that opens "What's Your Rush?" to its mutation into $\hat{6}$-$\hat{2}$-$\hat{3}$, repeated four times, by the end of the same song.[7] And it bears repeating that Sondheim's motivic impulse—seen in songs such as "Saturday Night," "Comedy Tonight," "There Won't Be Trumpets," "Company," "I'm Still Here," "Send In the Clowns," "Pretty Lady," "Pretty Women," "Our Time," "Beautiful," "No One Is Alone," "Everybody's Got the Right," "I Read," and "The Game"—began at Williams College as early as the piano sonata if not earlier. Sondheim became more conscious

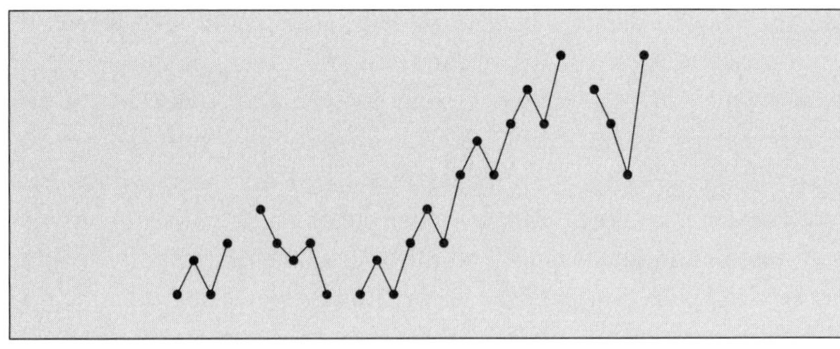

FIG. 3. A graphic representation of the melody of "My Friends"

of motivic processes in *Sweeney Todd* and beyond, but he has always been motivic in orientation.

Upon reflection, Sondheim's motivic propensity helps to explain why his melodies are less hummable than those of his fellow songwriters. It may at first seem counterintuitive that a melody derived from a motivic kernel should be less memorable than melodies that feature a rather wayward tunefulness, employ collections of motives, or even eschew motivic development altogether. But the classical repertory is rife with examples of motivic/melodic couplings where the melodic element is more easily retained than its motivic pair. For example, most people find it easier to sing the self-contained melodies that appear in the finales of Beethoven's Fifth and Ninth Symphonies and of Brahms's First Symphony than to sing the motivic jags that mark the opening movements of each of these works. As with "What Can You Lose?," variations in the motivic deployment in these movements make it difficult to reproduce accurately "tunes" that rely principally on motivic generation. (One could argue that the "Ode to Joy" melody of Beethoven's Ninth is a highly motivic melody, but the ends of the main phrases and the release all break away from the four-note figure that opens the melody. Like the tunes of the classic songwriters, it contains several motivic ideas memorably joined together.) The marvel of Sondheim's melodies is their close motivic unfolding rather than their expansive tunefulness, in keeping with the manner in which Western classical music unfolds.

A similar kinship to Western classical music rather than to American popular song is seen in the way a typical Sondheim song places less emphasis on rhythm than on melody (revealed through motivic outworking) and harmony. As has already been noted, Sondheim drew less from non-Western music, and especially black music, than did Ravel harmonically or Gershwin or Bernstein rhythmically. Sondheim's typical harmonic features will be discussed below, but his distinctive rhythmic features are almost nonexistent. Although vamps are commonplace in his accompaniments, there is no single rhythmic figure that recurs, whereas the motivic kernels are recycled from song to song. Latin rhythms appear from time to time, more frequently in the early part of Sondheim's career, but they hardly constitute a core rhythmic feature for Sondheim as they do for Porter. And syncopation and cross-rhythms occur more often as the result of pastiche (e.g., "Can That Boy Foxtrot!" and "That Old Piano Roll" [*Follies*]; "Who Wants to Live in New York?" [*Merrily*]; "More" [*Dick Tracy*]) than as a natural trait (e.g., the openings of "Don't Look at Me" and "The Road You Didn't Take" [*Follies*]; parts of "Poems" and "A Bowler Hat" [(*Pacific Overtures*]). Given that rhythm is such a powerful demarcation of character—often indicating ethnicity or, less dramatically, a character's affinity to a certain style of music, as in the case of Joanne's contemporary fascination with the bossa nova in "The Ladies Who Lunch" *(Company)*—it is not surprising that Sondheim's accompaniments and melodies shy away from highly rhythmic expressions; rhythmic deployment may make for a catchy tune, but it also affects the dramatic profile of a character. And Sondheim's focus has always been on the drama facilitated by the music, as later chapters will make even clearer.

In sum, then, a Sondheim melody is recognizable for its close development of relatively few motives, and very often of only one motive. These motives range from as short as two notes to as long as seven, with the preponderance of melodies generated from four- and five-note motives. And rhythm, while always a part of Sondheim's musical arsenal, rarely takes a prominent role in the melodies themselves. The accompaniments, as has already been noted, are much more active rhythmically, but even here, the principal interests lie in a realm that is somewhat unusual for one who writes for the popular stage.

Contrapuntal harmonies

If the melody of "What Can You Lose?" is difficult for the singer to memorize correctly, the accompaniment likewise lacks many musical mnemonics. At first glance it appears relatively sparse, but after several readings it reveals a number of chromatic lines, most often in the inner voices. The song manages to be both completely tonal, with its harmonies functioning in a conventional manner, and unconventional, with unusual and unexpected chords arising from these chromatic contrapun-

tal lines. In this and the other Sondheim songs for *Dick Tracy*, the standard commercial practice of providing a harmonic reduction of the accompaniment by means of chord symbols is abandoned, since much of the musical material is as linear as it is vertical. Much of the song's tortured message is contained, then, in these passages of "tortured" writing. Even the choice of key is unusual: the manuscript, the published score, and the recorded performance are all in B major. In comparison with other movie songs of the 1930s and 1940s, this is a difficult song to sing and play. It is a highly stylized realization, in Sondheim's own voice, of a vintage era movie song.

The harmonies of "What Can You Lose?" arise less through choices of block harmonies and more by contrapuntal alignments. This contrapuntal nature is made clear in the first two measures, where there are five different voices notated in the accompaniment. But this is not standard species counterpoint, as evidenced by the parallel fifths in the lower two voices at the end of the first measure and the obbligato figure in the second that mirrors the tenor line at the end. The counterpoint is quite free, with voices occasionally doubling each other (as the soprano and tenor do at m. 1) only to separate later on (as these same two voices do at m. 7). Voices also trade registers, as the soprano voice of the accompaniment in measures 3–4 (first half) is taken over by the alto in measure 4 (second half), thus completing the descending figure in the inner voice.

The "harmonically underneath" becomes critically important in this song. Already I have mentioned how the tenor voice, having begun in unison with the soprano, begins to harmonize in measure 7. But even before this, the notated nontriadic tones throughout the accompaniment provide particular colors that cannot be obtained through simple leadsheet formulations. From the subdominant in measure 2, which contains a ninth degree and receives a superimposed dominant, to the voicing of the suspended dominant chord in the pickup to measure 5, with its flattened ninth, to this chord's resolution into a tonic chord that initially is missing its third but has an added ninth, the voicings and the harmonies are quite specific and are derived from voice-leading rules (e.g., how the flattened ninth occurs when the soprano and alto voices trade registers in m. 4, second half, and the descending figure is completed). As Sondheim songs go, "What Can You Lose?" is rather straightforward, as this introduction comprising tonic, subdominant, and dominant chords suggests. But the manner in which these standard progressions are entered and exited are distinctly Sondheim's own contribution to the musical language of the theater, as the accompaniment continuously interweaves lines that create unexpected changes to the progressions.

Note, for example, how the alto D and the bass D♯ clash in measure 9; there is no obvious lead-sheet reduction for this sonority, which is a tonic chord in first inversion. The contrapuntal felicities continue as the whole-note descent B-A♯-G♯ in the baritone voice (mm. 9–11) moves the music quickly and unusually from the tonic B major to the dominant of the dominant (F♯), even as the tenor both underscores and undermines the secondary dominant in its half-note answer by first resolving a suspension to the dominant's leading tone (F♯ to E♯, m. 11) and then abandoning the secondary dominant altogether (E to D♯, m. 12). Indeed, this secondary dominant is spelled with the root in the soprano voice and the fifth in the bass, a rather unstable position in classic harmony but deliberately so, as it facilitates the unusual harmonic changes that occur because of the counterpoint.

Thus far, then, we have encountered commonplace progressions arrived at in uncommon ways, voiced in nonstandard positions, and ornamented with unexpected nonharmonic tones. To come up with a foolproof formula for these harmonies is next to impossible, but they already illustrate, in encapsulated form, the "wrong note" writing that so troubled Bernstein. The D♯-D clash is unnecessary in theoretical terms, and the failure to return to the E♯ in the secondary dominant is more willful than unavoidable. But in both instances, the logic is typically Sondheim; it is these harmonic clashes and abandonments that give a Sondheim harmony its distinctive sound.

The presence of moving inner voices, the legacy of Rachmaninoff as much as anyone else, permeates the songs. From the simple undulating tenor line in the chorus of "Lovely" *(Forum)* to the chromatic ascending line in "Losing My Mind," from the chromatic descending line in "Our Time" (see chapter 2) to the sung countermelody in "My Friends," from the burbling accompaniment figure to the soaring string obbligato in "Finishing the Hat" *(Sunday)*, Sondheim's songs are quite active in the "harmonically underneath" area. Sometimes, in fact, the complexity of the inner voices leads to some unorthodox spellings, as in the F𝄪 (opposite an F♯) in measure 16 and the D♮ in measures 17–18 of "What Can You Lose?" (they should be G♮ and C𝄪, respectively). But even these "misspellings" can be explained away through the contrapuntal behaviors of the lines in which they occur. In the former case, it can be argued that superimposing a B♯ dominant seventh chord upon an F♯ dominant seventh chord is an artful application of tritone substitution. Alternately, the arpeggio in the tenor voice at measure 16 could be explained as the introduction of the octatonic scale, given that seven notes of the scale are present in the first half of the measure.

Contrapuntal harmonies, tritone substitutions, and octatonic scales rarely feature in discussions surrounding theater music, let alone the notion of a songwriter composing in the key of B major and using double sharps. (There are eight of them in "What Can You Lose?" including two at the appearance of the D♯ major chord beginning with the pickup to m. 19 and two in the vocal line at mm. 41–42.) The web of inner voices results in remarkable harmonies and nontraditional (for Broadway) notations and references. But such visual, aural, and nomenclatural curiosities are commonplaces for Sondheim.

"What Can You Lose?" is somewhat anomalous in Sondheim's canon in its repeated use of standard dominant sevenths, but even here (e.g., in mm. 11, 13, 15–16, 34) the contrapuntal lines complicate the normal dominant functions and introduce altered dominants, including Sondheim's favorite, the suspended dominant. From the second measure forward, where there is a strong plagal motion, the song plays with the tonic-dominant relationship. The chord on the downbeat of measure 2 is clearly a subdominant in root position (from the bass, E-B-F♯-G♯), but its added ninth also makes it a doubly suspended dominant in third inversion (whose root position would be F♯-G♯-B-E). That the subdominant is functioning as a dominant is made plain by the superimposition of an arpeggiation of a dominant chord (with an added sixth) that ends on the dominant F♯, answers the rhythm in measure 1, and leads back to the tonic. The subdominant chord and dominant arpeggio repeat in measure 4, whereupon the bass moves up to the actual dominant and the harmony confirms the function here of the suspended dominant, albeit one now with a minor-mode inflection.

In this song, the standard dominant sevenths, where the dominant is treated as an arrival sonority and not the consequence of contrapuntal motion, typically appear in root position (mm. 18, 20, 30, 31–32, 40, and 41–42; the chord in m. 36 is in second inversion). Yet even some of these arrivals are disrupted by contrapuntal motion that leaves and then returns to the dominant seventh chord (mm. 31–32 and its parallel in 41–42), while the other dominant sevenths (mm. 18, 20, 30, 40) are enriched by added ninths, elevenths, and thirteenths. The finest illustration of the complex picture of the dominant function in this song is in the final measures (mm. 43–45), where, instead of the suspended dominant—the expected penultimate sonority in a Sondheim song—the music arrives at what sounds as if it will be a standard dominant seventh (here, ninth) chord, given the presence of the leading tone A♯. Upon closer examination, however, the chord reveals itself to be a substitute dominant built on the leading tone and using a flattened third (i.e., A♯-C-

E-G♯), a clear echo of the flattened third that appeared at the beginning of the song in measures 4 (interpreted as a subdominant) and 6 (i.e., E-G-B-D♯).

In addition to harmonies arrived at through contrapuntal devices and reinterpreted dominant chords, the song employs yet another harmonic maneuver that is common in a Sondheim song: the unaltered melody over the changing harmony. From the fourth beat of measure 16 to the third beat of measure 20, the melody comprises three notes, G♯-C♯-A♯, which are repeated five times. The chords that harmonize this figure, however, change. The sequence begins (m. 16) with one iteration on V (F♯^{sus7}, given that the third is missing), proceeds (m. 17) with the second iteration on I (B$^{maj\ 9\ add\ 6}$), moves (m. 18) to two more iterations on V/iii (A♯^{13}; the enharmonic spelling of D instead of C$^{\times}$ may also be a result of the bluesy C♯ in the melody and the added flattened F♯ in the harmony), comes to rest (m. 19) on III (D♯$^{maj\ 9}$), without an iteration, and then returns (m. 20) for the final iteration on V again (F♯^{13}), where the A♯ of the melody is now allowed to sound with the dominant, which itself has an added D♯. To state this analysis differently, Sondheim harmonized the three-note melodic figure G♯-C♯-A♯ three different ways, with chords built on B, A♯, and F♯. And this is not the only time he did so in this song: the melodic figure F♯-A♯-A♯-F♯ (or -G♯) is harmonized as I (B$^{maj\ 7}$/D♯, m. 9), iii (D♯^{m9}, mm. 10 and 29), and V/ii (G♯^{9}, m. 30).

The use of lead-sheet chord symbols in the preceding paragraph illustrates the complexity of Sondheim's chords and provides one reason why he himself never reduced his music to such crude approximations. His own blunt words on the subject embrace the notions of counterpoint, harmony, and putting music together.

> I've never used lead sheets, and neither has any self-respecting composer with any training. Give me a melodic line and I'll harmonize it one way, you may harmonize it another way. It's an entirely different song, even though it's got the same melodic line. Music is made up of a number of elements, and it is the putting together of all those elements that gives the song its flavor, character, quality, weight, texture, everything else. Lead sheets have nothing to do with anything as far as I'm concerned. If you leave it up to the orchestrator to fill in the textural details in the orchestra, it becomes essentially an arranger's score. That's what the word "arranger" really means: somebody who takes lead sheet and chords and makes an arrangement of a tune. Now, for my money that's the composer's job, otherwise he's not composing. A lot of people aren't trained to do that and need arrangers, but not any of the composers whose work I respect.

> An arrangement is not clothing (I don't even like the word "arrangement"). There is the song or there is *not* the song, and a song doesn't consist of a sketch, which is what a lead sheet is, any more than a scene consists of what is going to happen in the scene. No, give me the dialogue. I don't care what a brilliant idea for a scene it is, I've got to see the scene. In the same way, I don't care what the sketch of a song is, I've got to see the song, or hear what's going on in the music. It's more than chords, more than rhythm. Music consists of many elements blended together, making much more than the sum of the elements. It's a geometrical progression.[8]

(This appeal to geometry came from someone who originally considered being a math major in college.)

Sondheim's invocation of an almost mathematical precision in constructing music must therefore include those songs whose accompaniments are not as involved as the one in "What Can You Lose?" The repeated-chord vamp of "Good Thing Going" shows why Sondheim's insistence is more than the whining of a petulant artist. In this AA′BA″ song, the harmony in the second measure of the three main sections changes each time, as the disposition and distribution of the inner voices shift from one repeat to the next and the harmonies wander further away from the tonic. Though the block-chord accompaniment appears not to contain any obvious counterpoint, these changes in harmony indicate that Sondheim was keenly aware of what the inner voices were doing and, just as importantly, how they assist in conveying the information in the lyric. They help mark the fact that the song, like its protagonist, has undergone a journey, has been "going along"; the changes become harmonic mileposts that signify time elapsed and distance traveled. On one level, the changes are superfluous and would likely not occur to most songwriters intent on composing a thirty-two-bar song. An arranger might trick out a song with occasional and unexpected changes of harmony. But Sondheim operates on a different level, which is evident even in his most stripped-down accompaniments.

Sondheim's harmonic choices occur sometimes as the result of instinct and sometimes as the result of deliberation. In both cases, they spring from his exposure to counterpoint as well as his amalgamation and reinterpretation of the harmonic language and compositional techniques of Ravel, Gershwin, Arlen, and others. The contrapuntally derived harmonies, the frequent use of ninths, elevenths, and thirteenths, the particular use of the suspended dominant, and the shifts of harmony under a stationary melodic idea may be traceable to these early composers and studies. But Sondheim has made each of these practices his own harmonic friends.

Characteristic accompaniments

In his analysis of "A Bowler Hat," Banfield described two manuscript pages on which appear sketches for the song's accompaniment. He refers to these putative accompaniments by the name Sondheim often used, from his Williams days forward.

> All of these attempts at the primary vamps use too many notes in their striving for harmonic severity and kinetic motion. . . . We should, however, also consider how important to the way a song turns out is the *character* of a vamp: all five of these sketches have strong and highly differentiated characters. . . . One cannot say that they would have given rise to categorically better or worse songs, just very different or less appropriate ones.[9]

Sondheim took time to figure out an accompaniment figure for this song, because the nature of the vamp has a qualitative effect on how one perceives the person who sings to it. And this is true for all of Sondheim's music, where the accompaniment becomes an integral part of understanding the character. This is another reason why it is difficult to speak of characteristic rhythms for Sondheim. Even though he suggested that he at times accidentally slips into South American rhythms,[10] Latin rhythms after *Company* become difficult to find unless they are character-driven (as in the Guatemala sequence in "I'm On My Way" in *Bounce*). Different characters require different rhythms, different vamps.

At first glance, "What Can You Lose?" seems vamp-less, in that there is no "chug-chug" figure that accompanies the melody throughout. The improvisatory feel of much of the accompaniment is appropriate, given that, in the film, we see 88 Keys sing this song late at night, after the club has closed, in a somewhat desultory fashion. But even in a song as lyrical and free as this one, Sondheim concocted a vamp that underscores the lyric and, more importantly, the emotional state of 88 Keys.

The vamp, found in measures 1–2, is in two parts. First is the upward arpeggio from the low bass note to spell the chord for the first measure. Sondheim treated this arpeggio fluidly throughout the song; it is emblematic of 88 Keys improvising at the piano, portraying his distractedness as he rolls his chords from bottom to top. The second part, in con-

trast, is more emphatic. The three-note figure in the second half of measure 1 that is then tied over into measure 2 will likewise return. But its rhythmic emphases off the beat (including its dissolution of the bar line), its doubling in the soprano and tenor voices, and its descent of a third all convey leadenness of heart and futility of hope. The answer to his titular question is something 88 Keys already knows. When he asks it, the vamp answers him: you will lose.

Consider three late appearances of this vamp. It returns dramatically in augmentation at measure 35, where the last of the character's questions stops him (and the music) in its tracks. The vamp seems to stomp its feet: if she had to choose, you would be passed over. Don't go there, it says. Then in measures 43–46, with the last possibility of hope (on the word "win"), the vamp (in the tenor in m. 43, then in the alto in 45) reminds the character that there is no winning in his future.

One hesitates to call such a figure a vamp, but a look at the Williams papers on Ravel and Copland as well as the manuscripts of "Putting It Together" (which is analyzed in chapter 6) affirms the importance of the term for Sondheim. In the manuscripts, there are notations about various vamps: the "Gossip vamp," that is, the ostinato that accompanies the Gossip Sequence in act 1 and whose music is recycled in "Putting It Together"; the "B&F vamp," a figure meant to accompany two characters (whose names over the creation of the musical would change); the sketch for the "Finale vamp"; and another for "Vamp vars." It is the omnipresence of vamps in Sondheim's work that makes the identification of a vamp in "What Can You Lose?" possible.

And though these various accompaniment figures pose compositional problems for Sondheim to solve (i.e., how to wed melody, counterpoint, and rhythmic figure), their primary role in his music is to establish identity. Banfield looked at Sondheim's work in the early 1950s and gave this assessment of the songs in *Saturday Night*. "They show two striking and interacting advances over those of *Climb High:* the characterization of musical styles, especially through vamps, and the extent and texture of wit."[11] I would go even farther and say that, once Sondheim had ceased to compose classical music with its nonspecific accompaniments, he began to explore how effectively a vamp can flesh out a character for the stage. He had little need to write distinctive vamps for his Williams shows, but already in 1954—before the highly characteristic vamps in *West Side Story*—we see him growing in his ability to get under a character's skin through the accompaniment.

Sondheim has spoken about the care with which he writes musical scenes; much of it is lavished upon finding, in Banfield's words, the most appropriate vamp at any given time. One sees again why lead-sheet reductions cannot do Sondheim justice. Recall the wrong-note guitar playing at the beginning of "Unworthy of Your Love" for an obvious example of this practice. For Sondheim, the accompaniments are integral to the songs.

Flexible structures

In chapter 2, Sondheim was quoted as admiring, besides Arlen's harmonic language, the "freedom of structure" that occurs in many of Arlen's "tapeworms." And Sondheim throughout his career has excelled at creating songs that show a wide range of structural freedom. Even when adhering to traditional forms, he has honored those forms in the breach.

"What Can You Lose?" provides a succinct example of the type of extended structure that Sondheim created and how those structures admit multiple readings. The first phrase (mm. 5–12) is laid out in a straightforward eight bars, and when the third phrase parrots the first nearly note-for-note (mm. 25–32), the natural assumption is that this is a standard 32-bar song in ABA′B′ form. But the first B section is twelve bars long (mm. 13–24), which seems to skew the musical weight of the song into the B section. Moreover, the last four bars of this section are almost identical with the opening four bars of the song, which were initially heard as an introduction and not necessarily of great structural importance. With their reappearance here (mm. 1–4 = mm. 21–24), the question arises whether the first phrase actually includes the first four measures, thus making it a twelve-bar phrase. As has been suggested, the eight-bar third phrase seems to confirm that the first phrase likewise is only eight bars long. Nevertheless, the integration of the introduction into the second phrase makes the introduction as notated structurally necessary. And if the structural weight initially shifted to the second section because of its length and its incorporation of the introduction, the fourth section, at fourteen measures (mm. 33–46), bests the second section.[12] It, too, incorporates the introduction, but now the introduction enters at the fifth measure of the section (instead of at the ninth measure in the second section). Indeed, from the third measure of this fourth section, the music ceases to follow the paths laid out by the previous sections. The melody charts a new course at measure 35. The melodic profile of the introduction is retained in measures 37–40, but the harmonies have changed. The introduction also returns a second time, at the

very end and again with altered harmonies (mm. 45–46). And while the melody and harmonies here resemble earlier gestures in the song, in the course of four measures this final section compresses the entire song's trajectory of opening up a minor third (m. 40; cf. pickup to m. 5) to the plaintive yearning captured in the minor sixth (mm. 42–43).

Viewed synoptically, the "32-bar song" reveals itself to be a 42-bar song (or a 46-bar song, counting its integral introduction). "What Can You Lose?" is almost a third longer than it initially appears to be. And yet this structural expansion occurs with no sense of distention. The music naturally fits the expanded structure. Or, to look at it differently, the structure naturally expands to fit the musical and dramatic narrative of the song.

Although Sondheim (perhaps intuitively) learned much about structuring music while at Williams, he attributed his understanding of form and his ability to organize his ideas to his lessons with Babbitt. "How do you hold something together for three minutes, five minutes, ten minutes . . . forty minutes . . . [and] make it *not* sound like another overture? . . . The reason . . . that I feel I can handle ten and twelve-minute musical sequences is because of what Milton taught me."[13] Those lessons, as already noted, covered composers as disparate as Mozart and Kern, and through their examples, Sondheim mastered the ability to handle large expanses of musical time.

This provides one explanation of why he rarely stayed within the standard 32-bar format when composing a stereotypical song. Motivic expansion and harmonic exploration were skills he mastered under Babbitt, and he naturally applied those skills to his own work. Even in the scores where one would most likely expect to see 32-bar songs, namely, the early scores and those with a great deal of pastiche in them (e.g., *Follies*, *Assassins*, *Bounce*), few of the songs fit the snug 32-bar frame; among those that do are "Lovely" *(Forum)*, "Beautiful Girls" *(Follies)*, and "What's Your Rush?" and "The Best Thing That Ever Has Happened" *(Bounce)*. Without question, the 32-bar song was subjected to expansion by composers well before Sondheim composed his mature shows, and even some of his early songs, such as "So Many People" and "What More Do I Need?" from *Saturday Night*, reveal a tendency from the beginning to make the final sections longer than the others. But other early songs, such as "Exhibit A" (also from *Saturday Night*), also demonstrate an ability to compose songs that are quite expansive in their structures.

Part of this expansive quality comes from the modular construction of many of Sondheim's songs. "What Can You Lose?" fails to demonstrate this characteristic well, but another song from *Dick Tracy*, "More," is highly modular, with its opening verse, a "standard" 32-bar song (which, given its notation and expansion, is actually a 78-bar song), and a partial repeat of the main song that comes after a bridge passage and before a lengthy tag. This modularity is seen in numerous songs in *Saturday Night* (e.g., the title song, "Exhibit A," and "In the Movies," among others) and continues all the way through Sondheim's career, suggesting its seminal position in his compositional philosophy. (The piano sonata also exhibits a strong modular aspect, thus undercutting the notion that, because some of the *Saturday Night* songs may have been composed after Sondheim's collaboration with Bernstein on *West Side Story*, Sondheim learned modular construction through emulation of Bernstein.)

What distinguishes Sondheim's modularity from that of other Broadway composers who wrote extended songs and ensembles is the relative brevity of the various modules. Since motives form the crux of the material Sondheim uses, it naturally follows that his individual modular units will be shorter than more traditionally melodic modular units. For example, Rodgers and Hammerstein's famous Bench Scene (from *Carousel*) has several ariosos, a reprise of an earlier song ("You're a Queer One, Julie Jordan"), and a new song that is itself reprised in the course of the scene ("If I Loved You"). Similarly, Billy Bigelow's "Soliloquy" from the same show strings together no fewer than four distinct songs into one long scene. In contrast, Sondheim's modules rarely contain melodies that can stand alone as separate songs. "Side by Side by Side" in *Company*, with its central section ("What would we do without you?"), is a notable exception. In contrast, consider how "Please Hello" from *Pacific Overtures* depends on the other modules to make coherent musical and dramatic sense, or how "Opening Doors" from *Merrily* fails to complete the embedded song, "Who Wants to Live in New York?" Sondheim's modular songs—such as "A Weekend in the Country," "Chrysanthemum Tea," the Johanna quartet, "Into the Woods," "I Read," and "I Love This Town"—tend to keep all melodies save for the main one aphoristic, a feature that, paradoxically, allows for considerable modular expansion provided that the main melody is adequately and frequently presented (as is the case in all of the examples listed above).

Coupled with this modular expansion is Sondheim's tendency toward metrical expansion, where the music temporarily changes meter, usually in the direction of adding time rather than taking it away. In the title song from *Company*, for example, the modularity of the song is complemented by shifts in meter from two to three (e.g., at "Late nights, quick bites") that add musical time into the modules. But such metrical shifts are not limited to modular songs. The end of "Sorry-Grateful" (also from *Company*) introduces a four-beat measure in what has been a song in three, and "In Buddy's Eyes" has a striking passage where Sally lapses into 5/4 and 6/4 in what is a 4/4 song. Nor do all of Sondheim's metrical shifts involve expansion; the shift from the 4/4 of the wedding soloist to the cut-time music ("Getting Married Today") emphasizes Amy's angst, and Petra's broad 3/4 musings on miller's sons, businessmen, and the Prince of Wales contrast with her urgent 3/8 commitment to seize the moment ("The Miller's Son"). But if meter can flex in a song—perhaps most famously in the 9/8 "tenuto" measures in the predominantly 12/8 "Send In the Clowns"—the structure of the song must also be flexible to accommodate the changes in meter. And Sondheim's songs use meter in novel ways, for example, the extended 5/8 passages in *Sweeney Todd* (the openings of "Ladies in Their Sensibilities" and "Pretty Women," where the music also uses three 4/8 and 6/8 measures) and the metrical fluidity of "My Friends" from the same musical (with its 4/4 insertions in a predominantly 3/4 song).

In chapter 6, more will be said about how Sondheim structured his ensembles. It is useful to be reminded, though, that he emerged at the end of an era where thirty-two-bar songs were still the norm. These songs would be supplanted by another structure, one that apparently wasn't covered in his lessons with Babbitt: the refrain-oriented song. From "Maybelline" and "Rock Around the Clock" forward, popular song in the latter half of the twentieth century would place its emphasis on a repeated refrain. Even though such repeats are inherently antidramatic, in that closely repeated words and music are usually static dramatically, the refrain-oriented song has become the standard for many younger Broadway songwriters (e.g., Andrew Lloyd Webber, Claude-Michel Schönberg, Frank Wildhorn). Sondheim, in contrast, has written few refrain-oriented songs, and on the rare occasion that he has (e.g., "Unworthy of Your Love," from *Assassins*), dramatic reasons have compelled him to do so.

At the heart of Sondheim's melos—his construction of melodies and harmonies—is kinesis. Melodies are constantly materializing from musical motives. Harmonies come and go as voices approach, meet, and depart. Unaltered shards of melody take on new patterns in a harmonic kaleidoscope. Chords perform *trompe l'oreille*. Structures expand and meters collide. This is not merely dramatically effective music, although it is most certainly that. This is kinetic music, music on the move, which is all the more striking for its general lack of a driving rhythmic component. What caused Sondheim to write music that embodies so much fluidity? Upon examination, one must conclude that his sound was profoundly affected not only by what he heard but also by what he saw and what he learned from the things he saw.

Kinetic characters

David B. Beverly interviewed composer John Adams some years after the premiere of Adams's second opera, *The Death of Klinghoffer* (1991). Beverly was intrigued by the seemingly schizoid nature of Adams's music, where apparently facile pieces like *Fearful Symmetries* and *Grand Pianola Music* exist cheek by jowl with *The Wound-Dresser* and *Klinghoffer*. Adams: "I acknowledge the bipolar nature of my music, but I am not anxious to make too much of it. I don't want people to always listen to John Adams's work and decide whether it's black or white, green or blue." Apparently, Beverly wasn't completely convinced by Adams's answer, as he advanced his own theory in a follow-up question. "Do you think too maybe you're starting to integrate these styles?" Adams:

> I don't think it's really any different than it ever has been. What I notice in recent pieces is that I've become even more openly embracing of a certain ambiance or tonality in American music. And I don't mean a tonality like B minor, I'm talking about a tonality of mood. I'm very deeply attached to American art, painting, literature, poetry, and, for sure, American music. Lately I've been reading a lot of contemporary American works of fiction. You know for years I read fiction from the nineteenth century or eighteenth century—a lot of German literature and French literature, but lately I've been reading works by novelists like Russell Banks (I read his *Continental Drift* [1985]), Paul Auster, Cormac McCarthy. Right now I'm reading Ralph Ellison's *Invisible Man*. These things always have a way of finding a route into my music, no matter how subliminal the influence or the reference may be. So I think I'm going through a very strong, possibly even self-consciously American phase right now.[14]

The idea that nonmusical stimuli can influence musical language is as old as music itself, and some of the ancients explored how music mirrors human emotions. Yet Adams here referred to something that stands somewhat outside the realm of the philosophy and aesthetics of music, outside the realm of music as mimesis. He spoke about digesting literature and witnessing the fruits of its nourishment in the music he wrote, in ways that are almost impossible to measure. His musical transmutations are not attempts to render Auster, McCarthy, or Ellison as sonic sketches, akin to Virgil Thomson's series of musical portraits. It appears that, on a less conscious level, Adams's reading habits affect his compositional choices. Perhaps the ways authors tell stories in novels inform the ways Adams communicates through music. And communicate is the right word here, as Adams interacts with the novels and then invites people to interact with his music.

In a similar fashion, Sondheim's choices of study found a route into his music. The preceding chapters traced the most obvious aural connections, those between Sondheim and the musicians who came before him. The following chapters trace connections that, while more difficult to establish, nevertheless are present in his compositional language: how kinetic languages helped to shape Sondheim's sound.

And *kinetic* is similarly the right word here, for movement in theater and film propelled Sondheim. To speak of the dramatic alone is to narrow the topic unnecessarily; one doesn't ordinarily speak of the genre of film as "dramatic," and there are many cinematic (and even theatrical) conventions that run counter to traditional conceptions of dramatic unities. From Sondheim's earliest years, fluidity becomes an important driving idea, and clearly talk about drama differs from talk about fluidity. A Sondheim musical may be very directional in terms of character development, but the track the characters take may be synchronous (a typical forward linear plot, as in *Forum*), diachronous (different linear plots stacked on top of each other, as in *Assassins*), achronous (the abandonment of linearity, as in *Company*), or even retrochronous (reverse linearity, as in *Merrily*). Time may be a flexible commodity—and this fluidity owes as much to literature that precedes theater and film as it owes to theater and film directly[15]—but in all these situations the characters undertake a journey. Addison Mizner sums up the typical Sondheim character when he sings, "I'm on my way." And that way typically is a convoluted yet dynamic path.

The question from the start, then, about these paths, about Sondheim's kinesis, is this: How much of this kinesis is due to the influence of his collaborators and how much of it is his own contribution? The musical is a highly collaborative art form, and attributions of influence are almost impossible to determine with any degree of certainty. And yet consider Sondheim's detailed answer to the question, "How do you work with a book writer, particularly on structure?"

> I like to work very closely with the book writer and structure everything for weeks before we start writing. We talk about it at great

length, not just because I like the dramatizing—and I have a good sense of storytelling, I think—but also because it helps me get into the playwright's mind, in terms of his approach to the material. So we do a great deal of talking and note-taking. With Jim Lapine [book writer for *Sunday in the Park with George*, *Into the Woods* and, after this interview, *Passion*], we met once a week for maybe two months before we started to write; with John Weidman on *Assassins*, many months, because finding the form was so tricky.

Then I like the book writer to write at least a scene, so that I can get into the characters as seen through his eyes and ears, especially as regards their diction. I like to subsume my collaborators and have them subsume me. That always makes for an integrated piece, which is something I was brought up to do by Oscar Hammerstein. What satisfies me the most in the musical theater is the sense of one piece.

Meanwhile, I start collecting musical themes to get the sensibility that will match what we've been talking about. Once the diction is there, once I have a scene or two and I can see that Brenda speaks this way and Sam speaks that way, and that sort of thing, and can even ask the playwright, "Why does she use contractions while he does not?," we can talk about very specific details. Then I can find my way into a lyric-writing style, and having done that I can start to write.

Another thing: I always tell somebody I haven't worked with before that I like to "raid" the material, so that there will always be a join between the dialogue and the songs. In the case of *Sunday in the Park With George* and *Into the Woods*, I asked Lapine to write monologues. For example, for those three sections for Little Red Riding Hood and Cinderella and Jack, where they step forward, he wrote monologues. We talked about what we wanted, how we wanted them to talk not about the adventures they'd had but about the *effect* the adventures had on them, so that people who knew the adventures wouldn't get bored. For "Color and Light," in *Sunday in the Park With George*, and even for the title song, James wrote interior monologues never to be spoken. They were sort of stream-of-consciousness pieces that I could take from. I use Lapine particularly as an example, because he's a generation younger than me, and he's a poet, and he thinks in different ways than I do. I was used to working with people of my own generation or older than myself. In order to get into his style and mind, I asked him to write things out, and it was fine.

I've done that before. I did a TV musical called *Evening Primrose*, and I planned a song called "I Remember Sky," and I asked James Goldman to write out a monologue for it. I find it useful to work closely with every book writer. I think that's necessary if you want to write a piece that holds together. It's also fun.[16]

Sondheim here spoke of a mutual subsuming, but it should be obvious that a book writer cannot raid music the way a composer can raid dialogue. More fundamentally, most book writers cannot comment intelligently about musical choices. Motivic development, harmonization, chord voicing, structural balances, and the like, to quote Hammerstein, are things beyond the ken of most playwrights. But playwriting, understood as storytelling, is not beyond Sondheim's understanding or ability. The plurals in his comments are genuine, yet his talent at subsuming his collaborator's material explains why we talk about a Sondheim musical in the first place. He stands as a playwright of his musicals as much as do the writers of the libretti. And just as the musical materials take on some common forms across the whole corpus of Sondheim's career, so the dramatic materials also fall into shapes that suggest that, in the talking phases with his collaborators, Sondheim has been smoothing the story into a form that suits his particular storytelling strengths.

It is accepted practice to refer to musical theater works (opera and musicals) by the composer's name. Accordingly, I speak of "Sondheim musicals." I do not want the reader to think, however, that I believe Sondheim single-handedly conceived and wrote his mature musicals. It would be a gross mistake to overestimate his contribution as a dramatist. But it would also be a gross mistake to underestimate that contribution. The accepted practice presumes that the composer does matter; witness how a skilled librettist—Arrigo Boito, for example—can nevertheless experience varying success, depending on the talent of the composer—Boito's own *Mefistofele*, Ponchielli's *La gioconda*, and Verdi's *Otello*. The documentary evidence for this last example, in fact, shows that Verdi not only wrote a brilliant score but also took an active hand in shaping the libretto.[17] As Sondheim himself attested, accounting for his skill as a composer-lyricist does not take the full measure of his abilities.

In what ways did Sondheim's apprenticeships in theater and film set the consistent tonality of mood in his works and help Sondheim find his sound? Chapters 4 and 5 offer some answers.

4

Sondheim the Dramaphile

The received story reexamined

Let's start at the very beginning, and let us hear it from Sondheim's mouth.

> Oscar Hammerstein gradually got me interested in the theater, and I suppose most of it happened one fateful or memorable afternoon. He had urged me to write a musical for my school (George School, a Friends school in Bucks County). With two classmates I wrote a musical called *By George*, a thinly disguised version of campus life with the teachers' names changed by one vowel or consonant. I thought it was pretty terrific, so I asked Oscar to read it—and I was arrogant enough to say to him, "Will you read it as if it were just a musical that crossed your desk as a producer? Pretend you don't know me." He said "O.K.," and I went home that night with a vision of being the first 15-year-old to have a show on Broadway. I knew he was going to love it.
>
> Oscar called me in the next day and said, "Now you really want me to treat this as if it were by somebody I don't know?" and I said, "Yes, please," and he said, "Well, in that case it's the worst thing I ever read in my life." He must have seen my lower lip tremble, and he followed up with, "I didn't say it wasn't talented, I said it was terrible, and if you want to know why it's terrible I'll tell you." He started with the first stage direction and went all the way through the show for a whole afternoon, really treating it seriously. It was a seminar on the piece as though it were *Long Day's Journey into Night*. Detail by detail, he told me how to structure songs, how to build them with a beginning and a development and an ending, according to his principles. I found out many years later there are other ways to write songs, but he taught me, according to his own principles, how to introduce character, what relates a song to character, etc., etc. It was four hours of the most *packed* information. I dare say, at the risk of hyperbole, that I learned in that afternoon more than most people learn about song writing in a lifetime.

He saw how interested I was in writing shows, so he outlined a kind of course of study for me which I followed over the next six years, right through college. He said, "Write four musicals. For the first one, take a play you admire and turn it into a musical." I admired a play called *Beggar on Horseback* by George S. Kaufman and Marc Connelly, and we actually got permission to do it for three performances at college [as *All That Glitters*].[1] Next, Oscar told me: "Take a play that you don't think is very good or that you liked but you think can be improved and make a musical out of it." I chose a play called *High Tor* by Maxwell Anderson—I couldn't get permission to put it on in college because Anderson wanted to do a musical of it with Kurt Weill (they never got around to it), but it taught me something about playwriting, about structure, about how to take out fat and how to make points.

Then Oscar said, "For your third effort, take something that is non-dramatic: a novel, a short story." I landed on *Mary Poppins* and spent about a year writing a musical version. That's where I first encountered the real difficulties of playwriting, which is one of the reasons I am not a playwright. It was very hard to structure a group of short stories and make a play out of them, and I wasn't able to accomplish it. Finally Oscar said, "For your fourth, do an original," so right after I got out of college I wrote an original musical [*Climb High*] whose first act was 99 pages long and the second act 60-odd. Oscar had recently given me a copy of *South Pacific* to read and the entire show was 90 pages long, so when I sent him my script I got it back from him with a circle around 99 and just a "Wow!" written on it.[2]

This is the standard story that tells how Sondheim learned about the theater, and quite a good story it is. It lays out a course of study that would benefit any would-be writer of musicals. It shows Sondheim's initiative and industry. It shows Hammerstein's interest in a young protégé.

Fundamentally, it focuses on Sondheim's relationship with Oscar Hammerstein II, his surrogate father from the time they met in the early 1940s until Hammerstein's death in 1960. There is no denying the importance of both Oscar and his second wife, Dorothy, in providing equilibrium for Sondheim, the only child of divorced parents. (Sondheim had two half-brothers from his father's second marriage.) Oscar and Dorothy served as foils to his absent father and monster mother. In later life, Sondheim weighed their contribution as meaning more to him professionally than personally, but the personal effect they had on him was undeniable. "The Hammersteins were more than a balm. They were not only comforting. They gave me an outlet; they opened up all the worlds of creative possibilities."[3] Those creative possibilities were the legacy the Hammersteins—and Oscar in particular—bequeathed to Sondheim. "The watershed, the landmark musical was indisputably *Oklahoma!* Everything that followed can be seen as a development of it—either a rejection or a carrying on. Me, I'm carrying it on, making variations."[4] In being a writer of musicals, Sondheim is merely filling his mentor's shoes.[5]

The problem with the story is that it is incomplete. Relying on repetition as a substitute for critical inquiry, writers have failed to address the story's obvious omissions. There was Sondheim's theatrical apprenticeship at the Westport County Playhouse in the summer of 1950, and Sondheim had had not a little theatrical experience before then. Moreover, he had studied modern drama at Williams, and many of his subsequent comments on Ibsen, Chekhov, Pirandello, and other modern dramatists unquestionably stem from his early exposure to their works and his understanding of their construction of drama through his experience in classes at Williams College.

Most significantly, the story fails to take into account a principal distinction between the two men: One was a lyricist-librettist; the other was a lyricist-composer. Hammerstein, who was steering Sondheim toward writing, indirectly helped him land a job in Hollywood to write for television.[6] While Sondheim was in California, Hammerstein read over the script for *Climb High*, and, in a letter to Sondheim, emphasized the latter's work as a playwright, saying little about his music (and, surprisingly, nothing about his lyrics).[7] One might argue that talking to Hammerstein about music would have been a waste of time. Sondheim: "I don't really remember talking to Oscar about my music very much. He never heard any of the so-called mature scores. All he heard was *Saturday Night*, and I don't remember. I think he certainly encouraged me, but he died before *Forum*, so of my professional work he only knew *Saturday Night* (if you call that professional) and *Gypsy* and *West Side*."[8] Yet, by Sondheim's own admission, straight writing was never his forte,[9] and, unlike Hammerstein, he never provided the book for a professional musical, even though this was the clear objective of Hammerstein's course. Hammerstein may have deferred to Rodgers in matters of music, but his implicit wish that Sondheim work with Rodgers after Hammerstein's death (and after Sondheim's work on *West Side Story* and *Gypsy*) provides some indication of what Hammerstein must have thought of Sondheim's early music: it wasn't "Broadway" (i.e., standard) enough.

At the same time, Sondheim developed a very clear concept of drama, which demanded a different kind of music from the norm on

Broadway when he was coming of age. The immediate catchiness of Cy Coleman or Jerry Herman would have likely worked at cross purposes to the dramatic trajectories in his musicals. Sondheim almost sounds like Wagner when he defends his musical perspective. "I'm accused so often of not having melodic gifts, but I *like* the music I write. Harmony gives music its life, its emotional color, more than rhythm."[10] Any discussion of his dramatic apprenticeship must take into account how Sondheim developed his understanding of the way *music* contributes to *drama*, how his distinct voice emerged. The first three chapters concentrated on Sondheim's amalgamation of classical motivic writing, contrapuntal techniques, and popular song form, a mélange that he has consistently employed in his compositions; that is, these chapters concentrated on music. This chapter and the next will focus on his blending of theater and film, that is, on drama. Chapter 6 will bring together these amalgamations, showing how Sondheim's strong musical personality merged with a strong dramatic personality to create his musicodramatic language.

The dramatic personality, however, may seem hard to trace at first, given that, as a collaborator, Sondheim appears to be more reactive than directive. *A Little Night Music*, *Sweeney Todd*, *Passion*, and *Bounce* were ideas that originated with Sondheim; the other musicals first took seed in the minds of his collaborators, and Sondheim "entered their visions."[11] He has freely cannibalized the work of his book writers, taking their words and turning them into songs. He has spoken of how his ideal way of working would be first to "stage" a "musical" without its music, so he could see the drama and then have months to write the score.[12] He has said that "what is required [of collaboration] is that everybody sit down together from the first day of the inception and talk about what the show should be. The hardest aspect of writing a musical is to be sure that you and your collaborators are writing the same show. Now, that sounds like sophistry but it is *very* difficult."[13] More than this, Sondheim has also relied on his collaborators to "supply the stimulation and encouragement . . . as well as the criticism. . . . I don't think I could *not* talk to people about my work. I need too much encouragement."[14]

Yet, as the final section of the previous chapter asserted, Sondheim's craft is so comprehensive that the work of his collaborators hinges more on Sondheim's contribution than his work hinges on theirs. In these shows, the tautness of the drama is expressed not in the book, direction, or scene design but primarily in the score. Said differently: the dramatic efficacy of the music makes the shows revivable. Moreover, one finds a certain consistency in the dramatic treatments and themes that the works explore. So, while Sondheim was not a librettist like Hammerstein, he has proven to be a dramatist unlike most musical theater composers. His service on behalf of the Dramatists Guild—including a stint as president (1973–81)—and his creation of the Young Playwrights Festival in 1981 speak volumes about the esteem in which he is held by other dramatists. Perhaps Sondheim himself was not adept at writing a play, but he, like Verdi or Puccini before him, knew how to get the best work out of his collaborators.

His apprenticeship, therefore, entailed learning from Barrow and others how to create dramatic tension in music as well as learning from Hammerstein how to create dramatic tension on stage. But there are at least two other factors that the story still omits. First, whenever Sondheim has spoken of Hammerstein's influence on him, he has turned to a seminal experience working on a particular musical. Second, in speaking of that experience, he has invoked language that points to yet another significant course in his apprenticeship. I sum up his education with three hypotheses.

> He learned how to write music mainly from Barrow.
> He learned how to create a character mainly from Hammerstein.
> He learned how to structure a scene mainly from film.

The first hypothesis was the subject of the first three chapters.[15] As to the other hypotheses, no one has ever disputed Hammerstein's importance to Sondheim, but no one, to my knowledge, has discussed extensively the importance of film, though it has hardly been a secret. With the caveat that the author has limited facility in the areas of theater and film scholarship, this chapter and the next address the remaining two hypotheses.

From *By George* . . .

In addition to the four apprentice musicals, Sondheim wrote *Phinney's Rainbow*, which was to Williams College what *By George* was to the George School: a lighthearted send-up of people and events on campus. Scripts for *By George*, *All That Glitters*, and *Climb High*, as well as songs and sketches for most of the apprentice musicals (and *By George*), are currently held by the Wisconsin Center for Film and Theater Research at the University of Wisconsin.[16] Other than the handful of published songs from *Phinney's Rainbow* and *All That Glitters* (see chapter 2), the scores for these two shows have disappeared from the public eye, as has the book for the former. In looking at the historical records and remaining documents, one might presume that Sondheim completed only the first of the four musicals laid out in Hammerstein's course. Yet the possibility exists that, with the exception of *Mary Poppins*, all of these early musicals might one day be reconstructed and shed additional light on how Sondheim grew as a musical dramatist.

As it happens, the class history in the 1950 Williams yearbook, the *Gul*, unexpectedly details Sondheim's maturation during his apprenticeship. One reads of a growing dismay on the part of the unnamed author as Sondheim becomes more and more serious in his pursuits. Sondheim's sophomore year featured *Phinney's Rainbow*, an oblique reference to Burton Lane's *Finian's Rainbow* (1947)—still on Broadway at the time—and a direct reference to Williams's president, James Phinney Baxter III. The *Gul* author singled out Sondheim for that sophomore (and somewhat sophomoric) production. "One of our boys, Steve Sondheim, wrote *Phinney's Rainbow*, which was brought to the AMT [Adams Memorial Theatre] stage over Spring Houseparties. We were sure he was a genius."[17]

If the author held this opinion then, he seemed less sure by the time of Sondheim's junior-year musical (the first in his course with Hammerstein), based on *Beggar on Horseback*, a play by George S. Kaufman and Marc Connelly. "That spring [of 1949] we enjoyed *All That Glitters* and had quite a sober spring house party, or we should say proper."[18] Perhaps the astute reader knew that Sondheim was the genius behind *All That Glitters*, but the author doesn't bother to identify him, even though the 1949 yearbook referred to the musical as a "resounding success."[19] The reviewer for the *Williams Record*, though, was as sober as the writer for the *Gul*.

> In general the songs were second-rate . . . *Phinney's Rainbow* made no attempt to be Serious Art; it was satirical throughout, and even poked fun at its love interest. Sondheim's new music, on the other hand, seeks to mix parody and social significance, to combine a straight romantic love affair with biting satire. To me it seems an unstable compound, and I believe that the play would have been better had it stuck to parody.[20]

Sondheim had tried to prepare the campus for a musical that was, in tone and execution, very different from his first Williams musical. "*All That Glitters* will be a 'book' show, thereby placing the focal emphasis on story, characters, and plot rather than on songs."[21] In *A History of Modern Drama* critics Barrett Clark and George Freedley called *Beggar on Horseback* "the first genuinely imaginative satire of its kind that, without heat or apparent moral indignation, attempted to expose the barren machine-age efficiency that had to some extent become a religion to Homo Americanus."[22] One can think of a number of Sondheim shows (*Follies, Pacific Overtures, Sweeney Todd, Merrily We Roll Along, Sunday in the Park with George, Into the Woods, Assassins*) that also engage in this type of imaginative satire. What the peer reviewer perceived as an unstable compound at Williams would become standard fare for the mature Sondheim, and it is easy to imagine that Sondheim had little time for those who lamented that, for *All That Glitters,* "the shabby-wigged, heavily busted, hairy legged chorus line of *Phinney's Rainbow* is gone with women being cast in female roles."[23]

All That Glitters, like *Beggar on Horseback,* features as protagonist Neil McRae, an impoverished composer-pianist. This character consumed Sondheim in his teens. Not only did the film *Hangover Square* (1945) have a similar protagonist in George Harvey Bone, but Sondheim's unfinished novel, *Bequest,* also featured a pianist-composer, Edward Gold, at the center of its story. All three suffer from severe psychosomatic episodes triggered by various means: Bone's, by harsh sounds; McRae's, by drugs; and Gold's, by paresis that implicitly is caused by syphilis. While there are clear autobiographical elements in these stories, and all the more so given Sondheim's precollege experience as a budding concert pianist,[24] there are other elements in *All That Glitters* that point to Sondheim's mature shows.

Few Sondheim musicals are overtly political, and the one that fits that description most, *Assassins,* deliberately places its political ideology in the background.[25] Other musicals, such as *Pacific Overtures* and *Sweeney Todd,* hint at their authors' political stance, but Sondheim's self-identification, according to Secrest, as a "fierce liberal" does not overwhelm these shows.[26] In contrast, *All That Glitters* finds Sondheim tipping his liberal hand throughout, albeit in a backhanded manner. Fred Cady is a plutocrat and the father of Gladys, Neil's fiancée-to-be. Although Neil is actually in love with his impoverished neighbor, Cynthia Mason, he has not yet come to terms with his affections or his continued poverty as a starving artist who takes on hackwork that impedes progress on his symphony. Cady tries to convince Neil that he would be better off writing for a broader audience and not limiting his efforts to art music. Cady enlists the help of Neil's old friend Albert Rice, a medical doctor who is checking on Neil's neurasthenia. Sondheim embellished Kaufman and Connelly's script with lines of his own (here and throughout in **boldface**).

> CADY: We've all got to please the public. Eh, Doctor?
> ALBERT: Oh, yes.
> CADY: I've got to in my business. **Especially since the New Deal and that Democratic administration.**
> **MRS. CADY: Mr. Cady's a Republican.** (S, P–18; K&C, 61)[27]

The contours of Cady's Republicanism, with the concomitant importance of being a loyal, true-blooded American, are more sharply drawn in the psychosomatic episode of Neil's trial. This patriotic emphasis begins with the Cadys' pestering Neil to play something for them—**"The Cadys! The Cadys! Two gentlemen and two ladies! / We're all one big, happy family, / Loyal Americans we!"** (S, 1–20)—and continues with Cady singing an apostrophe to **"That Good Old American Dollar"** (S, 1–25f.). Neil himself succumbs to the call to nationalism as he enlists the support of the jurors to nominate Albert as their foreman because he is "a man of the people, for the people, and by the people, and the stars and stripes forever in the good old U.S.A.! **After all, the main thing is to be an American, through and through! No foreigners for us!"** (S, 2–7; K&C, 179).

Little of this jingoism or xenophobia is found in the original play. Perhaps Sondheim is sending up Hammerstein, specifically the film *State Fair* (1944), with Neil's words, **"It's a great country, it's a great feelin'"** (S, 2–8), reminiscent of the song "It's a Grand Night for Singing," and with the original title of the show, *Dollars to Doughnuts,* recalling the title song of the film, "It's dollars to doughnuts that our state fair / Is the best state fair in our state." (The earlier title, crossed out on the title page of Sondheim's adaptation and replaced with the handwritten final title, has no basis in the Kaufman and Connelly play.) But coming in the shadow of the initial investigations of the House Un-American Activities Committee in 1947, Sondheim's patriotic tub-thumping and denunciation of foreigners in *All That Glitters* take on a darker hue.

Cady's conservatism extends beyond politics, and here Sondheim parroted the highbrow/lowbrow divide that plagued Bone in *Hangover Square* and would return, in autobiographical form, in *Merrily*. Cady: "I don't claim to know anything about music, but I think I represent about the average viewpoint. **I know what I like**—and what I like is a good lively tune. Something with a little snap to it. As I understand it, though, you sort of go in for highbrow music" (S, P-18, 19; K&C, 61). Cady tries to talk Neil into abandoning music altogether and joining his business, an arrangement Gladys seconds, but before Neil can consent, the drugs the doctor has administered take effect, and Neil's fantasy begins. In it, he kills Gladys, Mrs. and Mr. Cady, and their son, Homer, all because they disparage his symphony. Homer rises, threatens to sue Neil, and then dies a second time. Neil: "It won't do you any good! Not when they know why I did it! Not when I show them what you killed! Not when I play them my music!" (S, 1–48; K&C, 165).

The judge for Neil's trial is Mr. Cady. Neil is unable to play his symphony for the jury because Gladys has torn it up earlier, thus precipitating the murders. Instead, Neil plays his music for a pantomime, and Cynthia assures him: "They'll think it's better, anyhow" (S, 2–24; K&C, 201). It is unclear whether (or how much of) the pantomime (a "dream ballet" that was part of the original play) was performed at Williams, as some of the pages of the script that detail it are crossed out. But in both the play and the adaptation, Neil is found guilty of writing highbrow music and is sentenced by "Judge" Cady.

> This business of using the imagination has got to stop. We're going to make you work in the right way. You see, your talents belong to us now, and we're going to make you the most wonderful songwriter that ever lived. **Lively tunes—with a little snap to them! Something that you can whistle!**

Neil protests: "But I can't write that kind of music! You know I can't!" Cady: "You can do it by our system. You are sentenced to be at the Cady Consolidated Art Factory at eight o'clock tomorrow morning!" (S, 2–29; K&C, 210). And in an interpolation that has no cognate in the play, Gladys congratulates Neil for his good fortune. **"You're going to love working in Papa's factory. Just you wait. Writing big song hits! You'll be pretty well-known—famous, in fact"** (S, 2–30).

The factory is a warren of cells, with the world's greatest novelist, composer, artist, and poet all next to one another. The play deals with the impoverishment of art and its mechanical reproduction, as Kaufman and Connelly anticipate not only Walter Benjamin's famous 1935 essay, "The Work of Art in the Age of Mechanical Reproduction," but also the second act of *Sunday in the Park with George*, where the creation of art takes on an assembly-line sterility. Here, visitors touring the factory stop before Neil's cell. Neil writes a "pathetic" song for them (i.e., full of pathos, but in actuality a double entendre). When asked if he writes other types of songs, he answers, "Oh, yes—mammies, sweeties, and fruit songs. The ideas are brought from the inspiration department every hour on the hour. After I turn them into music, they are taken to the purifying department, and then to the testing and finishing rooms. **Then** they are **simplified and** packed for shipment" (S, 2–35; K&C 220).

Thus the battle between high art and "lowly" commerce, the questions of compromise and simplification, and the pressure to write big song hits entered Sondheim's dramatic imagination at an early age—before Bernstein penned his own lament along these lines, "Why Don't You Run Upstairs and Write a Nice Gershwin Tune?"[28]—and continued to resonate throughout his career. Techniques that appear in *Beggar on Horseback*—extended passages of simultaneous dialogue, a penultimate scene where the events of the play are recapitulated by the characters who experienced them—similarly recur in Sondheim musicals. The absurdity of Neil's hallucination leads him at one point to ask, "Are we all crazy?" The answer comes back, echoing *Anyone Can Whistle:* "Yes" (K&C, 127–28).

Clearly, there is more in Sondheim's choice of *Beggar on Horseback* than a foil for his own life or an attempt to try his hand at the "by-now-familiar theme of youthful promise in danger of being corrupted by worldly temptations," a theme the play shares with *Allegro.*[29] In his adaptation, Sondheim tested a number of dramatic possibilities and musical techniques to which he would return later in life. One final example of the latter is found in the character of Mrs. Cady. Her musical tastes resemble neither Neil's nor those of her husband. "For my part I like hymns. There's nothing like the old familiar hymns. (SHE sings "Nearer, My God, To Thee.")." Later, "to the tune of the hymn," she sings, "Yes, tea time! It's tea time! It's tea time!" (S, 1–15). It may seem a small thing to point out that, in the original play, Mrs. Cady sings four hymns but not "Nearer, My God, To Thee." It is difficult to know precisely why Sondheim made this substitution—the melody does not easily fit Mrs. Cady's paean to tea time—unless he associated the hymn with death, even the mock death that Mrs. Cady would experience. But this small point reinforces a later concordance between the melody of "The Ballad of Czolgosz" *(Assassins)* and "Nearer, My God, To Thee." Leon Czolgosz successfully assassinated President William McKinley. On his deathbed, "McKinley . . . mumbled the last verse of 'Nearer, My God, To Thee,' and died about 2:15 A.M. on September 14. . . . 'Nearer, My God, To Thee' became more popular."[30] The greatest melodic concordance between "The Ballad of Czolgosz" and the hymn occurs at the mention of the president's name in the ballad and at the words "nearer my God" in the hymn.[31] If, for Sondheim, the hymn became a sonic representation of impending death (and its use on the sinking *Titanic* would further this connection), then it is notable that he (instinctively?) employed it when he was nineteen years old.

In the shadow of *Allegro,* and with the intensity of late adolescence, Sondheim brought a morality tale to his campus that mirrored his personal life at the time even as it helped shape his professional life for years to come. And with the success of *All That Glitters* (at least in the eyes of *Variety* and BMI), Sondheim was on a roll. It was time to begin his second apprentice musical, an adaptation of "a play that you don't think is very good or that you liked but you think can be improved."

How Sondheim decided on *High Tor* is unclear. It is highly unlikely that he saw it during its Broadway run, as he was six going on seven at the time.[32] It is tantalizing to imagine that he may have come upon the play indirectly through his acting. In May 1947, when Sondheim appeared in a Williams production of Anderson's *Winterset,*[33] the college library owned at least four different volumes that contained *High Tor,* three of which also contained *Winterset.*[34] Still another possibility is that Hammerstein suggested it to him when Sondheim was working on *Allegro* or that Sondheim asked Jo Mielziner, the set designer for *Allegro,* to direct him to a play; Mielziner had designed *High Tor.* However he was drawn to it, Sondheim chose a play as fantastic as *Beggar on Horseback,* with echoes of Wagner's *Der fliegende Holländer.* "Mixing fantasy and reality, Anderson tells a tale of grubby real-estate developers trying to flimflam the young owner of a mountain above the Hudson River into selling them his property. The mountaintop is also apparently inhabited by the ghosts of a Dutch captain, his wife, and his crew, who have waited two centuries for the ship that will take them back to Holland."[35]

Although there is no mention of Sondheim or *High Tor* in the yearbook class history recitation of senior-year milestones, the musical is mentioned at least once elsewhere in that yearbook, suggesting that people within the campus community were aware that Sondheim wrote three musicals while at Williams.[36] Given the paucity of material from this apprentice musical that is publicly available—two songs in the Wisconsin archives—one might conclude that Sondheim had not progressed far in his adaptation before Anderson refused his permission. But the correspondence surrounding *High Tor* indicates that this work was substantially complete, and Sondheim recalled that he had written about fifteen songs for the show.[37]

In fact, Anderson refused Sondheim not once but twice. Most of the correspondence in 1949 occurred between David Bryant, the director of the Adams Memorial Theatre, and Anderson's representatives, who gave Bryant little hope that permission would be granted. Two years later, Sondheim wrote Anderson directly. Clearly, he would not have endeared himself to Anderson had he shared the true nature of his assignment (i.e., fix a play you think needs fixing), so even as he obliquely mentioned the other apprentice musicals, he refrained from telling Anderson the reasons for choosing *High Tor* and honeyed his words about the play. As Sondheim's letter has not appeared elsewhere in print, it is reproduced here in full.

November 21, 1951
Dear Mr. Anderson—

In December of 1949 I wrote to you through Mr. David Bryant (Director of Theater at Williams College) to ask for permission to put on, at college, a musical adaptation I had made of your play, *High Tor*. Your reply was a very kind but firm "no." At that time I was not discouraged, because I had written it largely as an exercise in adaptation for myself, on the theory that one should adapt good plays before attempting adaptations of short stories, original ideas, etc. I had not expected to have it produced at college and therefore had not asked your permission before starting work on it.

A little while after your letter, Mr. John Wharton (a graduate of Williams) visited us at college. He asked to read some of the lyrics and hear the music. He seemed favorably impressed and said you might be interested in seeing my work. Mr. Oscar Hammerstein, under whose watchful eye I have been writing, also suggested that you might like to see it.

I am therefore sending it along to you in the hope that you will read it. If you have the time and inclination to look it over, I would be much obliged for any comment you might make, either critical or approbatory. Also, if you are interested, I would very much like you to hear and/or see the music. If so, perhaps you would let me play it for you some time.

I have revised the adaptation somewhat during the last two years, although I have retained almost all of your original dialogue. I sincerely hope that I have done no injustice to either the mood and characterizations of your play or the exigencies of your business and time.

By the way, since I am no longer in college (I am studying Musical Composition in New York), rest assured this letter is in no way a request for production of any kind.

Thanking you for your attention, I am

Sincerely,
Stephen Sondheim
1010 Fifth Avenue,
New York City, N.Y.[38]

Wharton (Williams class of 1915) was a "combination business adviser, legal counsel, mediator, and—after his official role was ended—historian for" the Playwrights' Company, of which Anderson was a founding member. Wharton was also on the board, where he "read every script, offered criticism, and passed on whether a given play reached the stage."[39] With Wharton and Hammerstein encouraging him, Sondheim had good reason to believe that Anderson would read the script he enclosed with his letter.

As it happened, his hopes were misplaced.

November 30, 1951
Stephen Sondheim
1010 Fifth Avenue,
New York City, N.Y.
Dear Mr. Sondheim:

I'm sending your script back without reading it for a reason which will perhaps come to you as a shock—so brace yourself. If *High Tor* is done as a musical I may want to do the book and lyrics myself, and it would be unfair of me to read another man's work on the same venture. I'm sorry that this may make your work seem wasted, but I guess nothing's ever really wasted. That's the best I can do in the way of comfort.

Sincerely,
Maxwell Anderson

This letter suggests that Anderson's original refusal to grant permission had little to do with his idea of turning *High Tor* into a musical. In his letter, Sondheim made no mention of this possibility, and it would have been disrespectful on his part to persist in asking Anderson to review his musicalization if Anderson had previously made it clear that he himself was intending to do the same. Anderson warned Sondheim to brace himself, further suggesting that this was the first time he gave Sondheim notice of his intentions, which may have motivated his firm "No" but which appears not to have been articulated.

Anderson also makes no mention of Kurt Weill, whom Sondheim had suggested as Anderson's likely collaborator. Around the time Sond-

heim began his adaptation, Weill and Anderson had finished their second musical together, *Lost in the Stars*, and had begun work on a third, *Raft on the River*, based on the Huckleberry Finn stories of Mark Twain. Weill, though, died suddenly on April 3, 1950, and therefore could not have been the collaborator Anderson had in mind. Anderson did write the book and lyrics for a musical version of *High Tor*, which CBS-TV aired on March 10, 1956. As with *Gypsy*, where Sondheim was passed over and an older, more established man of the theater was tapped (Jule Styne), so here Anderson chose Arthur Schwartz (1900–1984) instead of Sondheim as the composer.[40]

It is telling that, after Anderson's refusal in late 1949, Sondheim did not try to write a replacement show. While *High Tor*, *pace* Secrest, did not win the Pulitzer Prize,[41] it was a serious play, and Sondheim no longer seemed interested in writing another *Phinney's Rainbow*. Sondheim (and Bryant with him) realized how long it would take him to write the kind of musical he desired to write and concluded he did not have enough time. The autobiographical echoes in "Opening Doors" (*Merrily:* "We haven't got time . . . Let's do a revue of our own") thus may go deeper than has been previously posited by others. After the demise of *High Tor*, Sondheim and his friends elected to put on a revue of their own, *Where To From Here*, to which Sondheim contributed one song, the melancholic "No Sad Songs for Me."[42] By that time, the *Gul* author had cooled toward Sondheim. The student who, as a sophomore, was hailed as a genius was voted the second most original student on campus by the end of his senior year.[43] It appears that the genius may have become a bit too serious—or, perhaps, too prickly—for his fellow students, at the same time that his music became increasingly sophisticated and less accessible to his peers.[44]

It is, however, possible that, after Anderson's refusal, Sondheim immediately turned to *Mary Poppins* as both a backup show and his third musical in Hammerstein's course.

> I did about two-thirds of it and realized I couldn't complete it because I could not solve the problem of taking disparate short stories, even though they are interconnected, and making a larger form. A footnote to that is that about ten years ago, when I was in London for some purpose, I had a call from P.L. Travers [creator of *Mary Poppins*], who said, "Mr. Sondheim, I would like you to adapt *Mary Poppins* for the stage," and I said, "Funny you should call, because when I was nineteen years old this is exactly what I did." She was astonished; I was flattered and astonished.[45]

In his remarks from 1974 that opened this chapter, Sondheim said he had worked on the adaptation for about a year, so if he did begin work on it when he was nineteen, this means he started before March 1950, well before he left Williams. Sondheim was already committed to write an honors thesis in music (his piano sonata), and as the prospect of staging *Mary Poppins* receded, it is no surprise that, of the four apprentice musicals, *Mary Poppins* is the least complete.

In addition to the musicals on which Sondheim worked and in which he performed during his years at Williams, there were the thirteen productions in which he appeared as an actor or staff member. (See table 1.) Sondheim obviously had little say in the choice of plays early in his Williams career, but his heavy involvement in Cap and Bells and the collaborative spirit of the organization (evident in their willingness to mount two Sondheim musicals and the attempt to mount a third) surely meant that Sondheim influenced the choice of plays as an upperclassman. Whoever brought *Night Must Fall* to the attention of Cap and Bells—and there is reason to believe that Sondheim himself might have suggested the play—its selection was likely made with the presumption that Sondheim would star as Dan, a homicidal psychopath. Sondheim coveted the role ("There was only one part I ever wanted to play, and I played it in college: Danny in *Night Must Fall,* an insane murderer")[46] and acquitted himself splendidly in it.[47] Dan is not only kin to Sweeney Todd, whom Sondheim would musicalize nearly thirty years later, but also to George Harvey Bone, the delusional killer in *Hangover Square* (1945), whose score (by Bernard Herrmann) so thrilled Sondheim. The appeal of playing Dan, with his resemblance to a certain strand of Hitchcockian noirish film characters, shows Sondheim's emerging preference for drama and film that was more dark (and at times surreal) than merely troubled, a preference also revealed in the revue song inspired by the 1950 movie, *No Sad Songs for Me,* where Margaret Sullavan's character is dying of cancer.

Then there are the various plays and playwrights Sondheim encountered as part of his Williams curriculum. After the war years, the college slowly expanded its courses to return them to prewar levels. (The provision for music was exceptional here, in that the department grew considerably immediately before the war and kept its courses throughout the war, even though no major was offered in 1944 and 1945.)[48] Only a handful of courses was available through the drama department at the time Sondheim was enrolled; dramatic works were studied through the English literature department. According to his college transcript, Sond-

Table 1. Sondheim's Theatrical Career at Williams, 1946–50

Playwright	Play	Sondheim's Role	Dates of Production
Freshman Year			
Noël Coward (1899–1973)	*Family Album* (from *Tonight at 8:30*, 1936)	Richard Featherways	December 6–7, 1946
Sophocles (ca. 496 B.C.–406 B.C.)	*Antigone* (5th c. B.C.)	One of two members of the chorus of Theban elders	January 18, 1947
Thornton Wilder (1897–1975)	*The Skin of Our Teeth* (1942)	Henry Antrobus	March 20–22, 1947
Peggy Lamson (1912–1996)	*Trade Name* (1947?)	A spy	March 28, 1947
Maxwell Anderson (1888–1959)	*Winterset* (1935)	Garth	May 15–16, 1947
Sophomore Year			
Noël Coward	*Ways and Means* (from *Tonight at 8:30*, 1936)	Stage manager	December 5, 1947
Sophocles	*Oedipus Rex* (5th c. B.C.)	Tiresias	January 23, 1948
Jean Cocteau (1889–1963)	*The Infernal Machine* (1934)	Tiresias	March 27, 1948
Stephen Sondheim et al.	*Phinney's Rainbow* (1948)	Pit pianist	April 30–May 1 & 7–8, 1948
Emlyn Williams (1905–1987)	*Night Must Fall* (1936)	Dan	May 28, 31 & June 1, 1948
Junior Year			
Clifford Odets (1906–1963)	*Waiting for Lefty* (1935)	Agate Keller	December 17–18, 1948
William Shakespeare (1564–1616)	*Julius Caesar* (1599–1600)	Cassius	February 18–19, 1949
Stephen Sondheim, after George S. Kaufman and Marc Connelly	*All That Glitters* (1949)	Pit pianist	March 18–19 & 21–22, 1949
Senior Year			
Irwin Shaw (1913–1984)	*The Gentle People* (1939)	Harold Goff	February 23–25, 1950
Stephen Sondheim et al.	*Where To From Here* (1950)	Production coordinator	May 11–13, 1950

heim completed ten English courses (both literature and composition), the number required for a major in English, although his selection of courses differed slightly from those outlined for the major. (By way of comparison, he completed sixteen music courses.) His choices are instructive.[49] He skipped the courses on English literature of the seventeenth, eighteenth, and nineteenth centuries; he did not take the course that was "a study of major works of the chief figures of American literature before the Civil War"; he passed on "The English Novel: Richardson to Meredith," "Chaucer," and "Shakespeare," all courses offered during his junior and senior years. Rather, he took every course that touched upon modern literature and drama.

His freshman year found him in the entry-level yearlong course (the equivalent of two courses), "Analytical and Critical Study of Poetry, Fiction, and Drama," whose purpose was "to teach the student to read intelligently and develop a critical capacity." In his sophomore year, he stepped outside of the English major sequence and enrolled in a second yearlong course, "Masters of English Literature," which covered "works by the major writers . . . from Shakespeare to the present day." His first elective, in the fall of his junior year, was "Modern Drama," which studied "(Continental, British, and American [works]) from Ibsen to the present day," followed by two courses the following spring. "Modern British and American Poetry" focused on the work of Auden, Stevens, Eliot, and Yeats; in "The English Novel: Hardy to the Present Day," Sondheim (presumably) read "a representative work of each of the principal novelists" and attended "lectures on the Victorian and continental influences and on the contemporary social, psychological, and literary background." Sondheim waited until his final semester to take "Contemporary American Literature," which concentrated on the development of the novel in America since the Civil War.

Coupled with his apprenticeship with Hammerstein, Sondheim's college curriculum demonstrates how focused he was in his desire to emulate Hammerstein as a contemporary dramatist. (One might speculate further and imagine that Sondheim consulted with Hammerstein about what courses he should take at Williams.) Without question, his exposure to literature and drama during his years at Williams was broad, even if, ironically, the references in his lyrics to literature wander outside of the modern Anglo-American orbit, given what his characters read. The Italians Giorgio and Fosca *(Passion)* exchange books and discuss them; the Japanese Kayama *(Pacific Overtures)* finds Spinoza *formidable* (given the word's French pronunciation, Kayama may be reading in French); the Swede Fredrik *(Night Music)* rapidly fires off a list of authors, con-

temporary and less recent, high and low, with whose works he is intimately familiar (Stendhal, Maupassant, Brontë, Hans Christian Andersen). If the Americans are slightly less literate, they still favor Continental and pre–Civil War American literature. Mary *(Merrily)*, with her writer's block, caustically compares herself to Balzac; Amy *(Company)* surprises us with her education by making a passing reference to *Uncle Tom's Cabin* ("Why watch me die like Eliza on the ice?"); and Ben *(Follies)* disparages those who "try to be profound / by reading Proust and Pound," even though, according to his wife Phyllis, he has "shelves of the world's best books." Still, such literary acumen on the part of these characters redounds upon their creators, and especially (in all the above cases) upon the lyricist.

A larger irony is that, for all their collective modernity, a third of Sondheim's mature musicals are set in the nineteenth and early twentieth centuries (*A Little Night Music*, nearly all of *Pacific Overtures*, *Sweeney Todd*, the first act of *Sunday in the Park with George*, the three central characters—Booth, Czolgosz, and Guitteau—in *Assassins*, *Passion*). They are early modern in their mise-en-scène, to be sure, but perhaps not as contemporary as some of the plays Sondheim studied at Williams. Add to these his one Shakespeare musical (*West Side Story*), which had been chosen before Sondheim signed on, and his two ancient classical stage works (*Forum* and *The Frogs*), both of which steer away from the high tragedy of Sophocles and Aeschylus in favor of the low comedy of Plautus and Aristophanes, and Sondheim emerges as a modern playwright who values the past. Of course, he relied on his collaborators in choosing stories for musicals, so the settings in time and place of these musicals cannot reflect his education alone.

All the same, Sondheim schooled himself in modern drama through studying it as well as creating it, and given his desire to create, his undergraduate diligence in his studies, and his retention of the knowledge he gained, the impact of his coursework on his creation would be difficult to underestimate. As but one example, Sondheim, according to Ted Chapin, "wanted to try for a Pirandello moment in Ben's song ["Live, Laugh, Love" from *Follies*], in which somehow the character and the actor get confused and the audience wouldn't be sure what was going on."[50] The song breaks down, as Ben sees through the characters he has adopted in self-defense and rejects them in search of his real self. The reference, of course, is to Pirandello's *Six Characters in Search of an Author* (1921), where "characters that have been rejected by their author materialize on stage, throbbing with a more intense vitality than the real actors, who, inevitably, distort their drama as they attempt its presentation."[51] Sondheim might have seen the Pirandello in real life, but it is also likely that he studied it in his "Modern Drama" class, nearly twenty years before he set out to write the "Pirandello moment" for *Follies*.

. . . to *Climb High* . . .

With *Climb High,* we encounter yet another wrinkle in Sondheim's chronology. *All That Glitters* premiered in March 1949. Sondheim worked on, and ultimately abandoned, *High Tor,* a project that had sufficient visibility that the 1950 *Gul* mentioned it. *Mary Poppins* followed, and he "spent about a year writing a musical version" before he abandoned it. At the same time, he wrote his senior thesis, the projected three-movement Sonata for Piano in C Major. (The outer movements were completed and submitted as his thesis; as of this writing, all that Sondheim has been able to locate for the second movement is a 32-bar sketch.) He began writing *Climb High* "right after I got out of college." (Secrest writes that *Climb High* was a project "he began in his senior year and worked on for the next two or three years.")[52] In the middle of his work on this, the last of the apprentice musicals, he continued to tinker with the second apprentice musical and wrote Anderson to ask for feedback on it, suggesting that he was open to reworking *High Tor* yet again. Some time after he abandoned *High Tor* (for the second time), but possibly before he shelved *Climb High,* he wrote three out of a projected four movements of his Concertino for Two Pianos. *A Very Short Violin Sonata,* a four-movement, 137-bar work for solo violin, may also date from this period.[53] Sondheim was indeed a busy young composer.

Because of its near-completeness and the plethora of material that documents its creation, *Climb High* deserves a study all its own. It is the only part of the Hammerstein course for which we have evidence of the teacher interacting with the student. Hammerstein annotated his copy of what appears to be at least the third draft of the script, and after returning that script to Sondheim, he followed up with a letter further expressing his concerns. Others have commented on the resemblance between David Alton, the protagonist in *Climb High,* and Joseph Taylor Jr. in *Allegro* and Franklin Shepard in *Merrily*.[54] In those musicals, the protagonist takes decades to go from a likable, idealistic fellow to someone who has deeply compromised himself and injured others; in *Climb High,* David becomes despicable in a mere two years. Hammerstein spared no words in cutting David down to size.

> David is not deeply involved in a big love story. . . . [T]his play is all about a boy out of college who would, like many others, like to make his mark in the theatre. But no excitement surrounds the issue. (1–78; act-page pagination comes from the script that Hammerstein annotated)

> What then is good about him? I don't mean that he should be a pure and noble hero. Billy Bigelow in *Carousel* is not, but his faults contain elements of grand tragedy. David's are little, mean, untragic faults. (1–91)

> Why spend an evening worry[ing] over a louse like this? (2–29)

And in his letter to "Stevie," Hammerstein expanded on his resentment and spelled out the reasons why he was so frustrated by David.

> My basic irritation lies in my deep faith in you and in your future. This faith is endorsed and substantiated by so much of the good writing that has been put into this play. What I resent is the story itself and the characters. They are getting far better treatment than they deserve, and so whatever irritation I have against the play is felt on behalf of the author, not on my own behalf. . . .
>
> In a curious way [this play] enhances my confidence in you. It proves to me that you can and will some day write a very brilliant play which will be a thing very much your own, and I hope you will follow it up with many more.[55]

Hammerstein's other comments deal with word choices, lines to cut, the pace and length of the first act, and the unoriginality of some of Sondheim's ideas for the staging. At some points, he marked the work as good, "not to balance the 'bad markings,' but in the interest of truth and fairness."[56] One of his most effusive marks ("Very good") comes for a song where an older woman sings of how she has succumbed to David's charms ("I'm in Love with a Boy"). The lyric bears more than a passing resemblance to "The Gentleman Is a Dope" from *Allegro*, so perhaps Hammerstein is unwittingly praising Sondheim for how well the student has emulated the teacher. The most fascinating "exchange" comes when Sondheim's characters talk about marriage. David wants Chris, his college sweetheart, to announce their engagement and to marry him soon, but Chris demurs. "We don't love each other the same way. I can't be your mother and sister and wife! That's no basis for a marriage!" (2–50). Hammerstein wrote in the margin: *"Oh, yes it is!!!!!"* Two subsequent comments find him further lecturing Sondheim about love and marriage. One can only imagine that Hammerstein, like other commentators, would have found *Company* a disturbing musical.

Hammerstein's annotations and letter show how he hoped to shape Sondheim. He spent little time critiquing the songs. Rather, he saw these four musicals—and the musical he encouraged Sondheim to write after *Climb High*—as opportunities for Sondheim to sharpen his storytelling abilities. For Hammerstein, this required that Sondheim make a connection with his audience above all other concerns. "I want you to say: 'Can I interest an audience in this to the extent that I am interested in it?' "[57] Hindsight shows that Hammerstein's audience and Sondheim's audience do not overlap completely, with the former unashamed to wallow in sentiment and the latter undeterred by intellectual complexity. Had he lived, it is likely that Hammerstein would not have always been a willing member of Sondheim's audience, so his comments about audience appeal, while valuable, are also limited.

Audience connection, Hammerstein argued, comes from solid writing, and he presented Sondheim with three main characteristics of solid writing. "I know that the smallest kind of story can be made to be earth-shaking if the characters are examined closely enough, and if the choice of incident is ingenious enough, and if the narrative of the incident is told with enough depth and human observation."[58] That Sondheim met these three conditions in all his mature shows reveals the extent of his indebtedness to Hammerstein's tutelage.

The first and third characteristics cannot be stressed enough in relation to Sondheim. The ingenuity of his shows has led many commentators to overlook the characterizations in favor of lauding their conceptual infrastructure. In 1971, critic Martin Gottfried indirectly created the term "concept musical" to describe *Company*, and since then writers have been quick to pigeonhole several of Sondheim's shows in the newly created category, even though, as early as 1976, Sondheim had expressed his disdain for the term. (See appendix.)[59]

His disdain is easy to understand. A musical like *Assassins* does not work because of its unusual construction; it works because Sondheim, through his humanization of his characters and his sympathy to their stories, allows (and even forces) the audience to connect with these characters. "If [*Assassins*] had been just a political tract, I wouldn't have wanted to do it. One of my objections to the works of Brecht is that it's always the politics to the forefront and the characters to the rear, and what I hope we have done with *Assassins* is to put the characters to the forefront and the political and social statements all around."[60] The label "concept

musical" diminishes the humanity of the characters who populate Sondheim's shows and ignores the sensitive ways he and his collaborators tell their stories. In the case of *Company* in particular, off-Broadway and West End revivals in the 1990s have shown Robert, the central character, to be wholly sympathetic and not the cipher that some thought him to be. We recognize Robert—an affable but noncommittal single person—and know someone (maybe ourselves) who has been, or currently is, Robert. He and his entourage are far from being dated.[61] The 2002 Kennedy Center Sondheim Celebration was revelatory in allowing Robert, Kayama *(Pacific Overtures)*, and Giorgio *(Passion)* to emerge as three-dimensional characters. One came away from those productions with the impression that the depth of character and story had always been present in these works but had been downplayed (because of choices by previous directors) and disregarded (because of critical biases that had labeled *Company* and *Pacific Overtures* "concept musicals").

To repeat, using Sondheim's own words, Hammerstein taught Sondheim, through example and guidance, "how to introduce character, what relates a song to character, etc., etc." If Sondheim's dictum—content dictates form[62]—means anything, it means primarily that the characters precede the concept, that, to use Hammerstein's language, there is enough human interest in these characters that their stories cry out to be told. Moreover, Sondheim's dictum suggests that certain characters and narratives profit from certain concepts, from particular ways of telling their stories. Robert's relatively static life corresponds with a freeze-frame presentation. Kayama's growing sense of his own individuality achieves greater impact when set against the timeless formalities of traditional Japanese theater. Giorgio's epistolatory flights of fancy appear onstage so that his denouement—a mélange of undifferentiated thoughts, a projection of an addled mind—is immediately recognizable as being a part of his native, dreamlike discourse. In every case, the concept augments the story and the characters within it; characters are not shoehorned into concepts. Sondheim: "My main goal is to tell a story and if I tell that story well, tell it with resonance, the inferences to be drawn will take care of themselves."[63]

In many respects, from *Show Boat* to *Passion*, teacher and student tell the same basic story: of couples and communities coming together despite the pressures around them that try (sometimes successfully) to force them apart, and of individuals who fail to find community. Sondheim's stories are darker than Hammerstein's because the mood in the 1970s and 1980s seemed less optimistic than in the 1940s and 1950s. "I feel *any* relationship with one person is increasingly difficult these days (1976), as the world shrinks and we are pushed and pushed by time. Yet it's more important than ever before to make personal contact."[64] This idea of connection appears across a variety of disparate shows. Robert needs to add it up to see that he needs "someone to hold him too close." George desperately tries to make a connection with both his art and his sense of communal obligation. The assassins reach across decades to join arms, and fairy-tale characters reach across their stories to work together. (Even Sweeney Todd makes a profound connection, albeit not with another person but with his inanimate—and animated—razors.) Similarly, disconnection comes at a cost. Sally and Ben *(Follies)* are emotionally shattered when they try to cut themselves off from the people who truly love and care for them (Buddy and Phyllis, respectively). Japan risks cultural suicide by becoming too enamored of the West. Frank *(Merrily)* lost touch with the person he was in his youth. These are the stories of Magnolia and Julie in *Show Boat* and of Jud in *Oklahoma!*

If the idea of connection binds Sondheim's stories to Hammerstein, one significant difference between them is the point at which the (dis)connection occurs. For Hammerstein, the crucial decision to (dis)connect usually occurs near the end of the second act. Laurie chooses Curly *(Oklahoma!);* Nellie chooses Emile *(South Pacific);* Anna and the King separate *(The King and I);* the Captain first chooses Maria over the Baroness, and then together they choose freedom over tyranny *(The Sound of Music)*. The bulk of the play sets up the circumstances that lead to the decision made in the second act.

For Sondheim, the crucial decision usually happens in the first act and at times precedes the actions we see on stage. Rather than showing the events that build to a critical choice, as in Hammerstein, Sondheim's dramas usually show the consequences of having made a particular choice or embarked on a course of action that may or may not have been of great importance at the time the decision was made. *Company, Follies, Night Music,* and *Passion* all begin with at least two marriages that either have failed or are in trouble.[65] Having chosen marriage before the curtain goes up, these characters and those they touch are forced to wrestle with their choices. *Sweeney Todd* also centers on marriage, as the Judge's unilateral decision to separate Benjamin and Lucy Barker animates the story (as the flashback reveals). The remaining marital decisions are despicable (Judge–Johanna), laughable (Sweeney–Mrs. Lovett), and noble (Anthony–Johanna), and all these decisions are made, if not consummated, in the first act. In addition, Sweeney announces his homicidal intentions in the first act. *Sunday in the Park with George* and *Into the*

Woods famously reach their "conclusions" at the end of the first act, only to have the second act deconstruct the meaning of finality. Commodore Perry comes to shore before the first act is over *(Pacific Overtures)*. The assassins (with the exception of Lee Harvey Oswald) have made their pact before the first *song* is over; they individually wait their turn for the remainder of the show.

That Sondheim's first-act epiphanies represent a profound departure from the theater of Hammerstein can be seen in the relatively straightforward stories of *Climb High* and the musical that followed it, *Saturday Night*, whose protagonist, Gene, is a gentler and kinder version of David Alton. Although Sondheim was not responsible for the book for *Saturday Night*—it was written primarily by Julius J. Epstein, based on a play he had written with his twin brother, Philip—both here and in *Climb High*, at the final curtain the guy gets the girl, and all unpleasant circumstances are either set right or forgotten. They are both very Hammersteinian in their trajectories, unlike Sondheim's mature musicals, where, to paraphrase his lyrics, he explores roads not taken and worlds that are shaken. And not only do the mature musicals foreground choice and shift dramatic weight to the center. Both *The Last of Sheila* (screenplay with Anthony Perkins, 1973) and *Getting Away with Murder* (play with George Furth, 1996) have deaths in the first half that, in each case, determine the rest of the play.

Sondheim's stories and depth of characterization pay homage to Hammerstein, but his foregrounding of choice and shift of dramatic weight come from another source. Upon reflection, one could indirectly attribute these dramatic differences to Hammerstein, for it was the innovations of a particular Rodgers and Hammerstein musical that opened up for Sondheim a new perspective on storytelling. *Allegro*, as innovative as it may have been, became a mythic container, into which Sondheim poured dramatic impulses that he learned from a different medium. Hammerstein taught Sondheim how to tell a tale, but film taught him how to structure a story. "Movies were, and still are, my basic language."[66] Sondheim made this statement in 2000, on the eve of his seventieth birthday, and yet few writers have attempted to translate his language using the dictionary of film. The translation is easy to make and illuminates much in Sondheim's dramatic language. For a single example, compare his mature musicals with the storytelling devices and denouement of Michelangelo Antonioni's *L'Avventura* (1960). Film was yet another one of his apprenticeships, and its importance emerges clearly with his comments on *Allegro*.

It would be nice if *Allegro*, Rodgers and Hammerstein's third stage collaboration, neatly demarcated Sondheim's true musical juvenilia from his apprentice works, but only *By George* came before Sondheim worked as Hammerstein's assistant on *Allegro*. Williams had never done a musical before Sondheim had asked to do one, and given the tradition of musical lampoonery on other campuses, perhaps Sondheim felt that he needed to prove himself with *Phinney's Rainbow* before he could begin Hammerstein's course in earnest. Whatever nonsense Sondheim indulged in his first Williams musical, his remarks about *Allegro* make it clear how formative the summer of 1947 was, when he worked for Hammerstein as a "glorified office boy, for $25 a week."[67] "Somebody said to me once, 'Your whole life has been fixing *Allegro*.' That's what I've been doing. I've been trying to fix *Allegro* all my life."[68]

Since *Allegro* is so seminal for Sondheim, it is worth recalling his words on the show.

> I think *Allegro* is a watershed musical. The fact is, it was not popular, so it's not viewed as such, because it had no direct effect. However, it affected very seriously the fluidity of the staging of *South Pacific*, which changed musical theater 180°. The notion that you didn't have to bring a curtain down and play something in one[69] while they changed the scenery backstage may seem like a simple concept now, but it wasn't. . . . And it was that fluidity which, incidentally, Hal Prince—who trades in that kind of staging—says was his seminal experience. Well, if he'd seen *Allegro*—which he probably did—that would've told you, because *Allegro* was the experimental thing that did that.
>
> *Allegro* was also the one that attempted to break down the sheer plot-telling chronology, to make an epic style out of a series of scenes. You could call it a "concept musical"—a phrase I loathe, that was invented by critics. But you could say that *Allegro*, in that sense, was the first commercial concept musical. And another one was *Love Life* [by Weill and Alan Jay Lerner]. . . . Most people didn't see them, so they don't think of them as having the kind of impact that *Oklahoma!* had. But I think they did. And particularly *Allegro*. And it was Oscar, working with Jo Mielziner, who created a whole new way of staging. A whole new way.
>
> It was, in fact, using cinematic techniques for the stage, which nobody had done before. Now, [Elia] Kazan had done it in straight plays—he did it in *Death of a Salesman*. The staging of *Death of a Salesman* was very cinematic. But not in musicals. . . . *Death of a Sales-*

man . . . may not have been the first of the straight plays; it may go back to the '20s—I don't know what I'm talking about now. But I do know, in terms of commercial musical theater that I'm aware of, *Allegro* was the first to try to take the influence of movies and the whole notion of dissolves.[70]

For Sondheim, then, the element from *Allegro* that influenced him most was its *fluidity,* which he compares first to epic theater ("a whole new way of staging") and then dramatically to cinema ("the whole notion of dissolves"). It is neither the music nor the story of *Allegro* that impressed Sondheim. It was the way that Hammerstein structured the story—the way he told the tale—that grabbed him. To understand the structure and the telling of *Allegro,* one must look first at the theatrical contribution of Jo Mielziner, then consider the text of the "musical play" (Hammerstein's preferred description of his works), and finally linger in the universe of film that Sondheim inhabited.

There were scenic designers before Jo (né Joseph) Mielziner (1901–76) who created cinematic effects where "each scene could segue into the next like motion picture dissolves, [creating] a theatrical spectacle that few were able to forget."[71] But Mielziner has been credited with consistently bringing the language of film to the theater. His design ideas for *Death of a Salesman* were so critical in the early planning that Arthur Miller agreed to do some rewriting based on Mielziner's vision of the play,[72] and their intertwined success has been a touchstone for all scene design that seeks to use cross-fades, dissolves, and wipes in a cinematic fashion. Mielziner, however, came to use cinematic techniques well before the late 1940s. Already in 1934, he and director-producer Guthrie McClintic sought "cinematic-style dissolves and quick changes" for the twenty-nine scenes of Sidney Howard's docudrama *Yellow Jack.*[73] In 1938, Mielziner applied film language to a musical. For the Rodgers and Hart musical *I Married an Angel,* which "demanded a great number of scenes," he created a design "to allow the speediest of scene changes" with "equal fluidity in the lighting, with one scene cross-fading into the next in full view of the audience, and no blackouts."[74] That same year he provided quick changes for *The Boys from Syracuse,* another Rodgers and Hart musical. Such transitions had become Mielziner's trademark by the time he collaborated with Rodgers and Hammerstein, first on *Carousel,* then on the next five musicals (including *South Pacific,* 1949, and *The King and I,* 1951).

Parenthetically, it is striking how, in his invocation of scenic design, Sondheim spoke of Mielziner and not Boris Aronson, with whom Sondheim had collaborated on four shows (from *Company* to *Pacific Overtures*). In his book *The Theatre Art of Boris Aronson*, noted Sondheim commentator Frank Rich quotes Sondheim sparingly, with most of Sondheim's remarks focused on how the mechanics of Aronson's stage design would affect the timing of various songs.[75] Rich drew comparisons between Mielziner and Aronson, quoting director Elia Kazan, who said that he turned to Mielziner to solve "the complexity of mechanical problems" and Aronson for "subtle or deep mood."[76] Aronson's comments about "A Bowler Hat" *(Pacific Overtures)* show that he was aware that Sondheim was also quite capable of portraying mood. "It didn't need scenery. In miniature, it conveyed the conflict of being contemporary and of being of another time."[77] Aronson, who was Prince's choice ("Hal always goes to the set designer first"),[78] had given Prince successes with *Fiddler on the Roof* (1966) and *Zorba* (1968). Furthermore, Sondheim's recollection of *Love Life* in tandem with *Allegro* suggests that he remembered the Weill-Lerner musical mostly for Aronson's work with Lerner, just as he praised *Allegro* for Mielziner's work with Hammerstein. It is worth noting that Mielziner was at least a year younger than Aronson (ca. 1900–79), so in working with Aronson, Prince (and Sondheim) reached back to the generation of Hammerstein's collaborators.

Mielziner's success at cinematizing the theater led authors to cinematize their plays. "The greatest change in the construction of plays in this century has resulted from the desire of the dramatist to be able to move his story along in an unlimited number of short scenes, and not to be held up by slow scenic changes."[79] Certainly *Allegro* was constructed in such a fashion—a concatenation of short scenes—and Sondheim was right to attribute much of the show's magic to Mielziner, who stressed the importance of collaboration.[80] The failure of *Allegro* has been variously attributed to Agnes de Mille's direction (Hammerstein eventually took over), Hammerstein's unfocused second act, and Rodgers's unremarkable music. But for Sondheim, the fluidity of the play's dramatic execution branded itself in his conscience even more than the story. In spending his life trying to "fix" *Allegro*, he has been about the business of getting its fluidity right.

This is not to say that the story of *Allegro* failed to make an impression on Sondheim. *Allegro* echoed through the stories of *All That Glitters*, *Climb High*, and *Merrily*. Moreover, the list of characters in Sondheim musicals who resemble Joseph Taylor Jr. suddenly increases when one reads Hammerstein's preface to *Allegro*.

The assault on [Taylor's] integrity is so subtly veiled that a good chunk of it is nibbled away before he knows what is happening to him. It is difficult for a man to recognize the gentle transitions of his own deterioration, the millions of small steps whereby he becomes less and less a doctor, more and more . . . everything but what he started out to be, studied to be, struggled to be. . . . Such problems as these are not confined to doctors. An equivalent story could be told about a lawyer, an artist, a businessman, an engineer—anyone who is good at his job.[81]

Ben Stone, politician and diplomat *(Follies);* Fredrik, lawyer, and Desirée, famous actress *(Night Music);* Kayama, samurai turned government functionary *(Pacific Overtures);* George, artist *(Sunday);* even Giorgio, professional soldier *(Passion):* all these characters experience the slow erosion of their convictions, some before the curtain rises. All, like Joe Taylor, face a moment of crisis, where they confront (and usually move through) their fears. Sondheim has spent much of his life embedding equivalent stories in his musicals, so much so that the non-equivalent stories—*Sweeney Todd* and *Assassins*—seem anomalous, despite their brilliance.

Yet the dissolution of the protagonist is hardly a novelty in drama. *Allegro* broke new ground (for Sondheim, at least) in its dramatic and visual fluidity. Hammerstein's text speaks to the quest for fluidity. "There are no stage 'sets' in the conventional sense, but backgrounds for action are achieved by small scenic pieces on a moving stage, by light projections, and by drops."[82] Neither are there "scenes" in the conventional sense, as one location blends into the next and as characters "appear" and "disappear" through the raising and lowering of lights and the flying on and off of props.

Sondheim recollected how Hammerstein and Mielziner achieved these effects. "[They] created an S-shaped curtain to slide on a wide floor-length track all along the stage to accommodate several sets at once; the action could then flow from one to the other with almost cinematic effortlessness."[83] The book gives some indication of how fluid the change from location to location must be. The action begins in Marjorie Taylor's bedroom (Joe's mother), where "there is no detailed stage set—no walls, no windows, no other furniture except the bed itself [Marjorie has just given birth to Joe]. . . . Soon another light comes up on the opposite side of the stage, revealing a CHORUS group,"[84] which, in effect, is located nowhere (or, literally, is located on stage). Throughout the play, locations are more hinted at than established, with even the "real" locations indicated in the script taking on a fantastic form. (In the first act alone, the identified locations include Marjorie's bedroom, the Taylors' porch, the college gym, the football field, the campus, Joe's study, a composite of five classrooms, two distinct places in a woodland, a garden, outside a church, and inside the church.) And time, while handled chronologically, flies by. Joe goes from birth to toddler stage to his high school graduation at lightning speed (and does so invisibly, as we do not see him until the dance at the college gym, thirty-five pages into the book).

Then there is the "unreal" chorus. "The singing chorus is used frequently to interpret the mental and emotional reactions of the principal characters, after the manner of a Greek chorus."[85] Sondheim:

> It occurred to Oscar to use a Greek chorus as a chorus. I don't think anybody had put those two ideas together before. The chorus in *Allegro* is used not only to comment on the action but to explore the inner thoughts of the main characters; something two thousand years old, but I don't think anybody's done it in the commercial theater. . . . Right away I accepted the idea of telling stories in space, of skipping time and using gimmicks like the Greek chorus.[86]

A look at the Sondheim musicals shows how influential *Allegro*'s chorus was. If the function of the chorus is akin to a narrator who stands outside of the story and substitutes exposition for action, Hammerstein's chorus turns up in almost every mature Sondheim show.[87] "The Little Things You Do Together" *(Company)* finds Joanne commenting on the activities of Harry and Sarah, and Marta's "Another Hundred People" encircles scenes between Robert and his other two girlfriends. In *Follies,* the ex-chorines sing "their" old songs that interrupt the linear stories of the leading characters but comment on those stories. *Night Music* features the Liebeslieder Singers, whose musical asides grow ever more trenchant as the show progresses. There are actual narrators in *Pacific Overtures* and *Into the Woods* (and a quasi narrator in the Balladeer in *Assassins*) and Greek choruses in *The Frogs, Sweeney Todd,* and *Merrily* (and quasi choruses in the soldiers and the final flashback in *Passion*). All that remains from the mature musicals is *Sunday,* where the "painting" addresses the audience in act 2 in order to bridge the action of 1880s France to that of 1980s America. Even *Bounce,* that throwback to an earlier Broadway era, fits the pattern (cf. the interjections from the ensemble in "Gold!," "The Game," and "Boca Raton").

Sondheim is also accurate in describing his almost immediate adoption of this chorus technique. *All That Glitters* gave him ample opportunity for choral commentary through the dancing teacher-jurors, and through it builds on the original play. *Climb High,* of course, is completely original, so the fact that there are two choruses of sorts is Sondheim's invention. The opening scene features a cocktail party as David and his roommate seek backers for a play. The guests, in anticipation of their doppelgänger in *Merrily*, alternate between praising each other and cutting everyone down to size. (Both *Climb High* and *Merrily* are reflected in Marta's line from *Company* about "meet[ing] at parties through the friends of friends who they never know.") They are part of the scene while they comment on it, so they are not as detached as the chorus in *Allegro*. The next scene, however, introduces a second chorus. "Two Elizabethan troubadours enter, carrying lutes, by which they accompany themselves" (1–15), and they sing a faux-Elizabethan ballad. Given that the first scene happens in the present, their historical distance from that present prepares us to travel back in time for the bulk of the play, which is a long flashback. The troubadours also return before the final scene (2–55), which begins where the first scene ended. While the troubadours act more as a framing device to set off the present from the past, their song and reprise comment on the story being told and the interior lives of the two main characters, David and his love interest, Christabel.[88]

In his marginalia, Hammerstein expressed reservations about the confusing effect the troubadours might have on the audience. A second letter to Sondheim about *Climb High* finds Hammerstein more concerned about the rationale behind introducing the troubadours in the first place and sets out how Sondheim's structure of storytelling began to differ from Hammerstein's at an early age. This letter came after the one in which Hammerstein suggested that Sondheim drop *Climb High* and write a new musical play. It appears that, between the two letters, Sondheim's defense of his choice of subject caused Hammerstein to relent.

August 6, 1953

Dear Stevie:

Regarding *Climb High,* not only did we like the original conception, but only a couple of months ago when you restated your theme it sounded good then. At the time I suggested that it was perhaps the prologue [act 1, scene 1, set in the present] that started us off not liking the boy, whereas if you told the story in its proper chronology, without flashbacks, you could get the audience to like him and go with him.[89]

The story may have worked for Hammerstein, but Sondheim's structure kept Hammerstein from endorsing the play. For Sondheim, however, structural innovation was vital, and, by his own words, he learned such innovation from *Allegro,* where (to him) "the idea of telling stories in space [and] of skipping time" was first introduced in the musical.

Hammerstein's "skipping time" and Sondheim's, though, are of different magnitudes and further demonstrate Sondheim's indebtedness to film. In *Allegro,* diachronic time is highly compressed but is never abandoned, and no popular Hammerstein show dispenses altogether with diachronic linearity. (Dream ballets and supernatural events à la *Carousel* are either synchronous to the diachronic story line or suspended in time without disrupting the flow of time.) But Sondheim's very first apprentice musical, *All That Glitters,* radically breaks away from diachronic storytelling. The prologue (thirty-seven pages) and epilogue (six pages) happen in "real" time, but the rest of the play (ninety-two pages) is a barbiturate-induced hallucination that defies the unities of time and space.

Accounting for this diachronic break is not difficult. In making *All That Glitters* an extended fantasy, Sondheim followed his source. And in telling what is, in essence, a dream, Sondheim is following an established musical theater tradition of shows that featured externally induced dreams (*A Connecticut Yankee,* 1927; revival, 1943), psychoanalytic projections (*Lady in the Dark,* 1941), and fantasy lands (*Finian's Rainbow* and *Brigadoon,* both 1947). Nevertheless, *All That Glitters* already shows lines of demarcation that will separate Sondheim from the Hammerstein of *Allegro,* mostly in how time is handled. There are numerous cases of simultaneous dialogue or of multiple events occurring simultaneously, features in the Kaufman/Connelly original that nevertheless return in the interrogation of *Whistle* and in the lead-in and lead-out of the "Loveland" sequence in *Follies* and that find a musical parallel in Sondheim's contrapuntal ensembles. A "gaudy cabaret becomes a sunny summer cottage" without the drawing of a curtain (1–38), betraying *Allegro*'s influence. Here, Neil simultaneously plays out two scenes, one in the cabaret that is interrupted by the one in the cottage, and both of these scenes are hallucinations and are, thus, outside of diachronic time. *Climb High* continues Sondheim's play with time, where again there are scenes that are played simultaneously and where the troubadours border the central story, told as a flashback. *Climb High* also contains a second flashback, as the linearity of the main flashback—act 1, scene 2 to act 2, scene 3 (part 1)—is followed by a second flashback that, in terms of chronology, fits between act 1, scene 2 and act 1, scene 3. The play ends in the immediate present, as David retrieves an old college theater program from his pocket and looks over at a fifteen-year-old autograph seeker who appeared in the flashback-within-a-flashback (i.e., she is currently the projection of his memory of that college production). The similarity to the final scene of *Carousel*, where Billy Bigelow and the Stargazer look at earthly events from another dimension, is there, but there the dimensions were more metaphysical in nature. Here, different moments in time are superimposed upon each other, just as they will be later (and brilliantly so) in one of Sondheim's favorite songs, "Someone in a Tree" *(Pacific Overtures)*.

Since *Allegro* does not skip time as readily as Sondheim musicals do (even the apprentice musicals), perhaps Sondheim misattributes the function of time in Hammerstein. Hammerstein's second letter about *Climb High* suggests that he and Sondheim talked of another seminal stage experience for Sondheim, from which he drew inspiration.

> [T]here is no doubt that a story can be told about a man who instead of learning how to use the tools of his craft, learns only how to put on the proper costume for it, thinking that he is going on a shortcut, and finding in the end that you must always go back and learn how to use those tools. . . . This is your story and it is perfectly sound. In fact it is the story of *Death of a Salesman*. . . . I would like to talk this over with you at great length (not the salesman, but [*Climb High*]) when you return [from California].

It is certainly possible that Hammerstein mentioned Miller's play on his own, but given Sondheim's remarks about the play, it seems likely that, by August 1953, he and Hammerstein had discussed *Death of a Salesman* and its ramifications for musical theater. Hammerstein wanted Sondheim to rewrite *Climb High* as a traditional diachronic story. Sondheim, instead, was extending his ideas on time. To be sure, he borrowed design ideas from Hammerstein and Miller; the staging of *Climb High* on occasion reads like that of *Death of a Salesman*, as various parts of the stage are bathed at different times with light.[90] But if the look of Miller's play impressed Sondheim, part of that look entailed the use of flashbacks, which Sondheim called "cinematic." Indeed, for Sondheim, a dissolve would come to mean more than the seamless flow from one scene to the next. In his musicals, Sondheim learned not only how to dissolve space (and location) but also time. The similarity between Sondheim's dissolves and editing (Fr., *montage*) of scenes and the world of film is remarkable. Miller's play may have inspired Sondheim's work on *Climb*

High, but it was the world of film that Sondheim saw lying behind his work and Miller's play. To that world, attention must be paid.

Before leaving the theater, though, it is worth recalling the very different political worlds Hammerstein and Sondheim occupied. Hammerstein lived at a time when theater could afford to be—and was expected to be—didactic. The heavy-handedness of some of the moral teachings in a Hammerstein musical (from *Show Boat* forward) may cloy today, but many believed in theater as an ameliorative art. Sondheim similarly believed in didactic theater, up to a point.

> I was most concerned that we not soap-box [in *Sweeney Todd*]. [Harold Prince] was too, because we both like didactic theater but don't like soap-boxing. I try to do it by just inserting here and there throughout the lyrics words like "engine," basic images, not just inserting the words but using them as little motivating forces to make a slightly wispy connection with the industrial revolution.[91]

"Soap-boxing" is a thinly veiled reference to the political theater of Bertolt Brecht, whose style of theater Sondheim never could stomach in its entirety. (Similarly, Sondheim downplayed the importance of Brecht's longtime collaborator, Kurt Weill, for his own concept of musical theater.)[92] But if his works are not as didactic as Brecht's (or Hammerstein's), Sondheim's shows on occasion do attempt to draw moral lessons.

Without question, Sondheim's politically liberal tendencies have been on display. The study materials for *Assassins* clearly mark the musical as a pro-gun-control work;[93] he refused the National Medal of Arts in 1992, when George H. W. Bush was president, and accepted it in 1997, when Bill Clinton was president.[94] Nevertheless, his art avoids being overtly political. Neither the Vietnam War nor the civil rights movement nor feminism nor issues surrounding gays (with the notable exception of *Bounce*) seemed to inform Sondheim's stories at all. While some take great pains to find these things in Sondheim, Sondheim took great pains to play down these very things.[95] One author suggests that all of this is evidence of Sondheim's Jewishness, as though his cerebral work and political astuteness were distinctively Jewish.[96]

And yet Sondheim's early apprenticeship with Hammerstein occurred in the shadow of dark political times. "From 1947 to 1961, your ability to work in Hollywood's motion picture industry strictly depended on whether or not your name appeared on a list of suspected Communist activists or sympathizers."[97] Sondheim's theatrical appren-

ticeship with Hammerstein began at around the same time as the first set of hearings by the House Un-American Activities Committee (1947). He arrived in Hollywood to write for television shortly after Elia Kazan named names, and returned to Manhattan around the time Jerome Robbins named names.[98] Bernstein had been blacklisted, and in Sondheim's first professional outing as a composer as well as a lyricist, a formerly blacklisted actor, Zero Mostel, had top billing (and had to work with Robbins). It is difficult to believe that Sondheim never discussed these matters with Hammerstein and others or considered how the tenor of the times affected the work that was being done on Broadway and in Hollywood. For example, both *South Pacific* and *Lost in the Stars* are responses to the political climate of the time. Predictably, the former was more successful because its cloak of patriotism in its tacit approval of World War II partially hid its antiprejudice message.

Sondheim himself has been negatively affected by politics, though not to the extremes of those who were blacklisted. *Assassins* has had a tortured journey to Broadway, having been stopped twice from appearing on the Great White Way because world events ran counter to its message. (Gulf War I in 1991 caused it to close off-Broadway, and the terrorist attacks of September 2001 led to the cancellation of an announced November 2001 opening.) And one can appreciate how a man who lived his life outside of the spotlight by and large would choose not to make his works polemical lightning rods. Yet no doubt there is more that can be written about the didactic Sondheim and what he learned from Hammerstein and the world around him during his dramatic apprenticeships. It is far too simplistic to suggest that his supposed misanthropic view comes from his experience in his late teens through his twenties. But until such time as someone seeks to explore this possibility more fully, we shall have to wonder to what degree the "apprenticeship of real life" affected Sondheim and appears in his work to the present day.

5

Sondheim the Cinéaste

In this chapter, which traces Sondheim's cinematic loves and finds vestiges of them in his musicals, two ideas intertwine. First, while Sondheim did not propose most of the stories that he and his collaborators set to music, the stories bear striking similarities to films that he knew and loved. This suggests that Sondheim as collaborator favored stories that were familiar to him and helped to shape these stories in ways that were familiar to him. Second, Sondheim *as composer* borrowed concepts from the language of film and translated these concepts into *the music*. Thus, to talk about the music of Sondheim, one must use the language of film to describe musical processes.

Sondheim and film: some observations

In the audio commentary to *Sunday in the Park with George*, Sondheim marveled at William Parry, who played Texan curator Charles Redmond in act 2. "He looks like Teddy Roosevelt! And he has a voice like Teddy Roosevelt, too! He should do *Arsenic and Old Lace*." When Mandy Patinkin ("George") asked why, Sondheim reminded his fellow commentators (and those listening to the commentary) about the part of Theodore Brewster, the brother of the lead character Mortimer. Theodore thinks he is Teddy Roosevelt and is always charging up and down the stairs. In saying that Parry should play the part, he was referring to the Joseph Kesselring play that opened on Broadway in January 1941. But one can hardly think about *Arsenic and Old Lace* today and not also recall the 1944 Frank Capra movie starring Cary Grant as Mortimer and John Alexander as Theodore. Sondheim's offhand remark thus ties together his two dramatic apprenticeships and hints at how completely both apprenticeships suffuse his thinking.

Sondheim's fascination with film is well known. One reads how, in 1953, Sondheim traveled to Europe as hanger-on and clapper boy for

John Huston's *Beat the Devil,* during the course of which he played chess with Humphrey Bogart and poker with David O. Selznick. Selznick encouraged Sondheim, who owned a 16mm Ciné Kodak movie camera and was eager to learn film techniques. (Sondheim lost track of the film he shot on the set; some decades later, unbeknownst to him, some of his footage was used in a PBS documentary on Bogart.)[1] Sondheim later conspired with Bernstein and his wife, Felicia Montealegre, to "remake" *Golden Boy, Humoresque,* and *Whatever Happened to Baby Jane?* In addition, the trio re-created the last ten minutes of act 2 of Puccini's *Tosca,* in which Montealegre played the titular heroine and her husband was the evil chief of police, Scarpia. Sondheim: "It was really fun. Franco Zeffirelli . . . said it was the best opera film he ever saw."[2]

Then there was Sondheim's sojourn in Hollywood in 1953, when (with George Oppenheimer) he cowrote scripts for the television series *Topper.* His love of film carried over to his work on *Topper.* In the episode "George's Old Flame," a subsidiary character is a movie star, disdained by a matron who remarks that the last movie she bothered to see was *Birth of a Nation* (made in 1915). If his apprenticeship with Hammerstein had caused Sondheim to have second thoughts about his capacities as a "playwright in words," his experience with Oppenheimer seemed to confirm his general unsuitedness to such literary pursuits, though the deadlines in television and the theater are similar.

Nevertheless, from the beginning of Sondheim's career, film encroached upon his music. In *Saturday Night,* the song "In the Movies" compares and contrasts the glamorous lives on the silver screen with the humdrum existence of life in New York. With the musical set in 1928, the reference to Rudolph Valentino is timely, as is that to Stella Dallas (the eponymous film was first released in 1925; the sound version appeared in 1937). Sondheim's immaturity as a "playwright in song" shows in his choice of silent films and film stars over the talkies. One imagines that, in 1928, savvy young men and women would attend talking pictures and would be less rapturous about silent films and their stars.[3] Yet what is more striking than the name-dropping is Sondheim's cinematic technique, as the song is a montage of scenes, alternating back and forth between the bickering of the men, the sycophantic rhapsodizing of the women for the screen stars, and the A-to-B comparisons of the movies and Brooklyn. This type of crosscutting will appear in other Sondheim songs (for example, Buddy's music in *Follies,* "Epiphany" in *Sweeney Todd,* "Unworthy of Your Love" in *Assassins*), and one might reasonably wonder whether Sondheim's contrapuntal proclivities in his ensembles owe a debt to film as well as to music, especially considering how the tropes of music in general and counterpoint specifically inhabit the vocabulary of filmmakers.[4]

Film techniques continue to make their presence felt in his later work. At the end of "A Bowler Hat" *(Pacific Overtures)*, Sondheim created a triple entendre with one word. "It's called a cutaway," Kayama sings, and all three meanings of the word, as listed in the *Oxford English Dictionary*, are on display here.[5] Kayama dons a morning coat, with its "skirt cut back from the waist in a slope or curve, as contrasted with a frock-coat." Thus he displays not only his sartorial elegance but also his lexical erudition (as does Sondheim), for the term did not come into usage until the mid–nineteenth century, that is, at the same time as the events in the musical. We have also witnessed the surgical amputation of Kayama's life as, over the course of the song, he becomes less and less the man whom we first met. The song thus functions as "a model or drawing of a piece of apparatus, etc., in which part is cut away so as to reveal the interior," here modeling a man's soul and the effects of Western capitalism upon that soul. Lastly, we watch as Kayama physically ages over the course of the song. An obvious cinematic parallel is the breakfast-table sequence in *Citizen Kane* (1941). There, in two minutes of actual time, years elapse as Kane and his first wife move from the playful repartee of young love through the comfortable boredom of companionship to the passive hostility of two people riven by ambition. In those two minutes, we see, multiple times, "the process of making a quick transition to another scene," the cinematic definition of a cutaway.

Nor is "A Bowler Hat" the only example of a cinematic cutaway in Sondheim. "The Little Things You Do Together" and "Another Hundred People" *(Company)* have already been discussed as examples of detached, "Greek-chorus" narration. But their visual presentation resembles the crossfade, montage, and cutaway of filmic language. We quickly move from one "shot" to another. The same type of theatrical cinematography occurs with "Liaisons" *(Night Music)*, as Madame Armfeldt sings her song as a continuation of her action (she had earlier told her granddaughter that she would recount her affair with the Baron de Signac at dinner) and as an interruption of the action between Fredrik and Desirée (who are busily renewing their sexual acquaintance). *Night Music* in particular so skillfully translates the cinematic cutaway to the theater, from the opening trio ("Now"—"Later"—"Soon"), played out in three different locations, to the minireprises that the Liebeslieders provide, that it is surprising that Hal Prince, the director of both the stage and film versions of the musical, stumbled so badly in the latter. Elsewhere, the musicals feature scenes that move away from the larger action, as in the case of *Follies* ("Bolero d'Amour," "I'm Still Here," "One More Kiss"), or, like "A Bowler Hat," can contain several scenes within one number, as in *Sweeney Todd* ("Kiss Me"/"Ladies in Their Sensibilities," the act 2 "Johanna" quartet, "City on Fire") and *Into the Woods* (the opening number).

One imagines that the decision to make these songs cinematic cannot have been Sondheim's alone but that he and his collaborators discussed their staging even before Sondheim had composed them. The directors, in fact, take credit for the cinematic aspects of *Company* and *Follies*.[6] One expects directors to be the principal voice when it comes to making a stage work cinematic. But we have already seen that other collaborators (such as Mielziner in stage design) also affect the nature of staging. And one would expect that Sondheim, steeped as he was in film and so affected by the cinematic staging of *Allegro*, would hardly be silent when he and his collaborators talked about what a show would look like on stage.

Yet in his work up through *Follies*, it is as though Sondheim were in full retreat from the cinematic techniques he had used in *All That Glitters* and *Climb High*. Perhaps the ghost of Hammerstein had dampened Sondheim's zeal for bringing cinematic language to the theater; had he adopted Hammerstein's suggestions for *Climb High*, he would have de-cinematized his own musical. Neither *Saturday Night* (1954) nor *Forum* (1962) nor *Anyone Can Whistle* (1964) is especially cinematic in structure or look. It took the prodding of his collaborators on *Company* and *Follies* to get Sondheim to use cinematic techniques in his musicals again.

Cinematic language saturates Sondheim musicals. One can conclude that the earlier collaborations so affected all of musical theater that Sondheim's later collaborators came to cinematic techniques on their own, and with the increasing use of these techniques in straight theater (James Lapine's natural home), such a conclusion is valid. Yet, since film language is a consistent component of Sondheim musicals, another conclusion is that Sondheim, once he recovered the importance of this language in structuring his stories, returned to it after Prince and Michael Bennett had left him. While there may be no need to choose between these two scenarios (and, undoubtedly, other scenarios exist), Sondheim's own investment in film is so thorough that film would have found its way into his dramatic language eventually. A further exploration of that investment is in order.

Sondheim at Telluride

If there were doubts about the place of cinema in Sondheim's life, they were dispelled when he served as the guest director of the 2003 Telluride Film Festival—the first time, according to Bill Pence, cofounder and codirector of the festival, that a composer had done so. Sondheim was invited "because of his stature as an artist and his reputation as a cinephile. Guest directors in a similar category have been Salman Rushdie and [performance artist and composer] Laurie Anderson."[7] If one can speak of film informing the work of Rushdie or Anderson, one can speak of film informing the work of Sondheim.

In newspaper stories before the festival and in a conversation during the festival with Elvis Mitchell, film critic for the *New York Times*, Sondheim showed how deeply he loves film. He spoke glowingly of Krzysztof Zanussi's *Contract* (1980): "It's a movie of his I find so extraordinary, I want to share it with everybody." He recalled a French director of the 1930s and tossed off the names of other directors as if no one needed to ask who they were.

> I thought it'd be fun to lay [Julien] Duvivier on people. And also I could get to see some of those movies again that I saw in my teens . . . *La Belle équipe* . . . really knocked me out in my early 20's, and I want to make a musical out of it, too. I love Duvivier's stuff; it's always one inch short of opera. It's romantic melodrama, which is exactly what *Sweeney Todd* is. If you see any of the French melodramas of the early 30's and 40's, like Clouzot, Carné, many have that dryness. And cigarette smoke. The cigarette smoke in those movies. The Zanussi, of course, is high comedy, which has nothing to do with those other movies—it's satirical. And we'll show *The More the Merrier*, because there should be a George Stevens.[8]

At the festival, three Duvivier films were shown. *La Belle équipe* (1936) relates the story of a group of unemployed workers who win a lottery and open a working-class dance hall and restaurant together. The arrangement, however, goes sour. In the original ending, one man kills another in a jealous rage over a woman they both love; in Duvivier's revised ending, the two men reject the woman and save their enterprise. Neither the tragic nor the happy ending was well received in Duvivier's time,[9] and one can only wonder which ending Sondheim adapted in his imagined musicalization of this story. *Un carnet de bal* (1937) follows a newly widowed woman as she reestablishes contact with the men with

whom she had danced twenty years earlier at her first ball, a pursuit that has unsatisfactory results. And in *Panique* (1946), an old maid is murdered and her murderer and his girlfriend harass a Jewish neighbor to death because the neighbor knows the truth about the murder.

According to Alan Williams, Duvivier was drawn to "the often tragic plights of isolated individuals" and to "the failure of an embattled individual trying to break out of some sort of trap. . . . virtually all of his French sound films, even those that end happily, are bathed in a pervasive, ultimately nihilistic pessimism."[10] Roy Armes goes on to speak of *Panique* as a *film noir*, "characterized by the theme of doomed lovers, the setting of urban backstreet squalor and an all-pervading air of fatalism."[11] Sondheim, as we shall see, also expressed an affinity for *film noir*. As with the play *Night Must Fall*, Sondheim showed a preference for dark and unlikable characters, and his affection for Duvivier and free association of the director and *Sweeney Todd* give an indication of which aspects of Duvivier's stories Sondheim enjoyed.

Yet, what to make of Sondheim's comment that Duvivier's "stuff [is] always one inch short of opera"? The fact that *Sweeney* and Duvivier both engage in romantic melodrama helps illumine his understanding of Duvivier, who is feted for his narrative sense, cinematic virtuosity, and ability to create the memorable scene and the striking confrontation, the *coup de théâtre* that is a staple of nineteenth-century Italian opera.[12] Sondheim's comment thus further defines his idea of opera as heightened, even exaggerated, drama, which all the while is handled with consummate technical skill.

If Sondheim sympathized with Duvivier in the types of characters that peopled his dramas and in the ways the stories unfold, he also learned something about the demands of the studio system and the film world of yesteryear. His love of film unexpectedly explains his relatively detached attitude about the success of his works, for success alone was not always the animating force behind film, at least as Sondheim understood it.

> I loved that professionalism. Prolificness is something I really envy, and someone like Duvivier just kept making the movies and moving on to the next one. We had the same thing here, too, with studio directors like Michael Curtiz and Raoul Walsh. They were heroes of mine. They went from movie to movie to movie, and every third movie was good and every fifth movie was great. There wasn't any cultural pressure to make art.[13]

Given that Sondheim's comments were made after *Bounce* had closed in Chicago to less-than-positive reviews, one can appreciate more fully the type of work Sondheim tried to do not only in *Bounce* but also throughout his career. He has written solid, professionally crafted musicals. Some have been hailed as good; some, great. But in lifting up the careers of these professional directors, who (according to Sondheim's math) came out with more mediocre movies than good ones, Sondheim invited the critic to judge his record in a similar fashion and called into question the "cultural pressure" put upon any professional. The craftsman comes before the artist, reminding one of his days at Williams, where craft supplanted inspiration, and where Sondheim's compositional philosophy revolved around technique rightly applied.

In his conversation with Mitchell at Telluride, Sondheim lamented how, after World War II, directors went from making movies to self-consciously making "works of art," signaled mostly by making movies longer. The demise of the double feature coincided with Sondheim's declining interest in film. (The Thalia and the New Yorker were among Sondheim's favorite movie palaces, and he routinely spent four hours watching movies there.) But he also expanded on how cinema informed his work. Again, he turned to *Allegro*.

> I can pinpoint exactly when the movies influenced musical staging. It was a show called *Allegro*. . . . It was a set of dissolves, a series of dissolves. Nobody ever thought of doing it before. The show was a flop, but it influenced the next show they did, which was *South Pacific*, which used exactly that technique. And Hal Prince says that was the turning point in his life. That's when he realized you can stage a show like a movie.

He also recalled his experience with Jerome Robbins on *West Side Story*, when the director was frustrated in figuring out how to block "Maria," which seemed to him dramatically static. Sondheim learned from that experience. "I think cinematically when I'm writing songs and I stage them . . . in my head. And I realize that I stage them like a movie."

In one of his most revealing comments, he explained what made *The Last of Sheila* exciting for him. "It's about camera angles. The climactic murder scene with the three confessionals is all about the angle that you shoot it from. The point of view of the character makes the audience think that something is happening that isn't happening." In the left margin of the screenplay, Sondheim drew camera angles for director Her-

bert Ross to follow. He attempted to direct the eye, and in his songs, he similarly directs the eye. By his own admission, his music operates the way a cameraman operates, which (it must be emphasized) is distinct from the way cinema has affected staging. *Allegro* and *South Pacific* may have made theater more cinematic, but Sondheim uniquely has made Broadway music more cinematic, and may have done so less deliberately and more intuitively. At Telluride, he talked about striving to write "songs in drama." "I'm not talking about songs that are just out there to take a moment and have fun with it or dance with it or have a repeat of a comedy lyric or something. I'm talking about songs that are meant to carry the story forward or to explore character or meant to create suspense." In other words, Sondheim wrote songs that do what movies traditionally have done: capture and project the kinetic aspects of the story and the characters within it.

Film noir

Sondheim clearly loved film. His early attempt at a novel, *Bequest*, is a cross between the events of *Hangover Square* and the result, by his own account, of watching "too many Bette Davis movies." Sondheim remembered which day his mother married former Paramount Films executive Ed Leshin because it coincided with the day that *All About Eve* opened at the Roxy. And his comments to Secrest about Margaret Sullavan movies are almost comic in their fawning adoration, even though most of her movies were made before Sondheim reached his teenage years.[14] Sondheim was not only a Broadway baby; he was also a cinemaniac.

Secrest noted Sondheim's love for a specific film genre, one reflected in his Telluride remarks about the *Thin Man* series and one that opens up a whole vista of possibilities: *film noir*.[15] On first glance Sondheim's affinity with the genre may seem to find little immediate resonance in his musicals. Secrest complicates the issue when she suggests that *Hangover Square* "was an early example of *film noir*";[16] few film scholars list the movie in that category, and its 1945 premiere positions it after other early classic *noir* films, such as *The Maltese Falcon* (1941), *Gaslight*, *Double Indemnity*, *Laura*, and *Murder My Sweet* (all 1944). (The existence of the Hollywood branch of the Office of War Information, which encouraged films that would support the war effort, accounts for the gap in *film noir* production in the early 1940s.)[17] One could drop the ubiquitous description of *Sweeney Todd* as "Grand Guignol"—a description made primarily because of the blood-squirting razors[18] and partially repudiated by

Sondheim[19]—and call it a *musicale noire,* given its similarities to the classic *film noir Out of the Past* (1947): a partial flashback; assumed identity; a powerful and corrupt womanizer; six deaths (including the male and female leads); the ingénue couple brought together at the end; and the presence of the childlike innocent.

Other aspects of Sondheim's life confirm his interest in *noir.* At Williams, he wrote for the college magazine, the *Purple Cow,* where one of his parodies, "The Wade Caper," appeared under the pseudonym Hashiell Dammit, a clear pun on the name of the author and founder of the hard-boiled detective novel that was a staple of *film noir.*[20] In addition, Sondheim (according to Secrest) longed to do his own version of the *Thin Man* series of films, which anticipate *film noir.*[21] *The Last of Sheila* and *Getting Away with Murder* filter *noir*-ish elements through the strainer of Agatha Christie murder mysteries. And (as noted above) Duvivier was also a *noir*-ish director.

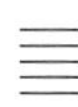

Michael Walker suggests that "*film noir* is ultimately a generic field rather than a category to which films may or may not belong"[22] and outlines the contours of this field. *Film noir*

> combines a number of elements in a way which makes it peculiarly complex and interesting: a distinctive and exciting visual style, an unusual narrative complexity, a generally more critical and subversive view of American ideology than the norm. For these and other reasons—the films' lack of sentimentality, their willingness to probe the darker areas of sexuality, their richly suggestive subtexts, the emotional force of the downbeat—*film noir* as a phenomenon continues to fascinate.[23]

Clearly, some of the elements Walker enumerates are present in Sondheim musicals. *Pacific Overtures* and *Assassins* take a critical stance toward American ideology, and while *A Little Night Music* and *Passion* are probably Sondheim's most sentimental musicals, many of the others are decidedly unsentimental, with *Follies* being markedly antisentimental.

Still, the dramatic results in Sondheim musicals and *film noir* seem at odds with each other. There are no femmes fatales. With the possible exception of Sweeney Todd and some of the assassins, paranoia does not drive any of the characters. There are few spectacular murders. Ironically, the most convoluted plot in a Sondheim musical is found in what is arguably the funniest of the shows, *Forum.* Perhaps Sondheim's love for *film noir* found no echo in his work. (And one must recall that the loves of Sondheim's collaborators are also reflected in these musicals.)

The musicals also differ from *noir* in that the films usually have a lone protagonist around whose life and actions the plot is organized. While romantic entanglements are common in *noir,* very often a single character emerges as central to the story. In the musicals, by contrast, ensembles of characters propel the drama. *Sweeney Todd*—and, to a lesser degree, *Company* and *Sunday*—are the only mature shows that have clear solitary leading characters, thus resembling the ensemble work in a late *films noir* like *Touch of Evil* (1958) more than the typical star-driven *films noirs* of the 1940s and 1950s. (This lack of a central character in Sondheim musicals exacerbates the lack of an emotional connection that some critics experience. Unlike most Hammerstein musicals, a typical Sondheim musical does not give the audience a clear indication of which ensemble member deserves their sympathy or disdain, which one is the star and which the villain.)

Yet one prominent aspect of *film noir* appears repeatedly: the struggle against an inexorable fate. This puts the choices that the characters must make in a harsh spotlight. If outcomes are predetermined—if there truly is no other way—then decisions would not seem to matter. Sondheim and his collaborators emphatically assert, however, that they do, that the impending doom that awaits the characters does not obviate the making of hard choices. Thus, despite the absence of certain *film noir* tropes—the gritty realities of urban settings or the triangles involving one man and two women (a domesticated and domesticating woman versus a siren)—the musicals adhere to a core ideology of *noir:* the search for a solution to an insoluble situation (e.g., *Detour* [1945] and *D.O.A.* [1950]). Whereas a *noir* character is murdered or hauled off to jail, most of Sondheim's *noir*-ish characters have an even crueler fate awaiting them: they must somehow go on with their lives. In *noir,* characters wrestle with their inner demons and lose more often than not; in Sondheim (e.g., *Company* and *Follies*), their fights end in a draw.

This sense of fatalism in both *film noir* and Sondheim musicals is reinforced by the convention of the flashback. In several *films noirs,* the story is not told linearly, from a point in time going forward, but rather from a present moment with recollections of the past. The audience sees early on the consequences of actions and decisions that have already been made. Only in the course of the film are those prior actions and decisions recounted. (*Double Indemnity* provides a classic example of this convention.) Flashbacks also inhabit Sondheim musicals. Sometimes the past is literally reenacted (as in the masked ball in *Sweeney Todd* or the narration of Fosca's past in *Passion*), but often it is stylized, recounted more by allusion than by illustration ("Remember" in *Night Music,* sung by the Liebeslieder Singers; the various pastiche numbers in *Follies,* where present and past are conflated). Seen through the lens of *noir*, *Merrily We Roll Along* is not only a musical based on Kaufman and Hart's reverse chronology play. It is also a series of flashbacks, with each flashback going farther back into the past than the flashback that preceded it. (In its original Broadway version, with the framing device of the two graduation scenes—the first in 1981 and the second in 1955—this structure of consecutive flashbacks emerges more clearly.)

In the musicals, the flashback, derived from the film world, replaces the dream ballet, derived from the dance world. Both conventions disrupt the forward linear progression of chronological time in the larger story even as they themselves unfold in a linear fashion. At their best, both provide information that proves crucial in understanding the events occurring in the putative present of the story. Seen in this light, it is not so odd, as Sylviane Gold suggests, that "Sondheim, who cut his teeth on Broadway writing the lyrics for *West Side Story*, one of the greatest dance shows ever, has rarely composed a pure dance number for a show."[24] Gold forgets that Bernstein was primarily an instrumental composer—*On the Town* (1944), for example, was an adaptation of the ballet *Fancy Free*—and that Sondheim has always been more wedded to the word than many of his peers. Furthermore, in Prince's trenchant words: "It's hard to dance in depth what's going on with characters,"[25] and Sondheim musicals are character-driven. (One also cannot ignore Prince's frustration in sharing directorial duties with Bennett on *Follies;* few Prince shows spotlighted dance after this experience.) Beyond this, though, Gold overlooks the indebtedness to film.

Thus, differences between the flashback and dance further illuminate why Sondheim musicals stand apart from other works. Dance emphasizes precision and athleticism on the part of the choreographer, dance corps, and soloist(s). *West Side Story* is emblematic of these features, but they are present in 1930s Busby Berkeley routines as well as in *The Will Rogers Follies* (1991) and *The Producers* (2001). Dance can also emphasize individuality. Bob Fosse's solo in the film version of *Kiss Me, Kate* (1953)—at a time before his name and style became legendary—shows how a soloist can make a singular impression.

In contrast, the flashback works to make invisible the efforts of those who create it (screenwriter, director, cinematographer, film editor, at times film score composer). The time-space continuum has been broken, but the focus is rarely placed on the virtuosity of the flashback, though all of its elements may demonstrate a high level of virtuosity. Moreover, the performance in a flashback typically does not occupy a different plane of reality. A flashback is usually told in the same voice as the narration of the present, whereas dance literally and figuratively steps outside of the standard narrative. Thus, the artificiality of the flashback is less noticeable than the artificiality of dance; everyone recollects, but not everyone dances. And while dance can be integrated into the story (the breakthrough in *Oklahoma!* and the particular genius of Jerome Robbins),[26] dance is rarely integral to the story (exceptions include *On Your Toes, Silk Stockings,* and *A Chorus Line*). If dance is a fundamental component of American musical theater history, as Gold suggests, the consistent substitution of the relative naturalness of the flashback for the artificiality of the dance makes Sondheim musicals seem less approachable to a general audience than a standard musical. This choice of fantasy vehicle stands outside the norm of the musical tradition, and a cursory review of musicals will confirm that Sondheim musicals, from *Company* forward, consistently use flashback.

Nevertheless, these flashbacks share a trait more commonly associated with dance than with film. In film, the time and location of the flashback are often fixed. In *Double Indemnity,* for example, the narrator (Fred MacMurray, who is talking into a dictating machine) recounts past events with, presumably, no distortion of fact, time, or place. The past is immutable and subject to little or no interpretation. In dance, and particularly in dream ballet sequences, fact, time, and place are blurred. Dance already is a stylized form of movement subject to various readings, and as with dreams, dream ballets distort time and place. Thus, while a film flashback advances the plot by means of concretizing the past and placing it in sharp focus, dance advances the plot by means of allusion and suggestion in soft focus (at best). (I am speaking about flashbacks in the Hollywood film tradition. As I shall explore below, Sondheim musicals borrow also from foreign films, whose use of flashback differs from that of Hollywood, especially the Hollywood of the *films noirs.*)

With the line "The vision's getting blurred," Stella in *Follies* pithily sums up many of the recollections in Sondheim musicals. Verities of time and space are often difficult if not impossible to establish in the flashbacks. When, at their reunion, Stella and her fellow chorines do the Mirror Number (one of the few dance sequences integral to a Sondheim musical), their younger selves also appear and dance with them as their mirror image. Are we witnessing a projection from the imaginations of the older women? Nothing visually or musically has signaled that we have traveled back in time, nor has the space suddenly been transformed into the theater of yesteryear. This uncertainty, this multiple reading that dance permits, occurs in flashbacks as well. Here in *Follies,* dance and flashback conspire together to blur the past, but elsewhere the flashback alone blurs and elucidates simultaneously.

The central flashback in *Passion* illustrates this propensity to blur and elucidate. It is introduced in the present, as the commanding colonel and Giorgio recount the history of Fosca and how the colonel became her guardian. Characters from her past appear—her parents; suitor "Count Ludovic" from Austria; the false count's wife—and elaborate chronologically on Fosca's past. At the same time, Fosca, as we have seen her, comments on her past. What we are experiencing is clearly a flashback (and the score labels it thus), but it violates the Hollywood verities of time and place. At least three locales appear simultaneously (and, given the limitations of the theater, contiguously): the site of the soldiers' walk; the site of Fosca's narration (since she is not seen by the soldiers); and the site of the flashback. As with the chorines projecting their pasts, so here the colonel projects, summoning not only characters from the past but also Fosca from the present to narrate his narration. Additionally, while we are fairly certain that the flashback represents an accurate picture of the past, that past is filled with enough lies and self-delusions that we may believe that the flashback has tinted the past in ways to incline it toward the present. It is not the clear-cut flashback of Hollywood but, rather, a more elastic retelling of the past that, in turn, offers more possibilities for living in the present.

If in *film noir* the flashback underscores the inexorability of fate, in the musicals the flashback simultaneously underscores and undercuts fate. The darkness of the stories may wrongly lead to the conclusion that a sense of fatalism pervades Sondheim's work. The characters make hard choices, which may initially seem futile in a closed universe. That universe, however, is permeable. Characters must choose in the present because the past, in Lawrence Levine's wonderful description, is so unpredictable.[27] Pasts are misremembered; presents are never completely predetermined (even in *Merrily*). Even when events seem unstoppable, there is always another way, another road to take.

These possibilities depend upon the possibility of time being refractory. Nonlinear time is a prominent feature of nearly all Sondheim musicals. Hear his words about *A Little Night Music*.

> Our original concept was that of a fantasy-ridden musical. It was to take place over a weekend during which, in almost game-like fashion, Desirée would have been the prime mover and would work the characters into different situations. The first time, everybody would get

> mixed up, and through farcical situations, would end up with the wrong partner. Then magically, the weekend would start again. The next time, everything worked out, but Henrik committed suicide. The third time, Desirée arranged everything right but this time when she was left alone with Fredrik, he put on his gloves and started to walk off the stage because she hadn't done anything to make him want her.
>
> The way all this worked was that Madame Armfeldt, who was like a witch figure, would reshuffle the pack of cards and time would revert and we'd be back at the beginning of the weekend again. The characters would then re-form, waltz again, and start over. It was all to be presented like a court masque with a music-box quality. But Hugh Wheeler finally gave up on it. He just couldn't make it work to his satisfaction. The show also began differently from the approach of the songs. I saw it as a *darker* Chekhovian musical. Hal didn't and admittedly it was a willful lack of communication on my part. I had already written six songs that were much bleaker, more reflective, almost out of Strindberg, and Hal finally persuaded me that instead of being as dark as Bergman, we should go entirely in reverse. And of course he was right. . . . I usually love to write in dark colors about basic gut feelings, but Hal has a sense of audience that I sometimes lose when I'm writing. He wanted the darkness to peep through a whipped-cream surface. Whipped cream with knives. And, quite simply, I was writing for Bergman's film, not Hugh Wheeler's play.[28]

This quote reveals Sondheim's knowledge of classic theater, and the intersection between his musicals and classic theater needs greater interrogation from scholars.[29] Here, in the discussion of time-play, Sondheim sheds light on his role in encouraging the nonlinear time ("our original concept," but "[Wheeler] just couldn't make it work") and the nature of that use of time ("the first time . . . the next time . . . the third time"; "Madame Armfeldt . . . would reshuffle the pack of cards and time would revert"). This use of time is quite distinct from classic Hollywood *film noir* and finds a model in another strand of film that Sondheim admired, the French *nouvelle vague*.

Before exploring that field of film more fully, consider a second example of the use of time and space in nonlinear ways. If, in *Night Music,* Wheeler was unable to shuttle back and forth along the time-space continuum, Sondheim, in his next musical collaboration, elected to provide an example of such travel, this time with the help of John Weidman, the book writer. Sondheim has repeatedly referred to "Someone in a Tree" *(Pacific Overtures)* as an achievement of which he is particularly proud.[30] No doubt his pride stems in part from the manner in which he handles time and space. The four characters who relate the events of

Commodore Perry's visit to Kanagawa occupy no fewer than three different time planes: (1) the at-the-moment reporting of the Boy in the tree and the Warrior under the Treaty House; (2) the decades-removed recounting of the Old Man (formerly the Boy); and (3) the atemporal comments from the Reciter (i.e., narrator). The song also presents the distortion of memory that occurs over time (in the case of the Old Man), the *Rashomon*-like differences that appear among firsthand observations (in the cases of the Boy and the Warrior), and the cold dismissal of such data in certain analyses (the Reciter). Time plays tricks—sometimes deliberately—with fact.

The characters' locations are similarly difficult to establish. It would have been impossible to see the Warrior at the time the Treaty House was in place; hence, we "see" him "under" an invisible Treaty House. According to the laws of physics, the Old Man and the Boy cannot be in the same location at the same time, although both the Old Man and the Boy talk to the reciter. The Boy and the Warrior (who sings, "I am here") appear to be located at the Treaty House. "I was there," the Old Man says, thus suggesting that neither he nor the Reciter is currently at the original location of the Treaty House. Yet the Old Man also says that the Treaty House was "very near"; the Reciter asks, "Over here?" and the Old Man answers, "Maybe over there." The Warrior also interrupts the other three characters, an act that argues that all four are at the original site of the Treaty House, despite the uncertain location of the Old Man and the Reciter.[31]

On one level, "Someone in a Tree" and *Pacific Overtures* in its entirety parallel the reading of American *film noir* provided by Raymond Borde and Étienne Chaumeton in their *Panorama du film noir américain* (1955), as summarized by James Naremore. The sense of discontinuity (the time-compressed "Please Hello"), the melding of realism and dreamlike states ("There Is No Other Way"), "an anarcho-leftist critique of bourgeois ideology" ("Next"), the eroticization of violence ("Pretty Lady"), and, fundamentally, "a psychological and moral disorientation, an inversion of capitalist and puritan values, as if it were pushing the American system toward revolutionary destruction" (here, the collapse of traditional Japan and the culpability of American values for that collapse): all these elements of *film noir*, as understood by Borde and Chaumeton, are recapitulated in *Pacific Overtures*.[32] Yet, on another level, it is too schematic to suggest that *Pacific Overtures* is a *musicale noire*—the very suggestion appears counterintuitive—or that its components are traceable to this universe of film only. In particular, the handling of time and space, in *Pacific Overtures* and elsewhere, is less realistic and more oneiristic than classic Hollywood *film noir*. The circularity of *Company*, for example, where linear time is obliterated, finds few precursors in American commercial film before 1970. *Assassins* similarly dispenses with linear time, and in *Follies*, *Sunday in the Park with George*, and *Passion*, characters regularly transcend boundaries of time and space. (In this light, *Merrily* is rather staid in its adherence to strict reverse linearity.)

Another strand of film parallels these experiments with time and space.

The *nouvelle vague*

In his "Biographical Dictionary of the French New Wave," Jean Douchet wrote:

> JEAN-LUC GODARD. The quintessential New Wave director, a filmmaker who has made reference (or quotation) one of the pillars of his cinematic style, Godard shows that we live within the disintegration of a civilization forced to navigate among fragments of culture that float around us as the ultimate signs of a world that is disappearing before our eyes.[33]

Douchet's words not only bring to mind the lyrics of "Beautiful" (from *Sunday in the Park with George*), where Seurat's fictionalized mother bemoans the beauty "disappearing as we look." This capsule biography of Godard describes Sondheim as well, who has made reference (or pastiche) a pillar of his compositional method, and whose musicals chart the disintegration of the worlds of individuals, communities, and even nations, all of which are forced (mirroring the coded references to Julian Schnabel, Basquiat, and other artists in act 2 of *Sunday in the Park with George*) to circumnavigate the sea of shit. By now, history has accorded Sondheim the place of a pioneer who initiated a new wave of American musical theater, as much heralded and vilified as were the achievements of the French New Wave in cinema. What historians have not yet established are the parallels between this school of French cinema and Sondheim's art, parallels that find support in Sondheim's love for cinema in general and in his words about the *nouvelle vague* in particular.

Young French film critics of the 1950s, who helped to create the concept of *film noir*, were enamored with the grittier tales that these films told. French essayist and director Éric Rohmer (né Maurice Schérer) observed, "Our immediate predilection tends to be for faces marked with the brand of vice and the neon lights of bars rather than the ones which glow with wholesome sentiments and prairie air."[34] Rohmer is talking about Hollywood film, but a transposition of his remarks to the Broadway musical is apposite, where "wholesome sentiments and prairie air" were staple commodities from *Oklahoma!* to the 1950s, as Siam, San Francisco, and the Austrian-Swiss border became the new prairie in the hands of Rodgers and Hammerstein. As early as *All That Glitters* (1949), though, with its pathetic protagonist, Sondheim began to distance himself from the sunny Hammersteinian view of the world. The comparatively dyspeptic *Anyone Can Whistle* comes into clearer focus in this longer view. As Sondheim said in his remarks about *Night Music,* he likes dark stories. And while his tales may not have the same degree of vice, neon, and booze that Rohmer and his confreres sought out, Sondheim, given the choice, chose *noir*-ish sentiments over wholesome ones.

In addition to the darkness of the tale being told, these French critics also focused on the telling of the tale and on who is doing the telling. For them, *film noir* provided the impetus to advance their idea of a *politique des auteurs*—that, while certain conventions may emerge in a selected group of films, the individual perspective of the director emerges even more clearly when that director's works are viewed *en tout*. Before these postwar French critics articulated their polemic, few writers thought to look beyond the factory-like mentality of the studio system to explore, beyond a handful of *auteurs* (Griffith, Lang, Eisenstein, for example), the impact the director has upon a film. Retrospectively, their critique led to reevaluation of older films, for example, the effect that Howard Hawks had on *The Big Sleep*.[35] Prospectively, they encouraged film directors to create unique cinematic idioms, and as many of these critics went on to become directors themselves, they had ample opportunity to put their polemic to the test. Thus, it is no accident that, as Hollywood *film noir* began to die out after 1955, French filmmakers began to take it in unforeseen directions. Hollywood employed a formula; Paris saw a chance for individuality. "In 1959, Jean-Luc Godard's *Breathless* was released, and [François] Truffaut's *Shoot the Piano Player* soon followed. Both films were fusions of . . . neorealism and surrealist disjunctions; both were littered with references to Bogart, *Gun Crazy*, *On Dangerous Ground*, and so on; and both made *film noir* available as a 'pretext' for directors who wanted to assert their personalities."[36]

Broadway had an analog for the studio versus the *auteur* film. With the success of *Oklahoma!* in 1943, the integrated musical as conceived by Rodgers and Hammerstein quickly became the norm, to such a degree that authorial distinctions, while ever present, become less important than adherence to the new Broadway formula. (The old formula consisted of a loose-limbed plot interspersed with various types of musical comedy song that played to the strengths of the performers, around whom the musicals were usually built.) Old-school Broadway composers, like Berlin and Porter, wrote musicals that follow the new formula (*Annie Get Your Gun* and *Kiss Me, Kate,* respectively). Similarly, younger composers, like Styne (*High Button Shoes, Gentlemen Prefer Blondes, Bells Are Ringing*), Loesser (*Guys and Dolls, The Most Happy Fella*), and Loewe (*Brigadoon, Paint Your Wagon, My Fair Lady*), did their best to imitate the masters. While musicals got darker as the decades passed, the formula of the integrated musical continued to entice composers of Sondheim's own generation (Jerry Bock and Jerry Herman) and beyond (Andrew Lloyd Webber and Claude-Michel Schönberg).

Against this foil of the integrated musical, where traditional and conventional stories are told in traditional and conventional ways, emerges the idea of the concept musical. In its own way, this type of concept musical resembles *film noir,* as heuristic and taxonomic labels mask hermeneutical and cultural problems. The contours of the concept musical, like those of *film noir,* are difficult to establish, and most writing on the genre has failed to rise to the level of *film noir* criticism in its lucidity and persuasiveness. Attempts to write the history of the concept musical similarly resemble the histories of *film noir,* where progenitors of Sondheim's *Company* (1970) are as eagerly posited as are progenitors of John Huston's *The Maltese Falcon* (1941).[37]

Chapter 4 explored Sondheim's disdain for the term *concept musical* and for labels in general. Nevertheless, and at the risk of substituting one label for another, the real contribution of Sondheim and his collaborators is not the *concept musical,* a term that fails to circumscribe their work, but is rather a clear break from the formula musical to the *auteur* musical. One may possibly mistake a Lerner and Loewe musical for a Rodgers and Hammerstein musical; one is far less likely to mistake a Sondheim musical for anything else. The way the tale is told makes it unique. And in spite of the variety of collaborators with whom he has worked, the consistency of the musicals gives credence to the term "Sondheim musical."

Here we turn once again to the French *auteurs* of the 1950s and 1960s. At that time, the Broadway musical had not yet caught up to what Hollywood was doing, and Hollywood had not yet caught up with the *auteur*-driven French New Wave. *Nouvelle vague* directors were using a cinematic language that was consciously breaking new ground. Alain Resnais complained about the hidebound attitudes of older filmmakers (mostly French, but also American), who believed that the "grammar of film is complete; nothing new can be invented. Maybe we can change some things about the story or about the character, but from the point of view of form, of editing, everything has already been done—nothing new can ever be done."[38] Resnais invented new grammars of form and editing (*montage*, a word that appears on occasion in Sondheim's work, e.g., *Follies*), and had done so as early as his trailblazing documentary, *Night and Fog* (1955), where he juxtaposed past and present in ways that force the past onto the present. Peter Cowie remarked that "Resnais is a director who expresses emotions in his work *through* the montage and composition of the individual shots."[39] Consider the end of the narration for *Night and Fog*, written and spoken by Jean Cayrol, a survivor of the Holocaust: "[T]hose of us who pretend to believe that all this happened long ago, and in another country, who never think to look around us, who never hear the cry that never ends . . ."[40] Without question, a homicidal barber or a gang of presidential killers pales in comparison with the enormity of the Holocaust. Even so, the story of man's inhumanity to man is never far from the more politically engaged musicals *(Anyone Can Whistle*, *Pacific Overtures*, *Sweeney*, and *Assassins)*. Moreover, in keeping with the idea of montage and composition as conduits for emotion, nearly all Sondheim musicals pit the past against the present in ways that are unforeseen by the audience (and the characters in the story) but that, bit by bit, come together. This is yet another resonance with the language of the *nouvelle vague*.

French New Wave directors additionally adopted the *film noir* device of narration and adapted it reflexively. I have already noted the presence of narration in Sondheim musicals and its dual indebtedness to Hammerstein and *film noir*. Comparing the way that narration was used in the latter with its use by the *nouvelle vague*, Jean Douchet noted,

> Narration no longer whispers confidences; it comments for real. It describes (places, journeys, characters), analyzes the action, judges and measures conduct. It sees different things and sees them differently than the image. The New Wave based its dramaturgy, its sense of action, on this duality. Action was displaced, and no longer resided in the sequence of events unfolding on screen but in the reality of their unfolding, the "how" of their development. . . . Narration introduced criticism—an environment most of the New Wave directors were familiar with—as a means of driving the narrative forward.[41]

The tone of narration in Sondheim musicals is likewise critical. The narrator sees things in the present that the characters—and, at times, the audience—cannot (or will not) see and warns both characters and audience of likelihoods in the future (e.g., when the Narrator, at the end of act 1 of *Into the Woods*, interjects, "To be continued"). The narrator controls the story, reshaping action as necessary (e.g., the Liebeslieder Singers cause Fredrik to remember his past affair with Desirée or the Reciter-as-emperor acts as deus ex machina at the end of *Pacific Overtures*). The narrator does not shrink from taking sides, uttering opinions that vary in range from dazed incredulity (e.g., "How did you ever get there from here?" in *Merrily*) to bitter rebuke (e.g., "Damn you, Booth" in *Assassins*). Given the ubiquity of narration in Sondheim musicals, its relative dissimilarity to the "passive" narration of *film noir* (cf. *Double Indemnity* or *Detour*), and its greater similarity to the "active" narration of the *nouvelle vague* (cf. *Breathless* or *L'Année dernière à Marienbad*), these musicals amalgamate Hammersteinian, *film noir*, and *nouvelle vague* elements into a unique narrative style.

The uniqueness of this style is most apparent when characters talk back to the narrator, a rare feature in the bodies of work mentioned above but a regular one in Sondheim musicals. The confrontations between characters and narrator jeopardize the narrative as the characters hear and question the narrator's critical stance. In both *Into the Woods* and *Assassins*—original works (i.e., not adaptations from a previous source) that do not share book writers, directors, or producers—the characters eject the narrator and "rewrite" the narrative. Despite sharing the same dramatic coup, the two musicals proceed in dramatically distinct manners. The remainder of *Woods* unfolds as an improvisation of sorts; *Assassins*, in contrast, supplants the uplifting story of the Balladeer (i.e., narrator) with the assassins' conspiracy of confederacy.[42]

Even in the musicals where narrators are unidentified or disguised, characters often abruptly redirect narrative flow. In imitation of a director, Bobby (of *Company*) yells "Stop!" All activity ceases. Then, as though they represented the creative minds behind the story, the characters collectively shape the denouement. (Banfield gives an extremely insightful reading into the four songs Sondheim wrote for this moment,[43] and the songs themselves and their various shadings are analogous to alternative endings in a film.) By way of another example, the four main characters in *Follies* confront the ghostly commentary that has haunted them throughout the show. They argue with their past selves in an electrifying moment of time-space discontinuity that dissolves into Loveland, a place (in the original version of the song) where "time stops" and the month of June—the traditional month for weddings and thus for love—has seven hundred days. And after "It's Hot Up Here" (in *Sunday*), the "painting" breaks both its two-dimensional surface and the fourth wall by stepping forward and addressing the audience.

These moments parallel developments in the French New Wave, but alone they provide inconclusive evidence that the *nouvelle vague* influenced Sondheim. Only in retrospect can we appreciate the originality of the French New Wave directors. Similarly, Sondheim's indebtedness to them comes with hindsight. In 1998, I asked Sondheim whether he had a sense then of what the next reformation in musical theater might be. In one of his most expansive and revealing responses, Sondheim showed the breadth of his knowledge and the acuity of his thinking, and his response included a description of another reformation that seemed, upon reflection, to affect him profoundly.

> Overview is something you do later. It's always post-. . . . [T]here are shows that are originals and there are shows that are dead ends in and of themselves, because they respond only to the requirements—as *West Side Story* does—of that particular story. *Company* is a way of looking at story as an abstract idea. That is to say: How about telling a story this way—not chronologically, but a series of moments that contribute to an overall arch. That's one way of telling a story. And, incidentally, you know, it can even follow post-modernism in the novel and paintings and that sort of stuff. It's a kind of abstract—I won't say expression—but abstractness.
>
> But the theater's always way behind other arts, as you know, because it takes so long to get a show on. So, by the time you paint your fabulous painting that opens up our eyes [in] a new way, and I write a show saying, "Hey, I saw this great painting; I know what to do with the show," it's two years later, by which time you've painted something that goes a whole other direction. . . .
>
> Movies can follow a little quicker, but you know, the *nouvelle vague* is, if you look at it in terms of its place in the art of the last part of the 20th century, it's behind the fact. . . . In movies it was a new idea; in novels, it was not. And it's not a coincidence that a lot of the *nouvelle vague* stuff used novels by Marguerite Duras and Alain Robbe-Grillet, because they'd been doing this stuff before. A novel, you just write it and it goes in. A painting's even quicker. . . . It took how many years for "Les Demoiselles" to echo itself in other arts, because Picasso could just go "Slash!," . . . and there it is right in front of you.
>
> So, where musicals are going is for an overview. I don't know if they're going any particular place. What's nice about it is that (as far as I can tell) virtually all the categorical rules have been broken, torn

down and dissolved. And so, if you sit down and write a musical today, there's virtually nothing you have to avoid. In subject matter, in form, in tone, in the relationship of the music to the book, in terms of whether it's an "opera" (meaning that it requires a sort of an operatic sensibility), or it's . . . country-western or whatever it is. It seems to me the barriers are down.[44]

Though he here defined postmodernism as a direction to follow, Sondheim nevertheless adopted a postmodernist sensibility for the musical of the late twentieth century.

Beyond the catholicity of Sondheim's vision for musical theater in these remarks, the casual manner in which he introduced French cinema is nothing short of revelatory. Earlier in the interview, he referred to the great film composers of the 1930s, 1940s, and 1950s—Franz Waxman, Max Steiner, and especially Bernard Herrmann—as well as John Williams's double-bass theme of *Jaws* and its reappearance in *Saturday Night Live* skits.[45] In the context of the interview, these comments come as no surprise, as Sondheim was explicitly talking about film music. In contrast, his comments about the *nouvelle vague* arose in the context of innovation in the visual and performing arts; there was no necessary reason for him to introduce it into the conversation. Moreover, the matter-of-fact references to Duras and Robbe-Grillet are revealing, given that Sondheim by his own confession was not a reader and that not all of the novels of these two writers were widely circulated in English translations at the time the *nouvelle vague* made a splash in the film world.[46] He treats the two authors as though they were household names, when in fact they remain known primarily to a coterie of literary and cinematic enthusiasts. At a minimum, these remarks refine his other remarks in which he suggested that, around the mid-1950s, he lost all interest in Hollywood film. The naturalness of his discussion here suggests that, while the post-studio film industry may have wearied him, he remained interested in film after the mid-1950s. Sondheim's decision to base a musical—*Passion* (1994)—on Ettore Scola's 1981 film *Passione d'amore* also calls into question his professed noninterest in film post-1960.

Like other younger members of the French New Wave, Duras and Robbe-Grillet moved from writing to directing. Their success as directors was limited, however, and Douchet, in his comprehensive book, says little about either artist as director.

> Alain Robbe-Grillet, one of the best known practitioners of the nouveau roman, was the first writer, after Cocteau, to attempt to use cine-

> matic means to write with film . . . Robbe-Grillet made *L'Immortelle* in 1962, then in a succession of films, yielded to an increasing simplistic representation of his obsessions and fantasies. Unwittingly, Robbe-Grillet demonstrated that literary and cinematic style are unrelated. . . . Working with very little money, Duras created a written body of work intended for the screen. Her films are "modern" and ultimately very New Wave.[47]

Contrary to Sondheim's assertion, not many of their novels were adapted as films, and most of those films had little impact on the larger universe of the New Wave.[48] As screenwriters, however, Duras and Robbe-Grillet had a signal influence, and Sondheim's naming of them seems to identify them less as novelists and more as screen playwrights. Both authors had a profound effect on the *nouvelle vague* through their collaborations with Alain Resnais, whose first two feature-length films—*Hiroshima mon amour* (1959) and *Last Year at Marienbad* (1961)—had screenplays by Duras and Robbe-Grillet, respectively. I would suggest that these two screenwriters function as semantic placeholders and that, to Sondheim, one of the truly creative forces of the *nouvelle vague*—and thus on Sondheim's reimagining of the Broadway musical—is Resnais.

Alain Resnais

Of course, the pairing of Resnais and Sondheim makes sense prospectively. In 1974, Resnais released his sixth feature-length film, *Stavisky* . . . , with a soundtrack by Sondheim; this, the composer's first-ever film score and the only extended one he would ever write, was, in Sondheim's words quoted earlier, one of the "best writing experiences" he had ever had.[49] Resnais talked about Sondheim's work and music in an interview with Richard Seaver. Resnais lived in New York City in the early 1970s, and as he recovered from the artistic and financial failure of his fifth feature-length film, *Je t'aime, je t'aime* (1968), he became a Sondheim fanatic.

> RESNAIS: I've always wanted to do a film with [Charles] Boyer, whom I greatly admire. In fact, [screenplay author Jorge] Semprun said, "All Resnais wants to do is make a film starring [Jean-Paul] Belmondo and Boyer, with music by Stephen Sondheim. He couldn't care less what the subject is, so long as he has those three

elements in it." He's exaggerating, of course, but there's a kernel of truth there. . . .[50]

Q.: . . . Can we talk a little about the music? How you decided on Sondheim, and why?

RESNAIS: That's a question the film's producer, Alexandre Mnouchkine, asked me more than once: "Alain, why make things more complicated than they already are? Why do you have to have an American composer for a French film? And, to boot, someone who has never written any music for films before?"

I knew all Sondheim's music, but the deeper I got into the Stavisky, the more I knew his music was perfect. I remembered in particular one scene in *Follies* that has always remained with me: a scene that begins in gaiety and high spirits, with John McMartin in white tuxedo and top hat singing and dancing, a scene full of joy and hope, when all of a sudden the music deteriorates, the lighting turns funereal, the girls collapse and dissolve, and he, McMartin, can no longer remember the words or music. It's devastating, a scene I've never forgotten. The worm in the apple, death in the midst of life. For essentially that's the story of Stavisky: a man condemned to death, fully aware of it, yet madly in love with life. In the middle of preparing the shooting script I picked up the phone from Paris and called Sondheim in New York.[51]

. . . To give you an idea how important Sondheim's music was to me, when writing the shooting script I conceived certain key scenes rhythmically, in terms of his music. And on the first day of shooting, I had my tape recorder handy, with key passages of *A Little Night Music* constantly in my ear, to make sure that the rhythm of the scene coincided with Sondheim's music. That involved the speed with which the actors walked, Baron Raoul's gestures, the whole scene with the white airplane outside Biarritz.[52]

One may question whether Resnais knew *all* of Sondheim's music that had been published or recorded by 1974, but he clearly knew "Life, Laugh, Love" from *Follies*. There, McMartin's character, Ben Stone, crumbles in the middle of the number and precipitates a personal and theatrical meltdown where "everything we've seen and heard all evening is going on at once, as if the night's experience were being vomited."[53] One can also appreciate Resnais's perspicacity in recognizing the consistency of Sondheim's music from one show to the next. Given the 1930s mise-en-scène of *Stavisky* . . . , one might have expected Resnais to limit his listening to the interwar "American" sound world of *Follies* rather than the fin de siècle "European" sound world of *Night Music*. (As

I have already suggested in chapter 1, *Night Music* is consistent with Sondheim's overall musical language; English-speaking commentators have read too much Old World ambience and nostalgia into the score.)[54]

Resnais made Sondheim's work on *Stavisky . . .* easy. He sent Sondheim a videotape of the film, allowing the composer to work from his home rather than spend valuable time in an editing room. According to James Monaco, "When Resnais and Sondheim first looked at the film together, the director's careful attention to the structure of the music paid off. They were in complete agreement where the music should begin and end."[55] Given Sondheim's reputation on Broadway as a difficult composer for audiences to grasp, it is amusing to read Monaco's assessment that *Stavisky . . .*, "Resnais's most successful film to date at the box office . . . even has a successful soundtrack album, certainly a first for Resnais."[56]

Monaco continues with an observation that, likely unbeknownst to him, implicated Sondheim as well as Resnais. "Yet, surprisingly, despite all these obvious commercial elements [including Belmondo and Boyer as stars], it is still quite clearly a film by Alain Resnais, the director of *Marienbad*, *Muriel*, *Je t'aime*, and all those cerebral 'art' films of the sixties. It is specious to think that a film can't be intellectually complex just because it is popular."[57] Indeed, when the complexities of the Sondheim musicals of the seventies and beyond are bracketed by the French New Wave films on one side and by Sondheim's own comments about the *nouvelle vague* on the other, the influence of the French New Wave upon Sondheim virtually establishes itself. Sondheim trafficked in a popular medium and yet brought to it an intellectual severity, a *politique d'auteur*, and even a manner of visualization that resemble Resnais's films in particular. A further exploration of French New Wave criticism strengthens the linkage between the two *auteurs* that extends beyond (and began before) *Stavisky. . . .*

Writers disagree about the importance of *Hiroshima mon amour* and *Last Year in Marienbad*, Resnais's first two feature-length films. Douchet begins his biographical entry on Resnais by stating unequivocally, "*Hiroshima mon amour* (1959) remains one of the three landmark films of the New Wave,"[58] whereas Leo Bersani asserts that "*Hiroshima* is Resnais' weakest film" and attributes its failure to Duras's bourgeois romance at the center of the film.[59] Bersani goes on to say that *Marienbad* "may strike us as a decadent period piece,"[60] and in a review, Peter Baker remarked that *Marienbad* "is to be enjoyed like a beautifully printed book. But it is a limited edition, with little to say to the vast majority of readers."[61] Contrast these comments with those of Monaco and John Ward, who find in *Marienbad* a work of such startling originality that it upsets the entire tradition of film.[62] These critical disagreements eerily parallel the arguments that greeted Sondheim's first two mature shows—*Company* (1970) and *Follies* (1971). Were the shows theatrical breakthroughs or brilliant exercises in a decaying genre? The critics were mixed.[63] Add to these critical similarities the coincidence that Resnais and Sondheim created their works in their late thirties; Resnais was born in 1922, and Sondheim started to work on what would become *Follies* when he was thirty-five and eventually set it aside to finish *Company*. In the case of both men, their work reoriented their respective disciplines, and for much the same reasons.

As Sondheim pointed out, before *Company*, not many musicals had sought to tell a tale in a nonlinear fashion, "a series of moments that contribute to an overall arch." The same could be said about cinema: prior to Resnais, not many films had sought to make the fracture of time and space an organizing principle. In the early films of Godard (*Breathless*, 1960; *A Woman Is a Woman*, 1961) and François Truffaut (*The 400 Blows*, 1959; *Shoot the Piano Player*, 1960; and *Jules and Jim*, 1962), linear story lines predominate, and flashbacks (when they occur) are lengthy (as in the central episode in *Shoot the Piano Player*). Thus, time-space discontinuity is not a paramount feature of the French New Wave. It is, however, a paramount feature of Resnais's films, where nonlinearity frequently occurs (most famously in *Marienbad* but also from *Night and Fog* through to *Mon oncle d'Amérique*, 1980) and where short flashbacks and quick cutaways constantly disrupt the sense of time and space. In his extended essay that attempts to link Resnais's sensibility of time and space to that of the French philosopher Henri Bergson, Ward may overstate the correspondences between the two, as Resnais has explicitly distanced himself from the philosopher.[64] Even so, Ward's description of Resnais's style—"Rapid cutting to correspond to involuntary memory and imagination, over-exposure, overlapping dialogue to portray the connections between two scenes in the protagonist's mind, off-screen narration to represent interior monologue"[65]—resembles Bergson's handling of time and space, most notably in the value placed upon intuition and free association, both characteristics of the stream-of-consciousness movement.

> Bergson must be considered as one of the progenitors of the stream of consciousness novel, surrealism and Sartrean Existentialism. . . . Rejection of intellect in favor of life and experience, particularly mental life which is characterized by its continuity and its susceptibility to

intuitive understanding, is neatly compatible with the belief that through dreams, drugs or automatic response we can arrive at some deeper awareness of ourselves.[66] The external world represents a threat to man's personal identity. Intelligence is powerless to defend this; so we must turn inward to discover the vitality of our lives. And when we do so we shall find impulses, ideas and symbols which will at first confuse us but which, as we come to be more familiar with them, will form patterns and meanings which make up our true selves.[67]

Intellect organizes life neatly according to clock time. Still, we experience life messily according to "the mental time of interior monologue, streamed consciousness and associated ideas."[68] Intellect is articulate, while impulses, ideas, and symbols initially confuse. Resnais, who is unquestionably intelligent, chooses to focus upon the messy and confusing nature of real life. He "treats film time as a completely malleable material, rather than following a strict and literal narrative line."[69] He "work[s] within an internal temporality where a future nourished on the memory of the past shapes a hypothetical present in which every encounter is part of the infinite play of possibilities, and becomes a simple element of chance that moves the pawns on the board."[70] His films are visually and narratively confusing, requiring work on the part of the viewer to make sense of the whole. They resist simple descriptions and the traditional linearity one expects from cinematic storytelling. They especially emphasize "the Bergsonian dilemma of the tension between the tenses," where "the past impregnates the present" and the past and present collide, often with tragic results.[71] That past intrudes upon the present and, at times, threatens to disrupt the present altogether through its dogged visual interference. Indeed, linearity is impossible, as the past and the present at times become inseparable (as in *Marienbad* or the first two acts of *Providence* [1976]) and memory is false (e.g., *Muriel, ou le temps d'un retour* [1963] is "more about the lives people imagine that they lead rather than the ones they do").[72]

These narrative and visual techniques find cognates in the narratives and characters that inhabit Sondheim musicals. "Two lovers are drawn together by their memories and at the same time are separated by them. They both have a need to remember and yet also a need to forget." Thus Ward described the central characters in *Hiroshima mon amour*,[73] but he could have been describing Fredrik and Desirée *(Night Music)* or the scene in *Follies* where Ben thinks he is singing to Sally—and Sally thinks he is singing to her—yet he holds Young Sally, the physical representation of his memory, in his arms and thus separates himself from present-

day Sally ("Too Many Mornings"). Many of Sondheim's characters actively resist the reality of the external world. Just as Perry's ships are an illusion to the priests in *Pacific Overtures,* so is the physical world an illusion to many of the characters in a Sondheim musical. They retreat into the false continuity they impose upon the present through their projection of the past onto the present.

Follies is one of the most persistent of the musicals in developing this idea of projection, so it is no wonder that, in his review of the original Broadway production, theater critic T. E. Kalem invoked the name of someone who, like Bergson, played with time, space, and memory. "[It is] the first Proustian musical—an act of dramatic creation even more daring than making a Proustian film."[74] Film critic Stefan Kanfer picked up the same thread in his review of Éric Rohmer's *Claire's Knee* (1970; United States, 1971). "Modern French films have risen from Proust's *Remembrance* [which] is clustered with optical allusions, accounts of the distortions of love in the fourth dimension of time. In its way it was the end of a line that could not be continued on the page—that needed the liberation of the camera."[75] (Or, as Kalem suggests, the liberation of the stage.)

Memory's distortions can corrupt the present. "If our memory deceives us about the past, and our memory of the past forges our present, then not only will our past be an illusion but our present also."[76] If one objects to calling the present illusory or corrupt, certainly it is fluid, as George recognizes after his encounter with an illusion of the past at the end of *Sunday in the Park with George:* "white, a blank page or canvas . . . so many possibilities."

Past memories affect present conceptions of space as well as time. In the same ways that "Someone in a Tree" plays with physical space, so do the examples above from *Follies* and *Sunday in the Park with George.* When, in the title song from the latter, Dot escapes from her dress and muses about artists in general and George in particular, she has also escaped from the spatial and visual plane that George occupies. She has already complained that he does not look at *her,* does not *see* her, and during her fantasy sequence in the middle of the song, he clearly fails to "see" what we in the audience see: the visible representation of Dot's interior thoughts. This sequence resembles a cinematic flashback, in that it steps out of the clear linearity of the story. Unlike a flashback, though, the fantasy occurs at the same time as the linear story, that is, simultaneously with George sketching Dot. It unites two spatially unrelated activities in a fashion that resembles the split screen of film, a technique that is Resnais-like in spirit if not in actual practice. As with the multiple approaches into A's boudoir near the end of *Marienbad,* where Delphine Seyrig turns again and again in an overexposed image that amounts to an ecstatic embrace of the camera, so Dot disrupts the conventions of physical space by cavorting across the stage. The effect is dizzying in both instances; in the musical, it is not only Dot who feels like fainting, but the viewer also is disoriented, thrust into a vertiginous world (corroborated by the coruscating music) that disappears when Dot returns to the dress and allows herself to be swallowed up by banality.

It is impossible to say precisely how, and to what degree, Resnais's work influenced Sondheim's. It could simply be that the two of them happened upon similar dramatic solutions to similar dramatic situations. The guests at Marienbad—who wear formal dress, who are often frozen in place as if they were props as much as humans, and who attend a play within the context of their coming together—bear a striking resemblance to the Liebeslieder Singers of *Night Music,* who wear formal dress, freeze the action around them rather than are frozen by it, and attend a play within a play. Even before *Night Music,* the "live mannequins" of the television musical, *Evening Primrose* (1966), echo the people in *Marienbad,* including their donning of formal dress at the end. Resnais's tendency to accelerate the intersections of past and present in the second half of his films *(Marienbad, Muriel, Stavisky . . .)* is paralleled in similar accelerations in *Follies, Night Music,* and *Sunday in the Park with George,* all musicals where time-space discontinuities abound. Resnais's films also end inconclusively. Does Marianne meet Diego in Barcelona and warn him in time *(La guerre est finie* [1966]*)*? What happens to René after he recovers from his failed suicide attempt *(Mon oncle d'Amérique)*? Do Bernard and Hélène thrive, and does Simone find Alphonse *(Muriel)*? And these are the films whose narrative structures are relatively clear; *Hiroshima* and *Marienbad* resist any attempts toward definitive conclusions, let alone interpretations. In similar ways, many Sondheim musicals end without ending; they conclude with question marks *(Sweeney, Assassins)* or ellipses *(Pacific Overtures, Passion)* more often than with periods. And the sense of montage in Sondheim musicals—skillful editing that interleaves material in novel and unexpected ways—exhibits the same sensibility that Resnais brings to film.

Sondheim clearly announced his love of Resnais at Telluride. "I'm a big fan of the early stuff, particularly *Muriel* but also . . . [Mitchell tried to assist Sondheim and suggested *Last Year at Marienbad.*] Yeah, that, and—what's the other one?—*La guerre est finie.*"[77] With such a clear preference for *Muriel,* the preceding discussion of Resnais's first two feature-length films may seem misplaced. But consider Monaco's remarks.

> In *Muriel, ou le temps d'un retour* everything comes together for Alain Resnais, and the experiments of the first two feature films pay off. *Muriel* shares with its predecessors a fascination with the phenomenon of memory and imagination; and like *Hiroshima* and *Marienbad* it situates its examination of the world of the mind in a geographical place which has its own concrete significance and which serves, in addition, as the locus for states of mind. But it is notable that the title of this, Resnais's third feature, is not as the previous pattern would indicate, "Boulogne." *Muriel* is named for a person, not a place; for the first time Resnais find a cinematic key that allows a human and deeply-felt emotional dimension. Characters are no longer identified by pronouns and algebraic symbols; they're allowed to live. They are liberated for the first time, no longer plot- and theme-ridden but free to "do things we don't approve of."[78]

Resnais honed his style of cinematic storytelling in the first two films and used it in novel ways in *Muriel*, *La guerre est finie* (which followed *Muriel*), and later films, such as *Providence* (1976), *Mon oncle d'Amérique* (1980), and *Same Old Song* (1999).

Bersani felt that *Muriel*, more than Resnais's first two films, was the breakthrough, and Bersani's comments on time and memory in the film not only reinforce the ideas outlined above but also point in the direction of Sondheim and illuminate why Sondheim may have "particularly" liked *Muriel*.

> *Muriel* . . . gives us characters unable to move ahead unless they somehow come to terms with their past, a past that is at once personal and collective. Consequently, the relation to the past is formulated as a question about the future: what kind of memory is necessary in order to move forward in time? . . . For all the characters in *Muriel* (except perhaps Françoise), going ahead seems to depend on being able to go back. . . . Once the past has been safely sequestered in its own intelligibility, they will be able to step into time again and recommence their lives.[79]

Taken together, Monaco and Bersani describe the characters in a Sondheim musical who are wedded to place (such as an old theater or Japan or an island in the middle of Paris), are liberated enough to transgress (e.g., sexual violation, murder, commercial compromise, filial abandonment), and must explore and conquer the past in order to move hesitantly into the future (e.g., the importance of the flashback). One need only substitute *Night Music* for *Muriel* to imagine that Monaco is describing the Sondheim musical here. "[It] is concretely a matter of comings and goings, small talk, dead time, quickly-eaten meals, aimless strolls, missed opportunities, compulsive entertainments, conversations with blunt ends, doors, open spaces, half-forgotten and mis-remembered pasts. It is more about forgetting than remembering, more about the lives people imagine that they lead rather than the ones they do."[80] And Monaco's criticism of the film—that "due to the masterful technique of the film, our attention is still more attracted to the teller than the tale"[81]—further explains Sondheim's fascination with a film that, with its almost one thousand different shots, exudes craft.

Though Sondheim expressed his appreciation for the visual aspects of Resnais, there are also similarities between the musical lives of these two *auteurs*. Resnais was not a musician himself, but he often spoke in musical terms about his work. "I'm not musical, I don't know how to write a score, but I should very much like to, if I could."[82] He was indebted to the music of Stravinsky and used "things like *The Firebird*" to accompany silent films.[83] Resnais also drew parallels between his first two feature-length films and music that are startling.

> I know nothing about musical composition but if it implies having a theme and building variations and counterpoints then this is quite true [about my work]. I think that if you analyzed *Hiroshima* with a diagram on graph paper you would witness something close to a quartet. Themes, variations on the first movement, from these repetitions and flashbacks which some people find insufferable and which besides may well be so for those who do not enter into the game. The last movement of the film is a slow movement, a decrescendo.[84]

Marienbad is "a musical comedy, without songs, that tries to deepen the forces of reverie."[85] In *Providence*, he had "arranged a quintet where Ellen Burstyn would be the violin, Dirk Bogarde the piano, David Warner would be the viola, Gielgud the cello and Elaine Stritch the double bass. In short, a group à la Schubert [cf. the "Trout" Quintet], although the internal sonority of the film was closer to Alban Berg or Bartók with its sudden breaks, its alternations between bitter and sweet."[86] With these views of music, it is easy to understand how Resnais worked with composers like Henze and Penderecki and why, once he found a kindred spirit in Sondheim, he did not hesitate to call Sondheim and offer him *Stavisky*. . . .[87]

If Sondheim had been reading about Resnais in the 1960s, he would have come across these references to musicality, and not only from Resnais's lips (found in Armes's 1968 book on Resnais). In *Antonioni, Bergman, Resnais* from 1963, Peter Cowie wrote,

The editing of *L'année dernière* seems deliberately to have been conducted along musical lines. Like a sonata, the film consists of a theme and variations; like a fugue, it could be defined as a polyphonic composition in which a short melodic subject is introduced by one of the parts and successively taken up by the others, thereafter forming the main material of the texture.[88]

He would have discovered Resnais's love of and indebtedness to Chester Gould, the creator of the *Dick Tracy* comic strip,[89] another node between Resnais and Sondheim, although it was Warren Beatty who drew Sondheim into Gould's universe on the 1990 film. Resnais, like Sondheim, once tried his hand at acting and gave it up because he wasn't good enough.[90] And while Resnais apparently was not into games the way that Sondheim was, the recurrent match game in *Marienbad* must have intrigued Sondheim, just as Resnais's comments about the "game" of *Hiroshima* would find sympathy with Sondheim the puzzler.

These suggestions are more than speculations. With his comments on the *nouvelle vague,* Sondheim invited the comparison of *Company*—and, by extension, his mature works—with the *nouvelle vague* as breakthroughs of similar magnitude. Those comments also stretch the time frame of his interest in film into the 1960s. His implicit invocation of Resnais (through naming Duras and Robbe-Grillet), his explicit naming of favorite Resnais films at Telluride, and his later work with Resnais create the possibility that he may have read up on Resnais in the 1960s, for if his knowledge of film was at one time encyclopedic, it follows that he did more than see the films of the French New Wave filmmakers.

I repeat these observations to advance what truly is a speculation: that the idea of *Sunday in the Park with George* finds a parallel inspiration in the work of Resnais generally and French film broadly. Early on for that musical, "Sondheim and [James] Lapine met once a week to talk through some ideas. They became interested in the notion of a show made up of a theme and variations, rather than one with a linear story."[91] The similarity between Craig Zadan's description and Resnais's remarks is coincidental, although the decision to write a nonlinear musical is telling. Over the course of their meetings, Lapine told Sondheim about Gertrude Stein's poem "Photograph," which he adapted for the stage and in which he used photographs of famous paintings. At some point,

Jim said, "Do you know Seurat's painting *A Sunday Afternoon on the Island of La Grande Jatte*?" And we realized that that painting was the setting of a play. All the people in that painting when you start speculating on why none of them are looking at each other . . . and maybe

> there's a reason for that . . . maybe someone was having an affair with another one, or one was related to someone else. And then Jim said, "Of course, the main character's missing." And I said, "Who?" And he said, "The artist." And once he said that, I knew there was a real play there. Once you get the idea that the artist has manipulated these people into this farcical afternoon they're having in which they're all pretending to be all pulled together, strolling apart, when actually all their passions are all over the place.[92]

Clearly, Lapine had brought his experience to the table, and Sondheim took to his concept.

Yet the idea of building a piece around a painter had also enticed Resnais. His first two documentaries (and, hence, his first two professional films) were on painters—*Van Gogh* (1948) and *Gauguin* (1950)—and his third documentary was on a painting: *Guernica* (1950). Given the limited distribution of those films, it is unlikely that Sondheim saw them. Even so, had he read Armes's book, he would have known about Resnais's three films.

> [*Van Gogh*] is not art criticism or scientific biography but "an attempt to tell the imaginary life of a painter through his painting" [Resnais]. . . . In its externals, [*Gauguin*] tells much the same story as *Van Gogh:* another journey undertaken by a painter in search of himself, his style and the sun, which again led to disappointment. . . . Whereas the works of Van Gogh and Gauguin were fused to make a single whole, in the film *Guernica* one painting is broken down into jagged, isolated fragments, each representing an image of suffering.[93]

And French film as a corpus is filled with films on painters, painting, and particular paintings.[94] *Sunday in the Park with George* shares correspondences with Resnais's aesthetic. Might the existence of this body of French films—"motion pictures"—about art and artists have encouraged Sondheim to consider making a theater piece—a hyperactive tableau vivant—in the same vein?

The last reel

Resnais has said, "For a film to interest me, it must have an experimental side."[95] For Herbert Ross's 1976 movie *The Seven-Per-Cent Solution*, Sondheim wrote "The Madam's Song" (as it is listed in the film's cred-

its). The setting is the parlor of an 1890s Viennese brothel. The camera focuses on the proprietress regaling her clients with three bawdy tales of her sexual exploits: one, with a captain of the guard and his St. Bernard; a second, with a baron who enjoyed sadomasochism; the last, with an abbot fond of entwining religious imagery and sex. The tales are all salacious—Sondheim's lyrics are deliciously scandalous—and are tossed off with insouciance by the madam, who celebrates the fact that, as she says, "I Never Do Anything Twice" (the name by which the song is known). Sondheim has said pretty much the same thing as the madam and Resnais. "I have always conscientiously tried not to do the same thing twice. If you're broken-field running, they can't hit you with so many tomatoes. . . . Being a maverick isn't just about being different. It's about having your vision of the way a show might be."[96]

Despite the constant invention that Sondheim invests in his shows, they share some common dramatic vistas. Indeed, the quest for invention sets Sondheim apart from his predecessors. He learned his craft from Hammerstein and borrowed liberally from film. Yet, he did so with no desire to follow a formula or intention to create a new one. Rather, he felt the freedom to establish his dramatic persona, to speak musically and dramatically in his own voice. What sets Sondheim apart from those who came before him—and from most of his peers and successors—is that he was the first American musical theater composer to do more than provide the score. Throughout his career, he has behaved like an *auteur*, and the unity of his musicals attests to the accuracy of calling him an *auteur*. He did not write book musicals or concept musicals; he wrote Sondheim musicals.

Trying to determine who deserves the designation of *auteur* can easily resemble the struggle of determining which musicals merit the designation of "concept musical." In collaborative work, identifying the person(s) who created and maintained the consistency of the "world" we see in a show is done in hindsight. In the case of *West Side Story*, for example, where dance was integral to the original conception and remains integral in revivals, Jerome Robbins is as much the *auteur* as is Bernstein. And Sondheim's comments about collaboration, with his talk of mutual subsuming and satisfying integration, make it clear that he refuses to take sole credit for the look of a show.[97]

But reticence and self-abasement are as much a Sondheim signature as are many of the musical, theatrical, and cinematic markers identified thus far. After having celebrated the idea that writers of musicals can establish their distinct styles, can "ride madly off in all directions," Sondheim continued his musings about the history of musical theater.

> You know, I think to be a young writer now [in 1998], from that point of view, is terrific. From other points of view, it isn't so terrific. Practical and financial and opportunity and that sort of thing. But, from freedom to say what you want to say, in the way you want to say it: boy, you can do anything. And that's been true, you know, for thirty years. As soon as *Hair* came out, and everybody said "Fuck" and "Shit," you thought, "All right . . . groovy."[98]

Sondheim's modesty comes through in his attribution of importance. Many believed that *Hair* would be the breakthrough musical. Time has shown otherwise. The *auteur* concept has proven to be the formula (inasmuch as one can call individuality a formula), and other younger composers—William Finn, Michael John LaChiusa, Jason Robert Brown, Adam Guettel, even Andrew Lloyd Webber—have Sondheim, not *Hair,* to thank for showing them the way. Banfield asked, "Might Broadway's recent history [i.e., the "poperettas" of Lloyd Webber and Boublil/Schönberg] have been different had Sondheim chosen to persevere with a role for himself as overall *auteur* rather than go along with the collaborative model that he has helped to further?"[99] The presumption here is that being an *auteur* and being a collaborator must be mutually exclusive. Sondheim musicals—and the musicals of those who have learned from him—argue otherwise. His dramatic influences are many, and their effects regularly turn up in his work at Williams as well as in his most recent "musical play." Mielziner wrote, "All of us working on a production—designer, producer, actor, composer, lyricist, choreographer—are spokes in a wheel. The hub is the dramatist."[100] Without denigrating any of his fellow spokes, especially the book authors and directors, Sondheim is the hub of his musicals. He was one of the first collaborative *auteurs,* unmistakably a team player and unmistakably original.

Sondheim's relationship to drama and cinema remains complex. Ibsen, Chekhov, Strindberg, and Pirandello represent a handful of the playwrights Sondheim has named in passing at one time or another. The Bergman "boom" of the late 1950s certainly informed Sondheim's work—*A Little Night Music* is "suggested by a film of Ingmar Bergman," *Smiles of a Summer Night,* 1955—although Bergman's views of morality and divinity are, in the main, absent from Sondheim musicals. (In the 1970s, Sondheim almost collaborated with Bergman on an anarchic film musical adaptation of *The Merry Widow,* but Bergman's tax and political problems, along with the difficulties in securing financing, brought this possibility to naught.)[101] No doubt, friendships also influenced how Sondheim envisioned drama. Anthony Perkins, for

example, had experience in both Hollywood and French film before his engagement to star in *Evening Primrose* and his collaboration on *The Last of Sheila*.[102] Like a playwright or film director, Sondheim has had to rely on others to help him bring his visions to life, and very often his role would appear, from the documentary evidence, to have been midwife to the visions of his collaborators.

Yet since much of the animation of the characters and the propulsion of the stories occurs in the music and lyrics, Sondheim's contribution cannot be easily dismissed. The songs uniquely wed soundscape, lyrics, characters, stories, and narration. Each individual component is handled with skill and passion, and together they are structured in unusual ways. Moreover, Sondheim's musicodramatic language has affected not only the way that composers write a theater song but also the way that dramatists shape a Broadway musical. Sondheim subsumes his collaborators more than they subsume him.[103]

Such a view deliberately takes Harold Prince and James Lapine—Sondheim's two main collaborators—down a notch. It is true that, with the exception of *Assassins*, these two men have shaped every Sondheim musical from *Company* forward. Their direction helped to establish the identities of the shows. Gottfried spoke of a non-Sondheim musical, *On the Twentieth Century* (book and lyrics by Betty Comden and Adolph Green, music by Cy Coleman), to illustrate Prince's importance. "This was an example of how much gifted professionals can do when greater demands are made on them. It was for such collaborative influence, expertise, and creativity that Prince became the most important musicals director of his time, a seminal figure. In many ways, the musical theater's continuing progress was in his hands." In summing up his chapter "The Director's Era," Gottfried concluded, "The seventies was not merely an era for the choreographer-director but for the person able to conceive shows whole. The director had become the musical's maker."[104] However, as the 2002 Kennedy Center's Sondheim Celebration demonstrated, the shows do not require the original direction, production, or scenic design in order to make their impact, a fact that questions some definitions of the concept musical. As impressive as Prince's list of directorial and collaborative accomplishments is,[105] and as extensive as Lapine's list of theatrical feats is,[106] Sondheim's shows continue to succeed (or, at a minimum, fascinate) because of his manner of addressing the drama in words and music. There is no questioning that his scores arose from discussions with collaborators, but other composers and lyricists have not amassed as consistent a dramatic body of work as has Sondheim. Just as critics have noted that Sondheim elicited from Bernstein *(West Side Story)* and Styne *(Gypsy)* their finest scores, so it appears that he elicited from Prince and Lapine some of their best dramatic work.

There is a simple reason why he waits until a script has been started before he writes a song. He wants not only to make his songs fit the emerging tone of the work but also to shape that tone. He doesn't want others to change or influence his work, but he is eager to change and influence the work of others. He wants to be the dramatic hub.[107]

Indeed, it is instructive that few composers after Sondheim have had as much sustained success on Broadway as he has had. The Broadway musical post-Sondheim has galloped off madly in all directions, with two main directions being "melody" shows and "message" shows. Lloyd Webber is the chief exponent of the former. He unquestionably has had megahits (*Evita*, *Cats*, *Phantom of the Opera*), but his overall contribution to musical theater has been uneven in dramatic terms (cf. *Starlight Express*, *Sunset Boulevard*, *Whistle Down the Wind*). Other composers who have followed Lloyd Webber into writing scores marked more by their tunefulness than by their dramatic effectiveness have rarely achieved more than one runaway success (Boublil-Schönberg and, perhaps, Frank Wildhorn are the obvious exceptions). Of the "message" shows, Frank Rich noted that Sondheim was "discouraged that recent musicals confuse his and Hammerstein's idea of the 'serious' musical with mere solemnity: 'They're so eager to make what they write important that they start with themes instead of stories and characters.'"[108]

Stories and characters. How to handle the stories of those characters. Sondheim's songs may not be immediately hummable as were the songs of old (though with their increased exposure, they are becoming more familiar to a wider audience), but Sondheim never was a musical theater composer cast from the melodic mold. His sustained success has as much to do with his skill as a dramatist as with his facility as a lyricist-composer. His self-definition as "a playwright in song" could hardly be more accurate, and few other composers merit this definition. The songs not only advance the drama; they are dramatic conceptions in themselves. How Sondheim put it all together—classical and popular music, Hammerstein and cinema—is the subject of the final chapter.

6

Putting It Together

"Bit by bit . . ."

> If you want your piece to be closely structured, allow for every single thing that should happen on the stage—a *very* important lesson and I think not a widely known one. . . . To avoid that static moment, plot and plan within an inch of its life every bar that you can. . . . Once the lyric starts to take shape, I don't want it to get too far ahead of the music, and vice versa. Then it's a matter of developing both simultaneously. I generally do it section by section, and I generally make a kind of long line reduction in the music, because I was trained in a sort of conservative school of composition about the long line. I generally make a reduction of the long line and know what the key relationships are going to be in the various sections of the song and how the general long line is going to go down or up or cover the third or fifth or whatever it is. But it is a matter of shaping a little bit at a time, like doing a jigsaw puzzle. It gradually closes in until it's all there.[1]

While Sondheim's comments here focus narrowly on the music (with its concomitant lyric), his description starts with the dramatic. The music must account fully for every action on stage. A song (which here is apposite to "piece" or "composition") may have a structure that follows a certain musical logic (long lines and key relationships), but musical logic is made subservient to the dramatic requirements of the piece in question. Structure is dictated by the drama; content dictates form.

Thus it is only now, with a better grasp of the components that inform Sondheim's understanding of content, that we can more fully appreciate how his syntax operates. The fleshing out of a character or a scene involves: the interplay of cinematic techniques imbibed and internalized over years and decades of movie watching; an eye for drama honed by Hammerstein and by Sondheim's studies of, scripts for, and experiences in theater, film, and television; an affinity with the working methods and constraints of the Broadway songwriters of yesteryear (especially Gershwin and Arlen); and a respect for (and a deep knowledge of) a stratum of Western art music that is both conservative (compared to other trends in art music) and progressive (compared to more commercial styles of music). Sondheim found his sound—and an amazingly consistent sound it is, from Williams College to the present day—by amalgamating these seemingly disparate components into his unique patois.

What better song, then, in which to examine Sondheim's amalgamations and his "bit by bit" manner of construction than that song that most closely scrutinizes the art of making art? By any manner of accounting, "Putting It Together," from act 2 of *Sunday in the Park with George* (1984), represents the pinnacle of Sondheim's abilities. Its size alone—47 pages in a 246-page vocal score (nearly one-fifth of the score)—gives it a unique place in Sondheim's oeuvre. (Only the finale of act 1 of *Anyone Can Whistle*—the interrogation sequence—is longer.) Soon after its completion, Sondheim joked about his Leviathan of a song.

> SONDHEIM: . . . "Putting It Together" is going be No. 1 on the Hit Parade.
>
> JAMES LAPINE: I know! Isn't that hilarious?
>
> SONDHEIM: And the hilarity is that, next to "Comedy Tonight" and "Send In the Clowns," "Putting It Together" has been recorded more than anything else.[2]

Horowitz's discography shows that this is not true,[3] but when Barbra Streisand released her version of "Putting It Together" on *The Broadway Album* (1985), the Xerox Corporation "was developing an advertising campaign that used a similar phrase. They changed their campaign, licensed the song and used it for over six years in all of their advertising. This was a tremendous opportunity for the song as it had a terrific recording and then great success as a commercial."[4] Such saturation virtually insured that Sondheim's tune would acquire a popular cachet that few of his songs have ever earned, however extensive their discographies.

Yet, there are other reasons to examine "Putting It Together." Despite its size and popularity, which make it rare among Sondheim's work, it exhibits a number of traits that are common to the bulk of his music. Its scope makes it easier to consider his manner of song construction, and its use as a commercial logo suggests that his art is not nearly as esoteric as its detractors would have one believe. It is classic Sondheim writ large.

Before I take apart "Putting It Together," let me remind the reader of its larger dramatic and historical context. *Sunday in the Park with George* tells two related stories that intersect at the end of the musical. The first story is a fictionalized account of the life of Georges Seurat.[5] All of act 1 and the opening of act 2 concern the imagined circumstances surrounding the creation of *A Sunday Afternoon on the Island of La Grande Jatte,* his second major work. George (abbreviated throughout) is so obsessed with the painting that his relationships suffer, not least that with Dot, his mistress. We watch as Dot, who is pregnant by George, grows estranged from him, to the point where she leaves Paris, with her new husband, Louis the baker, and her infant daughter, Marie, for Charleston, South Carolina. The fractiousness of this and the other relationships is both mollified and exacerbated in the tableau vivant that closes act 1 and opens act 2. All through act 1, we have seen George sketching the various people who frequent the island, and at the end of the act, these characters, augmented with various flats of trees, animals, and other persons, are assembled to re-create Seurat's painting. The imagined harmony and repose that is created by the completed painting ("Sunday") is interrogated at the opening of act 2, where the characters in the painting, frozen for eternity, complain about their surroundings, their companions, and the heat ("It's Hot Up Here").[6]

After these characters break their stances and eulogize Seurat (who is absent in act 2), the second story begins. Its central character is Seurat's great-grandson, also named George. Like his ancestor, George is an artist who has stretched the boundaries of art. He is an inventor-sculptor, whose works require the latest in technology ("I've installed a new state-of-the-art Japanese microcomputer which controls the voltage regulator") and cause his collaborators to have anxiety attacks ("I'm going back to NASA. There is just too much pressure in this line of work").[7] Unlike his ancestor, George craves money. For him, "the art of making art is putting it together," with "it" being the financing that underwrites his enterprises.[8] When George confesses in an aside, "It's time to get to work," we soon discover that his "work" is chasing down commissions. Money buys him the attention of the cognoscenti and the envy of his peers. A rival dismisses George's creation—the seventh of his Chromolumes, a light-emitting mechanism—by questioning whether it qualifies as art. A critic warns George that, as inventive as he may have been, his concept has grown stale. And George suspects that both his rival and critic are right: he has a gnawing feeling that he has not lived up to his potential as an artist even though he is successful in lining up financial support. Lastly, like his ancestor, he has difficulty with his relationships.

He is divorced from his wife, he is cool and even dismissive toward his collaborators, and he is patronizing to his grandmother, Marie (Dot's daughter). His artistic and personal alienation lead to a dramatic encounter with his great-grandfather's world, whose characters reappear and view the modern-day George as the same man they encountered on La Grande Jatte. In a dramatic arch, the show closes as it began, with the image of a blank canvas. "So many possibilities," one of which, the musical *Sunday in the Park with George*, we have witnessed.

By the time *Sunday in the Park with George* arrived on Broadway, Sondheim's star seemed to have grown dim. The seventies had been his heyday. Four of the five Sondheim musicals that premiered that decade ran over five hundred performances each (*Pacific Overtures* did not), each of those four won the Tony Award for Best Score, and three won for Best Musical (*Follies* was nominated for, but did not win, Best Musical). The eighties was a rockier decade. *Merrily* was a flop and precipitated Sondheim's creative break from his longtime collaborator, Harold Prince. The traditional manner of bringing a musical to Broadway was through out-of-town runs. Prince gambled on New York previews to tune up *Sweeney* and *Merrily;* he won on the former and lost on the latter. In contrast to these methods, *Sunday* and *Into the Woods* were created off-Broadway and had relatively long gestation periods and extensive rewriting before they opened on Broadway. Both of these musicals also developed a reputation among some audience members that has dogged them to the present day: their "perfect" first acts are sullied, if not ruined, by "unnecessary" second acts. *Sunday* in particular was initially passed over by the Broadway theater community. It received ten Tony nominations but won only two technical awards (Best Scenic Design and Best Lighting Design). Frank Rich's tenacious advocacy as theater critic for the *New York Times* helped to keep the show alive, and he and the show's creators were vindicated when *Sunday* received the 1985 Pulitzer Prize for Drama, becoming only the sixth musical to be so honored since the early 1930s.[9]

"Putting It Together" thus not only details the travails of the modern-day George in his pursuit of endorsements—or the work of the Parisian George, who "dot by dot buil[t] up the image." Not only does it comment on Sondheim's creative method, both in the small (the composition of a song) and the large (the slow gestation of *Sunday* and the gradual accretion of its songs and script are hinted at in the audio commentary). It metaphorically limns Sondheim's career, one that illustrates modern-day George's assertion that "art isn't easy." (Two major books on Sondheim take their titles from this song, further suggesting its connection to his life and career.)[10] Sondheim has never been as hungry for money as some of his characters have been. But his life story reveals a man who has been committed to, if not obsessed with, his work throughout his career. And "Putting It Together" gives evidence of Sondheim's own tenacity as a creator. (Think of the string of "-ition" rhymes in the song—ambition and exhibition, addition and tradition, fruition, coalition, commission, recognition, suspicion, competition and politician, position and composition—and the fact that Sondheim's lexical and grammatical use of them is flawless, despite the fact that he called lyric writing hellish.) Other songs from *Sunday* may pack more emotional punch—the initial appearance of "Sunday," for example, or "Move On"—but "Putting It Together" neatly subsumes so much of Sondheim the creator and Sondheim the man that it is a logical choice for analysis.

In terms of time and space, "Putting It Together" takes place after the activation of Chromolume #7 and before a dinner gathering. The script indicates that the location is "an American art museum"; later, we are in "the gallery where the painting hangs." (It is on permanent display at the Art Institute of Chicago.) Modern-day George has finished giving a short presentation in the museum's auditorium about the Chromolume and its tangential relationship to Seurat. (He invites the audience "into *my* 'Sunday: Island of Light' . . . on exhibition here in the upstairs gallery for three weeks.") The song occurs during the cocktail reception that follows George's presentation. As we surmise from the museum director's comments and from the identities of some of the guests, this is an invited and somewhat well heeled audience, although the presence of Alex and Betty, two bohemian artists, gives the postpresentation reception a certain edginess. With its underscoring and musicalization of cocktail conversation, "Putting It Together" embraces the entire reception; after the song ends, the museum director announces that dinner is served.

Sondheim the cinematographer

In considering "Putting It Together," one cannot dismiss the importance of Sondheim's collaborators in creating the final composition. It was Lapine's idea to have cutouts of George pop up to interact with various characters throughout the number, a conceit that reimagines the vaudeville routine of spinning china plates on wooden dowels, as George has to attend to the cutouts periodically to keep them from falling. Lapine was reprising a visual motif he established in the first act,

where cutouts appear and disappear for animals and scenery (most amusingly, for the Old Lady's tree) and substitute at times for humans (as in the tableau vivant of "Bathing at Asnières," which contained three actors as well as cutouts for other human figures, and again for the Soldier's deaf-mute and "very close" comrade). What is also remarkable about the mise-en-scène for "Putting It Together" in the original production, given Sondheim's complaint about the practice, is that it is played in one.[11] As cocktail parties and galleries go, it is a very narrow room, and this also must be attributed to Lapine, who was director as well as book author.

In the theater, the cinematic nature of "Putting It Together" can be obscured. But a look at the vocal score quickly reveals the song's structural complexity and similarity to a composite cinematic scene. There are seventeen identified parts for "Putting It Together," seventeen different angles from which to look at the reception. And whereas theatergoers may choose for themselves where to direct their attention, the video production of "Putting It Together" circumscribes the viewer's choice, agreeing by and large with the cinematic choices Sondheim made in his seventeen sections. (See table 1.)

Part I introduces seven characters, five of whom are new to us. (We met Robert Greenberg, the museum director, and Naomi Eisen, the composer, in the preceding scene.) While the clothing and entrances (in the original production) divide the seven into groups—a couple dressed in cocktail casual attire, two men with ties, three bohemians—it is possible at first to view them as one large group of seven, as their spoken conversations remain abbreviated. With Parts II–IV, the focus distinguishes the three groups from each other as the musical camera highlights each group for approximately twenty seconds. In these shots, these characters begin to emerge more clearly. The focus repeats the order of introduction that occurred in Part I and expands on the short conversations we heard there. First is the couple (Part II). We learn that, although they know something about art, George's Chromolume has left them at sea. We then cut away to the two men (Part III). They are even more knowledgeable than the couple, using French terms in their conversation,[12] yet they remain rather cool toward George. We cut away again, now to the three artists (Part IV). They are the most passionate, with one praising the Chromolume, one panning it, and the third—George's collaborator—trying hard not to offend. Parts II–IV thus inform the wide-angle images we saw in Part I. Part V pans across the room to take in all seven one by one, providing a second composite image of the situation, but now with the characters and the trajectory of the story clarified by Parts II–IV. In addition, at the end of Part V, where the musical lens is opened up to embrace the seven, three more characters are included (Randolph, the Photographer, and the Assistant), whom we saw during Part I. While their actual sung contribution is minimal, their presence intensifies the images already presented, suggesting that there are unseen others besides the seven shown to us in close focus who share their sentiments of confusion and uncertainty.

Part V abruptly ends; George enters (Part VI). In many respects, George functions as a narrator, indicating how the action has arrived at its current situation and where it will likely go from here. At no point in "Putting It Together" does he sing to another character. His singing externalizes his interior monologue; only when he speaks does he interact. In contrast, the other characters interact with each other in all their remarks, even those that are rhetorical. The interiority of George's remarks is reinforced here in Part VI, as the other characters are frozen in their tracks while George makes his comments. This stance, while reminiscent of the earlier tableaux vivants, differs fundamentally in that this "freeze-frame" does not fix a representation of an artwork (even a putative one, say, "Cocktail Reception at a Museum") but instead exists to allow the narrator to step outside of time and provide commentary while the other characters remain frozen. Its similarity to *Marienbad* is obvious, although other films and theater pieces have used this device. (The published script does not indicate that the characters should freeze at this point.)

What is important is that an abundance of cinematic techniques have been presented in these six parts of "Putting It Together," which together make up approximately one-fifth of the song. It would be impossible to attribute these techniques solely to Lapine, as they are found time and again in Sondheim's work in very different dramatic situations and with a variety of collaborators ("A Weekend in the Country," *Night Music;* "Please Hello," *Pacific Overtures;* "City on Fire," *Sweeney Todd;* the "Gun Song" and "Something Just Broke," *Assassins*). In fact, the cinematic fluidity of *Allegro* once again seems to be the driving force behind Sondheim's cinematic techniques, which he incorporated as early as *Climb High.* Given the early and consistent appearance of cinematic devices in his work, it is easy to concur with Sondheim about the importance for him of cinematic language.

Here again, though, it is necessary to mention Sondheim's collaborators, for not all of the music of "Putting It Together" is by Sondheim. Parts I, VII, IX, XIV, and a portion of Part XV contain "Cocktail Music." Diegetic music—music that one would expect to hear in the set-

Table 1. "Putting It Together," *Sunday in the Park with George*

Part	Subtitle/Characters	Tempo Marking	Key	Number of Mm. (total)[a]	Added/Subtracted Mm.?	Other Notes **Final Directions**	CD timing[b]	DVD timing[c]
Section 1								
I	Cocktail Music #1	Free, cocktail music feel	E♭	11	No	Short dialogue with Harriet, Billy, Redmond, Greenberg, Alex, Betty, and Naomi **Segue**	n/a	1:44:46
II	Harriet, Billy	Allegro con spirito (♩ = 144)	E♭, with modulation to:	12 (23)	Yes	**Segue**	0:24	1:45:22
III	Greenberg, Redmond	A tempo	C, with modulation to:	12 (35)	Yes	**Segue**	0:48	1:45:45
IV	Naomi, Betty, Alex	L'istesso tempo (♩ = 144)	A, with modulation to:	13 (48)	No	**Segue**	1:06	1:46:03
V	Company	L'istesso tempo (♩ = 144)	F, with modulation to D, then ??	11 (59)	No	**Segue**	1:27	1:46:25
Section 2								
VI	George	Allegretto (𝅗𝅥 = 100); Poco rubato; Con moto (𝅗𝅥 = 126)	E♭	22 (22/81)	No	Horn fanfare announces George's arrival; no indication in book that all other characters freeze **Cross-fade segue**	1:45	1:46:42
VII	Cocktail Music #2	Jazz waltz (♩ = 126)	E♭	20 (42/101)	No	Dialogue with Greenberg, Harriet, and Billy **Segue**	n/a	1:47:17

VIII	George	Allegretto con poco rubato (𝅗𝅥 = 100); Con moto (𝅗𝅥 = 126)	E♭	17 (59/118)	Yes	**Segue** followed by dialogue with Harriet, Marie, Billy, and Elaine (underscored by IX)	2:17	1:47:43
IX	Cocktail Music #3	Hot swing	E	8 (67/126)	No	Uses chord symbols: "Ad lib. jazz solo on chord changes" **Segue**	n/a	1:48:02
X	George	Allegretto (𝅗𝅥 = 100) con poco rubato; Con moto (𝅗𝅥 = 126)	E, with modulation to G♭	23 (90/149)	Yes	Interspersed with dialogue with (and lines for) Billy, Marie, and Elaine **Segue**	2:35	1:48:41
Section 3								
XI	George	L'istesso tempo (𝅗𝅥 = 126)	G♭	54 (54/203)	Yes: two extra mm. at opening; mm. 43–44 excised	Lines for Harriet and Marie during XI, dialogue with Redmond and (later) Greenberg during musical safety at end of Part XI and beginning of Part XII **Segue**	2:56	1:49:12
XII	George	L'istesso tempo	G♭	48 (102/251)	Yes: 2 added mm. between 34 and 35	No dialogue **Segue**	3:44	1:50:09
XIII	Company	L'istesso tempo (♩ = 116 [sic?]):	G♭, with modulation to	13 (115/264)	No	**Cross-fade segue**	4:26	1:50:56

TABLE 1. *Continued*

Part	Subtitle/Characters	Tempo Marking	Key	Number of Mm. (total)[a]	Added/Subtracted Mm.?	Other Notes **Final Directions**	CD timing[b]	DVD timing[c]
		should be 144; cf. Pt. V)	E♭, then ?? (same as Pt. V)					
XIV	Cocktail Music #4	Bossa nova (repeat ad lib. under dialogue)	G♭	4 (119/268)	No	Dialogue with Marie, Randolph, George, and Naomi **Segue**	n/a	1:51:16
XV	George	Come sopra (𝅗𝅥 = 126); Cocktail style, rubato (𝅗𝅥 = 100)	G♭, then abrupt shift to E (after shift, to Pt. X)	50 (169/318)	Yes: cocktail music is interpolated into score	Substantial cut in the CD, mostly of cocktail music; exchange between Dennis and George, concludes w/ remarks by Betty, Alex, and George **Segue**	4:45	1:51:30
XVI	George	L'istesso tempo (𝅗𝅥 = 126)	G♭	46 (215/364)	No	Begins with dialogue between George, Alex, and Betty; guests promenade (= circulate) at end **Attacca subito**	5:07	1:52:54
Section 4								
XVII	George, Company	Dictated; Poco rubato (𝅗𝅥 = 100); Con moto (𝅗𝅥 = 116)	G♭, with modulation to A♭	109 (473)	Yes	Conversation between Blair and George introduces final section	5:35 (ends at 7:16)	1:53:45 (ends at 1:55:56)

[a] Where two numbers appear in parentheses, the first number tallies the number of measures for the section (see Col. 1) and the second number tallies the number of measures for the entire piece.
[b] *Sunday in the Park with George*, Original Cast Recording, RCA RCD1-5042, 1984, Track 12, "Chromolume #7/Putting It Together."
[c] *Sunday in the Park with George*, Image Entertainment/Brandman Productions, Inc., ID4586MBDVD, 1986, 1999.

ting being portrayed—is a classic feature of film music. Just as we expect to hear cocktail music in the background at Rick's Place *(Casablanca)*, we expect to hear it at the reception to honor George. This written-out cocktail music is a realization of improvisations provided by Paul Ford and others for the original production. (In the audio commentary, Sondheim remarked: "Cocktail music. Paul Ford playing the cocktail piano.") The harmonic and contrapuntal language of these musical moments is noticeably different from the rest of "Putting It Together," but because the music is heard in the background, its stylistic incongruence is obscured. Part IX also uses chord symbols and tells the musicians "Ad lib. jazz solo on chord changes." The presence of these markings further argues against Sondheim's authorship, given his aversion to lead-sheet reductions of his music (chord symbols are a rarity in his scores). Nevertheless, the notion of diegetic music in a Sondheim musical is not new. The reunion at the heart of *Follies* features a small combo that, throughout the evening, plays "old Follies songs" for the guests (actually, they are Sondheim's songs, some of which he cut from the original production). Nor is the idea of someone else providing diegetic music and Sondheim providing the songs unusual. Though it comes after *Sunday*, *Dick Tracy* (1990) features this division of labor, with Sondheim's songs being in the foreground and original songs by Andy Paley coming out of radios in apartments, cars, diners, and hotels.[13]

"Putting It Together" is notable for the musical directions given in the last bar of each part. With the exception of the final part, with its final cadence, every part is marked with an instruction to move seamlessly into the one that follows. "Segue" is the most common indication, with two of the sections leading into a cocktail music segment marked "Cross-fade segue," as much of a studio music term as a cinematic one. The intent is for the eleven-minute sequence of musical events to play as a unified whole, a single scene comprising many discrete shots, joined through skillful montage.

The shifts to and from various "camera angles" slow considerably from this point (Part VI) forward. Appropriately, the remainder of the song principally employs a different cinematic technique: the tracking shot. In the tracking shot, a single camera records the action, as distinct from several cameras capturing the action and then editors piecing the footage together in the editing room. As its name implies, the camera often moves, or tracks, with the action. Standard though the technique is, tracking shots are usually not very long in terms of elapsed time because of the difficulty involved in creating them (e.g., coordinating the movement of camera and sound equipment to the movements of the

actors, working within the constraints of the shooting space). These difficulties in fact heighten the impact of such shots when they are successful, as their apparent ease is accompanied by their obvious virtuosity. The bank scene in Godard's *Breathless* (1960) and the elevator and hotel scene in his *Alphaville* (1965), for example (the latter making reference to an earlier hotel elevator scene in *Touch of Evil,* 1958), are remarkable for their visual continuity within the confines of extremely small spaces (in *Alphaville,* we follow the character through a lobby and up a glass-enclosed elevator to his room). And the lengthy tracking shots that open Robert Altman's *The Player* (1992; eight minutes) and Brian De Palma's *Snake Eyes* (1998; twenty minutes) are justly famous, as is Aleksandr Sokurov's *Russian Ark* (2002), a feature-length film shot entirely in one take from a single camera. An astute viewer recognizes the technical skill the filmmaker and his collaborators put into a tracking shot, even as a truly fine example should seem inconspicuous and inevitable and be a natural realization of the action we see.

Virtuosity and ease of execution are the key to appreciating Sondheim's own "tracking shots" in "Putting It Together." Parts VI–XII comprise a single four-minute musical camera shot that tracks George as he works the crowd at the reception. As has already been established, not all of the music here was composed by Sondheim; he (and Lapine) made room in their conception of this scene to utilize the skills and talents of their collaborators. Still, it is Sondheim, in consultation with Lapine, who decided how rapidly this tracking shot should unfold and how much action it should contain. What quickly becomes apparent is that Sondheim has slowed both the cinematic and dramatic action from what we experienced in Parts I–V. There, we had the constant shifting of focus from one group to another. Now we have the tighter focus on George. Consider also that, as George enters, two additional characters enter with him: his grandmother, Marie, and his ex-wife, Elaine. The audience needs time to assimilate them and their stories into the dramatic trajectory. To thrust them immediately into the center of the group of ten (from the end of Part V) might have been possible but would have likely been disorienting, not only for them (as characters) but also for the audience. Appropriately, Sondheim and Lapine limit the number of interactions in Parts VI–XII. The two men (Greenberg and Redmond) split up. Greenberg introduces George to Harriet (one of his board members, we discover) and Billy—the couple from Part II—and then momentarily disappears. Redmond does not make an appearance until the end of Part XI. Naomi, Alex, and Betty (cf. Part IV) and the three characters introduced at the end of Part V are completely absent. Not only are Elaine and Marie integrated more smoothly into the reception. The audience is also allowed to assimilate the new characters more deliberately through the absence and attenuation of the previously introduced characters. (The music also contributes to establishing a more deliberate pace through its use of a halting three-chord accompaniment and the persistent notation "ten." [i.e., tenuto] in the vocal part.) Here it is worth noting that, though temporarily eliminating the trio of artists, Sondheim and Lapine preserve the visual symmetry by introducing the trio of George, Marie, and Elaine and by returning to a grouping of seven.

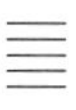

In this tracking shot, George's spoken interactions with the guests as he mills about the cocktail party are framed by his musical narrations directed to the audience. The similarity of these asides to those of a protagonist narrating his own actions in film is obvious. What differs is the manner of presentation. On stage, George's direct appeals to the audience are in keeping with the presentational nature of theater (and, especially, song). In film, we are accustomed to the protagonist providing voice-over narration instead of turning directly to the audience (here, camera). In both cases, the audience hears the protagonist's musings, both conscious and subconscious (the latter occurring, for example, when George accidentally says "you" instead of "your work" in his reference about going on exhibition).

Mundane though this all may seem at first, upon reflection one discovers the relative rarity of this type of tracking shot in Sondheim. Certainly there are other occasions where interactions and commentary on them are interleaved. In *Pacific Overtures*, the Reciter interjects himself periodically into the fabric of a song, but there the commentary is spoken, not sung as in "Putting It Together." *Company* provides an even more apposite example. In "The Little Things You Do Together," Joanne and the company comment in song upon the nonmusical actions of Harry and Sarah. But in these songs, there is a division between the commentator and the actor(s). The characters in action (Harry and Sarah, with Robert looking on) are not commenting on their own actions. And because we want to know who the commentators are, because we want to *see* them, we are likely to cut away to the commentators (the Reciter, Joanne, and the company) when they "speak."

In "Putting It Together," action and commentary are seamless because the musical camera is mounted on George's head and the microphone placed in front of his mouth. For four minutes, in Parts VI–XII, we never leave George as we see and hear the action from his point of view. Structurally, this is a cinematic recapitulation of first-act George's soliloquy, "Finishing the Hat," which was also a long tracking shot.

(Clearly it is a grammatical recapitulation—notice the gerundives—and it is a musical recapitulation as well, a fact that will be discussed below.) There, however, the shot was relatively simple, as only George occupied the frame. Here, George shares the visual, dramatic, and narrative space with six other actors. Again, the emphasis here is on the virtuosity in handling this sequence without drawing attention to its complexity. Its naturalness disguises its craft.

The fluidity of this long tracking shot is contrasted with Part XIII, where the company once again commands the musical camera's attention as it did in Part V. There, the musical camera panned the scene, catching each character one by one, and then zoomed out to include the entire ensemble. Here, Sondheim used a different device that, while it has cinematic resonances, is a recurrent feature in his writing for ensembles. Short utterances from the entire company alternate with reflections from the individual characters. Their statements are worth reproducing in full, as Sondheim managed, in this brief section, not only to express a collective frustration that these characters are experiencing but also to extend the character development that began in Part I and continued in Parts II–IV. Recall that Alex and Betty are bohemian artists, Harriet and Billy are the couple at sea, Greenberg and Redmond are museum curators, and Naomi provided the music for the Chromolume.

> ALL: Art isn't easy—
> ALEX, BETTY: Trying to make connections—
> ALL: Who understands it—?
> HARRIET, BILLY: Difficult to evaluate—
> ALL: Art isn't easy—
> GREENBERG, REDMOND: Trying to form collections—
> ALL: Always in transit—
> NAOMI: And then when you have to collaborate—!
> ALL: Art isn't easy any way you look at it.

For each of these four groups, art is problematic, but problematic in different ways. Sondheim thus united these disparate individuals around a common complaint.

Visually, then, we face a choice. Are we to emphasize the smaller groupings and cut away to them when they speak? Or is the focus upon the larger group, in the midst of which individuals speak up from different locations on the musical screen? As I suggested, this is a common occurrence in Sondheim's larger ensembles.

The same questions arise earlier in act 2 with "It's Hot in Here." There, the members of the tableau vivant collectively admit that "there are worse things than sweating by a river on a Sunday" and then, in rapid-fire delivery, thirteen different characters, one after the other, unload their observations. Sondheim wisely chose to distribute the observations from character to character, from audience left to audience right, so that the theatergoer can pan across the stage as the observations are rattled off. (For the video production, the editor chose to make seven shots of this musical section: one group of three, four groups of two, and two shots of individuals.)

At issue here is the density and intensity with which a typical Sondheim ensemble confronts both viewer and listener. In many of these ensembles, there is a moment about two-thirds of the way through the composition where an intensification of musical, lyrical (in terms of words), dramatic, and visual information occurs. The viewer-auditor is challenged to assimilate all of this information quickly, and in those cases where the information comes in layers (i.e., where several characters are singing at the same time), immediate assimilation is impossible. These moments, of course, are not strictly cinematic, as the contrapuntal ensemble has its own long history in musical theater (e.g., the Sextet in *Lucia di Lammermoor*, the Quartet in *Rigoletto*, the Quintet in *West Side Story*). And yet they also borrow from cinema the idea of crowd scenes, where multiple conversations occur, some of which are intelligible, while others are not. In Part XIII, the movement between group song and the utterances of smaller character units is slow enough for us to catch every word, even if we fail, upon first hearing, to see how well Sondheim kept his characters in character. All the same, in moving away from the relative consistency of George's long tracking shot to this busier interaction of characters, we are suddenly asked to process information much more quickly than before. Sondheim's close-cutting here helps to underscore his message here: Art isn't easy. (The video production treats Part XIII neither as a single wide shot nor as nine quick shots but strikes a compromise between the two, occasionally employing pans to join the various sections of Part XIII together.)

Part XIV through the first half of Part XVII constitutes a second cinematic unit that focuses on George. The entire piece, from a cinematic point of view, can thus be divided as follows:

Part I—small crowd
Parts II–IV—focus on individuals from within the crowd
Part V—a larger crowd
Parts VI–XII—introduction of George and his views of the people around him
Part XIII—a still larger crowd

Parts XIV–XVII(a)—return to George and his views of the people around him
Part XIV(b)—the entire crowd

As we shall see later, this cinematic structure does not parallel the musical structure, a fact that enriches the piece. Still, the symmetry of the cinematic structure, where crowd scenes are interleaved with more intimate ensembles, appears to be deliberate, as does the fact that Part XIII, which plays out in microcosm the alternation from crowd to solos and duets, falls near the midpoint of the entire piece (see DVD timings on table 1).

Parts XIV–XVII(a) comprise a second tracking shot from George's point of view. The slow unfolding of Parts VI–XII is reversed in Parts XIV–XVII(a). There, the first half (Parts VI–X) slowly coalesced into a more solidified commentary (Parts XI–XII), and the entire sequence followed the organic growth of George's relationships with the people in the gallery. In Parts XIV–XVII(a), even though there are fewer notated parts, there is greater atomization within the parts, as the relationships exhibit signs of decay. Here again are musical sections that come from hands other than Sondheim's: Part XIV and the central section of Part XV are transcriptions of cocktail improvisations. But whereas the first tracking shot ended with a sense of George's control over his environment—he interacted smoothly with the guests and his commentary was crisp—the second tracking shot shows an increase in frustration. In this section, Lapine's cutouts of George are unstable, either sinking into the ground or drifting into the wings. George is spread too thin and is having difficulty keeping the guests entertained. It is all yet another confirmation that art isn't easy.

Harriet's a cappella line, "But he combines all these different trends," signals the second half of Part XVII, and in typical Sondheim style, the moment encompasses more than its immediate referent (i.e., George's postmodern aesthetic). To stay with the cinematic aspects of the song: it neatly brings together the various techniques that Sondheim and Lapine employed here, from narrative commentary to live action, from quick edits to longer tracking shots. Ultimately, these techniques affect the visual presentation—the way we see the song—but it cannot be stressed enough that these techniques were written into the music. As the opening quotation in this chapter made plain, Sondheim had a vision of this song that he brought to life through his music. And that vision was profoundly shaped by cinematic ways of looking at the world.

Before turning to the theatrical elements of "Putting It Together," I should conclude this section by saying that Sondheim's use of cinematic techniques was not flawless. There are moments where the musical camera seems to focus too long on a character or, as noted above, the musical camera moves too quickly. To call these flaws may be to judge them too harshly, for Sondheim was not concerned with cinematic possibilities alone. At times, musical logic overtakes cinematic (or theatrical) logic in Sondheim's songs, and so a passage of music (usually instrumental in nature) may occur that is too long or too short for the drama but which makes sense musically. In the case of "Putting It Together," many of these musical passages are "papered over" by dialogue. The relative insignificance of the dialogue, however, becomes apparent when one hears the songs outside of the musical. The music makes sense without the dialogue (or action); the latter is a concession to the drama.

This is the case in the final seconds of the video production of "Putting It Together." In the audio commentary, Sondheim stated at the beginning of the song, "This is a number where, as you'll see, there is a cheat at the end of it because of a problem with shooting." Lapine explained, "We didn't have footage to cover [the action] musically, so what we did was [insert] freeze frames." It is hard to know what footage would have worked well here, as it is the music and not the drama that propels the song to its conclusion. At this moment, the important activity is in the pit, not on stage. At best, it can be compared to the final shot of a long cinematic sequence that ends with stillness on the set while the music surges underneath. What results is static action on stage; the freeze frame is more than appropriate. In a film, the visual would fade out. In musical theater, the music drives the scene to a close. It is a convention that necessarily abandons cinematic language for theatrical language, that is, the big finish.

Sondheim the playwright

Much of what has already been said about the cinematic Sondheim could be transferred to a discussion of the theatrical Sondheim, as issues of character development and dramatic balance are paramount in both realms. Sondheim delineates characters through his lyrics and balances them through his music; he gives characters time to develop and words that trace their development. The manuscripts for the song show Sondheim's attention to drama, as he specified when characters enter and exit, what lines actors speak, where an actor should direct his attention, and how the cutouts behave. Yet there are a number of dramatic gestures in

"Putting It Together" that cut across the cinematic structure and demonstrate attention to theatrical devices.

Throughout the song, dramatic intensification is achieved by threefold repetitions of a basic complaint. The first of these instances is found in Parts II–IV (an intensification of the conversation that takes place over the cocktail music of Part I). The basic complaint concerns the impenetrability of the Chromolume specifically and of modern art more generally. We are first introduced to Harriet Pawling, a patron of the arts whose family runs a foundation that is always looking for new projects, and Billy Webster, her friend whose chief dramatic role is to be more clueless about art than Harriet is. It is a cliché that art connoisseurs with money actually know little about art, and Harriet embodies that cliché. Thus we may dismiss her bewilderment as relatively unimportant: we do not expect her (or her déclassé friend, who can only say, "I'm not surprised") to hold an opinion of art that we should take seriously. (These actors play Louis the baker and the uncouth American Mrs. in act 1.)

The complaint is then repeated, this time by art professionals. Robert Greenberg is the director of the museum that has just installed Chromolume #7. Charles Redmond is a visiting curator from the County Museum of Texas who is interested in George's work. Greenberg (both characters are identified in the script by their last names), befitting his station in a prominent Midwest museum (presumably Chicago), is more polished than Redmond. He is also unctuous; we have already heard him talk when the Chromolume failed, whereupon he pitched the museum's high-rise condominiums to the audience. Redmond, in line with his Texas provenance, is more down-to-earth, with his oft-repeated slangy phrase, "You're telling me." Since they traffic in art for a living, we expect that their opinions carry more weight than do those of Harriet and Billy. And since they express reservations about George's work, we are more inclined to question that work ourselves.

The third and final repetition comes with the two artists, Alex and Betty, as they speak with George's composer-collaborator, Naomi. Betty found the Chromolume terrific; Alex thought it was terrible; Naomi is understandably ambivalent, not wanting to offend her current collaborator or to alienate potential future collaborators. Alex and Betty may also be a couple—while Alex dismisses his chances of securing a Texas commission, Betty chimes in that "Texas would be fun!" Couple or not, some of the tension they feel toward George is tied up in gender: Alex views George as a threat and belittles his intelligence, whereas Betty sees George as a bright and talented colleague. Because they themselves are artists and are thus uniquely positioned to comment on the work of a fellow artist, their opinion is particularly valuable. Their disagreement about George's work is much more intense and absolute than the judgments made by the previous two groupings.

(Consider the gendered roles that Alex, Betty, and Naomi play. In Sondheim and Lapine's original production, Betty is costumed as a refugee from the 1960s, with a red scarf tied across her forehead and a funky blouse-and-skirt combo that is literally held together by another scarf, this one of indeterminate length. She telegraphs a certain bohemian sexual allure and is marked as flighty, both by her dress and by her unrelentingly positive assessment of George's work. In contrast, Naomi is dressed in all black with some jewelry and a very unflattering haircut. She telegraphs little sexual allure and is marked as unattractive and possibly lesbian. Alex wears a sport coat, a multicolor crew-neck T-shirt, and blue jeans. His body language telegraphs that he is straight, and combined with his verbal language, marks him as volatile, both sexually and artistically. There are other ways of playing these characters—Alex and Betty as gay, for example—but in terms of dialogue, Betty is the nurturer and Alex is the competitor.)

The recapitulation of all the complaints in Part V—perhaps better understood as a fourth repetition, though another reading will emerge—comes after this intensification of the complaints. (And the lyrics of Part V, like those in Part XIII, do a remarkable job at developing the individual characters.) Their frustrations have reached a dramatic climax. George enters (Part VI), and the drama effectively starts all over. His entry temporarily deflates the frustrations and allows the characters time to recover from (or cloak) their grievances.

But George has grievances of his own that he voices in his own threefold repetition. Whether he knows that he has been the subject of contentious conversation is unimportant, because the other characters now expect George to control the conversation. In Part VI, he acknowledges that he has diverted the attention away from all others and onto himself. And he outlines what his line of conversation will be: funding for Chromolume #8. His first statement is thus preparatory to his reasoning, even though it clearly indicates his predatory intentions.

Part VII finds George brownnosing Harriet and Billy. Since we have heard George's comments in Part VI, we know his words here are slightly insincere. Part VIII focuses on that insincerity. In his second statement he repeats his predatory intentions by noting that "machines don't grow on trees," a twist on the aphorism that "money doesn't grow on trees" and thus making machines and money synonyms in his thinking. Key, then, to his securing the money is to schmooze with those who

have the money and make them feel good about giving that money to him.

Part IX puts George in an awkward position. Since his earlier presentation of the Chromolume featured a prominent part for his grandmother, Marie, he cannot afford to hide her or affront her at the reception. Marie and Elaine, George's ex-wife, now enter the conversation with George, Harriet, and Billy. Marie neither shares George's predatory instinct for money nor knows how to engage in the kind of oleaginous conversation that opens pocketbooks. In fact, after she boasts to Billy that George takes an entire year to build a single Chromolume, she unthinkingly blurts out, "The minute he finishes one, he starts raising money for the next." She is oblivious to the fact that she just revealed George's modus operandi for the evening, but George recovers by noting that he inscribes the names of his contributors on every machine, thus memorializing their role in creating art, and Elaine conspires with him by volunteering that there are "some very impressive people" named on George's machine. Translation: those with money should consider it an honor to be asked to assist George in the making of art.

Part X is George's third statement of his quest for money, but its intensification comes not from a ratcheting up of his predation but from his attaching the predation to a higher purpose: the advancement of art. Visions, George laments, need money to allow them to come to light. He sees his grubbing for financing as an unfortunate reality of the modern art marketplace.

Here, then, are two repetitions and intensifications (Parts II–IV and Parts VI–X) that find structural parallels but focus on different complaints. In the first, the complaint centered on the quality of art; in the second, the potentiality of art is central. In a third set of repetitions, these two complaints are brought together by means of another dramatic device: the interruption.

Before looking at that set of repetitions, note that the second repetition takes almost the same amount of time as the first set. This structural balance is as much a musical as a theatrical achievement, as Part XI marks a new type of discourse for George, both musically and theatrically. I have already suggested that Part XI, cinematically speaking, is a continuation of Parts VI–X, and in terms of its orientation (i.e., from George's perspective), it is connected. Dramatically and musically, however, Sondheim shifted the emphasis here from more fragmentary utterances to a more extended soliloquizing. Whereas the characters in Parts I–V are not given the time or space to explore their opinions, George, as the central character, is allowed these luxuries. In spite of the occasional snatch of dialogue from other characters, Parts XI and XII represent George's first significant speech in act 2, his first soliloquy.

Part XIII, where the characters revoice the opinions they raised in Parts I–V, is less an interruption of George's monologue than it is an intensification of Part V. The true interruption comes at the end of Part XIII, when a new character is introduced. I have already posited that George's entry in Part VI redirected the dramatic trajectory. In a similar fashion, the three interruptions at the end of "Putting It Together" change the dramatic flow, and the fact that the interruptions grow in intensity, I believe, is self-evident. Less obvious are the parallels between these introductions-as-interruptions and the characters who surrounded the first act George.

The first interruption reintroduces two characters we have already seen. One is Lee Randolph, the museum publicist, who joined the ensemble in Part V. In that appearance he was nameless, and thus his opinion carried little importance. But now he declares, "There's a lot of opportunity for some nice press here," confirming George's hunch that this evening's gathering could help him secure financing for his next project. Randolph's conversation with George is interrupted by Naomi, George's collaborator. Having overheard Randolph's positive comment, she assures George, "That electrical foul-up didn't hurt our reception." Until this moment, the technical mishap that could have brought George's presentation to ruin has gone unnoticed. Now, however, in addition to the financial tightrope he is walking, George must confront the possibility of failure. As friendly as journalists might be, they would have to report George's glitch. And that might call into question not only his technical wizardry but his creative vision, personal relationships, and ability to raise money. From this point in the song, the possibility of George's failure grows more pronounced with each interruption.

The composite interruption of Randolph and Naomi focuses on a public relations failure narrowly averted. If their interruption begins to deflect the dramatic trajectory, Dennis's interruption affects the story more profoundly. Dennis is George's technician who, we will discover, has been with George since Chromolume #3 (by extrapolation, over four years). We saw him briefly when Chromolume #7 was unveiled and then heard and saw him again when the machine failed ("It's the regulator, George"). For whatever reason, he has been unable to join the reception until this moment. He immediately finds George, thinking that George will be brooding over the technical malfunction, when in fact the malfunction had not crossed George's mind until Naomi mentioned it

immediately before Dennis's entrance. Of little importance is Dennis's announcement that Naomi was at fault for the malfunction; of greater importance is his announcement that he intends to leave George. The script itself gives little indication of how Dennis and George are to play this scene, but in the video production, they behave very much like a couple who have been together for years, as Dennis tries to talk to a distracted George. George finally snaps at Dennis, and Dennis seeks cover. When Dennis expresses his intention to quit and his reasons for doing so, George verbally massages him into temporarily retracting his rash decision. One suspects, though, that these two know each other well and that they are aware that the decision is far from rash. Later we discover that Dennis has kept to his decision to leave.

The failure here concerns not a failure of machinery or publicity but a failure of humanity. Modern-day George, like his great-grandfather, has difficulty connecting with others, and now his relationship with Dennis carries echoes of the earlier George's relationship with Dot. Modern-day George has been using Dennis for what Dennis can provide. George has been insensitive to Dennis's needs and aspirations. He is stunned that Dennis would quit, just as the earlier George was surprised that Dot would walk out on him. Like his forebear, modern-day George thought his partner understood him. But unlike his forebear, George can at least tell him not to go, even if his request that Dennis stay is self-serving. We will discover that, with Dennis's departure, George will branch out in a different direction. In many ways, Dennis has been more than George's technician; he has served as George's muse, his enabler.

One could easily extend the homoerotic aspects of this relationship to Dennis's other interactions: his sniping with Naomi, who (in the video production) has lesbian shadings; his cowering at Alex's sarcasm, given that Alex (again, in the video production) comes across as a straight alpha-male; and his fondness for Marie, George's only living relative whom we see. (We are led to believe that Henry, George's father, may no longer be alive.) In the last case, it is Dennis who encourages George to inspect Marie's grammar book more closely, since he has already done so without George's knowledge or permission. (This was the book with which Dot laboriously taught herself to read and write, and in which she wrote down the words spoken by her lover, George's great-grandfather.) But the bigger, more significant issue is that, with his break from Dennis—even more than with the (offstage) death of Marie—George is cut off from others. Again and again, in the song "Lesson #8," George sighs that he was hoping to see people. Dennis's interruption in "Putting

It Together" signals George's relational demise, a failure far greater than any public relations calamity.

Earlier I mentioned that these three interruptions integrate the complaints from the previous set of interruptions, namely, that they deal with questions of the quality and the potential of art. In both the Randolph-Naomi and the Dennis interruption, the near nonpotentiality of art—the averted technical failure—did not detract from the perceived quality. Randolph speaks of the stir that George and Naomi have created, and Dennis congratulates George on the beauty of the light show. The third interruption, by far the most intense, interrogates the conflation of beauty and quality. As impressive or as inscrutable as Chromolume #7 may be to those assembled, one guest lets George know that not only is she unimpressed, but she is also profoundly disappointed in him.

Blair Daniels, an art critic, begins her conversation with George abruptly, trumpeting, "There's the man of the hour." Unlike the previous instances, where we were fleetingly introduced to the characters prior to their dramatic interruptions, Blair is an entirely new character we have not yet met in act 2. We quickly discover that she is more than an art critic. George praises her piece on neoexpressionism, suggesting that she is an art theorist with a formidable mind. George may truly have enjoyed the piece, as he tells Blair, but she rightly suspects that this is part of his game of working the crowd, and she dismisses it quickly. It is intriguing that Blair highlights "a certain humanity" that occurred when George and Marie shared the stage with George's light sculpture. George is struck by Blair's choice of the word "humanity": perhaps he recalled his relational failure with Dennis. Whatever the reason, Blair continues by pinning the technical failure not on the momentary electrical glitch but on the entire artistic project. She has reservations about not only the potential of the series but also its ongoing aesthetic value. George could have easily defended himself by invoking Monet's series of haystacks or the paintings of Rouen cathedral. But though he disagrees with Blair, he suspects that she may be right: "Even if it's true, George— / you do what you can do . . ." And while the cutouts had begun to "misbehave" after George's encounter with Dennis (that is, they began to sink into the floor or move too far away from people, necessitating George's ministrations to right them), George's encounter with Blair shows how powerful she is, as George is initially unable to summon a cutout to interact with her. He must go into the wings, retrieve a cutout, and plop it in front of Blair, even as the other cutouts continue to falter sporadically. Blair is formidable indeed.

As supportive as she is critical, Blair represents for the modern-day

George what the Old Lady and Jules collectively represented for the first-act George. The connection between Blair and the Old Lady (actually, first-act George's mother) are clear, as the same actress plays both of these outspoken characters. The connection to Jules should also be clear, as Blair's opinion of George's work—and the influence her opinion carries—matters greatly to modern-day George, just as Jules's opinion mattered to first-act George. Thus, along with Marie, Dennis and Blair emerge as pivotal characters in act 2, not least because they recall pivotal characters in act 1.

These three interruptions, all conveyed with spoken and not sung words, cause us to revisit the perennial question: Where does Sondheim stop and his collaborators begin? The actual words that these characters speak may not have originated from Sondheim's pen. For example, the score suggests that "Putting It Together" might have originally ended with Part XV, that is, before Dennis's interruption. The vocal line for Part XV (measure 5a) is marked "GEORGE: *(Last time)*," and the non-Sondheim cocktail music is interpolated midway in this part with numbering that accentuates its interpolation (measures 28a–h). Then, after Blair's interruption and the retrieval of the cutout (Part XVII, measures 1–32), the score is marked "GEORGE: *(Last time)*." The score thus suggests some last-minute additions to the score (and scene) that may not have been all from Sondheim's mind.

Even so, the plotting of the scene had to rest in part with Sondheim, and the use of music during the interruptions shows how Sondheim participated in the intensification that takes place. The Randolph-Naomi interruption takes place entirely over cocktail music (Part XIV); in other words, Sondheim's musical contribution was to leave space for Paul Ford and the pit band to improvise. Dennis's interruption (the cocktail midsection of Part XV) happens in part over improvised music, but the moment Dennis announces that he is quitting, Sondheim's music comes in. As Dennis raises the dramatic stakes, Sondheim supports him musically. (The music continues through Alex's snub of Dennis and underscores the conversation between George, Alex, and Betty, which in many ways is a continuation of Dennis's interruption, in that it highlights relational dysfunction within the creative community.) For Blair and her interruption, Sondheim appears to have provided all of the music (beginning of Part XVII), with its slightly off-key chords and the occasional jab of widely spaced intervals. Here, the music contributes to the tension that is brewing between Blair and George.

Whether it can ever be determined which part of the collaboration is

Sondheim's and which is Lapine's (or Ford's or that of Paul Gemignani, the music director for the show), it is likely that the threefold repetitions in "Putting It Together" occurred through a deep knowledge of the theater rather than from a deliberate plotting of threefold repetitions. If, for instance, the interruptions of Dennis and Blair came later in the concept (as the score suggests), the fact that, with the Randolph-Naomi interruption, they constitute a triad of interruption was a by-product of the determination that "something else is needed here." And yet the structural resilience of threefold repetitions emerges in one last iteration of the practice: in the three ensembles, Parts V, XIII, and XVII(b), where the acknowledgment that "art isn't easy" is thrice voiced with increasingly complex music. (In Part XVII(b), the music at one point breaks into nine parts.) However much input he received from his collaborators, it is Sondheim alone who is ultimately responsible for providing the theatrical frame that holds the song together.

One other theatrical aspect of the song, one small yet powerful moment, merits discussion. Its disarming brilliance gives it a special place in the entire Sondheim canon. Part III of "Putting It Together" is a musical transposition of Part II, so the rhythm and scansion for both parts is identical. In Part II, Harriet makes numerous attempts to articulate her understanding of George's work. Three times, her friend Billy responds, "I'm not surprised." In Part III, Greenberg expresses his concerns about art today, and his colleague Redmond concurs twice by saying, "You're telling me." The interchange between Greenberg and Redmond shifts in such a way that it is Greenberg, not Redmond, who is poised to utter the line, "You're telling me," at the same point where Billy earlier uttered, "I'm not surprised" for the third time. But instead of adopting Redmond's response, which is what we expect, Greenberg coolly utters, "There's no surprise." In that single line, Sondheim showed his brilliance, because it *is* a surprise when we hear those three words. They verbally tie Part III back to Part II. They distinguish the urbane Greenberg from the Texan Redmond and the neophyte Billy. And they send a small shock through the audience that has kept up with Sondheim's lyrics to that point, for the word "surprise" neither rhymes with nor parrots anything in Part III. There is even a hint of a cross-musical reference, as "Good Thing Going" from *Merrily We Roll Along* contains the words "with no surprise" set to a similar musical figure. The words are like an inside joke with an unexpected punch line. As with the rhyme in Part III of "new, though" and "nouveau," Sondheim has buried delights in places where they continue to surprise.

(The length of "Putting It Together" prohibits reprinting it here. My comments, however, are based primarily on the printed score and not on the original cast recording or the video production. I encourage the reader, even if s/he does not read music fluently, to have the score in hand while reading this section.)

Sondheim's proclivity to think structurally has served as a given in discussing the cinematic and theatrical aspects of "Putting It Together." Let us remind ourselves, then, of Sondheim's understanding of structure. In the quotation that opened this chapter, Sondheim stated that a piece should be "closely structured" and that, in order to achieve such close structure, one must "plan within an inch of its life every bar that [one] can." Without explaining how a piece is divided, Sondheim added, "I generally do it section by section, and I generally make a kind of long line reduction in the music, because I was trained in a sort of conservative school of composition about the long line."

One does not tend to think of Sondheim and conservative in the same breath. He has been cast in the role of Broadway's musical maverick, with commentators pointing to his lessons with Milton Babbitt as "proof" that he is avant-garde. But those lessons covered rather conservative topics, and Babbitt himself downplayed the effect the lessons had upon Sondheim's musical language.[14] Unquestionably, Robert Barrow was conservative in his teaching and his own compositions,[15] and while Sondheim attributed the emphasis on the "long line" and "architectonics" to Babbitt,[16] his pre-Babbitt compositions and term papers make it clear that Sondheim was sympathetic to long-line composition and structural integrity while he was at Williams. Taken all together, then, Sondheim's description of his training as conservative is accurate.

Two other terms move Sondheim away from the realm of songwriter (in the Tin Pan Alley understanding of the term) and into the realm of the classical composer. Few speak of "schools" of tunesmiths, though differences exist between, say, the wide-ranging lyricism of Kern and the blues-inflected repetitions of Arlen. "Schools" usually refer to groupings of classical composers, and given that Sondheim highlighted the conservatism of his school in the 1950s, its opposite would almost certainly be the so-called Second Viennese School of Schoenberg, Berg, and Webern, with its followers (and extenders) at musical institutes in Darmstadt and Paris. Similarly, his description that he usually works "section by section" in tandem with "mak[ing] a kind of long line reduction in the music" fits a classical composer more than a songwriter, whose sections are conceived in the relatively small units of verse and 32-bar refrain (most familiar in the first half of the twentieth century, especially the 1920s through the 1940s) or of verse-refrain-verse-refrain-break-refrain (seen in many pop and rock songs from the 1960s to the present day).

The manuscripts for "Putting It Together" provide ample evidence of his sectional approach to composition and how these long lines join larger units. The manuscripts appear in two separate folders, suggesting that Sondheim may have originally thought of two distinct songs. "The Museum—Party Sequence" contains the music for what will become Parts II–V; "Putting It Together—II-3" contains what will become Parts VI–XVI. "II-3" means that it was the third scene in the second act; the "Party Sequence" does not have a similar number attached to it. The manuscripts do not have the cocktail music, yet another indication that they are not from his hand. (See table 2.)

This two-song background explains the overall architecture of the song: a metaverse (Parts I–X) is followed by a metarefrain (Parts XI–XVII). One can even see how the metaverse is really two introductions, as the manuscript version of "Putting It Together" had its own verse (in the mss., Parts I–III). Though obscured by the size of the song, the song structure serves as an underpinning. In terms of elapsed time in performance—that is, with the cocktail music interludes—the division between metaverse (approximately 4′30″) and metarefrain (6′40″) fulfills the expectation that the latter will be longer than the former. And since there are more interludes in the verse section, where they are generally longer than in the refrain, their removal further highlights the introductory aspect of Parts I–X when one considers Sondheim's contribution alone.

This also explains how and why Sondheim restructured the song in two of its most prominent performances outside of the musical: the revue *Putting It Together* (1999) and Streisand on *The Broadway Album*. (In both cases, Sondheim rewrote the lyrics, removing direct references to George's situation and inserting references to the new circumstances, e.g., vocal projection for the theater revue vs. studio techniques and realities for the recording.) In both versions, material from Parts I–IX is almost completely absent. Variants of Part VI appear, but given that this music itself is recapitulated later in the metarefrain (in Parts XV and XVII), one understands why Sondheim, in rewriting the song for these other ventures, did what many performers do: he discarded the verse.

There is, of course, the irony of rewriting a song about art as business in order to create more business for the song and, in the process, question the song's status as "art." Skillful though the rewrites are, they nev-

TABLE 2. Manuscripts for "Putting It Together"

Heading	Key	Pages	Notes	Score (ke
From folder "The Museum — Party Sequence"				
Party Sequence— Part I (Harriet & Billie)	E	3	Same key as "Gossip Sequence"; key change to F♯, with additional notation: "(i.e., up a tone from previous key)"	II (E♭)
Party Sequence— Part II (Blackmun, Green)	D	2	Discussion of loaning paintings	III (C)
Party Sequence— Part III (Jed, Naomi, Alex)	C	2	Version from which copyist made copy, which is transposed to A major	IV (A)
Party Sequence— Part III (II-3)—revised (Betty, Alex, Naomi)	A	2	Second page crossed out; says "cf. INSERT"	IV
Insert—Part: Part III (12/19/83)		1	Alex and Betty quarrel; Naomi interjects; "Segue to Part IV," which is in G♭	IV
Party—Part 4— Alan and Linda	C	2	Resembles published IV in melodic contour and Harriet-Billy affectionate exchanges ("darling")	
Party Sequence – Part IV (Billie, Greenberg, Alex, Harriet, Betty, Redmond)	G♭	3	Ends with 𝄋 chord (see Example 11)	V (F)
From folder "Putting It Together—II-3"				
Putting It Together— Part I (George)	E♭	2	Fanfare is in flute range, not horn; "Allegretto non rubato (h.n. = 100)"; "ten." marked for every vocal entrance and every held chord	VI (E♭)
Putting It Together— Part II (George)	E♭	2	Accompaniment is marked "non legato"	VIII (E♭
Putting It Together— Part III (George)	E	5	Notation in m. 2: "(raises cutout)"; many erasures; dialogue is given rhythmic contour At key change, at the word "light," figure from "Color and Light": this measure is crossed out and rewritten on next page with accompaniment corresponding to final version "Segue to Part IV"	X (E/G
Putting It Together— Part IV (George, Billie, Harriet)	F♯	9	On p. 5: "Transpose to G♭"; every page thereafter has "in G♭" underlined "Art of making (art)": pointillistic language from "Color and Light" appears in quarter notes "Segue to Putting It Together Part V"	XI (G♭)
Putting It Together— Part V (George, Greenberg, Redmond)	F♯	11	Notation in upper left-hand area, enclosed in a box: "Transpose to G♭" "Segue to Party Sequence, Part V"	XII (G♭
Party Sequence—Part V	F♯	2	Lyrics differ from final version; ends with 𝄋	XIII (G
Putting It Together— Part VI (George)	F♯	6	In a 5/4 measure, a notation to George: "(glances at cutout)"	XV (G♭
Putting It Together— Part VII	E/F♯	15	At Alex's comment, "Little technical fuck-up tonight, Dennis?" Sondheim wrote,	XV–XV (E/G♭)

TABLE 2.—*Continued*

Heading	Key	Pages	Notes	Score (key)
			"Putting It Together Part III" and provided m. no. from the earlier part Key changes for B section to G♭ At end, a four-bar sketch for choral ending, starting in G but returning to G♭ "Segue to Putting It Together Part VIII"	
Putting It Together—Part VIII	G♭/A♭	22	Refers to earlier m. no. for musical repeats; indicates when characters enter and exit, including "(cutout droops)"; chorus sings a tonic chord but accompaniment has § Revision, 3/23/84: reworking of contrapuntal section Revision, 3/24/83: chorus now ends with suspended dominant, which resolves in last measure	XVII (G♭/A♭)

ertheless obscure the craft Sondheim invested in the original. For it is in the metaverse that he set forth the materials for the main part of the song.

Each half of the metaverse contains a threefold dramatic repetition, with the last repetition intensified. Looking only at the Sondheim musical material, we see that he reinforced the repetitions and intensifications through his musical choices. Parts II–IV and Parts VI–X (even numbers) are cast in AA′B form, a common formal choice for the verse to a 32-bar song, especially in Gershwin's songs (cf. the verses to "Someone to Watch over Me," "They Can't Take That Away from Me" and "But Not for Me"). Here, in "Putting It Together," the shift to new material in the third section of each introduction creates musical tension through novelty. The musical structure thus simultaneously recapitulates the dramatic structure and conforms to standard song-form practice.

And the manuscripts show how the metaverse is derived from other pieces. "Party Sequence—Part I" is in the key of E♭ major. While this will be transposed to E major in the published score, the manuscript's key makes the music's debt to act 1's "Gossip Sequence" even clearer. There in act 1, Celeste #1 relates rumors she has heard about George's private life, and Celeste #2 responds, "I'm not surprised." (See Example 1.) Not only is the music from the "Gossip Sequence" repeated in Parts II and III of "Putting It Together," but Sondheim also brought over some of the lyric as well, even though the lyrics from the manuscript to the published version will not be identical.

The remarks in the "Gossip Sequence" are also ad hominem: the Celestes know George, not his work, and they disparage him. The

Example 1. "Gossip Sequence," mm. 35–38.

reprise neatly reverses this relationship: the guests at the reception critique the Chromolume, not George. But the music's reprise also invites us to conflate person and work and read the guests' criticism as an indictment of George himself, in the same manner that Celeste #1 derides George. Indeed, modern-day George later conflates himself with his work going on exhibition, and the three interruptions at the end of the song increasingly point to a personal failing on his part. The musical reprise, then, admits numerous dramatic possibilities.

Even so, there are a number of musical devices employed by Sondheim that make the reprise a new musical statement. First, he rewrote the exclamation heard in the "Gossip Sequence" that "artists are so crazy / artists are so peculiar" (Example 2a). In Parts II and III, it becomes the twice-affirmed remark about the state of the art (Example 2b). Though the words have been changed significantly, the sense of peculiarity remains, expressed directly at art and obliquely at the artist. Second, Sondheim interposed a rhythmic figure that positions the music in the pop culture of the early 1980s. The ostinato that accompanied the "Gossip Sequence," with a right-hand four-note figure superimposed upon a left-hand three-note figure, is turned into a vertical sonority with a more contemporary sound. Sondheim updated the gossip, if you will. (See last measure in Example 2b.) Lastly, with this update comes a "new" figure in the bass, which is another superimposition, this time of the first three notes of the bass figure that appears in measure 49 of "The Day Off (Part I)."

Much of the remaining music in Parts II–X of "Putting It Together" will derive from different sections of "The Day Off," raising the question of what parallels exist between celebrating a cessation of work and criticizing a work of art. The chief element that links these two songs is their multisection construction put to the service of multiple character

EXAMPLE 2a. "Gossip Sequence," mm. 55–58.

EXAMPLE 2b. "Putting It Together," Part II, mm. 11ff

development. It is a structural parallel, not an inherently dramatic one.[17] Still, the music invites comparison between the earlier crowd scene and this one. The superimposition provides one more example of Sondheim's contrapuntal tendencies. This trait is given its fullest treatment in Part XVII, where it has a particular structural significance in light of Sondheim's oeuvre. But this layering of musical material can be traced back to his piano sonata at Williams and occurs with such regularity in his work—the montage in *Follies*, the trio in "Soon" *(A Little Night Music)*, the "Johanna" quartet *(Sweeney Todd)*, the final scene in *Passion*—that this contrapuntal device unquestionably lies at the core of the Sondheim sound.

If the borrowing from "The Day Off" is obscured in Parts II and III of "Putting It Together," Part IV spotlights the connection. This B section of the first introduction is a rearrangement of measures 1–10 of "The Day Off (Part V),"[18] and the two moments share dramatic similarities as well. In act 1, the music accompanies Franz and Frieda, the servant couple, as they have a disagreement of sorts, and precedes Franz's apostrophe on work. In "Putting It Together," the music accompanies the disagreement of Alex and Betty over the artistic worth of the Chromolume. In both cases, the music and the pace of communication are atomized, more suggestive than expository. But whereas in act 1 the moment unfolded into something more substantial musically, in act 2 its truncated state and its distinction from what came before accentuate the pitch of the disagreement between Alex and Betty and, indirectly, the tension that the other guests feel toward George's art. Indeed, though the accompaniment is very familiar—it runs through much of "The Day Off," beginning in Part I—the difference between how the vocal lines scan in the two acts ("Second bottle" vs. "He's an original") nearly obscures the earlier appearance as the exact model for Alex and Betty; it is a musical intensification when compared to its earlier appearance. And as with Parts II and III of "Putting It Together," Part IV ends with the exclamation, "That is the state of the art" (again, with music derived from the "Gossip Sequence"), but here Sondheim turns the exclamation into an interrogative, not only in the lyrics but also in the music, which fails to resolve and ends on a dissonance (before Naomi hesitantly says, "Well . . .").

Part V, as stated before, is a structural coalescence and intensification of Parts I–IV, and here, too, Sondheim put act 1 material in new musical clothing. Because of the relationship between Part V and Part X, I will postpone discussion of Part V. Instead, a reminder of Sondheim's attitude toward reprises in general is in order.

> I find the notion that the same lyric can apply in the first act and the second act *very* suspect. . . . I have found places [in my work] where the music could be reprised, but I've never found one where the lyric could be reprised.
>
> I'm not downgrading reprises. I'm saying it's very difficult to find a way that is honest for the evening and therefore doesn't break the audience's concentration and doesn't remind them that they are in a Broadway theater listening to a reprise. . . . I remember when we were writing *Do I Hear a Waltz?* Dick Rodgers wanted a reprise of "Take the Moment." I asked why. He said, "I want them to hear the tune again." For me, that isn't enough reason.[19]

Sondheim here exaggerated, for in fact, well before he said this, he had reprised not only music but lyrics also. The most notable instance is "Lovely" from *Forum,* where the song is first sung by Philia, the beautiful if dim-witted courtesan with whom Hero falls in love. In the reprise,

Hysterium is dressed to look like Philia. He is uncertain that his disguise is effective, so Pseudolus tries to calm him by singing that (s)he is lovely. There is little need for Sondheim to change the words (and the lyric isn't changed much), so significantly have the circumstances altered around the song. What was sweet and touching and only slightly comic in its original presentation becomes ridiculous in its reprise. It is the same song, and it is not. Sondheim also used both music and lyrics in the minireprises in act 2 of *A Little Night Music*, where the beginnings of four songs from act 1 return as commentary for the events on stage. (Members of the Liebeslieder Singers reprise these songs.) And those songs that serve their musicals as frames that separate commentary from action—the larger ensemble numbers in *Sweeney Todd*, *Merrily We Roll Along*, *Into the Woods*, and *Assassins*—likewise reprise both music and lyrics.

Yet Sondheim's remarks demonstrate that, in his manner of working, lyrics and music convey information in profoundly different ways. To begin with, those remarks help to explain why Sondheim could be so amenable to changing or adding lyrics to music that has been removed from the original dramatic context. For him, song (recall the opening quotation) encompasses more than the popular notion of a discrete musical composition with a relatively fixed set of measures containing a limited vocabulary of musical gestures and a concomitant fixed set of words. If the words can be detached from the music and new words can be fitted to the music, do we then have two different songs or two versions of the same song? For example, is Part II of "Putting It Together" the same song as the "Gossip Sequence," or is it an entirely new song? In his willingness to treat lyrics and music separately, Sondheim discarded the traditional understanding of song altogether. This is not to say that he never wrote traditional songs, for clearly he did, both as pastiches—"Sooner or Later (I Always Get My Man)" and "Unworthy of Your Love"—and in his nonpastiche musical idiom—"Good Thing Going" and the opening portion of "Gun Song." But with Sondheim, reprises are suspect because the song itself is suspect. It is more fluid than fixed, and not just when the song emerges from the musical in which it first appeared (or for which it was first written).

Sondheim's dramatic sensibilities use music in three ways. First, it serves as a lyrical container, as a vehicle for projecting verbal information. For many, if not most, of Sondheim's admirers, this is the primary feature of his music: the music exists to highlight his wit as a lyricist. And yet, when recasting his songs for performances outside of their original contexts, Sondheim almost never rewrote the music. (He often restruc-

tured the music, a phenomenon I shall take up shortly, but I cannot think of a single instance where he changed the music as radically as he changed the words.) This fact alone supports his assertion that reprising lyrics is of a different order from reprising music.

Second, music serves as a dramatic mirror for Sondheim, as a vehicle for projecting dramatic information. The fracturing of "Hail to the Chief" at the opening of *Assassins* is more than a musical puzzle à la Stravinsky's "Greeting Prelude." The images associated with this interpolated song are brought to bear on the images we see in this show, where the hail of greeting metamorphoses into a hail of bullets. This is an instance of Sondheim using preexistent musical material for its associative characteristics. The bulk of his music, however, sets its own associative referents, either through its attempt to capture a mood or atmosphere or through its direct association with a character or both. Thus, in *Sweeney Todd,* the music that accompanies the Beggar Woman on her first appearance conveys a mood of agonizing despair and forever thereafter is associated with her, even when she is not visible. In the case of *Sunday in the Park with George,* we are encouraged to draw comparisons between the characters in acts 1 and 2 because of when and where Sondheim reprised the music. In other words, the musical reprise, without its original lyric, takes on a dramatic function, as associations originally attached to the music are carried forward at its reprise.

As I have already suggested, there are times when Sondheim reprised music where there does not appear to be a clear dramatic relationship between the original appearance and the reprise. This brings up the third of his uses of dramatic language: as a vehicle to explore the plasticity of music itself. To take a single melodic idea and develop multiple harmonizations of it; to take an accompaniment figure and compose multiple melodic lines to it; to change the tempo or key or meter of a musical figure, to turn a musical motive upside down or inside out in order to discover new uses for the same material: Sondheim routinely engaged in these and other musical tricks not because the lyrics demanded it nor because the drama suggested it but because the musical material allowed it. In fact, "tricks" is the wrong word, as it unnecessarily leads to accusations of Sondheim's "cleverness," as though such an attribute is a negative thing (and perhaps it is in a medium traditionally understood as being more sincere than clever). Sondheim respected music as a discipline with a set of theories and principles that have been honed over the centuries. As he wrote in his senior-year paper on Copland, craft and technique are among the "greatest virtues" any composer can display, and Sondheim must be understood as being first and foremost a composer who sought to practice these virtues himself.[20]

It is, paradoxically, the thoroughness of Sondheim's compositional skill that enables parts of a single composition to be rearranged in new and various ways. Because pieces are conceived architecturally as related sections held together by a long line, the possibility arises that a different long line can result in a different ordering of the sections. Sondheim famously referred to the score of *Merrily We Roll Along* as being

> built in modular blocks, and the blocks were shifted around instead of having transitions from number to number or interweaving themes the way the songs functioned in *Sweeney Todd*. You take a release from one song and you make that a verse for a different song, and then you take a chorus from a song and make that a release for another song, and then you take an accompaniment from yet a different song and make that a verse in another song. . . . It's like modular furniture that you rearrange in a room: two chairs become a couch, two couches at an angle become a banquette.[21]

As Banfield noted, "[T]his same approach will become evident in *Sunday in the Park* and, more pervasively, *Into the Woods*."[22] But modular construction is only an extension of Sondheim's proclivity to move around musical material in multisectional works. Again, this is traceable to his earliest years: consider the developmental sections in the outer movements of the piano sonata or the recycling of material in the multisectional songs from *Saturday Night* (e.g., the title song, "Exhibit A," "In the Movies," and "Class"). Sondheim's penchant for recasting musical material acts as a framing device in *Pacific Overtures*, where the final song, "Next," is not merely a Westernization of the opening number, "The Advantages of Floating in the Middle of the Sea," but is also a thoroughgoing recomposition of the song. (This also is an example of the dramatic aspects of music, as Sondheim speeds up and abbreviates the earlier song as a musical parallel to the accelerated modernization of Japanese society through its contact with the West.)[23] So pervasive is the recomposition and rearrangement of materials in Sondheim's work that it seems to be almost a musical reflex for him. Thus, the commercial versions of "The Day Off" (the original cast album) or "Putting It Together," in which entire sections are moved around, added, or omitted, are part of Sondheim's compositional aesthetic. There is no song per se, only pieces of songs that are assembled and disassembled throughout the course of a show, or even the course of an individual song. (In "Live,

Laugh, Love" *(Follies)*, the multisectional form of that song lays the foundation for the spectacular dismantling of the song, story, and show.)

This emphasis on section instead of song separates Sondheim's sound world from the more traditional scores of American musical theater. While his musical characterizations are arguably more incisive than those of his more melodic contemporaries and successors (Coleman, Lloyd Webber, Schönberg, Wildhorn, Stephen Flaherty), his modularity figuratively and literally deconstructs traditional understandings of popular songwriting. Sondheim's focus is upon music, not tunes. And those composers who have followed his penchant toward musical modularity (Finn, Guettel, LaChiusa) likewise suffer from a lack of infectious tunefulness. Musical structures rather than soaring melodies fire their imagination, which, to critics like John Lahr, is a betrayal of the very nature of American musical theater.[24]

Be that as it may, Sondheim's structural bent comes from his study with his "conservative" teachers, Barrow and Babbitt, as does his adherence to, and practice of, the laws of Western music generally and counterpoint especially. These features suffuse all of his work in ways that lead the musically untutored to call his music "complex." With Part VI of "Putting It Together," some of that complexity is laid bare.

The manuscripts throughout contain an uncanny amount of musical detail, especially here. All of the "ten." markings in George's vocal part are present, as are instructions of tempo (Allegretto non rubato) and attack (non legato). One imagines Sondheim upstairs in his studio being George, dictating his pace and mood by musical means.

Certainly he dictates his entrance. Part VI begins with the horn fanfare that is derived from the five-note figuration from the "Opening Prelude (Example 3)."

Example 3

There, orchestrator Michael Starobin assigned the music to the piano, synthesizer, percussion, and sustained strings, saving the horn sound for the dramatic arrival on the word "harmony" in the tonic key of E♭, that mellifluous key for brass. But the horn there doesn't play the fanfare; instead it prefigures the main melodic idea from the act 1 finale, "Sunday." Given that the "Opening Prelude" was written before the rest of the first act had been composed, Sondheim (and Starobin with him) foreshadowed a number of aural and visual items in the prelude: the fanfare that emerges from the five-note figuration (and appears, un-fanfare-like, in m. 7 of the prelude); the murky image of the horn player in Seurat's painting; the concept of tension (and dissonance) with its (harmonic) resolution; and the importance of the horn sound in the orchestration. When the fanfare is finally assigned to the horn, it is in the introduction to "The Day Off (Part II)." The stage directions are explicit: "HORN PLAYER rises from the stage. Two horn calls. Music continues under."[25] What is almost comical is that Sondheim and Lapine have little other dramatic use for the Horn Player. There is no mention of how or when he is supposed to exit, and the video shows him walking slowly and somewhat awkwardly stage left behind the cutout trees and into the wings. The heraldic nature of the fanfare also seems out of place here; while we meet Franz's wife, Frieda, for the first time, Franz, the two Celestes, and the Nurse are already familiar to us, and none of these characters strike us as requiring a fanfare announcing their arrival. Moreover, after the fanfare it is George who sings what amounts to a musical and thematic continuation of the previous scene, in which he impersonated the two dogs, Spot and Fifi. We have seen him in the previous scene; he hardly needs a fanfare. The moment seems like a miscalculation, and all the more so given that the live Horn Player never appears again, his place being twice assumed by a cutout. He is not listed in either the dramatis personae in the book or the final credits for the video. (The fanfare is cut in the original cast recording of "The Day Off.") He is a dramatic contrivance that corresponds to an image in the Seurat.[26]

But he becomes a very helpful musical contrivance, for the undramatic fanfare of act 1 is put to dramatic use in act 2. In Part VI of "Putting It Together," it functions in the way we expect of a fanfare, as it announces the arrival of George and musically suspends all other activity. It also signals the end of the direct borrowing from "The Day Off," a song principally focused on the nonartistic characters (Jules has a spoken exchange with George between Parts IV and V, Yvonne appears near the end of the song, as do Dot and Louis, and George throughout the song is a vessel for the sentiments of his models, both human and animal.) From here on, "Putting It Together" will borrow its musical materials primarily from music associated either with reverie (daydreaming) or with the creation of art.

The musical shift parallels the cinematic and dramatic shifts that make George the central focus. Accordingly, the music functions as yet another introduction, and just as Parts VI–X paralleled Parts I–V dra-

matically as a threefold repetition with a final intensification, so does the musical structure of the second introduction parallel that of the first. Excluding the fanfare, Parts VI and VIII are basically the same music, with Part VIII experiencing an elision in measure 10 of measures 11 and 13 in Part VI. (Parts VII and IX are cocktail music not written by Sondheim.) In both parts, the instrumental music that follows George's solo is a diatonic version of the pointillistic motive we first hear when we see George painting in his studio—"Color and Light (Part I)"—and which becomes principally associated with George's painting or sketching. Its recurrence here reinforces not only the artistic relationship between the two Georges but also their genealogical ties to each other. Part X recapitulates different music from that recapitulated in Parts VI and VIII, so the three parts taken together make up an introduction in AAB form, the same as the introduction contained in Parts II–IV.

When it comes to the parallels between Parts V and X, the matter of choice becomes more explicit. In terms of cinematic or dramatic structure, there is no clear reason to link the ensemble's uncertainty about the nature of art (Part V) with George's musings about the difficulties of securing financing (Part X). At this point in the song, George is not self-critical enough to wonder whether his vision is valid or not. At this stage, his only concern is that if the vision is "only in your head . . . it's as good as dead." For the time being, it remains the concern of the ensemble to question George's artistic validity in terms of the words we hear.

But the words do not tell the whole story, and here we must now look at the music of Part V, its recomposition for Part X, and its structural significance for the entire piece. To begin to address the last of these, Part V is structurally distinct from the two introductions. Cinematically, it is needed to amalgamate the opinions of the diffuse ensemble. But musically, it initially seems somewhat unnecessary in its localized context: one could segue from Part IV to Part VI with no tear of the musical fabric. But Part V exists for more than cinematic reasons. Musically, it acts as the ensemble's musical answer to the musical questions they raised in Parts II–IV; it is the "refrain" the first "verse" introduces. Formally, this is clear, as the AA′B of Parts II–IV are followed by the new material in Part V. And in the larger structure of the song, the ensemble's "refrain" is reprised in Part XIII. We shall look later at how Sondheim interleaved the two "songs" in the one piece.

While the melody line of Part V seems relatively new (temporarily discounting the family resemblance of all of the music from the show), the underlying accompaniment is decidedly not. It retains the updated rhythm of Parts II–IV, with its interpolation from "The Day Off (Part I)," measure 49, and the harmonic language and structure of Part V of "Putting It Together" point clearly to a later section of "The Day Off (Part I)," specifically measures 55–65. What is telling in both instances is how the melodies are constructed. After the melody is presented in the first two measures over a tonic chord, it is shifted down a step for the next two measures, which occur over a dominant chord. The fifth through eighth measures repeat the music of the first four measures. For the ninth and tenth measures, the melody is shifted down a third from its original position (which is the same as another step down from the seventh and eighth measures), and the final measure brings the proceedings to an abrupt halt. These two moments from the two acts provide yet another instance of Sondheim's composing multiple melodies to the same accompaniment, something he had done earlier in the "Gossip Sequence," where the Celestes, the Old Lady, and the Boatman all have different melodic figures set to the same repetitive accompaniment figure.

Are we supposed to associate the frustration of the art community in "Putting It Together" with the drama in this section of "The Day Off"? It would seem a stretch, given that, in the latter, the music accompanies the escapades of Spot and Fifi on their day off. Here again is a section of music where there appears to be no clear dramatic relationship between the two moments. And yet the melody in act 2, for all of its putative newness, does bear a passing relationship to the main melodic figure in "Beautiful" from act 1.

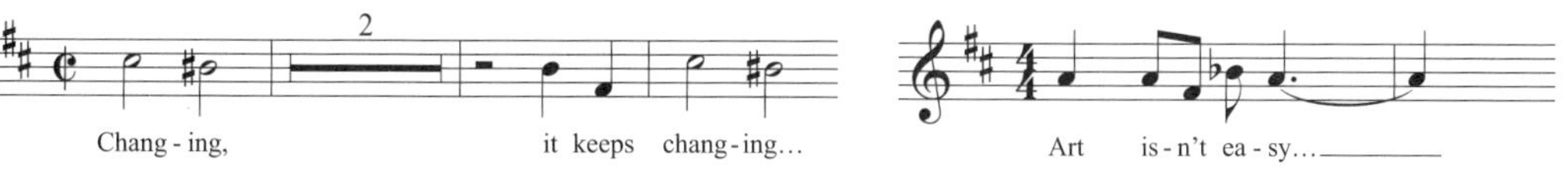

EXAMPLE 4. Motives from "Beautiful" and "Putting It Together (Part V)"

There, the Old Lady complains that the world she knew and understood—"when things were beautiful"—is "disappearing as we look." The ephemera of beauty lead her to command George, "Quick, draw it all," in other words, capture her aesthetic and make it normative for others. She is uneasy about the changes, just as the art community is kept off-balance by the fact that "something new pops up every day." The Old Lady's lament, then, is not far from that of the art community in act 2, which suggests that here the melodic resemblance may be more deliberate than it appears at first glance. Assuming a deliberate melodic borrowing here, it is yet another instance of Sondheim's layering of musical materials, with the melody from "Beautiful" placed over an accompaniment that uses a figure from "The Day Off."

The layering of materials is a central feature throughout "Putting It Together," and Parts VI and VIII provide another example of this practice. After the fanfare in Part VI, the accompaniment consists of four iterations of the same three-chord figure. (The third and fourth iterations add a B♭ above the A♭ in the right hand, and the fourth goes down to a low F in the left hand.) Its proximate source is from Part II, where it served as the updated rhythmic overlay to the bass line that was borrowed from "The Day Off." There, the descending line in the alto voice was chromatic; here, it is diatonic. But in the manner that Sondheim recycled and recomposed these materials, the accompaniment manages to sound new and familiar at the same time.

Example 5a. From "Putting It Together (Part VI)"

Example 5b. From "Sunday in the Park with George"

On top of this accompaniment, Sondheim placed a melody that has appeared many times already in the musical and merits chronicling.

Table 3 traces its use throughout the score. Its first appearance comes when Dot has transcended the realm of the visible and is acting out her fantasy. George is busily sketching "her" in the dress, even though the dress dramatically opened up and freed her just a moment before. He doesn't see what we see, and so he cannot see (or hear) Dot addressing him directly. She is lost in reverie as she contemplates George's eyes, beard, and size, moves on to rhapsodize about his painting, and then, feeling faint, recovers by remembering that she has, in fact, been in the dress all along. This association with daydreaming and contemplation leads me to call this the "reverie" motive, and as table 3 shows, its other appearances throughout the musical occur at moments when the characters are deep in thought or lost in reverie. Most often, it appears as both a harmonic and a melodic component: the former, a tolling of two chords back and forth; the latter, a descent of a step in the melody. Often Sondheim elaborates the melody, adding passing tones and arpeggiations, but in nearly all the appearances of the motive, both its harmonic and melodic components are present.

It is too narrow to say that this "repeated two-chord progression . . . represents George."[27] When, for example, Dot compares her physique to that of a Folly girl, she does not seem to have George in mind; when Marie is referring to all of the images of her mother (Dot) in the Seurat painting, her primary focus is not upon how much her father loved her mother but upon how beautiful her mother was and how much Marie loved her; and when George reads Dot's grammar, he is missing Marie and only near the end of this introduction (in "Lesson #8") does he begin to focus upon himself ("George misses a lot"), whereupon the music changes ("George is alone"). The music accompanies reverie much more consistently than it refers to George. That reverie and thoughts of George collide in Part VI of "Putting It Together" is a happy coincidence, but the musicodramatic lesson Sondheim drew for the attentive listener was that, with George deep in thought about how to move conversations in favorable directions, it was natural for his character to take on the "reverie" motive.

Is the three-chord accompaniment of Part VI an elaboration of the two-chord progression that so often accompanies this "reverie" motive? Perhaps, but even if it is, that doesn't remove the fact of its proximate similarity to Parts II and III. And in the motive's first appearance, harmony and melody were later separated, with the melody continuing over an accompaniment that will take on a life of its own throughout the musical. What makes Sondheim's sound world distinctive is this remarkable economy of material coupled with the plasticity of the material itself,

TABLE 3. The "Reverie" Motive in *Sunday in the Park with George*

Song	Measure Numbers	Incipit	Harmony? Melody? Both?
"Sunday in the Park with George"	77–94	Dot: "Your eyes, George. . ."	Both (77–86); Melody (87–94)
"Color and Light"	Part II: 84–91	Dot: "If my legs were longer . . ."	Both
	Part II: 128–33	Dot: "If I was a Folly girl . . ."	Harmony
	Part III: 194, 196, 198–203 (204ff.)	Dot: "But it's warm inside his eyes . . ."	Both
"The Day Off"	Part I: 7–12	George: "If the head was smaller . . ."	Both
"Everybody Loves Louis"	5–14	Dot: "Hello, George . . . Where did you go, George? . . ."	Both
	51–58	Dot: "The bread, George . . ."	Both
	97–104	Dot: "We lose things . . ."	Both
"Finishing the Hat"	12–15	George: "Yes, she looks for me . . ."	Both
"We Do Not Belong Together"	1–4 (includes a safety)	(under dialogue)	Harmony
	25–31	George: "What I feel? . . ."	Both
	98–101	(under scene change)	Harmony
"It's Hot Up Here"	53–64	Dot: "Hello, George . . ."	Both
"Putting It Together"	Part VI: 3–10	George: "All right, George . . ."	Melody
	Part VIII: 2–9	George: "Say 'cheese,' George . . ."	Melody
	Part XVII: 16-49	George: "Be nice, George . . ."	Melody
"Children and Art"	a–b (introductory vamp)	(under dialogue)	Harmony
	27–35	(under dialogue, then) Marie: "Isn't she beautiful? There she is . . ."	Harmony (both?)
	62–63	Marie: "The child is so sweet . . ."	Harmony (both?)
"Lesson #8"	1–10	George: "'Charles has a book' . . ."	Harmony (both?)
"Move On"	1–8	Instrumental version of "We Do Not Belong Together," mm. 25–31	Both
	55–60	Dot: "Look at what you want . . ."	Both
	103–10	Dot: "Look at what you've done . . ."; George: "Something in the light . . ."	Both
	155–60	Dot: "Anything you do, . . ."	Both (incomplete)

which allows a previously heard melody to migrate to a new accompaniment. Such is the case in the second halves of Parts VI and VIII, where the pointillistic melodic figure from "Color and Light" is now accompanied by an ostinato figure (derived from the fanfare which opened Part VI) that will serve as the principal accompaniment figure for the main part of "Putting It Together." Thus does an old melodic fragment appear with a vamp yet to bloom fully. Just as in the piano sonata from the Williams days, in which he carved three movements out of one six-note idea, so Sondheim more than three decades later created a large musical canvas by manipulating a small handful of musical ideas.

One last section needs to be addressed before we look at the first ten parts as a unit. Part X begins by retaining the accompaniment of Parts VI and VIII and interspersing a solo woodwind obbligato derived from "Color and Light." Later, at measure 11, an accompaniment figure from "Color and Light" appears and alternates with the Part VI accompaniment. And the piece ends with the vamp that closed Parts VI and VIII. In terms of accompaniment, then, Part X shows its indebtedness to the other sections of this second introduction, while it, like those parts, freely borrows and modifies material from act 1. Indeed, the dramatic link between Part X and "Color and Light" is underscored in George's last remark here: "[The vision] has to come to light!"

Yet I have already mentioned that Part X is also a recomposing of Part V, itself a reassembling of other, earlier musical ideas. The principal element linking these two parts is the melody (and the lyric) with which both parts begin. Given all the other musical elements already crowded into Part X, it is hardly surprising that Sondheim made some adjustments in the Part V melody to place it in this new musical context. Now, the melody no longer starts on the fifth of the harmony but on the sixth; the intervallic content of the melody has been redistributed; the music is no longer solidly in the major mode; and its repetition moves up a tone rather than down a tone (Example 6).

Art is-n't ea-sy–
Fight-ing for pri-zes–
Art is-n't ea-sy.
E-ven when you're hot.

EXAMPLE 6. From "Putting It Together (Parts V and X)"

These first three changes help to explain why, on the original cast album, Mandy Patinkin sounds tonally insecure in the opening of Part X. Picking out the fifth of a chord is relatively simple; picking out the sixth is less intuitive, and Patinkin is not helped by the three-chord figure that precedes his entrance, as the chords contain every pitch *except* the sixth. In addition, the basic contour of the melody is the same in Parts V and X, but whereas Part V has (1) a downward leap of a third followed by (2) an upward leap of a fourth and ending with (3) a stepwise descent, Part X reverses the order. It is technically a retrograde inversion of the original melody, and while it is perfectly singable, the redistribution of intervals is disorienting at first. Lastly, while the overall harmonic scheme for the first nineteen measures of Part X (from m. a to m. 17) appears to be E major (by virtue of the key signature of four sharps), the first ten measures obscure the major mode—and even key—by vacillat-

ing between minor-key (F♯ as root) and suspended-dominant (B as root) sonorities. (It could be argued that the melody in m. 1 begins on the second of the harmony, if F♯, rather than B, is understood as the root of the chord. Seconds are no easier to sing than are sixths.)

It would be impossible to know why Sondheim made all of these changes (and the composer himself may not recall why), but they do have a felicitous effect in making the fourth change more noticeable. In Part V, the opening five-note phrase (C, C, A, D♭, C) did not include the first note of the second phrase (B♭). There, the second phrase began a tone lower than the first phrase. In Part X, the second phrase begins a tone higher than the first phrase. Had Sondheim left the original melody intact, the first note of the second phrase would have been sounded in the first. (Using Part V pitches as an example, the second phrase would begin with a D(♭) if it was a step higher than the first phrase.) By redistributing the intervals, Sondheim created the first phrase in Part X (G♯, G♯, F♯, B, G♯) absent the first note of the second phrase (A).

There may be a dramatic reason that led Sondheim to make Part X a refraction of Part V as opposed to a reprise or transposition. While the art community and George both say that "art isn't easy," they seem to have in mind two very different concepts about what makes art hard. Yet the musical reasons for doing so remain: the materials are plastic enough for these kinds of manipulations.

With this in mind, let me close the discussion of the introduction(s) to "Putting It Together" with a look at its composite structure, for the stepwise ascent in Part X may be explained from a different perspective. Sondheim rewrote the measures from the "Gossip Sequence" ("Artists are so crazy . . .") for Parts II and III of "Putting It Together," but he retained two features that were prominent in the earlier music: a stepwise descent between the two phrases; and a cadence that temporarily positioned the music in a new key. In the "Gossip Sequence," the song proper begins in the tonic key of E major; at "artists are so crazy," the music moves to the subdominant (A); at "artists are so peculiar," the music begins a half-step lower (on G♯), using that sonority as the first half of an authentic cadence to C♯. After this cadence "on" C♯, the music starts up again in the key of E major. Sondheim overrode the modulatory aspects of the music in act 1; in act 2, he allowed the passage to take the music into new keys. Part II begins in the tonic key of E♭; at "that is the state of the art, my dear," the music moves to the subdominant (A♭); at the second "that is the state of the (art)," the music begins a half-step lower (G); on the final word, "art," not only have we completed the authentic cadence "onto" C, but the music (Part III) is now "in" the key of C major. Parts III and IV are similarly linked, with Part IV in the key of A major.

Given that the key for the main part of the song (XI–XVII) is G♭ (enharmonically the same as F♯), the first four parts seem headed logically to the main key, given that each modulation is a minor third lower. Had Sondheim completed the chain of modulations (E♭ to C to A), Part V would be in F♯, a minor third away from Part IV. The end of Part IV does feint in this direction, with its hovering, interrogatory final sonority of a supersaturated D major thirteenth chord. But instead of folding into F♯, the music overshoots its target and lands (in Part V) in F major. As if this miss were not bad enough, Sondheim here recomposed the material from "The Day Off" so that the fifth iteration of the idea—which in the earlier song moved down to the third of the tonic—still retains the descent of the third in its melodic contour but the harmony is now reinterpreted as if the fifth iteration still began on the fifth of the key and not the third, as it had before. To say this differently, in "The Day Off (Part I)," the fifth iteration did not result in a modulation; in "Putting It Together (Part V)," it does. And as the modulation now moves the music down a minor third, it is as though the actual modulations in Parts II and III and the aborted one in Part IV have polluted the material in Part V, making it modulatory as well.

By the end of Part V, not only have we missed the targeted tonic key but we are now spinning into a distant modulatory orbit. The fanfare that opens Part VI, then, abruptly stops the modulatory madness and returns us to E♭. This time, rather than approach our target key by downward motion of minor thirds (Parts II–V), the modulations are upward. The cocktail music of Part IX anticipates the new key in Part X, now a half step above Parts VI–VIII. Thus, the reinterpretation of the melody from Part V in Part X, specifically, its repetition up a tone, now has a larger framework in which to operate. It replicates locally what is happening between Parts VIII and XI. And as I have already pointed out, Part X contains an upward modulation, now not of a half step but of a whole one, putting the music in the key of G♭, the targeted key from the beginning (see Figure 1).

As pedantic as this all may seem, it squares with the quotation that opened the chapter. "I generally make a reduction of the long line and know what the key relationships are going to be in the various sections of the song and how the general long line is going to go down or up or cover the third or fifth or whatever it is." In this case, it also shows that Sondheim remained flexible in his long line; in the manuscripts, this song

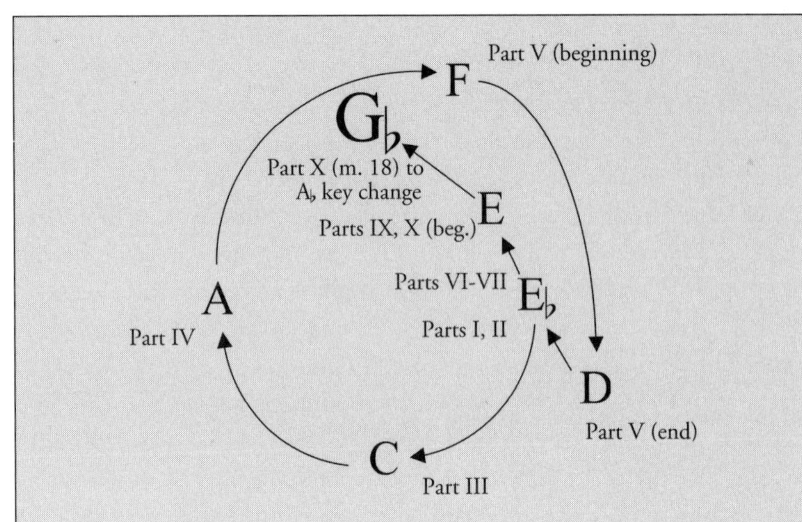

Fig. 1

begins in E major, modulates to D major, C major, and A major, lands in G major, and then goes to E major for the ascending modulation to G. Sondheim refined his long line by nudging his key areas while retaining the overall concept of modulatory suppleness. But the long line remains. Sondheim made his long-line remark in 1978, six years before the premiere of *Sunday in the Park with George*, but he volunteered that such thinking goes all the way back to his study with Barrow and Babbitt. Sondheim acknowledged that he adored the emphasis Barrow placed on technique and the dismissal of romantic notions surrounding the meaning of inspiration. With a song the size of "Putting It Together," one can scarcely imagine that its harmonic, melodic, and motivic construction were happy accidents of "inspiration," and both the manuscripts and the finished score suggest that craftsmanship was ever in Sondheim's mind as he wrote and refined this song.

". . . Putting it together"

Although the main part of "Putting It Together" is longer than its introduction, Parts XI–XVII are in many ways easier to talk about because of the large-scale repetition within these parts as well as their incorporation of materials from the introduction that have already been discussed. Let us begin, then, with a synoptic view of the structure of Parts XI–XVII.

Those sections marked by an asterisk are in keys other than the main tonic of G♭. (The interruptions are those discussed above in the section "Sondheim the playwright.")

A—"Bit by bit . . ." 20 mm. (XI, mm. 1a–20)
A—"Ounce by ounce . . ." 28 mm. (XI, mm. 23–52)
A—"Link by link . . ." 18 mm. (XII, mm. 24a–43)
B—"Art isn't easy . . ." 12 mm. (XII, mm. 44–55)
A—"Ev'ry time I start to feel defensive . . ." 12 mm. (XII, mm. 56–67)
Interpolation derived from V (XIII)
Interruption 1 (XIV)
A—"Dot by dot . . ." 24 mm. (XV, mm. 5a–28)
*Interruption 2 (XV, mm. 28a–h)
*Interpolation derived from X (from XV, m. 30 to XVI, m. 2)
B—"Art isn't easy . . ." 13 mm. (XVI, mm. 3–15)
A—"So you should support the competition . . ." 28 mm. (XVI, mm. 16–43)
Interruption 3 (XVII, mm. 1–15)
Interpolation derived from VI (at XVII, mm. 16–49)
*A—"Bit by bit . . ." 56 mm. (XVII, mm. 50–106)
Solo and ensemble references to II–IV are interleaved with A, mm. 68–106
*Coda—Reference to end of II–IV (XVII, mm. 107–18)

This overview omits a few measures of music that appear as brief introductions to sections or safeties that link sections. And as I have already mentioned, the numbering of measures throughout shows that some cuts and additions were made between the time Sondheim finished his fair copy and the time the vocal score was prepared. For example, in the vocal score Part XII begins with measure 8 and, five bars later, moves to measures 24 and 25, a safety, after which the vocal line begins in measure 24a.

"Putting It Together" is derived from the fanfare in a most ingenious way. While the fanfare's three middle notes span the octave, the first and last notes of the fanfare (circled in Example 7) span a second.

Example 7

These two elements are all Sondheim used to spin out the A sections of the song. The middle three fanfare notes open the song ("1") and then are immediately repeated with the addition of a second on either end of the figure ("2a"; seconds are circled). This second figure is then immediately repeated with its ending transposed up a third, followed by a descending scalar line ("2b"). Upon closer examination, the descending line is nothing other than the inversion and filling in of the ascending figure with which 2a begins (and which was derived from 1; see circles in 2b). Next, the inversion is extended further, now flipping the fifth at the end of 1 so that it descends ("2c"). And later, Sondheim removed most of the ascending notes of 2b and extended the last note, creating what feels like an augmentation of 2b, even though most of the quarter notes have not changed value ("2d").

EXAMPLE 8. Motivic Construction in "Putting It Together"

To appreciate how thoroughly Sondheim relied on these five figures, note that table 4 accounts for nearly all of the A material in "Putting It Together." (It omits the interleaved references to Parts II–V in the final appearance of this material; see above.) It shows how Sondheim made subsequent sections longer, typically by repeating 2c (though once he used 2b again) and how 2d, with its long-held note, is treated as a cadential figure, leading to the palindromic device of closing sections with 2a followed by 1. It also indirectly shows how 2c, the derivation farthest removed from 1, is also the most unstable figure and that it seeks har-

TABLE 4. Construction of "A" Sections in "Putting It Together"

Part Number	
XI, mm. 1a–20	1 2a 1 2b 2c 2b 2c 2c ——→ 2a 1
XI, mm. 23–52	1 2a 1 2b 2c 2b 2c 2c 2c 2c ——→ 2d 2a 1
XII, mm. 24a–43	1 2a 1 2b 2c 2b 2c 2c 2c
XII, mm. 56–67	2c 2c 2c 2c 2c 2c
XV, mm. 5a–28	1 2a 1 2b 2c 2b 2c 2c 2c 2c 2c 2c
XVI, mm. 16–43	2c 2c 2c 2c **2b** 2c 2c 2c 2c 2c 2c
XVII, mm. 50–106	1 2a 1 2b 2c 2b 2c 2c 2c 2c 2c 2c 2c 2c 2c 2c 2c 2c 2d 2a 1 1 1 1 1 1

monic and melodic resolution; a comparison of table 4 with the synopsis of the main song shows that every non-A event is preceded by an A phrase that ends with 2c.

This example of motivic economy and development is par for the Sondheim course. Until the complete scores for the student shows come to light and we can see to what extent he tied these scores together through motivic development, the piano sonata remains the first significant example of Sondheim's creating a vast musical canvas from a handful of musical motives. But it would not be the last. He referred to *Anyone Can Whistle* as

> sort of a music student's score. That whole score is based on the opening four notes of the overture, which is a second going to a fourth. All the songs are based on seconds and fourths and the relationship between a D and an E and a C and an F. The fallacy is that the music isn't continuous, so that it doesn't mean anything to the audience's ear *really*—except to some musicians who could possibly hear it. But the seed doesn't germinate the way it does in a symphony with a continuous spread. It germinates, and then there is dialogue, and then I remind everybody that it's based on the second or fourth . . . it's all too late. But it helped *me* make the score.[28]

Banfield suggested that Sondheim retrospectively viewed his statement as an exaggeration,[29] and it would be difficult to account for the pitch and intervallic features Sondheim mentioned across the entire score. But what remains essential is how this compositional construct assisted Sondheim in making the score. And one finds evidence later of motivic manipulations and overriding compositional constructs. The four-note melodic figure that opens "Side by Side by Side" (*Company:* the words are "Isn't it warm?"), which ends with an ascending figure, is recomposed midsection ("What would we do. . . ?") and goes downward. The pastiche songs the principals sing in *Follies* (original 1971 version) share significant musical gestures with the nonpastiche numbers assigned to these characters.[30] *A Little Night Music* is held together by the organizing principle of multiples of three. The association of certain musical gestures with certain characters in *Sweeney Todd* has an almost Wagnerian feel about it. In *Merrily*, the composer Franklin Shepard has only one tune in him, but that one tune gives us "The Hills of Tomorrow" (from the original 1981 version), "Who Wants to Live in New York?" "Bobby and Jackie and Jack" (both the opening section and the central waltz, "We're Bringing Back Style to the White House"), and "Good Thing Going." The central section of "No One Is Alone" (*Into the Woods:* at the words "People make mistakes") is an inversion of the "magic" motive introduced when the five beans are doled out.[31] In *Assassins*, pre-existent music ("Hail to the Chief," Sousa's "El Capitan March," "Nearer, My God, To Thee") is turned into new songs, and melodies once presented are themselves manipulated (e.g., the Balladeer's music in "The Ballad of Booth" is taken up by Booth when he sings).[32] The two main motives in *Passion*—the "obsession" motive that saturates the score and overtakes the "happiness" motive—are chiasms of each other.[33] And in *Bounce*, musical motives migrate from song to song. In all these instances, in a time period spanning four decades, Sondheim put the music together bit by bit, piece by piece, writing tightly composed, highly worked-out compositions. To someone like theater critic John Simon, such writing may seem pretentious,[34] but for Sondheim, there truly is no other way to compose.

The B sections of "Putting It Together" further illustrate the interrelatedness of musical material throughout the song. Its initial phrase, "Art isn't easy," moves past the refracted version George sang in Part X and adopts the original version the ensemble sang in Part V (and will sing again in Part XIII). With its long-held final note, it echoes phrase 2d in the musical example, which heralded the end of a long musical period, and sets the stage for the line's reappearance at the climax for the entire song, when the ensemble sings the line for the last time (Part XVII, mm. 97–106). In a sketch with the title "George—Verse III," one can see how Sondheim derived the larger musical idea for B from the "bum-bum-bum" sections in act 1. The B sections also employ the second-half downward shift of a minor third that figured in all of the ensemble moments in the introduction, although the remainder of the melodic material is yet another recrafting of the A material, specifically, the downward descent through the fourth that occurs in 2b–2d (Example 9).

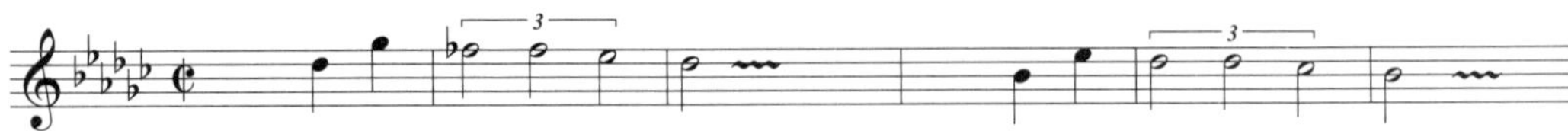

Example 9. Motive from "B" section of "Putting It Together"

Here, George seems to adopt not only the music but also the attitude of the ensemble. He remembers the importance of keeping his artistic vision clear, even as he recognizes that such clarity is subject to the whims of fashion. For a moment, he drops his pursuit of money. But after each B section, the music is arrested, and George, unable to find the cadence (in the sense of both lilt and ending) in pursuing an artistic vision, reverts to the "art" he knows best: the art of getting backing. Sondheim neatly portrayed the treadmill-like ordeal facing George in this pursuit by building the A sections that follow the B sections almost entirely out of 2c, the most worked-out inversion of the original idea as well as the figure that forever seeks a cadence but itself cannot bring the musical line to an end, as over the course of the song, 2c goes from two consecutive iterations in the first A section to a whopping twelve repetitions in the last.

This musical bloat on the level of phrase repetition also finds deliberate expression in the overall structure of this song. "Putting It Together" is a reworking on a massive scale of the standard verse-and-refrain Broadway song of the 1940s. Instead of one AAB verse, Sondheim provided two, with a linking section between them (Part V) that then recurs in the second verse (Part X). Instead of a classic 32-bar AABA refrain, with eight bars to every section, Sondheim expanded the sections, doubling and trebling them, and added an extra A section the first time through (Part XII, mm. 24a–43). Then the refrain is repeated a second time after an "interlude" derived from the verse (Part XIII, derived from "Party Sequence—Part V," which is not in the "Museum" folder but is inserted between Parts V and VI of the "Putting It Together" manuscripts). In the repeat, Sondheim made additional references to the verse, reaching back almost schematically to more and more distant parts of the verse (first Part X—even returning to the earlier section's key—then Part VI, then finally Parts II–IV). This ongoing reclamation of earlier music—the ever-unfolding reprise, if you will—recalls Sondheim's procedure in act 2 of *A Little Night Music*, but given its localization to one song, it has about it the construction of a symphonic poem by Liszt or the Franck D minor symphony. To call such structural expansion symphonic is not to hear "Putting It Together" as Western art music. And yet, such a sweeping architectural concept is much more common among writers of symphonies (or composers like Ravel) than among writers of song. Not only was Sondheim able to put this song together bit by bit, but he also created a structure that holds it together using the time-tested models of both Tin Pan Alley and the concert hall.

Sondheim's statements about song form are worth revisiting here. I have referred to "verse and refrain"; Sondheim used the alternate designation of "verse and chorus."

> The dividing line between verse and chorus is no longer what it used to be. Songs are much freer in form. The verse is a form of bridging dialogue into song and, if it's a fairly free-form verse, has a feeling to

it of a kind of heightened speech. It's a way of leading them in gently by the hand. I'd say keep it going as long as it's interesting, as long as you've got something to say. You can have a five-minute verse, fine, it will keep my attention. You want it not to overwhelm the chorus, however, if you really want a chorus feeling. If you want the sense of a refrain, then you don't want a top-heavy poem, but I wouldn't make any rule about that. It's like writing anything, it's good insofar as it holds your interest and no longer.[35]

Dialogue is interspersed through the entire song, not just the verse, although the link between Parts I and II is an especially successful bridging of dialogue and song. Sondheim's verse is "only" four and one-half minutes, but he did say much here. And in making the refrain so concentrated in terms of motives and key, Sondheim allowed it to have a "chorus feeling," that is, the sense of arrival.

There remain a number of other features that require consideration before we leave the song. While the refrain stays fairly well anchored to G♭ throughout, in Part XVII, at the end of the Part VI reprise, the music modulates to A♭, and the song concludes in this key. This modulation was prefigured in Part X, where the music also modulated up a whole step from E to G♭ (enharmonically, F♯). But what makes the modulation in Part XVII a classic Sondheim modulation is the manner in which the melody is harmonically reinterpreted. In Part VI and initially in its reprise in Part XVII, the high point of the melody represents the seventh of the tonic key (in Part VI, a D in E♭; in Part XVII, an F in G♭). Instead of rewriting the melody to modulate, Sondheim simply changed the key underneath the melody. When George sings, "You do what you can do," the final note—F—is identical with all the other high notes he has sung in the reprise. But the harmony has shifted; it is now the sixth of the new key. I have already pointed out Sondheim's penchant for reharmonizing melodies or remelodizing harmonies. But this particular feature, of leaving a melody intact while changing its key, is on a different order of difficulty and appears more rarely in Sondheim. But appear it does, as early as the recapitulation in the first movement of the piano sonata (see chapter 1) and as late as Little Red Riding Hood's interjections in "Hello, Little Girl."[36] A similar phenomenon occurs in "Green Finch and Linnet Bird" *(Sweeney Todd)*, where, when the main melodic material returns (at "Ringdove and robinet . . ."), the melody has modulated up a whole step, while the accompaniment initially tries to stay in the song's original key, only to join the singer four bars later (at "Have you decided . . .").

This ability to create a tune that can appear unaltered in more than one key is fundamentally a contrapuntal trick, akin to the canons at different intervals in J. S. Bach's *Goldberg Variations,* and it has already been established how central counterpoint is to Sondheim's compositional aesthetic. "Putting It Together" has several examples of Sondheim plying his contrapuntal craft, so to select only two may give the impression that these are exceptional examples, when in fact, they are not. In the first example, Sondheim added an inner voice that complements the melody (see Example 10). More than this, the ascending chromatic nature of this countermelody works to increase the tension during this section—one of the chains of 2c iterations—and significantly is introduced after the first statement of the A material; that is, Sondheim held this device initially in check. In his orchestration, Starobin accentuates the ascending line by giving it to strings, which sustain each note. And Sondheim himself said that "occasionally, in fact, some of the orchestrations are merely the piano scores with instruments assigned to the contrapuntal lines."[37]

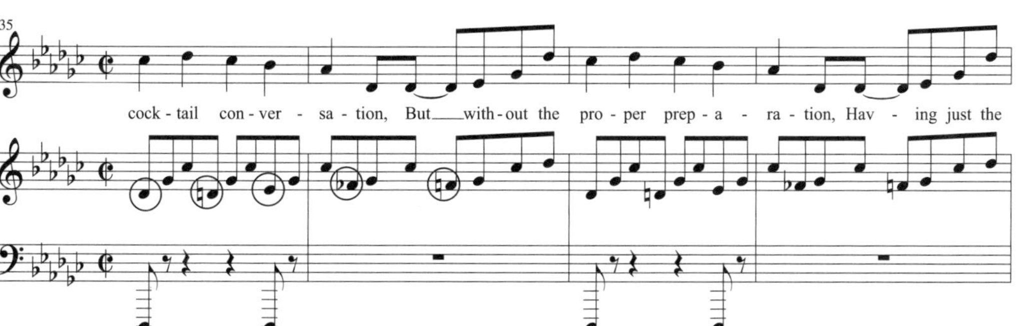
35
cock - tail con - ver - sa - tion, But with - out the pro - per prep - a - ra - tion, Hav - ing just the

Example 10. Contrapuntal countermelody in "Putting It Together"

The inner lives of Sondheim's songs would require more space than can be allotted here. But one can easily think of a number of salient examples: the descending chromatic line at the end of the verse in "Our Time" *(Merrily)* that then emerges, in diatonic form, as the main tune of the refrain; the various inner voices in "Not While I'm Around" *(Sweeney Todd)* that comment on Toby's sincerity and Mrs. Lovett's duplicity; the languid line in "What Can You Lose?" *(Dick Tracy)* that, in musical terms, seeks to answer the question the lyric poses; the undulating line that accompanies the word "Lovely" in the song of the same name *(Forum);* the skipping line that accompanies Desirée and the rocking one that accompanies the Liebeslieders in "The Glamorous Life" (*A Little Night Music,* stage version) or the descending line, straight out of Rachmaninoff, that occurs in the release of "Send In the Clowns." These inner lines—and the involved accompaniments that house them—are integral to Sondheim's songs and provide yet another reason why his music is irreducible to the traditional lead-sheet structure of melody and chord symbols.

The inner lines spill into Sondheim's extended ensembles in ways that become almost geometric, to use the term Sondheim applied in referring to how music ought to be put together.[38] Most of these extended ensembles fall into three parts. First, a long opening section presents the main musical ideas, sung individually by the various characters in the ensemble. Second, a shorter section follows, in which fragments of the melodies are treated contrapuntally. (Typically, only the head of each melodic idea is used, distributed among the singers.) This method of handling musical material differs from the quodlibet, where melodies ordinarily begin and end at the same time (e.g., "An Old-Fashioned Wedding" from *Annie Get Your Gun*, "Tradition" from *Fiddler on the Roof*, or "Cocktail Counterpoint" from *La Cage aux Folles*), nor is Sondheim's technique strictly canonic (e.g., "Fugue for Tinhorns" from *Guys and Dolls*). In these central ensemble sections, musical entrances are terraced to reinforce the contrapuntal texture, and these fragmented melodies accelerate both musically and dramatically the trajectory of the song. Third, this contrapuntal section gives way to group song, normally reprising either the chief melodic idea for the ensemble or a song from another part of the musical, or both. Although Sondheim often incorporates old material in this last section, the reprises are seldom an exact repetition of the original material. These ensembles also tend to be through-composed, once again in contradistinction from quodlibets, with their base structure (the length of the principal melodic line) repeated at least as many times as there are additional individual lines. A classic example of this type of extended ensemble is "It's a Hit" *(Merrily)*; the finales for both acts of *Into the Woods*, the opening and closing "Ballad of Sweeney Todd," and "Please Hello" *(Pacific Overtures)* also employ this device.

While Part XVII of "Putting It Together" is more solo song than ensemble writing, it nevertheless tends toward this tripartite structure of a long opening section followed by a shorter section of intricate counterpoint based on fragments of earlier melodies and then ending in a homophonic ensemble statement. Here, the second section is set apart as a parenthesis to George's musings. Harriet interrupts George's chain of 2c iterations and repeats a line from Part II, the second line she uttered and the third musical vocal line of the entire song: "But he combines all these different trends." From there, Betty, Alex, Greenberg, Redmond, Harriet, and Billy each reprise both the words and the music that they pre-

sented in Parts II–IV, and the others join them with a brief and newly composed line of their own. Because of the thickness of the writing here, the speed with which it all goes by, and the preferential amplification often provided for George, it is impossible to hear just how intricately Sondheim wove all of these melodic fragments. More than this, these twelve measures (82–93) seem inordinately difficult to learn, given that the result is a Babel-like cacophony where individual expression is unrewarded. Sondheim could have written something simpler or more transparent, but he did not, for part of the Sondheim sound world is the collective din that comes from the collision of contrapuntal lines.

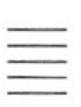

Again, a detailed remark from Sondheim is in order, as he talks about his relish for this type of device (this time in a more transparent ensemble) and his disdain for the quodlibet.

> As for the three songs going together ["Now," "Later," and "Soon," *A Little Night Music*], well, I might as well confess. In those days I was just getting into contrapuntal vocal and choral writing—I had done a little in *Company* and a lot in *The Frogs*—and I wanted to develop my technique by writing a trio. What I *didn't* want to do is the quodlibet method, where you hear one tune, and then you hear another, and you know they're going to go together, and to your dismay they do. I thought, wouldn't it be nice to have three songs you *don't* think are going to go together, and they *do* go together. . . . The trick was the little vamp on "Soon" which has five- and six-note chords in it, and therefore it's like spaghetti sauce—it'll cover almost anything. And in fact, if you listen carefully, the tunes go together until a certain point, and then suddenly one note goes off and then another one a little later, and so on. I made them work together for a while, and it still comes out all right as a trio, but it's not exactly what I intended to do. Nevertheless, I'm still glad I sacrificed the neatness for the surprise, because otherwise the trio would have been an anticlimax.[39]

One can equally imagine that the contrapuntal episodes in the extended ensembles don't always do what Sondheim intended them to do. Yet they stand as testament to his interest in counterpoint in general and contrapuntal vocal and choral writing in particular.

The manuscripts and the published score provide other examples of how Sondheim derived musical elements from previous motives, constructed longer songs, conceived accompaniments, wrote drama literally into the music, and searched for the right sounds. The final five measures serve as a fitting conclusion to this compendium of ideas and techniques. In the manuscripts for the "Party Sequence" and "Putting It Together,"

Sondheim came up with this chord as a final harmony (Example 11, designated § in table 2):

Example 11

As the concluding chord of a piece that ends in A♭, it is decidedly a nonstandard substitution for the tonic. Sondheim will preserve this color but animate it in the ostinato accompaniment that runs throughout the song (Example 12).

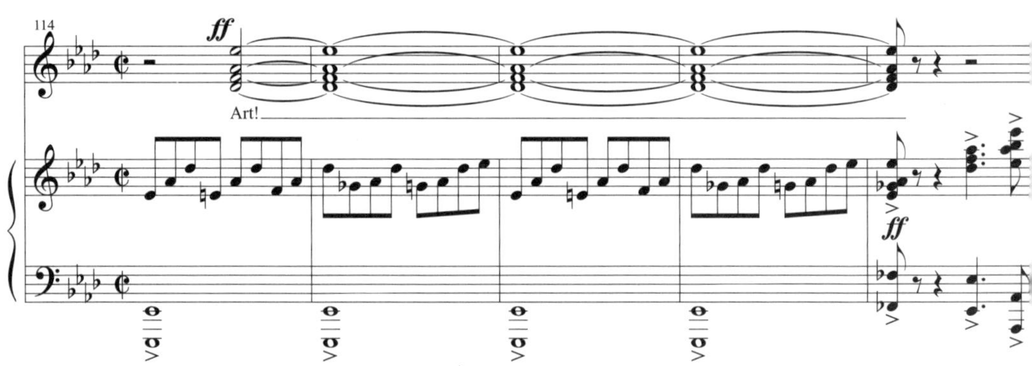

Example 12. Conclusion of "Putting It Together"

In addition, the vocal chord originally was a tonic chord, second inversion, with an added second. In a revision, Sondheim changed it to the suspended dominant (in the preceding example), but resolved it in the final measure. Poetic niceties occasionally occur, as here, where the word "art" is joined to the sonority most illustrative of Sondheim's sonic language. As for the final three chords, they do not appear in the manuscripts contained in the folders. If they are a later addition by Gemignani or another hand, they invoke, both gesturally and harmonically, the "Alleluia" from the *Symphony of Psalms*, that touchstone of Sondheim's youth.

". . . and that is the state of the art"

To close this exploration of Sondheim's sound, consider the lyrical device Sondheim used to frame the entire song. The words "state of the

art" have been used in the scene before this song, where George spoke of the microcomputer that controlled the voltage regulator. (In saying it was made in Japan, Sondheim and Lapine slyly referred to the end of *Pacific Overtures,* where the ensemble asserts that Japanese technology has outstripped American technology.) There, with hyphens linking the words, it refers to something at the vanguard of its industry. When the guests at the reception take up the words (this time with hyphens missing), it describes the condition, if not chaos, in which the art world finds itself at that moment. Given the state of the art (world), it is impossible for them to determine what is state-of-the-art. By the time George uses the term, at the end of the song, we know that the quest for patronage lies at the heart of his understanding of the art world; as Sondheim referred to George, he is "the face of fund raising." Thus, Sondheim's recapitulation of "the state of the art" as the very last gesture in the song invites a wealth of interpretations, as both the guests and George sing the words together—and not to music associated with those words, but rather, to a continued repetition of the fanfare figure (1) that begins with George's dyspeptic catalog of minks and drinks. What is at the vanguard of the art movement? Celebrity art? Postmodernist collage? The equitable distribution of money and attention to all serious artists? No answers exist to these questions, because Sondheim refused to provide a single answer, either cinematically or dramatically or musically. (The music in fact hints at a kaleidoscopic approach to reading what constitutes the state of the art, since the figure that carries these words at the end of the song—1—is the inversion of the figure at the ends of Parts V and XIII, where it is set to words that say that art isn't easy "any way you look at it"—for example, looking at it upside down.)

But in yet another reading of the phrase, the entire song, "Putting It Together," represents the state of the art in musical theater. The song, with its cocktail music insertions, interpolations from other parts, and dramatic interruptions, takes more than eleven minutes to perform. Sondheim stands as the principal author for the entire song, and yet the song also gives indisputable evidence of the work of other authors. It is unapologetically collaborative, and it shows what can result from successful collaboration. On this level, it is at the vanguard of musical theater writing.

Sondheim's specific contributions are also at the vanguard. The lyrics, as is nearly always the case with Sondheim, are brilliant, but the lyrics alone do not tell the story. "Music writing and lyric writing are very different skills," as Sondheim noted, and few authors, solo or multiple, would attempt to create as broad a musical canvas as Sondheim did here, in large part because few authors know how to. "Music writing is a technique on which you have to spend a number of years of training in order to know what you're doing; otherwise you're at the mercy of insufficient tools. Many composers write with no tools at their disposal, and their music is dull."[40] Clearly, Sondheim possesses the musical technique to control all this material.

The audio commentary provides an example of how sophisticated that musical technique is. As "Putting It Together" is proceeding, Mandy Patinkin invites Sondheim to recount act 2's references to act 1. "It was the party to celebrate your last performance. And . . . I made some remark about 'Putting It Together' and 'Finishing the Hat' being the same tune. And Mandy looked at me, *startled*. He had sung it for two years or a year and a half and hadn't consciously [made the connection]." Patinkin then sings the words "putting it together" and "finishing the hat," one after the other, underscoring the similarity.[41] One can appreciate that Patinkin could go through the run and not make the connection, given that he probably never saw the music, where the similarities between the two songs could hardly be clearer. But those who can read music should revel in Sondheim's accomplishment, both here in this song and score and throughout his body of work. His ability to handle and manipulate music is remarkable, and the number of times he has displayed this ability is legion.

More than this, his musical control is placed in league with his theatrical control, with his sense of dramatic pacing and cinematic feel. These multiple filters are only partially instinctual for Sondheim. More often, these vectors of control are the result of deliberation.

> I like to be able to justify verbally everything I do, because I think by being forced to justify it you discover what might be the danger of it. But there are times when you are reduced to saying, "I don't know. It just . . . it just feels right to me. Let me do it and see if you don't think I'm right." Usually I am, because sometimes your instinct takes over and it's not immediately analyzable. Most of the time, though, I think you can say, "That's the moment. That's the moment for a song."[42]

In the case of "Putting It Together," the issue becomes not only whether this was a moment for a song but whether it was a moment for a song of such immense proportions. Sondheim revealed some of the larger structural implications of "Putting It Together" when he said that "most people don't realize that this entire sequence ("Putting It Together") is a replay of 'The Day Off,'" the first act's extended multisection song.[43] But Sondheim's statement isn't entirely true, in that the act 2 song reprises other moments in act 1 and the act 1 song is not a self-contained unit (it segues into "Everybody Loves Louis," and Part IV is recapitulated and developed in "The One on the Left"). Sondheim would be among the first to point out how the songs differ. He would also be one of the last to talk about the amount of plotting and craft that went into either song, given his general modesty and inclination to be self-effacing.

In the audio commentary, Sondheim's only comment directly about "Putting It Together" as a whole is his response to Lapine's statement, "This is a fun number," to which Sondheim replied: "Mm-hm." It is a fun song, filled with fun moments. But the sense of fun needs to be placed next to Sondheim's conception of writing music narrowly and writing for the theater more broadly. In 1991, when asked whether he ever thought of writing only lyrics, as in *Gypsy*, Sondheim answered:

> No. First of all, I have too much fun writing music. I've said it before: I find lyric writing one of the most unpleasant professions in the world, whereas music is fun—not that it isn't hard, too. You can sweat a lot over music, but it's very fulfilling. I was trained and started out as a composer, and I fell into lyric writing, so to speak. I wanted to do both, but music was my joy.[44]

Those who focus on Sondheim's lyrics seem to do so because they more easily understand the joy that comes from writing words than the joy that comes from writing music. Without question, Sondheim the composer owes a perennial debt to Sondheim the lyricist, Sondheim the theater aficionado, and Sondheim the cinephile. All of these factors inform the music, which is what makes Sondheim's music so rewarding (as well as fun) to study.

Still, there are those who loathe Sondheim. Principal among them is critic John Lahr:

> In the sung-through musical that Sondheim pioneered and that Andrew Lloyd Webber popularized, the narrative function has been taken away from the playwright and given to the songwriter. . . . The musical increasingly is not telling a narrative story. Its telling is through song, and song is not sufficient to establish character; it cannot carry the burden of psychology and situation. You need prose and plot. With all he's given the musical, Sondheim, by deconstructing it, has taken it narratively to a place where it can't function.[45]

If Lahr mistakenly joined Sondheim and the "poperetta," he perspicaciously identified the core issue. Song alone may be unable to narrate, but opera composers would argue that music is able to narrate. And Sondheim, the playwright in song, has shifted narrativity to music and not song as understood by Lahr. As Herbert Ross noted, "[T]he audience has become more familiar with [Sondheim's] style . . . the harmonics, the rhythms . . . [and the fact that] his work is moving more and more to the opera and growing less dependent on prose to carry it."[46] It is not that Sondheim's music is more serious than other musical theater composers or even more operatic. It is that it consistently endeavors, *pace* Lahr, to establish and develop character.

Sondheim is upstairs, trying to become the character he's creating. This means knowing how the character walks, talks, breathes, thinks, behaves. It means translating these actions and thoughts into notes and time signatures and tempo markings. It means embedding into the music glances and gestures, camera angles and points of view. "That's something I'm good at and that I'm sensitive to"—Sondheim remarked—"musical dramatization, musical playwriting."[47]

In this book, I have attempted to take Sondheim's sound world apart, bit by bit, in the hope that the reader might better appreciate how, bit by bit, it is put together. There are clearly musical gestures and techniques that make Sondheim's sound what it is. But to focus on these alone is to risk succumbing to the fallacy that, in isolating these musical techniques, we have managed to explain what make Sondheim's sound so fascinating. Instead, I have sought to argue that the fusion of the musical and nonmusical aspects of Sondheim's creative life, the manner in which he weds *melos* and *kinesis*, music and drama, is what makes Sondheim distinct. His sound is not aural alone, and one must have eyes to see as well as ears to hear in order to grasp how Sondheim found his sound.

Appendix: The Concept Musical and Sondheim

While writers have tried to define the concept musical, few have troubled to trace the genesis of the term. In his dissertation Eugene Robert Huber cited Martin Gottfried's 1979 definition of the concept musical and asserted that the term "seemed to enjoy a great popularity in the sixties, seventies and the early part of the eighties."[1] Huber, however, offers no evidence to bolster his assertion. Moreover, by marking the term's genesis in the 1960s, Huber implicitly suggests that the term was not unique to Sondheim; Sondheim was relatively inactive between 1964 and 1970. Joanne Gordon, in contrast, squarely situates the term in Sondheim's work. "*Concept,* the word coined to describe the form of the Sondheim musical, suggests that all elements of the musical, thematic and presentational, are integrated to suggest a central theatrical image or idea."[2]

But the term wasn't coined expressly for Sondheim. John Bush Jones gives a short history of the term, relating that Gottfried, in his review of *Zorba,* began to formulate the notion of a concept musical. "Conception is the big word here—it is what is coming to replace the idea of a 'book' . . . there is even less room than in the usual musical [for story] because Prince's concept . . . apparently won out on every question about cutting."[3] Gottfried further developed his ideas of concept in his review of *Company.*

> [*Company*] isn't a story musical but an alternative to the "book show," which any sophisticated (and there aren't many) musical theatre person knows is silly, passé and doomed. It is also without singing and dancing chorus so that the 14 people in it do everything. That is, it is an ensemble or chamber musical with words and music and musical movement and dance that flow, organically, from the same source. Yet, it hasn't the self-conscious look of an "experimental musical" because it is so sleekly professional.[4]

With his review of *Follies,* Gottfried consolidated his ideas.

> This story is the weakest part of the show, grasped by its makers as a device to hold it together despite their every impulse to throw it away. Stephen Sondheim and Harold Prince finally did throw such stories away (with *Company* which, though produced last year, was conceived after *Follies*) because that is where their theatre has been leading. Sondheim and Prince are up to their ears in dance music theatre but *Follies* was not quite ready to rely completely on concept as the organizational replacement for a book, and so it falls back on the shaky support of a story. James Goldman wrote this story and he was given short shrift by Prince and Sondheim, who were obviously more interested in the concept.[5]

As for which musicals are "concept musicals," it depends on whether the writer is focused on Sondheim. Gottfried, writing broadly, named *Fiddler on the Roof* (1964), *Cabaret* (1966), and *Chicago* (1975);[6] Scott Miller, writing narrowly on Sondheim, named *Company, Follies, Pacific Overtures, Merrily We Roll Along,* and *Assassins.*[7] Dan J. Cartmell, also writing narrowly, omitted *Merrily* but included *West Side Story* as well as *Fiddler on the Roof, Cabaret,* and *Chicago.*[8] Stephen Citron names "*Sunday in the Park with George* (how an artist rearranges reality)" as a concept musical.[9] Foster Hirsch wrote as follows.

> Someone who should know what a concept musical is has his own list.
>
> "*Love Life* and *Allegro* were the first concept musicals," said Hal Prince, who directed a series of landmark concept musicals, including *Cabaret* (1966), *Company* (1970), *Follies* (1971), and *Pacific Overtures* (1976). "They were the first of their kind. Subconsciously, when I first saw them, I noted that they were shows driven by concepts. They didn't work, though I was too young at the time to realize that. (Weill's score is swell, by the way.) Were the shows upstaged by their concepts? In both cases you were so aware of the concept and the craft."[10]

But despite Hirsch's imputation of concept musical to shows that Prince directed, Prince himself repudiated the term.

> The whole label that was put on our shows, the whole notion of the "concept" musical, was one that I really resent. I never wished it on myself. . . . I kept hearing, "We're sick of the goddamn concept musical." And I kept thinking, "Leave me alone . . . I never called it that." It's called a "unified" show, an "integrated" show.[11]

And Sondheim didn't think much of the term either.

> When they say a show is a concept show, what they really mean is that it is some kind of presentational approach—that it's all done in red, or it's all done with mirrors, or it's all a metaphor for . . . war, or whatever. The idea of "concept" comes from wanting to reduce things to simplicities. "Concept" is this decade's vogue word, just as 'integrated' was the vogue theatrical word of the '40s, referring to an approach in which a story is told and characters are advanced through song.[12]

Cartmell suggested that "the concept musical is conceived from inception through performance around a central concept which informs not only the physical production but the actual writing of libretto, music and lyrics."[13] But Sondheim did not distinguish between concept and "nonconcept" musicals when he stated that "in every show there should be a secret metaphor that nobody knows except the authors. . . . In collaboration, we talk about the material until we eventually get down to that terrific moment, after a number of weeks, when the secret metaphor becomes clear."[14] Cartmell also asserted that "a strong director is the most important figure in all aspects of the show, encouraging a real collaboration of the librettist, lyricist, composer, choreographer and designers" and "the concept imbues the script with a built-in staging mechanism and interpretation,"[15] yet he complicated his assertions by stating that directors could impose a concept on *Hamlet*.[16] Shakespeare was also a collaborative artist, but today it is typically Shakespeare's text, and not a reconstruction of a particular performance, that is produced and directed. By extension, directors of revivals of Sondheim's shows could de- or reconceptualize them, thus diminishing Prince's or Lapine's importance to the continued success of the show while retaining Sondheim's score.

Notes

Introduction

1. Mark Eden Horowitz, *Sondheim on Music: Minor Details and Major Decisions* (Lanham, Md.: Scarecrow Press, 2003), 79. Wilson Mizner is one of the characters from *Bounce*, which premiered in Chicago in June 2003; Sondheim's remarks date from October 1997.

2. Stephen Sondheim, conversation with Elvis Mitchell, as part of the Telluride Film Festival, Sunday, August 31, 2003, in Telluride's County Courthouse (hereafter "Sondheim at Telluride"). I thank Bill Pence, cofounder of the Telluride Film Festival and director of the Dartmouth Film Society, for making a videotape of this fifty-minute conversation available to me.

3. Horowitz, *Sondheim on Music*, 25.

4. Marni Nixon, "Soundtracks," episode 7 of *Popular Song: Soundtrack of the Century*, Bravo Network, n.d.

5. Horowitz, *Sondheim on Music*, 25.

6. Sondheim: "The two best writing experiences I've ever had in terms of fun were *The Last of Sheila* and the movie score for *Stavisky* . . . because it didn't involve lyrics, which are hell. They're just no fun to write." "Sondheim at Telluride."

7. Sondheim's remark (found in Steven Robert Swayne, "Hearing Sondheim's Voices," Ph.D. diss., University of California, Berkeley, 1999, 347) comes from Stephen Leacock, "Gertrude the Governess: or, Simple Seventeen," in *Nonsense Novels* (New York: Dover, 1971), 30. In the story, Lord Knotacent (pronounced "Nosh"), father of Lord Ronald, commands Ronald to marry a woman neither one of them has seen.

> "Listen, Ronald, I give one month. From that time you remain here. If at the end of it you refuse me, I cut you off with a shilling."
>
> Lord Ronald said nothing; he flung himself from the room, flung himself upon his horse and rode madly off in all directions.

8. Joseph Straus, *Remaking the Past: Musical Modernism and the Influence of the Tonal Tradition* (Cambridge: Harvard University Press, 1990), 9–14.

1. Sondheim, personal communication with the author, December 20, 2003.

2. Meryle Secrest, *Stephen Sondheim: A Life* (New York: Alfred A. Knopf, 1998), 17–25.

3. Hugh Fordin, *Getting to Know Him: A Biography of Oscar Hammerstein II,* introduction by Stephen Sondheim (New York: Da Capo, 1995), xii–xiii.

4. Tony Sloman, ed., "The Sondheim *Guardian* Lecture," reprinted in *Biased: Newsletter of the Sondheim British Information and Appreciation Society,* spring–summer 1988, 56.

5. Personal communication with Mark Eden Horowitz, January 3, 2004.

6. His compact disc collection is cataloged in a computer database. There as well, the emphasis is on classical music, and the same proclivities toward composers and eras appear. Given that the advent of compact disc technology came well after Sondheim's musicodramatic language was established, I will refrain from making extensive mention of that collection.

7. "Interview with Stephen Sondheim," in David Savran, *In Their Own Words: Contemporary American Playwrights* (New York: Theatre Communications Group, 1988), 229.

8. Craig Zadan, *Sondheim & Co.,* 2d ed. (New York: Harper & Row, 1989), 384.

9. Sondheim, personal communication with the author, December 20, 2003.

10. Sondheim: "I was never one for collecting different performances of the same piece. Whatever I heard the first time around was the performance that would remain the standard for me, and I have very little interest—and still do—in getting different performances of given pieces that I like. . . . I certainly listen to everything I've bought at least twice." Sondheim, personal communication with the author, November 15, 2001. See also nn. 13 and 30.

11. "The Sondheim *Guardian* Lecture," 56. Sondheim: "I like seventh chords—I live on seventh chords. (Ravel gave us that gift.)" Horowitz, *Sondheim on Music,* 43.

12. Swayne, "Hearing Sondheim's Voices," 340–41.

13. Stephen Sondheim, *Desert Island Discs,* BBC Radio 4, December 31, 2000. The "thesis" was in fact a paper written for a class during Sondheim's senior year.

14. Swayne, "Hearing Sondheim's Voices," 338.

15. Stephen Banfield, *Sondheim's Broadway Musicals* (Ann Arbor: University of Michigan Press, 1993), 400. Presumably Banfield wrote Sondheim about the waltzes in *A Little Night Music,* as the notion of "dark" and "romantic" is broached there (219).

16. Roland-Manuel, "Une esquisse autobiographique de Maurice Ravel," *La Revue musicale,* December 1938, as translated in *A Ravel Reader: Correspondence, Articles, Interviews,* ed. Arbie Orenstein (New York: Columbia University Press, 1990), 31–32.

17. Ravel to Jean Marnold, February 7, 1906, as quoted in Orenstein, *A Ravel Reader*, 80.

18. Orenstein, *A Ravel Reader*, 423 and 434.

19. Deborah Mawer, "Ballet and the Apotheosis of the Dance," in *The Cambridge Companion to Ravel*, ed. Deborah Mawer (Cambridge: Cambridge University Press, 2000), 150.

20. G. W. Hopkins, "Ravel, Maurice," in *The New Grove Dictionary of Music and Musicians*, ed. Stanley Sadie (London: Macmillan, 1980) (hereafter *NGDM I*), s.v. G.W. Hopkins, "Ravel, Maurice," 15:617.

21. See Secrest, *Stephen Sondheim*, esp. 44–60 and 270.

22. Secrest, *Stephen Sondheim*, 68.

23. Charles Michener et al., "Words and Music—by Sondheim," *Newsweek*, April 23, 1973, 61; emphasis added.

24. George Benjamin, "Last Dance," *Musical Times*, July 1994, 432.

25. See Swayne, "Hearing Sondheim's Voices," 244–316.

26. The variations are performed by Dominic John on the recording *Sondheim Tonight: Live from the Barbican Centre, London*, Jay CDJay2 1313, 1999.

27. For more on the sonata, see Steve Swayne, "Sondheim's Piano Sonata," *Journal of the Royal Musical Association* 127 (2002): 258–304.

28. Mark DeVoto, "Harmony in the Chamber Music," in Mawer, *Cambridge Companion to Ravel*, 105.

29. My numerous attempts to locate the source for this quotation, including searching the Williams College Library collection, have been thus far unsuccessful.

30. See n. 10 in this chapter for Sondheim's opinion of multiple versions of a performance.

31. Stephen Sondheim, "The Art of the Musical," *Paris Review* 142 (spring 1997): 276.

32. See Banfield, *Sondheim's Broadway Musicals*, 20 and 106.

33. Personal communication, December 20, 2003. Mark Eden Horowitz attended some of the recording sessions for *The Frogs* and related to me that Sondheim may have referred to the first "Evoe" as being reminiscent of Milhaud. But when asked, Sondheim said to me, "There's nothing in *Frogs* that is consciously influenced by Milhaud" (December 20, 2003).

34. Banfield, *Sondheim's Broadway Musicals*, 360.

35. Geoffrey Chew, "Gymnopaidiai," in *NGDM I*, 7:864.

36. Banfield, *Sondheim's Broadway Musicals*, 158, 190 and 205, 232, 74, and 400, respectively.

37. Banfield, *Sondheim's Broadway Musicals*, 215.

38. Sondheim, "Art of the Musical," 276.

39. "The Sondheim *Guardian* Lecture," 56.

40. The George School was a Friends high school in Newtown, Pennsylvania, that Sondheim attended from 1942 to 1946. For the nickname, see Stephen Citron, *Sondheim and Lloyd-Webber: The New Musical* (Oxford: Oxford University Press, 2001), 32. Sondheim: "I liked playing the piano part of the first movement of the Rachmaninoff C minor [concerto, op. 18], which I

played in high school, toured, and gave recitals in Pennsylvania." Sondheim, personal communication with the author, November 20, 2001.

41. Stephen Sondheim, *Bequest* (unfinished novel), Stephen Sondheim Collection, Wisconsin Center for Film and Theater Research at the University of Wisconsin, U.S. Mss 66AN, Box 19, 10 (hereafter "Wisconsin").

42. Swayne, "Hearing Sondheim's Voices," 345.

43. Swayne, "Hearing Sondheim's Voices," 345.

44. For more on Rachmaninoff's counterpoint and its relation to Sondheim, see Swayne, "Sondheim's Piano Sonata."

45. For the identification of the Kitson, see Steve Swayne, "Hindemith's Unexpected Grandson," *Hindemith-Jahrbuch* 32 (2003): 225.

46. For Sondheim's remarks about "Send In the Clowns" as a rhapsody, a piano prelude, and a deliberate imitation, see Swayne, "Hearing Sondheim's Voices," 336.

47. Horowitz, *Sondheim on Music*, 96.

48. See William McBrien, *Cole Porter: A Biography* (New York: Alfred A. Knopf, 1998), 282 and 287–88.

49. For more on the autobiographical aspects of "Opening Doors," see Joanne Gordon, *Art Isn't Easy: The Theater of Stephen Sondheim* (New York: Da Capo Press, 1992), 258; Paul Salsini, "Sondheim, on Campus, Talks about Opening Doors," *Sondheim Review* 1, no. 3 (1995): 6; and Frank Rizzo, "Sunday on a Campus with Sondheim," *Sondheim Review* 3, no. 4 (1997): 4.

50. Sondheim, *Desert Island Discs*.

51. "The Sondheim *Guardian* Lecture," 56.

52. Sondheim, personal communication with the author, March 15, 2001.

53. Banfield, *Sondheim's Broadway Musicals*, 99 and 292.

54. Anthony Tommasini, "A Little Classical Music from Sondheim's Youth," *New York Times*, May 17, 2001, E5.

55. Tommasini, "A Little Classical Music."

56. Sondheim, personal communication with the author, May 8, 2001.

57. For a fuller description of Sondheim's indebtedness to Hindemith, see Swayne, "Hindemith's Unexpected Grandson," 215–34.

58. Heinz-Jürgen Winkler of the Hindemith-Institut provided these facts about Barrow and about other American students on September 12 and 19, 2001, in email correspondence.

59. Eckhart Richter, "Training Prospective Composers to be *Compleat* Musicians: Hindemith's Teaching at the Berlin Musikhochschule," *Hindemith-Jahrbuch* 20 (1991): 28 and 38–39.

60. Sondheim, "Art of the Musical," 263–64.

61. Sondheim, personal communication with the author, March 15, 2001. See also n. 45.

62. Frederick J. Bashour studied at Williams from 1965 to 1969. Personal communication with the author, August 27, 2003.

63. Zadan, *Sondheim & Co.*, 121–22.

64. See Ted Chapin, *Everything Was Possible: The Birth of the Musical "Follies"* (New York: Alfred A. Knopf, 2003), 64, 169, 217–18.

65. "Stephen Sondheim in a Q & A Session: Part II," *Dramatists Guild Quarterly* 28, no. 2 (1991): 12.

66. Horowitz, *Sondheim on Music*, 29.

67. Howard Pollack, *Aaron Copland: The Life and Work of an Uncommon Man* (New York: Henry Holt, 1999), 211.

68. Zadan, *Sondheim & Co.*, 6.

69. Secrest, *Stephen Sondheim*, 102. Secrest also incorrectly identifies the second movement as using "experimental techniques, such as plucking the piano strings"; the first movement alone uses this technique.

70. Sondheim, personal communication with the author, March 15, 2001.

71. Sondheim, personal communication with the author, November 20, 2001.

72. Secrest, *Stephen Sondheim*, 86.

73. For an overview of the remarks by Banfield and Secrest, see Steve Swayne, "*Music for the Theatre*, the Young Copland, and the Younger Sondheim," *American Music* 20, no. 1 (spring 2002): 82–83 and 97–98.

74. James M. Keller, "*Sweeney Todd, the Demon Barber of Fleet Street:* A Musical Thriller," brochure notes for *Sweeney Todd,* Live at the New York Philharmonic (compact disc: NYP 2001–2), 16

75. "The Sondheim *Guardian* Lecture," 56.

76. Pollack, *Aaron Copland*, 210.

77. Banfield, *Sondheim's Broadway Musicals*, 106. I thank Howard Pollack, who reminded me that the Coplandesque section of "Free" appears in the musical's overture.

78. Swayne, "Hearing Sondheim's Voices," 331. See also Stephen Sondheim, John Weidman, and Loren Sherman, *"Assassins": An MTI Video Conversationpiece* (New York: MTI Enterprises, no catalog number, 1991).

79. See Swayne, "Young Copland and Younger Sondheim."

80. See Horowitz, *Sondheim on Music*, 50–51.

81. Banfield has expanded upon his previous statements, offering hints, but not proof, of Copland's influence on Sondheim. See Stephen Banfield, "Copland and the Broadway Sound," in *Copland Connotations: Studies and Interviews*, ed. Peter Dickinson (Woodbridge, Suffolk: Boydell Press, 2002), 153–57.

82. But see Swayne, "Young Copland and Younger Sondheim," 101 n. 41, for a possible explanation of Sondheim's inclusion of the Copland.

83. Savran, "Interview with Stephen Sondheim," 229.

84. Alan Poulton, "Sondheim's Island Choice," *Sondheim News*, April 2001, 7.

85. "The Sondheim *Guardian* Lecture," 56.

86. "Probably what I had in mind is Gösta Nystroem, who was, of course, Swedish, and not Norwegian, and Montsalvatge, who was, indeed, South American. They have written some of my favorite pieces, so, naturally, I lump them together." Sondheim, personal communication with the author, November 20, 2001. Montsalvatge was in fact Catalan.

87. Sondheim, personal communication with the author, December 20, 2003. I thank Jim Leve for initially making me aware of these concordances. At the Wall-to-Wall Sondheim event at New York City's Symphony Space on Saturday, March 19, 2005, violinist Christina Sunnerstam introduced the violin sonata by asserting that the music of Swedish composer Dag Wirén has profoundly influenced Sondheim's work. Mark Horowitz asked Sondheim about Sunnerstan's remark during a break. Sondheim responded that, though he liked Wirén's music—especially the Serenade for Strings, op. 11 (1937)—Sunner-

stan was mistaken, whereupon he reaffirmed the influence of Nystroem generally and the *Sinfonia del mare* in particular. Mark Eden Horowitz, personal communication with the author, March 23, 2005.

88. As quoted in Willi Reich, *Alban Berg's "Wozzeck": A Guide to the Text and Music of the Opera* (New York: Schirmer, 1952), 22.

89. Sondheim referred to Berg and *Wozzeck* still later in life. See Horowitz, *Sondheim on Music*, 16, 22–23.

90. Hindemith composed "The Four Temperaments" in 1940, but because of World War II, his German publisher Schott did not immediately publish the work. It was published in 1947, and Schott's American agent, Associated Music Publishers, published it a year later. According to the first supplement of *The World's Encyclopaedia of Recorded Music*, the first commercial recording (with Lukas Foss at the piano) was released on American Decca as a long-playing disc at some time between April 1950 and May–June 1951 (the dates of the supplement). Thus, for Sondheim to have listened to the Hindemith at the time he wrote his concertino, he would have had to be familiar with this recording.

91. Horowitz, *Sondheim on Music*, 19.

92. Zadan, *Sondheim and Co.*, 7.

93. Secrest, *Stephen Sondheim*, 56–57.

94. See David Drew, "Weill, Kurt," in *NGDM I*, 20:308–9.

95. For other reasons, writers about Weill attempt to hitch him to Sondheim's star. See chap. 14, "Before Sondheim," in Foster Hirsch, *Kurt Weill on Stage: From Berlin to Broadway* (New York: Alfred A. Knopf, 2002).

96. Sondheim, personal communication with the author, December 20, 2003.

97. See Larry Gelbart, introduction to *A Funny Thing Happened on the Way to the Forum*, by Burt Shevelove, Larry Gelbart, and Stephen Sondheim (New York: Applause, 1991), 9.

98. See Swayne, "Sondheim's Piano Sonata," 319.

99. Kim Kowalke, review of Joanne Gordon, ed., *Stephen Sondheim: A Casebook*, in *Theatre Journal*, 50, no. 4 (1998): 553.

100. Sondheim, personal communication with the author, November 20, 2001.

101. Sondheim, "Art of the Musical," 276.

Chapter 2: Sondheim the Tunesmith

1. See Alec Wilder, *American Popular Song: The Great Innovators, 1900–1950* (New York: Oxford University Press, 1972); and Allen Forte, *The American Popular Ballad of the Golden Era, 1924–1950* (Princeton: Princeton University Press, 1995). Martin Gottfried elected to omit Arlen and spoke instead about "the 'big five' musical theater composers" of the same period. See his *Broadway Musicals* (New York: Abradale Press/Harry N. Abrams, 1984), 249.

2. Richard Rodgers, *Musical Stages: An Autobiography* (New York: Random House, 1975), 243.

3. See Charles Hamm, "The Theatre Guild Production of *Porgy and*

Bess," *Journal of the American Musicological Society* 40 (fall 1987): 495–532, for more on these versions.

4. Sondheim, personal communication with the author, November 15, 2001.

5. Secrest, *Stephen Sondheim,* 32, 53–56, and 84–85.

6. "Benatzky wrote the bulk of the score including the title song, but others of the best-known numbers were by Robert Stolz, Robert Gilbert and Bruno Granichstaedten." Andrew Lamb, "Benatzky, Ralph [Rudolph Josef František]," *The New Grove Dictionary of Music Online,* accessed December 14, 2001.

7. Secrest, *Stephen Sondheim,* 20; and Gerald Bordman, *American Musical Theatre: A Chronicle,* 3d ed. (New York: Oxford University Press, 2001), 570.

8. Secrest, *Stephen Sondheim,* 388.

9. Secrest, *Stephen Sondheim,* 68–69. While the last three shows all predate Shainman's arrival at Williams in 1948, *Me and Juliet* opened in 1953, well after Sondheim had left Williams.

10. Banfield, *Sondheim's Broadway Musicals,* 22; and Secrest, *Stephen Sondheim,* 87.

11. Banfield, *Sondheim's Broadway Musicals,* 22–23; see also Secrest, *Stephen Sondheim,* 87.

12. Stephen Sondheim, brochure notes for Paul Weston, *The Columbia Album of Jerome Kern,* Columbia C2L-2, ca. 1957, reissued as Sony Special Projects AK 47861.

13. See Zadan, *Sondheim & Co.,* 147.

14. Zadan, *Sondheim & Co.,* 147.

15. Bordman, *American Musical Theatre,* 128–29 and 146.

16. Secrest, *Stephen Sondheim,* 87.

17. Frank Rich, "Conversations with Sondheim," *New York Times Magazine,* March 12, 2000, 42.

18. Sondheim, brochure notes for Weston, *Columbia Album of Kern.*

19. Sondheim, brochure notes for Weston, *Columbia Album of Kern.*

20. Rich, "Conversations with Sondheim," 42.

21. Sondheim, personal communication with the author, December 20, 2003.

22. Horowitz, *Sondheim on Music,* 170.

23. Secrest, *Stephen Sondheim,* 106.

24. Sondheim also commented on the Mizner musical in 1979. See "On Collaboration between Authors and Directors," *Dramatists Guild Quarterly* 16, no. 2 (1979): 30.

25. Secrest, *Stephen Sondheim,* 133.

26. Secrest, *Stephen Sondheim,* 310.

27. See also Michael Phillips, "Theater Review: *Bounce* at Goodman Theatre," *Chicago Tribune,* July 1, 2003, URL accessed July 1, 2003.

28. In *Cole Porter* McBrien provides both a history of Linda's Williamstown property, known as Buxton Hill, and a photograph of the main house (236–38).

29. Secrest, *Stephen Sondheim,* 73–74. The lyrics alone would have left Cole Porter in no doubt that Sondheim was imitating him: "Once you do it,

you will really be cooked— / It's something that Cole Porter must have overlooked!" (*All That Glitters* [typescript], 1–35).

30. Secrest, *Stephen Sondheim*, 136. In his conversations with Frank Rich, Sondheim told the same story with a slightly different nuance. "He chortled. . . . He got such a moan of pleasure, it was absolutely sexual. It was *great! It was a great moment!*" Rich, "Conversations with Sondheim," 43.

31. See Banfield, *Sondheim's Broadway Musicals*, 179ff., for a further discussion of Porter's list songs and Sondheim's opinion of and affinity to them.

32. Banfield, *Sondheim's Broadway Musicals*, 147. The song's similarity to Weill's "The Saga of Jenny" has been noted elsewhere; see n. 110 in this chapter.

33. In *The Richard Rodgers Reader* (Oxford: Oxford University Press, 2002), editor Geoffrey Block not only reprinted the material Craig Zadan amassed on *Do I Hear a Waltz?* (in *Sondheim & Co.*) but also provided a short but insightful summation of the issues that arose during the collaboration of Rodgers and Sondheim (224–30). See p. 325 for an additional recollection from Rodgers on *Do I Hear a Waltz?;* also see Arthur Laurents, *Original Story By: A Memoir of Broadway and Hollywood* (New York: Alfred A. Knopf, 2000), 213–19.

34. See William G. Hyland, *Richard Rodgers* (New Haven: Yale University Press, 1998), who borrows largely from Mary Rodgers Guettel's introduction to *Musical Stages* (see n. 35); and Meryle Secrest, *Somewhere for Me: A Biography of Richard Rodgers* (New York: Alfred A. Knopf, 2001), who relies more on the Columbia oral history of Mary Rodgers Guettel.

35. This introduction is reprinted in Block, *The Richard Rodgers Reader*, 255–58. According to Stephen Citron, Mary Rodgers said, "[I]t was my fantasy that my parents would die and I would be adopted by the Hammersteins" (*Sondheim and Lloyd-Webber*, 29).

36. Fordin, *Getting to Know Him*, 222.

37. Secrest, *Stephen Sondheim*, 172.

38. See Secrest, *Somewhere for Me*, 177 (Mary's confiding in Sondheim; Dorothy Rodgers on homosexuals) and 325 (Mary's infatuation with Sondheim); Zadan, *Sondheim & Co.*, 104 (Richard Rodgers on homosexuals).

39. Myrna Katz Frommer and Harvey Frommer, *It Happened on Broadway: An Oral History of the Great White Way* (Madison: University of Wisconsin Press, 2004), 97.

40. Walter Kerr, as quoted in Block, *The Richard Rodgers Reader*, 239–40.

41. As quoted in Secrest, *Somewhere for Me*, 371. See also "The Musical Theater: A Talk by Stephen Sondheim," *Dramatists Guild Quarterly* 15, no. 3 (1978): 20–21.

42. Rich, "Conversations with Sondheim," 41.

43. See Zadan, *Sondheim & Co.*, 102.

44. See Secrest, *Stephen Sondheim*, 53–56; Rich, "Conversations with Sondheim," 41–42; Swayne, "Hearing Sondheim's Voices," 348–49.

45. As quoted in Fordin, *Getting to Know Him*, 257–58.

46. See Secrest, *Stephen Sondheim*, 53–56; Swayne, "Hearing Sondheim's Voices," 348; Rich, "Conversations with Sondheim," 42.

47. "Sondheim Interview," *Williams Record*, March 12, 1949, 2. Earlier in the "interview," the journalist revealed that Hammerstein had worked with Sondheim in drafting the book for *All That Glitters*.

48. Block, *The Richard Rodgers Reader*, 325. "He," in Leish's comment,

probably refers to Sondheim but could be a reference to Arthur Laurents, who, as author of both the book and the play on which the musical was based, was responsible for making the heroine "unsympathetic" and "unpleasant."

49. Rodgers, *Musical Stages*, 238.

50. Rich, "Conversations with Sondheim," 41.

51. Rodgers, *Musical Stages*, 239.

52. Zadan, *Sondheim & Co.*, 7.

53. Swayne, "Hearing Sondheim's Voices," 338.

54. Stephen Sondheim, "Side by Side by Side (An Interview with Stephen Sondheim)," interview by Frank Rich, *American Theatre* 19, no. 6 (July–August 2002): 68.

55. Swayne, "Hearing Sondheim's Voices," 340.

56. As quoted in Edward Jablonski, *Harold Arlen: Rhythm, Rainbows, & Blues* (Boston: Northeastern University Press, 1996), 309 (hereafter *Rhythm, Rainbows, & Blues*).

57. Jablonski, *Rhythm, Rainbows, & Blues*, 114. See also p. 262, where this statement is repeated.

58. Hollis Alpert, *The Life and Times of "Porgy and Bess": The Story of an American Classic* (New York: Alfred A. Knopf, 1990), 195–97.

59. As quoted in Jablonski, *Rhythm, Rainbows, & Blues*, 262.

60. See Edward Jablonski, *Harold Arlen: Happy with the Blues* (New York: Da Capo, 1986), 219–30 (hereafter *Happy with the Blues*); Jablonski, *Rhythm, Rainbows, & Blues*, 302–5; and Alpert, *Life and Times*, 283–85. Alpert provides a picture from a rehearsal of *Free and Easy*, which includes the young Quincy Jones as musical director.

61. Swayne, "Hearing Sondheim's Voices," 340.

62. Sondheim, personal communication with the author, November 15, 2001. The 1998 City Center Encores! Great American Musicals in Concert performance obviously influenced Sondheim in his positive identification of *St. Louis Woman*. In the notes to the original cast recording, musical director Rob Fisher revealed that the production necessitated the reconstruction of the score, as both the piano-vocal score and orchestrations have been lost. Also noteworthy in this 1998 production is the female lead, Vanessa L. Williams, who would go on to star as the Witch in the 2002 Broadway revival of *Into the Woods*.

63. Banfield, *Sondheim's Broadway Musicals*, 41.

64. Secrest, *Stephen Sondheim*, 39.

65. Sondheim, *Desert Island Discs*.

66. Horowitz, *Sondheim on Music*, 170.

67. Horowitz, *Sondheim on Music*, 48.

68. For more on the crap-game fugue, see Paul Nauert, "Theory and Practice in *Porgy and Bess:* The Gershwin-Schillinger Connection," *Musical Quarterly* 78 (1994): 9–33, esp. 21–25; and Wayne Shirley, "'Rotating' *Porgy and Bess*," in *The Gershwin Style: New Looks at the Music of George Gershwin*, ed. Wayne Schneider (New York: Oxford University Press, 1999), 21–34, esp. 25–30.

69. For the lessons with Barrow, see the "Ravel" section in chapter 1. For the undated sketch, see Swayne, "Hearing Sondheim's Voices," 190–91. For the sonata, see Swayne, "Sondheim's Piano Sonata."

70. Steven E. Gilbert, "Nice Work: Thoughts and Observations on Gershwin's Last Songs," in Schneider, *The Gershwin Style*, 70–71.

71. Gilbert, "Nice Work," 68.

72. Savran, "Interview with Stephen Sondheim," 229.

73. Sondheim, *Desert Island Discs.*

74. Bordman, *American Musical Theatre*, 546.

75. See John Simon, *Uneasy Stages: A Chronicle of the New York Theater, 1963–1973* (New York: Random House, 1975), 292–93 ("Sondheim seems happiest writing a typical show tune like 'Side by Side by Side' or a patter song like 'Getting Married Today,' to which he adds a little dissonance or antimelodiousness. Otherwise, the toe-wetting forays into the sea of modernity [in *Company*] merely produce some peculiar tonal intervals to make things harder for the performers"), 327 ("Sondheim's music [for *Follies*] is mostly over-cerebral parody, always cluttered up with an overlay of fussiness"), and 391 ("Stephen Sondheim's score [to . . . *Forum*] remains his best because it is his least pretentious").

76. William V. Madison, review of *Sweeney Todd* (performed by the Chicago Lyric Opera), in *Opera News*, March 2003, 83–84.

77. Carol Oja, in "Gershwin and American Modernists of the 1920s," *Musical Quarterly* 78 (1994): 646–68, gives an account of how Gershwin was seen by the music industries of his day (both classical and popular).

78. Clive Barnes, "*Porgy & Bess* and How! Gershwin Opera Hits Great Stage of Music Hall," *New York Post*, April 8, 1983, as reprinted in *New York Theatre Critics' Reviews, 1983*, ed. Joan Marlowe and Betty Blake, vol. 44, no. 5 (New York: Critics' Theatre Reviews, 1983), 318.

79. Harold Prince and Stephen Sondheim, "Author and Director: Musicals," in *Broadway Song & Story: Playwrights / Lyricists / Composers Discuss Their Hits*, ed. Otis Guernsey Jr. (New York: Dodd, Mead, 1985), 361. See also Zadan, *Sondheim & Co.*, where Sondheim is quoted as saying that *Sweeney Todd* "was going to be virtually an opera" (246).

80. Michael John LaChiusa, "Genre Confusion," *Opera News*, August 2002, 73.

81. LaChiusa, "Genre Confusion," 15.

82. Terry Teachout, "Sondheim's Operas," *Commentary*, May 2003, 57–61.

83. Jablonski, *Happy with the Blues*, 19–20.

84. Jack Viertel, "*St. Louis Woman* and the Harold Arlen Curse," in the brochure for Harold Arlen, *St. Louis Blues*, original New York cast recording, Mercury 314 538 148–2, 1998, (12–13). See also Gottfried, *Broadway Musicals*, 253–55.

85. As quoted in Allen Woll, *Black Musical Theatre: From "Coontown" to "Dreamgirls"* (Baton Rouge: Louisiana State University Press, 1989), 197.

86. Swayne, "Hearing Sondheim's Voices," 338.

87. Swayne, "Hearing Sondheim's Voices," 338.

88. Horowitz, *Sondheim on Music*, 100.

89. See chapter 4 and n. 92.

90. Sondheim, "The Musical Theater," 22.

91. Jablonski, *Rhythm, Rainbows, & Blues:*

> One Sunday afternoon, at the Ryan's East Side apartment . . . Arlen was introduced to a young television scriptwriter (for the "Topper" series) and aspiring songwriter named Stephen Sondheim. . . . Arlen played and sang several songs, which Ryan recorded on tape. Sondheim then performed songs from his early musical *Saturday Night,* probably written in his teens (he was about twenty-five when he and Arlen met).
>
> As they left the Ryans, Arlen admitted that he was not impressed by Sondheim's juvenilia. Years later, he would change his mind. (263)

Whether it was the Ryans' or Harburg's apartment, Jablonski's tone is noticeably dismissive toward Sondheim, with Jablonski unaware of Sondheim's age either at the time of the meeting or when he wrote *Saturday Night.* Notice also that Sondheim (in Jablonski's prose) is a scriptwriter first and songwriter second. Later in his book, Jablonski bemoaned the lack of attention paid to Arlen's *Gay Purr-ee*—"the most original film musical of a year notable otherwise only for filmed Broadway fare, *The Music Man, Gypsy,* and *Jumbo.* Broadway that year—1962—did little better with Richard Rodgers's first solo venture . . . *No Strings;* likewise Stephen Sondheim with *A Funny Thing Happened on the Way to the Forum*" (314). In fact, both of the musicals Jablonski named had successful New York runs: *No Strings* ran for 580 performances; *Forum,* the Tony winner that year for Best Musical, ran for 964 performances.

92. Sondheim was visibly moved at this point in his recollection of Arlen.

93. Swayne, "Hearing Sondheim's Voices," 338–41.

94. See Banfield, *Sondheim's Broadway Musicals,* 22.

95. See Wilder, *American Popular Song,* 253–91, for a discussion of songs that exhibit these features.

96. Banfield, *Sondheim's Broadway Musicals,* 27.

97. Jablonski, *Happy with the Blues,* 220. Jablonski does not repeat this "possible" in his second book, *Rhythm, Rainbows, & Blues* (1996).

98. Nelson Pressley, "A Darker *Passion:* Sondheim's Solid Music of Obsession," *Washington Post,* July 23, 2002, C1; also http://www.washingtonpost.com/wp-dyn/articles/A47489-2002Jul22.html, accessed October 21, 2004.

99. Horowitz, *Sondheim on Music,* 169–70.

100. Stephen Holden, "Some Witchcraft from Cy Coleman and Friends," *New York Times,* January 24, 2002, http://www.nytimes.com/2002/01/24/arts/music/24POPS.html, accessed August 20, 2002.

101. Zadan, *Sondheim & Co.,* 83.

102. Swayne, "Hearing Sondheim's Voices," 337.

103. http://nfo.net/.CAL/tm1.html, accessed August 19, 2002.

104. Bordman, *American Musical Theatre,* 579. See also Gottfried, *Broadway Musicals,* 256–57.

105. Wilder, *American Popular Song,* 346.

106. Secrest, *Stephen Sondheim,* 100.

107. Sondheim, personal communication with the author, January 19, 2001.

108. Sondheim, personal communication with the author, December 20, 2003.

109. For Bernstein's linkages to Gershwin, Hindemith, and Copland, see David Schiff, "Bernstein, Leonard," *New Grove Dictionary Online*, accessed August 21, 2002.

110. See Geoffrey Block, *Enchanted Evenings: The Broadway Musical from "Show Boat" to Sondheim* (New York: Oxford University Press, 1997), 288, where it is suggested that a "more likely model" for "Lucy and Jessie" *(Follies)* is "The Saga of Jenny" from Weill's *Lady in the Dark* (1941). Block's footnote to this sentence advances the comparison still further: "In honor of Bernstein's seventieth birthday Sondheim composed the parody 'The Saga of Lennie,' [*sic*] which, according to a particularly helpful anonymous outside reviewer of this book, 'shows a good understanding and sympathy with the original 'Saga of Jenny.''" (390 n. 36). While he may not be the anonymous reviewer here, Kim Kowalke also tells the story about "Lauren Bacall singing 'The Saga of Lenny,' Stephen Sondheim's affectionately wicked account of the man who could never make up his mind what he wanted to be—a parody, of course, of 'The Saga of Jenny' from Weill's *Lady in the Dark*. But all of this is, indeed, another story." Kim H. Kowalke, "*The Threepenny Opera:* The Score Adapted," in Kurt Weill and Bertolt Brecht, *"Die Dreigroschenoper": A Facsimile of the Holograph Full Score*, in *The Kurt Weill Edition*, managing editor Edward Harsh, series 4, vol. 1 (New York: Kurt Weill Foundation for Music, 1996), 15. See also Hirsch, *Kurt Weill on Stage*, particularly chap. 14, entitled "Before Sondheim."

111. Rizzo, "Sunday on a Campus," 3–4.

112. Rich, "Conversations with Sondheim," 60. See also Steve Swayne, "In Search of the Gay American Musical," *Journal of Homosexuality* 43, no. 1 (2002): 108–11.

113. Woll, *Black Musical Theatre*, 253.

114. Woll, *Black Musical Theatre*, 229–48.

115. Reebee Garofalo, *Rockin' Out: Popular Music in the USA*, 2d ed. (Upper Saddle River, N.J.: Prentice-Hall, 2002), 130–31.

116. Woll, *Black Musical Theatre*, 247.

117. See n. 62 in this chapter for more on Vanessa L. Williams.

118. Arthur Laurents and Stephen Sondheim, *Anyone Can Whistle* (New York: Leon Amiel, 1976), 63–64.

119. For more on *South Pacific*, see Andrea Most, "'You've Got to Be Carefully Taught': The Politics of Race in Rodgers and Hammerstein's *South Pacific*," *Theatre Journal* 52, no. 3 (2000): 307–37. Another incident of race relations made right in the musical is the 1999 television version of *Annie* (Charles Strouse, music, and Martin Charnin, lyrics). There, marriage is in the cards for (white) Victor Garber (Oliver "Daddy" Warbucks) and (black) Audra McDonald (Miss Grace). For McDonald, this was a replay of sorts. In her role as Carrie Pipperidge in the Nicholas Hytner revival of *Carousel* (1994), McDonald was paired with (white) Eddie Korbich and memorably sang Carrie's song, "When I Marry Mr. Snow."

Chapter 3: Pulling It Apart

1. For more on the music from the film, see Steve Swayne, "So Much 'More': The Music of *Dick Tracy*," *American Music* 22 (spring 2004): 50–63.

2. In the manuscript, only "Lazy Blues" is present; no metronome mark or any indication to the pianist is given.

3. Secrest, *Somewhere for Me*, 284.

4. Frommer and Frommer, *It Happened on Broadway*, 251.

5. Steven Blair Wilson, "Motivic, Rhythmic, and Harmonic Procedures of Unification in Stephen Sondheim's *Company* and *A Little Night Music*," D.A. diss., Ball State University, 1983.

6. Banfield, *Sondheim's Broadway Musicals*, 152.

7. For more on the *Bounce* score, see Steve Swayne, "The Score: Brilliance under the Simplicity," *Sondheim Review* 10, no. 2 (2003): 10–11.

8. Sondheim, "The Musical Theater," 22.

9. Banfield, *Sondheim's Broadway Musicals*, 74.

10. Horowitz, *Sondheim on Music*, 151.

11. Banfield, *Sondheim's Broadway Musicals*, 28.

12. In the recorded performance of the song for the movie, a long pause—effectively the length of an entire measure—occurs on the word "choose" in m. 36.

13. Eugene Robert Huber, "Stephen Sondheim and Harold Prince: Collaborative Contributions to the Development of the Modern Concept Musical, 1970–1981," Ph.D. diss., New York University, 1990, 39, as cited by Banfield, *Sondheim's Broadway Musicals*, 22.

14. "*Klinghoffer* and the Art of Composing: An Interview with John Adams by David B. Beverly," http://www.earbox.com/sub-html/interviews/ja-on-kling-low.html, accessed September 30, 2003.

15. "[Arnold] Hauser suggests that this type of dramatic technique which allows the playwright to break with linear progression and rearrange the time sequence of a play has developed in the last century 'perhaps under the immediate influence of the film, or under the influence of the new conception of time familiar also from the modern novel.'" Laura Hanson, "Elements of Modernism in the Musicals of Stephen Sondheim," Ph.D. diss., New York University, 2001, 285. Hanson refers to Arnold Hauser, *The Social History of Art*, vol. 2 (New York: Alfred A. Knopf, 1952), 942.

16. "Stephen Sondheim in a Q & A Session: Part I," *Dramatists Guild Quarterly* 28, no. 1 (1991): 13–14.

17. "Verdi's *Otello*," in *Opera: A History in Documents*, ed. Piero Weiss (New York: Oxford University Press, 2002), 230–43.

Chapter 4: Sondheim the Dramaphile

1. There were actually four performances, on March 18, 19, 21, and 22, 1949.

2. Stephen Sondheim, "Theatre Lyrics," in *Playwrights, Lyricists, Composers, on Theatre*, ed. Otis Guernsey (New York: Dodd, Mead, 1974), 62–63. In fact, Hammerstein underlined the number "99" and wrote "Boy!" next to it.

3. Secrest, *Stephen Sondheim*, 51.

4. Guy Flatley, "When Stephen Sondheim Writes Words and Music, Some Critics Don't Leave the Theater Humming," *People*, April 5, 1976, 69.

5. See Secrest, *Stephen Sondheim*, 142, on Sondheim receiving Oscar Hammerstein's monogrammed slippers from Hammerstein's oldest son, William.

6. Secrest, *Stephen Sondheim*, 95–96.

7. Fordin, *Getting to Know Him*, 306–7.

8. Sondheim, personal communication with the author, November 15, 2001.

9. Sondheim, "The Musical Theater," 17; "Sondheim Q & A: Part I," 14; and Secrest, *Stephen Sondheim*, 236–37 and 402–3.

10. Frank Rich, "Conversations with Sondheim," 43.

11. Carol Ilson, *Harold Prince: From "Pajama Game" to "The Phantom of the Opera" and Beyond* (New York: Limelight Editions, 1992), 200; Sondheim, "Collaboration," 21; and Secrest, *Stephen Sondheim*, 379. *Bounce*, based on Alva Johnston's novel *The Legendary Mizners*, attracted Sondheim as early as the mid-1950s; see Secrest, 105–6.

12. Sondheim, "The Musical Theater," 28; Frank Rich with Lisa Aronson, *The Theatre Art of Boris Aronson* (New York: Alfred A. Knopf, 1987), 260.

13. Sondheim, "The Musical Theater," 11.

14. Sondheim, "Collaboration," 24.

15. I have also explored this hypothesis in greater depth elsewhere. See Swayne, "Sondheim's Piano Sonata"; "Hindemith's Unexpected Grandson"; and "Young Copland and Younger Sondheim."

16. These scripts are at Wisconsin, U.S. Mss 66AN, Box 1 *(All That Glitters)* and Box 5 *(By George* and *Climb High)*.

17. *1950 Gul* (Williams College yearbook), 35. "Much praise went to co-authors Steve Sondheim and T.S. Horton for an extremely successful and entertaining production." *1948 Gul* (Williams College yearbook), 122. The dates for *Phinney's Rainbow* were April 30, May 1, May 7 and 8, 1948.

18. *1950 Gul* (Williams College yearbook), 35.

19. "The sophomores . . . came out with the news that they were sponsoring a dance on the week-end of March 19. . . . This was the same weekend that Cap & Bells was presenting its second production of the year, *All That Glitters*, a musical written by Steve Sondheim. Both the dance and the musical were resounding successes, and as everyone expected, there was a slight snowfall." *1949 Gul* (Williams College yearbook), 73.

20. Edwin N. Perrin, "*All That Glitters* Shiner for Cap and Bells, Cast," *Williams Record*, March 23, 1949: 4.

21. "Sondheim Interview," *Williams Record*, 2.

22. Barrett Clark and George Freedley, *A History of Modern Drama* (New York: Appleton-Century-Crofts, 1947), 733, as cited in Rhoda-Gale Pollack, *George S. Kaufman* (Boston: Twayne, 1988), 31.

23. "Sondheim Interview," *Williams Record*, 2.

24. See Secrest, *Stephen Sondheim*, 57–60, and the "Rachmaninoff" section in chap. 1.

25. See "Sondheim Q & A: Part I," 10–11. In Sarah Schlesinger's *Music Theatre International Study Guide for Sondheim and Weidman's "Assassins"* (New York: MTI, 1993), numerous questions are provided concerning the role of media in violence and the effect of gun control legislation (see esp. pp. 13–15). This guide is one of a series designed as a resource to "provide an ideal vehicle for a foundation or corporation to sponsor a unique educational opportunity" and to allow schools to "incorporate the study of musical theatre into the curriculum" (in the foreword).

26. Secrest, *Stephen Sondheim*, 362. Secrest's writing here is slightly unclear. "Sondheim shared [*Assassins* book writer John] Weidman's political perspective—he characterized himself as a 'fierce liberal'—but was not attracted to the subject for this reason alone." "He" may refer to Weidman and not Sondheim; in either case, Secrest does not indicate in her notes the source of the designation "fierce liberal."

27. S = Sondheim, *All That Glitters* (typescript); P = prologue; 1 = Act 1; 2 = Act 2; numbering refers to prologue/act-page number. K&C = George S. Kaufman and Marc Connelly, *Beggar on Horseback: A Play in Two Parts* (New York: Boni and Liveright, 1924).

28. Leonard Bernstein, *The Joy of Music* (New York: Simon and Schuster, 1959). The essay, on pp. 52–62, was written in April 1955.

29. Secrest, *Stephen Sondheim*, 73.

30. James McKinley, *Assassination in America* (New York: Harper & Row, 1977), 55–56.

31. See Swayne, "Hearing Sondheim's Voices," 145.

32. Information from the Internet Broadway Database (www.ibdb.com), accessed October 30, 2002.

33. Secrest, *Stephen Sondheim*, 80.

34. *High Tor, A Play in Three Acts* (Washington, D.C.: Anderson House, 1937); John Gassner, ed., *Twenty Best Plays of the Modern American Theatre* (New York: Crown Publishers, 1939); *Eleven Verse Plays [by] Maxwell Anderson, 1929–1939* (New York: Harcourt, Brace, 1940); and *The Critics' Prize Plays*, introduction by George Jean Nathan (Cleveland: World Publishing, 1945).

35. Mary C. Henderson, *Mielziner: Master of Modern Stage Design* (New York: Back Stage Books, 2001), 112.

36. "The AMT Committee felt we ought to get familiar with the classics by going to see their *Agamemnon*, and Steve Sondheim was supervising a group of amateurs in the production of another Masse musical, following Maxwell Anderson's axe of his *HIGH TOR* adaptation." *1950 Gul* (Williams College yearbook), 90.

37. Sondheim, personal communication with the author, December 20, 2003. Sondheim suggested that Wisconsin has lost this material.

38. Sondheim's letter to Anderson is found at Wisconsin, U.S. Mss 66AN, Box 1.

39. Alfred S. Shivers, *The Life of Maxwell Anderson* (New York: Stein and Day, 1983), 168–69.

40. Anderson's letter and the information about the Anderson-Schwartz collaboration is found in Laurence G. Avery, ed., *Dramatist in America: Letters of Maxwell Anderson, 1912–1958* (Chapel Hill: University of North Carolina Press, 1977), 253.

41. Secrest, *Stephen Sondheim*, 79. In 1933, Maxwell Anderson won the Pulitzer Prize in drama for *Both Your Houses;* it was his only Pulitzer. Stephen Citron repeats Secrest's error in his book *Sondheim and Lloyd-Webber*, 37. *High Tor* won the 1937 Drama Critics' Circle Award, and some critics felt it should have won that year's Pulitzer Prize, which went instead to the George S. Kaufman and Moss Hart comedy, *You Can't Take It with You.*

42. "Cap and Bells sponsored and engineered [*sic*] Lillian Hellman's *Watch on the Rhine,* William Saroyan's *My Heart's in the Highlands,* and a student written musical, while the AMT Committee launched the season with *Faust* (Part I) in connection with the world wide celebration of Goethe's two hundredth birthday." *1950 Gul* (Williams College yearbook), 127. The dates for *Where To From Here* were May 11, 12, and 13, 1950. See also n. 36 and Secrest, *Stephen Sondheim*, 82–83.

43. In the *1950 Gul,* Sondheim received votes from his peers in a number of categories: Most Versatile, 22 votes (third place); Most Brilliant, 14 (sixth); Most Likely to Succeed, 29 (fourth); Done Most for Williams, 4 (last); Most Original, 32 (second).

44. See Banfield, *Sondheim's Broadway Musicals*, 16–20, for a discussion of the music from *Phinney's Rainbow, All That Glitters, High Tor,* and *Mary Poppins.*

45. Secrest, *Stephen Sondheim*, 79.

46. Sondheim, "The Musical Theater," 27.

47. Secrest, *Stephen Sondheim*, 80–82.

48. See *Williams College Bulletin,* December 1943, 94, and December 1944, 51.

49. The titles and descriptions of the English courses come from the *Williams College Bulletin* of March 1948 (academic year 1948–49) and March 1949 (academic year 1949–50).

50. Chapin, *Everything Was Possible*, 84–85.

51. "Pirandello, Luigi," Encyclopaedia Britannica, http://www.search.eb.com/eb/article?eu=61671, accessed October 30, 2002.

52. Secrest, *Stephen Sondheim*, 88.

53. Secrest, *Stephen Sondheim*, 102–3. The sonata was copyrighted in 1999 and performed that year by Christina Sunnerstam at the Barbican Centre, London, at a gala concert to celebrate the music of Sondheim. See *Sondheim Tonight: Live from the Barbican Centre, London,* Jay CDJay2 1313, 1999. Its four movements are marked Moderato poco rubato (37 mm.); Adagio sempre non legato (34 mm.); Rigadoon (43 mm.); and Allegro (23 mm.).

54. See Secrest, *Stephen Sondheim*, 88, and Banfield, *Sondheim's Broadway Musicals*, 24.

55. Fordin, *Getting to Know Him*, 306–7. The original of this letter appears to be lost.

56. Fordin, *Getting to Know Him*, 306.

57. Fordin, *Getting to Know Him*, 307.

58. Fordin, *Getting to Know Him*, 306.

59. See John Bush Jones, *Our Musicals, Ourselves: A Social History of the American Musical Theatre* (Lebanon, N.H.: Brandeis University Press, 2003), 270–73, for a short history of the "concept musical" and a proposal for an alternate term. For Sondheim's disdain for the term, see Flatley, "When Sondheim Writes," 69.

60. "Sondheim Q & A: Part I," 10–11.

61. Banfield provides a fascinating study of *Company* as concept musical (see *Sondheim's Broadway Musicals*, 147–49 and 160–73) and raises the possibility (before the revivals of the mid–1990s) that the show was dated.

62. Sondheim, "The Musical Theater," 13; Sondheim, "Collaboration," 21 and 26–28.

63. Flatley, "When Sondheim Writes," 69–70.

64. Flatley, "When Sondheim Writes," 70.

65. I am thinking of all of the married couples *(Company);* Buddy–Sally and Ben–Phyllis *(Follies);* Fredrik–Anne and Carl Magnus–Charlotte *(Night Music);* and Clara–her absent husband and Fosca–"Count Ludovic" *(Passion).*

66. Rich, "Conversations with Sondheim," 61.

67. Secrest, *Stephen Sondheim*, 53.

68. Rich, "Conversations with Sondheim," 42.

69. "In One: Refers to a scene which is played in front of main curtain while other scenes are being set up on main stage area." Willard F. Bellman, *Scenography and Stage Technology: An Introduction* (New York: Thomas Y. Crowell, 1977), 594. See also Jo Mielziner, *Designing for the Theatre* (New York: Atheneum, 1965), where he calls the "scene-in-one" "that ancient and tiresome convention of the musical theatre" that "halts the smooth progress of the story and drastically limits the director and the designer" (21).

70. Swayne, "Hearing Sondheim's Voices," 348–49.

71. Henderson, *Mielziner*, 22.

72. See Mielziner, *Designing for the Theatre*, 26.

73. Henderson, *Mielziner*, 82.

74. Mielziner, *Designing for the Theatre*, 21–22. See also Henderson, *Mielziner*, 117–18.

75. Rich, *Theatre Art of Aronson*. See 219–80 for the discussion of the Prince-Sondheim shows generally. For a discussion of how Sondheim's musical decisions were affected by Aronson's design, see 230 (*Company);* see also Zadan, *Sondheim & Co.*, 239–40 *(Company)*, 250 *(Follies)*, and 260 *(Night Music);* see n. 12 in this chapter.

76. Rich, *Theatre Art of Aronson*, 23.

77. Rich, *Theatre Art of Aronson*, 264.

78. Sondheim, "The Musical Theater," 14.

79. Mielziner, *Designing for the Theatre*, 12.

80. Mielziner, *Designing for the Theatre*, 9. See Henderson, *Mielziner*, 182, 217, and 223 for more on collaboration.

81. Oscar Hammerstein II, *Allegro: A Musical Play* (New York: Alfred A. Knopf, 1948), vi–vii.

82. Hammerstein, *Allegro*, 2.

83. Secrest, *Stephen Sondheim*, 54.

84. Hammerstein, *Allegro*, 3.

85. Hammerstein, *Allegro*, 2.

86. Secrest, *Stephen Sondheim*, 54 and 56.

87. In *Forum*, Prologus (who plays the part of Pseudolus) addresses the audience ("Comedy Tonight"), and after the deliberately off-kilter overture for *Anyone Can Whistle*, an offstage Narrator, who possesses a "humorously folksy voice," introduces the ramshackle sight of Mayoress Cora Hoover Hooper's town.

88. The choice of name for the leading female character allows a number of interesting readings. One can posit that Chris (full name, Christabel Longworth) is a surrogate for another male character and that David and Chris's relationship is a homoerotic one. The book doesn't read that way, but "Longworth" easily lends itself to gay discourse. Her given name can also go in other directions: (1) her archaic-sounding name "introduces" the troubadours; (2) the homonymic similarity between *Christabel* and *crystal ball* suggests that David's future is in Chris's hands, or, similar to this, (3) she is a Christ figure who, at the end, gives her life to save David, thus anticipating by forty years a similar situation in *Passion*, where Fosca gives her life for Giorgio.

89. This letter is at Wisconsin, U.S. Mss 66AN, Box 1.

90. Act 2, scene 3: "The following scenes take place in small spotlighted areas all over the stage, at times stationary, at times moving, at times alone, at times simultaneously. The locales are undefined. The scenes are to be played very fast, joining each other in quick succession, with no breaks except where indicated" (2–26).

91. Sondheim, "Collaboration," 16.

92. From a telephone interview conducted on December 20, 2003:

SONDHEIM: I never liked [Weill's] stuff except for *Threepenny*, and some of his American stuff I like. There's a rumba version of "Girl of the Moment" in *Lady in the Dark*—I mean, I like so little of his stuff I can pick out the pieces I like—and part of the overture to *Street Scene*—it's the theme that goes with the lyric [Sondheim sings:] "Hoping I'd discover some wonderful lover." And that about covers it. I've never caught on to his stuff. What I love about *Threepenny* is how harsh and dissonant it is. I like it when it's played by a small band. But outside of that, Weill's musical language is anathema to me.

SWAYNE: Anathema?!

SONDHEIM: Well, in the sense that I don't like it. I mean, anathema like those fruity chords with the added sixths. They make me come all over queasy.

93. See Stephen Sondheim, John Weidman, and Loren Sherman, "Assassins": *An MTI Video Conversationpiece* (New York: MTI Enterprises, 1991), and Schlesinger, *Study Guide for "Assassins."*

94. Secrest, *Stephen Sondheim*, 398–99.

95. For more on the gay issue, see my review of books by John Clum and D. A. Miller, "Gay American Musical." Whereas homosexuality is ancillary to *Company* in the optional scene between Robert and Peter, *Bounce* is the first show where the lives of gay people become integral to the play.

96. Stephen J. Whitfield, *In Search of American Jewish Culture* (Hanover, N.H.: Brandeis University Press, 1999), 83–87.

97. Larry Ceplair, "SAG and the Motion Picture Blacklist," http://www.sag.com/blacklist.html, accessed March 26, 2003. This article is also in a special edition of *Screen Actor*, January 1997, 18–27.

98. Walter Goodman, *The Committee: The Extraordinary Career of the House Committee on Un-American Activities* (New York: Farrar, Straus and Giroux, 1968), 303 and 537; and Greg Lawrence, *Dance with Demons: The Life of Jerome Robbins* (New York: G. P. Putnam's Sons, 2001), 201–11.

Chapter 5: Sondheim the Cinéaste

1. "Sondheim at Telluride."

2. See Secrest, *Stephen Sondheim*, 92–100, for information about Sondheim's interest in film and his work in Hollywood.

3. "In the Movies" may also point to an earlier song, "Dreams Come True" (*Billion Dollar Baby*, 1945), which makes references to pre-Depression movies.

4. I am thinking of Orson Welles's famous fifty-three-page memo concerning *Touch of Evil*, in which he writes about "making a short contrapuntal reference to what is going on across the border." Later, while Welles leaves out the explicit word, a contrapuntal idea remains. "What's vital is that both stories—the leading man's and the leading woman's—be kept equally and continuously alive; each scene, as we move back and forth across the border, should play at roughly equal lengths." Welles also talks extensively about how music is to be used throughout the film, often in a cross-cutting, "contrapuntal" fashion. See Orson Welles, *Touch of Evil*, Universal DVD 20470, 2000.

5. *Oxford English Dictionary*, accessed November 7, 2002.

6. Zadan, *Sondheim & Co.*, 141.

7. Personal communication, June 18, 2004.

8. Elvis Mitchell, "Sondheim, Film Devotee, Shapes Telluride Festival," *New York Times*, August 28, 2003, http://www.nytimes.com/2003/08/28/movies/28SOND.html?ex=1063072681&ei=1&en=209152758ceao7a2, accessed August 28, 2003. Sondheim's collaborators considered another French film from the 1930s, Jean Renoir's masterpiece *La règle du jeu* (1939), for musical treatment. Sondheim, however, preferred Ingmar Bergman's *Smiles of a Summer Night* (1955), and he prevailed. See Ilson, *Harold Prince*, 200.

9. Alan Williams, *Republic of Images: A History of French Filmmaking* (Cambridge: Harvard University Press, 1992), 239.

10. Williams, *Republic of Images*, 191–94.

11. Roy Armes, *French Cinema* (New York: Oxford University Press, 1985), 129.

12. Armes, *French Cinema*, 99.

13. Mitchell, "Sondheim, Film Devotee."

14. Secrest, *Stephen Sondheim*, 57, 64, and 77. On Broadway, Margaret Sullavan starred in *The Voice of the Turtle*, which opened on December 8, 1943, and ran for an astounding 1,557 performances; she was starring in *The Deep Blue Sea* at the time Sondheim was working on *Climb High*. The very first line in *Climb High*, where David talks about securing Sullavan's services for a new play, is more "insider" than Secrest lets on. *The Deep Blue Sea* closed on February 28, 1953, after 132 performances, and thus Sullavan would be able to star in the show the producers are hawking (and Sondheim was writing). She went on to star in *Sabrina Fair* later that year (Nov. 11, 1953–Aug. 21, 1954, 318 perf.), and her last Broadway appearance was in *Janus* (Nov. 24, 1955–June 30, 1956, 251 perf.). From www.ibdb.com, accessed November 7, 2002.

15. Secrest, *Stephen Sondheim*, 100.

16. Secrest, *Stephen Sondheim*, 57. *Hangover Square*, though, might be classified as a "*noir* version of the story about a psychologically unstable or disturbed hero," a category Michael Walker calls "the *noir* amnesiac films." See Michael Walker, "Film Noir: Introduction," in *The Movie Book of Film Noir*, ed. Ian Cameron (London: Studio Vista, 1992), 15.

17. See Clayton R. Koppes and Gregory D. Black, *Hollywood Goes to War* (New York: Free Press, 1987), esp. 58–72.

18. See Mel Gordon, *The Grand Guignol: Theatre of Fear and Terror* (New York: Amok Press, 1988), 47.

19. Sondheim: "I saw some Grand Guignol in Paris in the 1960s, although by then it was no longer what it once had been. I went because I wanted to see what Grand Guignol was like. There were three extremely bloody one-act plays. . . . The three plays were extremely boring because, bloody as the effects were, if you were squeamish, you hardened yourself, and if you weren't squeamish, it was just red tomato sauce and a lot of people in terrible make-up overacting. Melodrama, for me, has to be a great deal purer than that, and it has to be at least as interesting as other drama." Stephen Sondheim, "Larger Than Life: Reflections on Melodrama and *Sweeney Todd*," in *Melodrama*, ed. Daniel Gerould, vol. 7 of the *New York Literary Forum*, gen. ed. Jeanine Parisier Plottel (New York: New York Literary Forum, 1980), 4. I thank Daniel Colvard for making me aware of this source.

20. For more on Dashiell Hammett and his relation to film, see James Naremore, *More Than Night: Film Noir and Its Contexts* (Berkeley and Los Angeles: University of California Press, 1998), 48–63.

21. Secrest, *Stephen Sondheim*, 78 and 237. For a summary of the *Thin Man* films, see Tom Soter, *Investigating Couples: A Critical Analysis of "The Thin Man," "The Avengers," and "The X-Files"* (Jefferson, N.C.: McFarland, 2002), 149–52; and Robert L. Gale, *A Dashiell Hammett Companion* (Westport, Conn.: Greenwood Press, 2000), 245–49.

22. Walker, "Film Noir," 21.

23. Walker, "Film Noir," 8.

24. Sylviane Gold, "A Lot More Sondheim, a Little More Dancing," *Dance*, February 2002, 30.

25. Sondheim, "Collaboration," 31–32.

26. "What made Jerry's touch individual and so brilliant were his humor and his use of dance to express emotion. He would not choreograph a dance as a dance, he had to know what the dancing was about. . . . He was a brilliant choreographer, he was better at staging a musical than anyone." Laurents, *Original Story By*, 357 and 419.

27. Lawrence W. Levine, *The Unpredictable Past: Explorations in American Cultural History* (New York: Oxford University Press, 1993).

28. Zadan, *Sondheim & Co.*, 182.

29. Two fine examples of this closer questioning are found in Sandor Goodhart, ed., *Reading Stephen Sondheim: A Collection of Critical Essays* (New York: Garland, 2000): Thomas Adler, "The Sung and the Said: Literary Value in the Musical Dramas of Stephen Sondheim," 37–60; and Paul Puccio, "Enchantment on the Manicured Lawns: The Shakespearean 'Green World' in *A Little Night Music*," 133–69.

30. "Sondheim Q & A: Part II," 12.

31. Laura Hanson provides another revealing account of "Someone in a Tree," in "Elements of Modernism," 161–66.

32. Naremore, *More Than Night*, 22.

33. Jean Douchet, in collaboration with Cédric Anger, *French New Wave*, trans. Robert Bonnono (New York: Distributed Art Publishers, 1999), 242. The "Biographical Dictionary of the French New Wave" is a self-contained chapter in Douchet's book (232–65), as is his "History of the New Wave" (164–73).

34. As quoted in Naremore, *More Than Night*, 25.

35. See Michael Walker, "*The Big Sleep:* Howard Hawks and Film Noir," in Cameron, *Book of Film Noir*, 191–202.

36. Naremore, *More Than Night*, 27.

37. See chap. 4 and appendix. Scott Miller identifies *Love Life* (1948) as the first "pure" concept musical; see his "*Assassins* and the Concept Musical," in *Stephen Sondheim: A Casebook*, ed. Joanne Gordon (New York: Garland, 1997), 188. Similarly, Foster Hirsch's chapter on *Love Life* (and *Down in the Valley*) is entitled "Before Sondheim" (in *Kurt Weill on Stage*, 276–99).

38. As quoted in James Monaco, *Alain Resnais* (New York: Oxford University Press, 1979), 10.

39. Peter Cowie, *Antonioni, Bergman, Resnais* (London: Tantivy Press, 1963), 142.

40. Monaco, *Alain Resnais*, 22.

41. Douchet, *French New Wave*, 182.

42. In the original 1991 off-Broadway version of *Assassins*, the "objective" narration never reappeared after the ejection of the Balladeer. For the London production of *Assassins*, Sondheim inserted the song "Something Just Broke" before the reprise of "Everybody's Got the Right." This ensemble reinstates an outsider perspective on the actions of the assassins and provides a faint echo of the voice (and moral stance) of the Balladeer. Sondheim scholars and enthusiasts can debate whether "Something Just Broke" strengthens or weakens *Assassins*, but Sondheim made it clear that, from the time of the off-Broad-

way version forward, he had always intended that "Something Just Broke" would be a part of the musical. See Miller, "*Assassins* and Concept Musical," 194–95; and Swayne, "Hearing Sondheim's Voices," 333.

43. Banfield, *Sondheim's Broadway Musicals*, 163–73.

44. Swayne, "Hearing Sondheim's Voices," 346–47.

45. Swayne, "Hearing Sondheim's Voices," 335 and 345.

46. See Robert Harvey and Hélène Volat, *Marguerite Duras: A Bio-Bibliography* (Westport, Conn.: Greenwood Press, 1997), 28–32; Roch C. Smith, *Understanding Alain Robbe-Grillet* (Columbia: University of South Carolina Press, 2000), 173–74.

47. Douchet, *French New Wave*, 250.

48. Five of Duras's novels—*Un Barrage contre le Pacifique* (1952), *Moderato cantabile* (1958), *Dix heures et midi du soir en été* (1960), *Le Marin de Gibraltar* (1952), and *L'Amant* (1984)—were made into films in 1958 (as *This Angry Age*), 1960, 1966, 1967, and 1991, respectively. The last three appeared after the heyday of the *nouvelle vague* in film, as did the two novels of Robbe-Grillet that were adapted for film: *Les Gommes* (novel, 1953; film, 1969) and *Dans le labyrinthe* (novel, 1959; television movie, 1976). Filmmaker John Waters paid homage to Duras in *Polyester* (1981); at a "high brow" drive-in movie theater, the marquee reads: "MARGUERITE DURAS NITE / THE TRUCK INDIA SONG / DESTROY SHE SAID". *Le Camion* premiered in 1977, *India Song* in 1975, and *Détruire, dit-elle* in 1969; all three have screenplays and were directed by Duras, with the last being her solo directorial debut.

49. For information about Sondheim's work on Warren Beatty's film, *Reds* (1981), see Sloman, "The Sondheim *Guardian* Lecture," 46–47; Bruce Kimmel, notes for *Sondheim at the Movies: Songs from the Screen*, Varèse Sarabande VSD-5805, 1997 (6), CD format; and Swayne, "So Much 'More.'" The quotation about the composition of the score for *Stavisky* . . . comes from Stephen Sondheim's conversation with Elvis Mitchell at Telluride; see also the introduction, n. 6.

50. Richard Seaver, interview with Alain Resnais, in *Stavisky*. . . , text by Jorge Semprun, for the film by Alain Resnais, trans. Sabine Destrée (New York: Viking, 1975), 156.

51. At Telluride, Sondheim said that they discussed *Stavisky* . . . at the 1973 Cannes Film Festival, where *The Last of Sheila* was shown ("Sondheim at Telluride").

52. Resnais, interview by Seaver, 160–61.

53. James Goldman and Stephen Sondheim, *Follies* (New York: Random House, 1971), 104.

54. In a comment that is germane to both *Follies* and *Night Music,* Resnais said, "la musique de Sondheim pour *Stavisky* c'était la joie de vivre et aussi la déchéance," "Entretien avec Alain Resnais sur *Providence,*" in Robert Benayoun, *Alain Resnais arpenteur de l'imaginaire: de Hiroshima à Mélo* (Paris: Stock, 1980), 242. Benayoun called the choice of Sondheim "inspiré" and the music (in words that defy translation) "lancinante et sinueuse, avec son orgeat désespéré, son air fin de party" (151–52).

55. Monaco, *Alain Resnais*, 183.

56. Monaco, *Alain Resnais*, 169. Compare Sondheim's neoclassical score with the tortured organ music Francis Seyrig provided for *Marienbad* or the modernist sound (with its unintelligible solo vocal "songs") of Hans Werner Henze's music for *Muriel* or even the less dissonant yet still unmelodic scores of Giovanni Fusco for *Hiroshima* and *La guerre est finie*. (Krzysztof Penderecki composed the music for *Je t'aime, je t'aime;* neither film nor soundtrack is commercially available as of this writing.) Perhaps his success with Sondheim led Resnais in new musical directions; his next film, *Providence* (1977), has what Leo Bersani calls "somewhat cloying, Hollywood music" by Miklós Rózsa. See Leo Bersani, *Arts of Impoverishment: Beckett, Rothko, Resnais* (Cambridge: Harvard University Press, 1993), 204.

57. Monaco, *Alain Resnais*, 169.

58. Douchet, *French New Wave*, 238. He does not identify the other two.

59. Bersani, *Arts of Impoverishment*, 189.

60. Bersani, *Arts of Impoverishment*, 190.

61. As quoted in Cowie, *Antonioni, Bergman, Resnais*, 153.

62. See Monaco, *Alain Resnais*, 53–73; and John Ward, *Alain Resnais, or the Theme of Time* (Garden City, N.Y.: Doubleday, 1968), 39–62. "*Marienbad*'s most important accomplishment is its shift of attention from the character axis to the author-observer axis. This implies that the observer has to work to complete the film. He must be an active participant. It is the strongest contradiction of Hollywood's *découpage classique*, in which it was taken for granted that the sole aim of cinema was to do as much as possible for the observer. Interestingly, it is in such a dreamplay as *Marienbad* that the viewer is freed from having his dreams provided for him by the filmmakers" (Monaco, 71).

63. *Company* was called "disappointing" (Richard Watts, *New York Post*), "quite simply in a league by itself . . . magnificent" (Martin Gottfried, *Women's Wear Daily*), and "the best musical of the year" (John J. O'Connor, *Wall Street Journal*). Clive Barnes was "antagonized by the slickness, the obviousness of *Company*" *(New York Times);* Walter Kerr "didn't like the show. I admired it, or admired vast portions of it, but that is another matter" (*New York Times*, Sunday edition). Edwin Newman of NBC-TV didn't particularly like the show; Leonard Harris of CBS-TV loved it. See Joan Marlowe and Betty Blake, eds., *New York Theatre Critics' Reviews, 1970*, vol. 31, no. 13 (New York: Critics' Theatre Reviews, 1970), 260–64. Sondheim said that "the anger and condemnation and snottiness and sneering that I got with *Company* quite startled me. Because I'd been dismissed before, which is not the same thing" (Rich, "Conversations with Sondheim," 60). *Follies* was "a welcome and joyous addition to the season" (Richard Watts, *New York Post*), "breathtaking . . . imaginative" (Douglas Watt, *New York Daily News*), "like a girl you love but do not always like" (Martin Gottfried, *Women's Wear Daily*). James Goldman's book takes a beating from most of the critics. And Jack Kroll *(Newsweek)* singled out Harold Prince, who "has created a generation of musicals which captures much of our time in a form that in his hands refuses to die." See Joan Marlowe and Betty Blake, eds., *New York Theatre Critics' Reviews, 1971*, vol. 32, no. 9 (New York: Critics' Theatre Reviews, 1971), 309–14.

64. "C'est comme Bergson que l'un de mes biographes m'attribue comme

source directe et que je n'ai absolument pas lu! Bergson, je ne connais pas!" "Entretien avec Alain Resnais sur *Mon oncle d'Amérique*," in Benayoun, *Alain Resnais arpenteur de l'imaginaire*, 251.

65. Ward, *Alain Resnais*, 113.

66. See Secrest, *Stephen Sondheim*, 265–66 and 274 about Sondheim's use of alcohol and drugs as a stimulant for his work.

67. Ward, *Alain Resnais*, 117.

68. Ward, *Alain Resnais*, 118.

69. Monaco, *Alain Resnais*, 11.

70. Douchet, *French New Wave*, 187.

71. Ward, *Alain Resnais*, 89 and 15.

72. Monaco, *Alain Resnais*, 87.

73. Ward, *Alain Resnais*, 17.

74. T. E. Kalem, "Seascape with Frieze of Girls," *Time*, April 12, 1971, 78. At the end of the review, Kalem quotes from Proust, perhaps forgetting Ben's lyric from "Live, Laugh, Love": "Some try to be profound / By quoting Proust and Pound."

75. Stefan Kanfer, "Hommage à Proust," *Time*, April 12, 1971, 94. Kanfer continues: "Directors such as Karel Reisz *(Isadora)* and Alain Renais [*sic*] *(La Guerre Est Finie)* acknowledge their debt to [Proust] in every temporal experiment, in every dissection of memory." Resnais, however, denied Proust any pride of place in his concept of time and space. "Dès dix, treize ans, j'ai été fasciné par le cinéma . . . Je n'ai jamais été quoiqu'on fasciné par Proust. J'ai lu tout Proust une seule fois dans ma vie, et je l'ai avalé d'un coup, en une semaine je n'ai rien fait d'autre. Je ne l'ai plus jamais rouvert, l'ombre de Proust depuis ne s'est jamais manifestée à moi, et je n'ai pas la sensation qu'il m'ait influencé en quoi que ce soit." As quoted in Benayoun, *Alain Resnais arpenteur de l'imaginaire*, 16.

76. Ward, *Alain Resnais*, 16.

77. "Sondheim at Telluride."

78. Monaco, *Alain Resnais*, 74.

79. Bersani, *Arts of Impoverishment*, 191, 194.

80. Monaco, *Alain Resnais*, 86–87.

81. Monaco, *Alain Resnais*, 89.

82. Roy Armes, *The Cinema of Alain Resnais* (London: A. Zwemmer, 1968), 77.

83. Armes, *Cinema of Alain Resnais*, 20 and 26. Resnais: "*Apollon Musagète* est pour moi une oeuvre capitale." As quoted in Benayoun, *Alain Resnais arpenteur de l'imaginaire*, 65.

84. As quoted in Armes, *Cinema of Alain Resnais*, 78. Resnais encouraged Marguerite Duras to write the screenplay for *Hiroshima* as if she were setting to music a piece originally meant for the theater, "comme Debussy avec le *Pelléas et Mélisande* de Maeterlinck." Benayoun, *Alain Resnais arpenteur de l'imaginaire*, 63.

85. As quoted in Monaco, *Alain Resnais*, 73. In "Entretien avec Alain Resnais sur *La guerre est finie*," Resnais remarked: "On a dit, aussi bien d'*Hiroshima* que de *Marienbad*, que c'était une espèce d'opéra sans musique." In Benayoun, *Alain Resnais arpenteur de l'imaginaire*, 223.

86. "Oui, j'ai déjà dit que j'avais disposé d'un quintette où Ellen Burnstyn [*sic*] serait le violon, Dirk Bogarde le piano, David Warner serait l'alto, Gielgud le violoncelle et Elaine Stritch la contrebasse. En somme une formation à la Schubert, bien que la sonorité interne du film soit plus proche d'Alban Berg ou de Bartók avec ses ruptures soudaines, ses alternances d'amer et de sucré." "Entretien avec Alain Resnais sur *Providence*," 243. A portion of Resnais's remarks are quoted in Bersani, *Arts of Impoverishment*, 206.

87. In his "Entretien avec Alain Resnais sur *L'amour à mort*," 261–67, Resnais spoke at length about his work with Henze as well as his appreciation for the Second Viennese School (in particular, "un très beau Trio de Schoenberg") and Mahler. In Benayoun, *Alain Resnais arpenteur de l'imaginaire*, 261–67.

88. Cowie, *Antonioni, Bergman, Resnais*, 150.

89. In the credits to *Toute la mémoire du monde* (1956), Resnais listed Chester Gould in the credits as one of the collaborators. According to Armes, Resnais discovered Gould and Dick Tracy around 1932. See Armes, *Cinema of Alain Resnais*, 22–24.

90. Armes, *Cinema of Alain Resnais*, 26–27.

91. Zadan, *Sondheim & Co.*, 296.

92. Zadan, *Sondheim & Co.*, 296–97.

93. Armes, *Cinema of Alain Resnais*, 39–40, 42, and 45.

94. See Alain Fleischer, *L'art d'Alain Resnais* (Paris: Centre Georges Pompidou, 1998).

95. Armes, *Cinema of Alain Resnais*, 42.

96. Rich, "Conversations with Sondheim." Sondheim: "I am not likely to be interested in something that doesn't try something new, because it is fun to explore unexplored territory and boring to go some place you've been." Sondheim, "Collaboration," 30–31.

97. "Sondheim Q & A: Part I," 13.

98. Swayne, "Hearing Sondheim's Voices," 348.

99. Banfield, *Sondheim's Broadway Musicals*, 25.

100. Mielziner, *Designing for the Theatre*, 9.

101. "Sondheim at Telluride."

102. Anthony Perkins starred in *This Angry Age* (1958; see n. 48), *Psycho* (1960), *Le glaive et la balance* (1963), *Une ravissante idiote* (1964), and *Paris brûle-t-il?* (1966), all of which predate his work on *Evening Primrose*.

103. Arthur Laurents outlined the collaboration on *West Side Story*, gave an example of how Sondheim seized a line of dialogue and "expand[ed] it into a lyric that works both dramatically and as a song," and volunteered that "[Sondheim] wrote lyrics that could be sung only by the characters they were written for at that moment—one of the many reasons he is unsurpassed as a lyricist." See Laurents, *Original Story By*, 348–50.

104. Gottfried, *Broadway Musicals*, 131 and 149.

105. See Citron, *Sondheim and Lloyd-Webber*, 156–58.

106. See Lois Kivesto, "The Theatre of James Lapine: Playwright, Librettist, Director," Ph.D. diss., New York University, 2001, esp. 104, 110, 124, 141–44, 150, 169–74, 176–79, 185–86, 231–32, and 382–86.

107. See Ilson, *Harold Prince*, 160–71, for Sondheim's role in shaping *Com-*

pany; Laurents, *Original Story By*, 219, for his desire not to be influenced by Laurents; and Lawrence, *Dance with Demons*, 247–48 and 343–44, for his opinions of Jerome Robbins.

108. Rich, "Conversations with Sondheim."

Chapter 6: Putting It Together

1. Sondheim, "The Musical Theater," 18, 19 and 24.

2. Audio commentary from Stephen Sondheim and James Lapine, *Sunday in the Park with George*, Image Entertainment/Brandman Productions, ID4586MBDVD, 1986, 1999. The commentary dates from 1999 and includes Mandy Patinkin (George) and Bernadette Peters (Dot/Marie).

3. Horowitz, *Sondheim on Music*, 187–340.

4. Paul McKibbins, "Protecting and Promoting Sondheim's Songs," *Sondheim Review* 4, no. 2 (1997): 22.

5. Stephen Sondheim and James Lapine, *Sunday in the Park with George* (New York: Dodd, Mead, 1986), xv.

6. Originally the "first act George" had a monologue that followed "It's Hot Up Here"; see Sondheim and Lapine, *Sunday*, 115 and 174.

7. Sondheim and Lapine, *Sunday*, 124 and 143.

8. The comparisons between "second-act" George and Franklin Shepard *(Merrily We Roll Along)* are striking. They share the same dramatic trajectory, from hard-boiled cynicism to starry-eyed anticipation, even though Frank's story is told in reverse chronology. The comparison is all the more remarkable because the creative teams behind *Merrily* and *Sunday* share only Sondheim in common and because it was Lapine's idea to tell a traditional, linear story for act 2 of *Sunday*. Sondheim had originally imagined something more elliptical, in the style of a theme and variations. See the audio commentary from Sondheim and Lapine, *Sunday in the Park with George*, DVD.

9. The five that preceded *Sunday* are *Of Thee I Sing* (1932), *South Pacific* (1950), *Fiorello!* (1960), *How to Succeed in Business without Really Trying* (1962), and *A Chorus Line* (1976). *Rent* (1996) also received a Pulitzer Prize. Years given are those in which the Pulitzer Prize for Drama was awarded. The special award for *Oklahoma!* in 1944 was made at the discretion of the Pulitzer Prize Board, the drama jury having been unable to agree upon a play. See John Hohenberg, *The Pulitzer Prizes: A History of the Awards in Books, Drama, Music, and Journalism, Based on the Private Files over Six Decades* (New York: Columbia University Press, 1974), 206.

10. Joanne Gordon, *Art Isn't Easy: The Achievement of Stephen Sondheim* (Carbondale: Southern Illinois University Press, 1990), later updated and republished with the subtitle *The Theater of Stephen Sondheim* (New York: Da Capo Press, 1992); and Horowitz, *Sondheim on Music*.

11. See chap. 4, n. 69.

12. "Sondheim enjoys the implantation of French words as a means of sharpening up contrasts or connections while at the same time deliberately letting them expose his own pretensions in putting French impressionism on the

stage. In the Act 2 cocktail dialogue 'new, though' is internally rhymed with 'nouveau,' and we hear that 'tomorrow is already passé'; in the studio Dot counters George's 'more red' with 'more rouge.'" Banfield, *Sondheim's Broadway Musicals,* 369.

13. See Swayne, "So Much 'More.'"

14. See Swayne, "Sondheim's Piano Sonata," 302.

15. See Swayne, "Hindemith's Unexpected Grandson."

16. Horowitz, *Sondheim on Music,* 101.

17. Sondheim: "The entire 'Day Off' sequence is mirrored in the entire art gallery sequence." Horowitz, *Sondheim on Music,* 99.

18. Note that, in the score, the first ten notated measures are mm. a–j; the measures to which I refer are designated as mm. 1–10, when, in actuality, they are the eleventh through twentieth measures of the piece.

19. Sondheim, "The Musical Theater," 20–21.

20. For more on the Copland paper, see Swayne, "Young Copland and Younger Sondheim."

21. Sondheim, in Zadan, *Sondheim & Co.,* 270.

22. Banfield, *Sondheim's Broadway Musicals,* 328.

23. Mark Eden Horowitz, "The Score: Tender, Funny, and Highly Dramatic," *Sondheim Review* 4, no. 4 (1998): 26.

24. John Lahr, "Sondheim's Little Deaths," *Harper's,* April 1979, 71–78.

25. Sondheim and Lapine, *Sunday,* 51.

26. A cutout of the Horn Player appears after "Finishing the Hat," where it could be argued that he "heralds" Dot's pregnancy. See Sondheim and Lapine, *Sunday,* 72, as well as no. 16, "Bustle," in the piano-vocal score. The cutout also emerges in the act 1 finale, "Sunday," where the book indicates that "the horn sounds" (102). See also Horowitz, *Sondheim on Music,* where Sondheim agreed that the horn call "grew out of . . . seeing that character in that painting" (102). The Horn Player's lack of development ultimately is a concession to the exigencies of the theater; Sondheim said that they could not afford an extra actor if he didn't double. Sondheim, personal communication with the author, December 22, 2003.

27. Banfield, *Sondheim's Broadway Musicals,* 376.

28. Sondheim, "The Musical Theater," 13–14 (ellipsis and italics in original).

29. Banfield, *Sondheim's Broadway Musicals,* 124.

30. See the discussion of these songs in Swayne, "Hearing Sondheim's Voices," 75–110.

31. See my article, "The *Woods* Score: Simple, Yet Enchanting," *Sondheim Review* 8, no. 4 (2002): 14–15.

32. See Swayne, "Hearing Sondheim's Voices," 120–58.

33. See Swayne, "Hearing Sondheim's Voices," 224–34. In addition to this relationship, Giorgio's confession to Fosca that "No one has ever loved me as deeply as you" is both a textual setting of Fosca's offstage piano solo and an inversion of her profession in "Loving You."

34. John Simon: "Stephen Sondheim's score [to . . . *Forum*] remains his best because it is his least pretentious" (*Uneasy Stages,* 391).

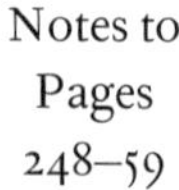

35. Sondheim, "The Musical Theater," 25.

36. For more on Sondheim's use of this in *Into the Woods*, see Swayne, "The *Woods* Score," 14–15.

37. "Sondheim Q & A: Part II," 10.

38. For "geometric," see Sondheim, "The Musical Theater," 22 (or the "Contrapuntal Harmonies" section in chap. 3). What follows is an abbreviated version of material from Swayne, "Hearing Sondheim's Voices," 188–209.

39. "Sondheim Q & A: Part II," 12.

40. Sondheim, "The Musical Theater," 21.

41. A different version of this story appears in Horowitz, *Sondheim on Music*, 99.

42. Sondheim, "The Musical Theater," 25 (ellipsis in original).

43. Audio commentary from Sondheim and Lapine, *Sunday in the Park with George*, DVD.

44. "Sondheim Q & A: Part I," 14.

45. Frommer and Frommer, *It Happened on Broadway*, 279.

46. Zadan, *Sondheim & Co.*, 387.

47. Horowitz, *Sondheim on Music*, 135.

Appendix

1. See Huber, "Sondheim and Prince," 7 and 12–13. Jones, *Our Musicals, Ourselves*, cites Huber citing Gottfried (270–71).

2. Gordon, *Art Isn't Easy* (1992), 7.

3. As quoted in Jones, *Our Musicals, Ourselves*, 270.

4. See Marlowe and Blake, *New York Critics' Reviews, 1970*, 261.

5. See Marlowe and Blake, *New York Critics' Reviews, 1971*, 310–11.

6. Gottfried, *Broadway Musicals*, 108–20.

7. Miller, "*Assassins* and Concept Musical," esp. 187–91. Miller says that *Company* and *Assassins* are "pure" representations of the concept musical "in which linear storytelling is completely discarded in favor of exploring one central idea."

8. Dan J. Cartmell, "Stephen Sondheim and the Concept Musical," Ph.D. diss., University of California, Santa Barbara, 1983, 1 (see also 93–131).

9. Citron, *Sondheim and Lloyd-Webber*, 42.

10. Hirsch, *Kurt Weill on Stage*, 297.

11. Zadan, *Sondheim & Co.*, 388.

12. Flatley, "When Sondheim Writes," 69.

13. Cartmell, "Sondheim and Concept Musical," 104.

14. Sondheim, "The Musical Theater," 13–14 (see also 15–16).

15. Cartmell, "Sondheim and Concept Musical," 104–5.

16. Cartmell, "Sondheim and Concept Musical," 94–95.

Bibliography

Adler, Thomas. "The Sung and the Said: Literary Value in the Musical Dramas of Stephen Sondheim." In *Reading Stephen Sondheim: A Collection of Critical Essays*, ed. Sandor Goodhart, 37–60. New York: Garland, 2000.

Alpert, Hollis. *The Life and Times of "Porgy and Bess": The Story of an American Classic*. New York: Alfred A. Knopf, 1990.

Anderson, Maxwell. *Dramatist in America: Letters of Maxwell Anderson, 1912–1958*. Ed. Laurence G. Avery. Chapel Hill: University of North Carolina Press, 1977.

Armes, Roy. *The Cinema of Alain Resnais*. London: A. Zwemmer, 1968.

———. *French Cinema*. New York: Oxford University Press, 1985.

Banfield, Stephen. "Copland and the Broadway Sound." In *Copland Connotations: Studies and Interviews*, ed. Peter Dickinson, 153–64. Woodbridge, Suffolk: Boydell Press, 2002.

———. "Sondheim and the Art That Has No Name." In *Approaches to the American Musical*, ed. Robert Lawson-Peebles, 137–60. Exeter: University of Exeter Press, 1996.

———. *Sondheim's Broadway Musicals*. Ann Arbor: University of Michigan Press, 1993.

Barnes, Clive. "*Porgy & Bess* and How! Gershwin Opera Hits Great Stage of Music Hall." In *New York Theatre Critics' Reviews, 1983*, ed. Joan Marlowe and Betty Blake, vol. 44, no. 5, 318. New York: Critics' Theatre Reviews, 1983.

Bellman, Willard F. *Scenography and Stage Technology: An Introduction*. New York: Thomas Y. Crowell, 1977.

Benayoun, Robert. *Alain Resnais arpenteur de l'imaginaire: De Hiroshima à Mélo*. Paris: Stock, 1980.

Benjamin, George. "Last Dance: Ravel's *La valse*." *Musical Times*, July 1994, 432–37.

Bernstein, Leonard. "Why Don't You Run Upstairs and Write a Nice Gershwin Tune?" In *The Joy of Music*, 52–62. New York: Simon and Schuster, 1959.

Bersani, Leo. *Arts of Impoverishment: Beckett, Rothko, Resnais*. Cambridge: Harvard University Press, 1993.

Block, Geoffrey. *Enchanted Evenings: The Broadway Musical from "Show Boat" to Sondheim*. New York: Oxford University Press, 1997.

———, ed. *The Richard Rodgers Reader*. Oxford: Oxford University Press, 2002.

Bordman, Gerald. *American Musical Theatre: A Chronicle*. 3d ed. New York: Oxford University Press, 2001.

Canby, Vincent. "Admirers and Fans, Take Note: *Passion* Will Divide You." *New York Times*, May 15, 1994, H1 et passim.

———. "Innovative Sondheim, Past and Present." *New York Times*, June 19, 1994, H5.

"Cap and Bells Season, 1949–50." *1950 Gul* (Williams College yearbook), 127.

Cartmell, Dan J. "Stephen Sondheim and the Concept Musical." Ph.D. diss., University of California, Santa Barbara, 1983.

Ceplair, Larry. "SAG and the Motion Picture Blacklist." http://www.sag.com/blacklist.html, accessed March 26, 2003.

Chapin, Ted. *Everything Was Possible: The Birth of the Musical "Follies."* New York: Alfred A. Knopf, 2003.

Citron, Stephen. *Sondheim and Lloyd-Webber: The New Musical*. Oxford: Oxford University Press, 2001.

"Comments on 'Songs I Wish I'd Have Written (at Least in Part).'" *New York Times Magazine*, March 12, 2000, 40–43.

Cowie, Peter. *Antonioni, Bergman, Resnais*. London: Tantivy Press, 1963.

DeVoto, Mark. "Harmony in the Chamber Music." In *The Cambridge Companion to Ravel*, ed. Deborah Mawer, 97–117. Cambridge: Cambridge University Press, 2000.

Dorfman, Joseph. "Counterpoint-Sonata Form." *Hindemith-Jahrbuch* 19 (1990): 55–67.

Douchet, Jean, in collaboration with Cédric Anger. *French New Wave*. Trans. Robert Bonnono. New York: Distributed Art Publishers, 1999.

Flatley, Guy. "When Stephen Sondheim Writes Words and Music, Some Critics Don't Leave the Theater Humming." *People*, April 5, 1976, 66–70.

Fleischer, Alain. *L'art d'Alain Resnais*. Paris: Centre Georges Pompidou, 1998.

Fordin, Hugh *Getting to Know Him: A Biography of Oscar Hammerstein II*. Introduction by Stephen Sondheim. New York: Da Capo, 1995.

Forte, Allen. *The American Popular Ballad of the Golden Era, 1924–1950*. Princeton: Princeton University Press, 1995.

Frommer, Myrna Katz, and Harvey Frommer. *It Happened on Broadway: An Oral History of the Great White Way*. Madison: University of Wisconsin Press, 2004.

Gale, Robert L. *A Dashiell Hammett Companion*. Westport, Conn.: Greenwood Press, 2000.

Garofalo, Reebee. *Rockin' Out: Popular Music in the USA*. 2d ed. Upper Saddle River, N.J.: Prentice-Hall, 2002.

Gilbert, Steven E. *The Music of Gershwin*. New Haven: Yale University Press, 1995.

———. "Nice Work: Thoughts and Observations on Gershwin's Last Songs." In *The Gershwin Style: New Looks at the Music of George Gershwin*, ed. Wayne Schneider, 67–94. New York: Oxford University Press, 1999.

Gold, Sylviane. "A Lot More Sondheim, a Little More Dancing." *Dance*, February 2002, 30.

Goldman, James, and Stephen Sondheim. *Follies*. New York: Random House, 1971.

Goldstein, Malcolm. *George S. Kaufman: His Life, His Theater*. New York: Oxford University Press, 1979.

Goodman, Walter. *The Committee: The Extraordinary Career of the House Committee on Un-American Activities*. New York: Farrar, Straus and Giroux, 1968.

Gordon, Joanne. *Art Isn't Easy: The Theater of Stephen Sondheim*. New York: Da Capo Press, 1992.

Gordon, Mel. *The Grand Guignol: Theatre of Fear and Terror*. New York: Amok Press, 1988.

Gottfried, Martin. *Broadway Musicals*. New York: Abradale Press/Harry N. Abrams, 1984.

Grant, Annette. "Line by Line by Sondheim: One Song, Start to Finish: A Music Lesson." *New York Times Magazine*, March 20, 1994, 41–43.

Green, Jesse. "A Complicated Gift." *New York Times Magazine*, July 6, 2003, http://www.nytimes.com/2003/07/06/magazine/06GUETTEL.html?ex=1058756584&ei=1&en=082a733898b4bc62, accessed July 9, 2003.

Greenspan, Charlotte. "*Rhapsody in Blue:* A Study in Hollywood Hagiography." In *The Gershwin Style: New Looks at the Music of George Gershwin*, ed. Wayne Schneider, 145–59. New York: Oxford University Press, 1999.

Hamm, Charles. "The Theatre Guild Production of *Porgy and Bess*." *Journal of the American Musicological Society* 40 (fall 1987): 495–532.

Hammerstein, Oscar, II. *Allegro: A Musical Play*. New York: Alfred A. Knopf, 1948.

Hanson, Laura. "Elements of Modernism in the Musicals of Stephen Sondheim." Ph.D. diss., New York University, 2001.

Harnick, Sheldon. "What Comes First in a Musical? The Libretto." In *Playwrights, Lyricists, Composers, on Theatre*, ed. Otis Guernsey Jr., 38–44. New York: Dodd, Mead, 1974.

Harvey, Robert, and Hélène Volat. *Marguerite Duras: A Bio-Bibliography*. Westport, Conn.: Greenwood Press, 1997.

Hedges, Inez. "Form and Meaning in the French Film, I: Time and Space." *French Review* 54, no. 1 (1980): 28–36.

Henderson, Mary C. *Mielziner: Master of Modern Stage Design*. New York: Back Stage Books, 2001.

Henry, William A., III. "The Century, Tryst by Tryst." *Time*, February 14, 1994, 67.

Herman, Jerry. "Jerry Herman in Conversation with Sheldon Harnick." In *Broadway Song & Story: Playwrights / Lyricists / Composers Discuss Their Hits*, ed. Otis Guernsey Jr., 197–209. New York: Dodd, Mead, 1985.

Hinton, Stephen. "Hindemith: Pedagogy and Personal Style." *Hindemith-Jahrbuch* 17 (1988): 54–67.

Hirsch, Foster. *Kurt Weill on Stage: From Berlin to Broadway*. New York: Alfred A. Knopf, 2002.

Hohenberg, John. *The Pulitzer Prizes: A History of the Awards in Books, Drama, Music, and Journalism, Based on the Private Files over Six Decades*. New York: Columbia University Press, 1974.

Holden, Stephen. "Some Witchcraft from Cy Coleman and Friends." *New York Times*, January 24, 2002, http://www.nytimes.com/2002/01/24/arts/music/24POPS.html, accessed August 20, 2002.

Horowitz, Joseph. *Understanding Toscanini*. Minneapolis: University of Minnesota Press, 1987.

Horowitz, Mark Eden. "The Score: Tender, Funny and Highly Dramatic." *Sondheim Review* 4, no. 4 (1998): 24–26.

———. *Sondheim on Music: Minor Details and Major Decisions*. Lanham, Md.: Scarecrow Press, 2003.

Huber, Eugene Robert. "Stephen Sondheim and Harold Prince: Collaborative Contributions to the Development of the Modern Concept Musical, 1970–1981." Ph.D. diss., New York University, 1990.

Hyland, William G. *Richard Rodgers*. New Haven: Yale University Press, 1998.

Ilson, Carol. *Harold Prince: From "Pajama Game" to "The Phantom of the Opera" and Beyond*. New York: Limelight Editions, 1992.

Jablonski, Edward. *Harold Arlen: Happy with the Blues*. New York: Da Capo, 1986.

———. *Harold Arlen: Rhythm, Rainbows, & Blues*. Boston: Northeastern University Press, 1996.

Johnson, John Andrew. "Gershwin's *Blue Monday* (1922) and the Promise of Success." In *The Gershwin Style: New Looks at the Music of George Gershwin*, ed. Wayne Schneider, 111–41. New York: Oxford University Press, 1999.

Jones, John Bush. *Our Musicals, Ourselves: A Social History of the American Musical Theatre*. Lebanon, N.H.: Brandeis University Press, 2003.

Kalem, T. E. "Seascape with Frieze of Girls." *Time*, April 12, 1971, 78.

Kanfer, Stefan. "Hommage à Proust." *Time*, April 12, 1971, 94.

Kaplan, James. "The Cult of Saint Stephen Sondheim." *New York*, April 4, 1994, 48–54.

Kaufman, George S., and Marc Connelly. *Beggar on Horseback: A Play in Two Parts*. New York: Boni and Liveright, 1924.

Keller, James M. "*Sweeney Todd, the Demon Barber of Fleet Street:* A Musical Thriller." Brochure notes for *Sweeney Todd*, Live at the New York Philharmonic. Compact disc: NYP 2001/2002. 14–23.

Kimmel, Bruce. Notes for *Sondheim at the Movies: Songs from the Screen*. Varèse Sarabande VSD-5805, 1997, (6), CD format.

Kivesto, Lois. "The Theatre of James Lapine: Playwright, Librettist, Director." Ph.D. diss., New York University, 2001.

Koppes, Clayton R., and Gregory D. Black. *Hollywood Goes to War*. New York: Free Press, 1987.

Kowalke, Kim H. Review of Joanne Gordon, ed., *Stephen Sondheim: A Casebook*. *Theatre Journal* 50, no. 4 (1998), http://muse.jhu.edu/journals/theatre_journal/v050/50.4br_gordon.html, accessed November 17, 2004.

———. "*The Threepenny Opera:* The Score Adapted." In Kurt Weill and Bertolt Brecht, *"Die Dreigroschenoper": A Facsimile of the Holograph Full Score*, ed. Edward Harsh, series 4, vol. 1 of *The Kurt Weill Edition*, managing editor, Edward Harsh. New York: Kurt Weill Foundation for Music, 1996.

LaChiusa, Michael John. "Genre Confusion." *Opera News*, August 2002, 12 et passim.

Lahr, John. "Sondheim's Little Deaths." *Harper's*, April 1979, 71–78.

Laurents, Arthur. *Original Story By: A Memoir of Broadway and Hollywood*. New York: Alfred A. Knopf, 2000.

Laurents, Arthur, and Stephen Sondheim. *Anyone Can Whistle*. New York: Leon Amiel, 1976.

Lawrence, Greg. *Dance with Demons: The Life of Jerome Robbins*. New York: G. P. Putnam's Sons, 2001.

Leacock, Stephen. "Gertrude the Governess: or, Simple Seventeen." In *Nonsense Novels*, 71–90. New York: Dodd, Mead, 1927.

Levine, Lawrence W. *The Unpredictable Past: Explorations in American Cultural History*. New York: Oxford, 1993.

Madison, William V. Review of *Sweeney Todd*, performed by the Chicago Lyric Opera. *Opera News*, March 2003, 83–84.

Mandelbaum, Ken. "The Year of the Wild Party." http://www.broadway.com/printablestory.cfm?id=51, accessed November 28, 2000.

Mawer, Deborah. "Ballet and the Apotheosis of the Dance." In *The Cambridge Companion to Ravel*, ed. Deborah Mawer, 140–61. Cambridge: Cambridge University Press, 2000.

McBrien, William. *Cole Porter: A Biography*. New York: Alfred A. Knopf, 1998.

McKibbins, Paul. "Protecting and Promoting Sondheim's Songs." *Sondheim Review* 4, no. 2 (1997): 22.

McKinley, James. *Assassination in America*. New York: Harper and Row, 1977.

Meredith, Scott. *George S. Kaufman and His Friends*. Garden City, N.Y.: Doubleday, 1974.

Michener, Charles, et al. "Words and Music—by Sondheim." *Newsweek*, April 23, 1973, 54–64.

Mielziner, Jo. *Designing for the Theatre*. New York: Atheneum, 1965.

Miller, Scott. "*Assassins* and the Concept Musical." In *Stephen Sondheim: A Casebook*, ed. Joanne Gordon, 187–204. New York: Garland, 1997.

Mitchell, Elvis. "Sondheim, Film Devotee, Shapes Telluride Festival." *New York Times*, August 28, 2003, http://www.nytimes.com/2003/08/28/movies/28SOND.html?ex=1063072681&ei=1&en=209152758cea07a2, accessed August 31, 2004.

Monaco, James. *Alain Resnais*. New York: Oxford University Press, 1979.

Most, Andrea. "'You've Got to Be Carefully Taught': The Politics of Race in Rodgers and Hammerstein's *South Pacific*." *Theatre Journal* 52, no. 3 (2000): 307–37.

Naremore, James. *More Than Night: Film Noir and Its Contexts*. Berkeley and Los Angeles: University of California Press, 1998.

Nauert, Paul. "Theory and Practice in *Porgy and Bess:* The Gershwin-Schillinger Connection." *Musical Quarterly* 78 (1994): 9–33.

Naughtie, James. "Sharp Operator." *London Times*, December 20, 2003, http://www.timesonline.co.uk/printFriendly/0,,1–1406–936249,00.html, accessed December 20, 2003.

Neumeyer, David. "Hindemith and His American Critics: A Postmodern View." *Hindemith-Jahrbuch* 27 (1998): 218–34.

———. *The Music of Paul Hindemith*. New Haven: Yale University Press, 1986.

Oja, Carol. "Gershwin and American Modernists of the 1920s." *Musical Quarterly* 78 (1994): 646–68.

Orenstein, Arbie, ed. *A Ravel Reader: Correspondence, Articles, Interviews*. New York: Columbia University Press, 1990.

Perrin, Edwin N. "*All That Glitters* Shiner for Cap and Bells, Cast." *Williams Record*, March 23, 1949, 4.

Phillips, Michael. "Theater Review: *Bounce* at Goodman Theatre," *Chicago Tribune*, July 1, 2003. http://metromix.chicagotribune.com/templates/misc/printstory.jsp?slug=mmx-030701-stagereviewbounce§ion=%2Freviews%2Fcritics, accessed July 1, 2003.

Pollack, Howard. *Aaron Copland: The Life and Work of an Uncommon Man*. New York: Henry Holt, 1999.

Pollack, Rhoda-Gale. *George S. Kaufman*. Boston: Twayne, 1988.

Popular Song: Soundtrack of the Century. Episode 7: "Soundtracks." Bravo Network. N.d.

Poulton, Alan. "Sondheim's Island Choice." *Sondheim News*, April 2001, 7.

Pressley, Nelson. "A Darker *Passion:* Sondheim's Solid Music of Obsession." *Washington Post*, July 23, 2002, C1.

———. "*Thou Shalt Not:* Sins and Lovers." *Washington Post*, October 26, 2001, C1 et passim.

Prince, Harold, and Stephen Sondheim. "Author and Director: Musicals." In *Broadway Song and Story: Playwrights / Lyricists / Composers Discuss Their Hits*, ed. Otis Guernsey Jr., 355–70. New York: Dodd, Mead, 1985.

Puccio, Paul. "Enchantment on the Manicured Lawns: The Shakespearean 'Green World' in *A Little Night Music*." In *Reading Stephen Sondheim: A Collection of Critical Essays*, ed. Sandor Goodhart, 133–69. New York: Garland, 2000.

Reich, Willi. *Alban Berg's "Wozzeck": A Guide to the Text and Music of the Opera*. New York: Schirmer, 1952.

Resnais, Alain. "Interview with Alain Resnais." By Richard Seaver. In *Stavisky . . .* , text by Jorge Semprun, for the film by Alain Resnais, trans., Sabine Destrée, 151–63. New York: Viking, 1975.

Rich, Frank. "Conversations with Sondheim." *New York Times Magazine*, March 12, 2000, 38 et passim.

Rich, Frank, with Lisa Aronson. *The Theatre Art of Boris Aronson*. New York: Alfred A. Knopf, 1987.

Richter, Eckhart. "Training Prospective Composers to be *Compleat* Musicians: Hindemith's Teaching at the Berlin Musikhochschule." *Hindemith-Jahrbuch* 20 (1991): 26–70.

Rizzo, Frank. "Sunday on a Campus with Sondheim." *Sondheim Review* 3, no. 4 (1997): 4.

Rodgers, Richard. *Musical Stages: An Autobiography*. New York: Random House, 1975.

"Russ." "College Show, *All That Glitters*." *Variety*, March 23, 1949, 52.

Sadie, Stanley, ed. *The New Grove Dictionary of Music and Musicians*. London: Macmillan, 1980.

Salsini, Paul. "Sondheim, on Campus, Talks about Opening Doors." *Sondheim Review* 1, no. 3 (1995): 6.

Schlesinger, Sarah. *Music Theatre International Study Guide for Sondheim & Weidman's* "Assassins." New York: MTI, 1993.

Secrest, Meryle. *Somewhere for Me: A Biography of Richard Rodgers*. New York: Alfred A. Knopf, 2001.

———. *Stephen Sondheim: A Life*. New York: Alfred A. Knopf, 1998.

Shevelove, Burt, Larry Gelbart, and Stephen Sondheim. *A Funny Thing Happened on the Way to the Forum*. Introduction by Larry Gelbart. New York: Applause, 1991.

Shirley, Wayne. "'Rotating' *Porgy and Bess*." In *The Gershwin Style: New Looks at the Music of George Gershwin*, ed. Wayne Schneider, 21–34. New York: Oxford University Press, 1999.

Shivers, Alfred S. *The Life of Maxwell Anderson*. New York: Stein and Day, 1983.

Simon, John. *Uneasy Stages: A Chronicle of the New York Theater, 1963–1973*. New York: Random House, 1975.

Singer, Barry. "Pop Self-Consciousness Finally Infiltrates Broadway." *New York Times*, August 26, 2001, sec. 2, p. 10.

Sloman, Tony, ed. "The Sondheim *Guardian* Lecture." *Biased: Newsletter of the Sondheim British Information and Appreciation Society*, spring–summer 1988, 34–61.

Smith, Roch C. *Understanding Alain Robbe-Grillet*. Columbia: University of South Carolina Press, 2000.

"Sondheim Interview." *Williams Record*, March 12, 1949, 2.

Sondheim Tonight: Live from the Barbican Centre, London. Jay CDJay2 1313, 1999.

Sondheim, Stephen. *All That Glitters*. Stephen Sondheim Collection, Wisconsin Center for Film and Theater Research at the University of Wisconsin, U.S. Mss 66AN, Box 1.

———. "The Art of the Musical." *Paris Review* 142 (spring 1997): 259–78.

———. *Bequest*. Stephen Sondheim Collection, Wisconsin Center for Film and Theater Research at the University of Wisconsin, U.S. Mss 66AN, Box 19.

———. Brochure notes for Paul Weston, *The Columbia Album of Jerome Kern*. Columbia C2L-2, ca. 1957, reissued as Sony Special Projects AK 47861.

———. *By George*. Stephen Sondheim Collection, Wisconsin Center for Film and Theater Research at the University of Wisconsin, U.S. Mss 66AN, Box 5.

———. *Climb High*. Stephen Sondheim Collection, Wisconsin Center for Film and Theater Research at the University of Wisconsin, U.S. Mss 66AN, Box 5.

———. Conversation with Elvis Mitchell, as part of the Telluride Film Festi-

val, Sunday, August 31, 2003, in Telluride County Courthouse. Videotape, courtesy of Bill Pence.

———. *Desert Island Discs*. BBC Radio 4 program broadcast by the British Broadcasting Corporation, December 31, 2000.

———. "Interview with Stephen Sondheim." In David Savran, *In Their Own Words: Contemporary American Playwrights*, 223–39. New York: Theatre Communications Group, 1988.

———. "Larger Than Life: Reflections on Melodrama and *Sweeney Todd*." In *Melodrama*, ed. Daniel Gerould, *New York Literary Forum*, gen. ed. Jeanine Parisier Plottel, 3–14. New York: New York Literary Forum, 1980.

———. "The Musical Theater: A Talk by Stephen Sondheim." In *Broadway Song & Story: Playwrights / Lyricists / Composers Discuss Their Hits*, ed. Otis Guernsey Jr., 228–50. New York: Dodd, Mead, 1985.

———. "On Collaboration between Authors and Directors." *Dramatists Guild Quarterly* 16, no. 2 (1979): 14–34.

———. "Side by Side by Side (An Interview with Stephen Sondheim)." Interview by Frank Rich. *American Music* 19, no. 6 (July–August 2002): 20–24 and 68–70.

———. "Stephen Sondheim in a Q & A Session: Part I." *Dramatists Guild Quarterly* 28, no. 1 (1991): 8–15.

———. "Stephen Sondheim in a Q & A Session: Part II." *Dramatists Guild Quarterly* 28, no. 2 (1991): 10–17.

———. *Stephen Sondheim's Crossword Puzzles from "New York" Magazine*. New York: Harper Colophon, 1980.

———. "Theatre Lyrics." In *Playwrights, Lyricists, Composers, on Theatre*, ed. Otis Guernsey Jr., 61–97. New York: Dodd, Mead, 1974.

Sondheim, Stephen, and James Lapine. *Sunday in the Park with George*. New York: Dodd, Mead, 1986.

Sondheim, Stephen, James Lapine, Mandy Patinkin, and Bernadette Peters. Audio commentary for *Sunday in the Park with George*. Image Entertainment/Brandman Productions, ID4586MBDVD, 1986, 1999.

Sondheim, Stephen, and John Weidman. *Pacific Overtures*. New York: Theatre Communications Group, 1991.

Sondheim, Stephen, John Weidman, and Loren Sherman. *"Assassins": An MTI Video Conversationpiece*. New York: MTI Enterprises, 1991.

Soter, Tom. *Investigating Couples: A Critical Analysis of "The Thin Man," "The Avengers," and "The X-Files."* Jefferson, N.C.: McFarland, 2002.

Straus, Joseph. *Remaking the Past: Musical Modernism and the Influence of the Tonal Tradition*. Cambridge: Harvard University Press, 1990.

Suleiman, Susan. "The Parenthetical Function in *A la recherche du temps perdu*." *Proceedings of the Modern Language Association* 92, no. 3 (1977): 458–70.

Suskin, Steven. *More Opening Nights on Broadway: A Critical Quotebook of the Musical Theatre, 1965 through 1981*. New York: Schirmer, 1997.

Swayne, Steven Robert. "Hearing Sondheim's Voices." Ph.D. diss., University of California, Berkeley, 1999.

Swayne, Steve. "Hindemith's Unexpected Grandson." *Hindemith-Jahrbuch* 32 (2003): 215–34.

———. "In Search of the Gay American Musical." *Journal of Homosexuality* 43, no. 1 (2002): 99–111.

———. "*Music for the Theatre,* the Young Copland, and the Younger Sondheim." *American Music* 20, no. 1 (2002): 80–101.

———. "The Score: Brilliance under the Simplicity." *Sondheim Review* 10, no. 2 (2003): 10–11.

———. "So Much 'More': The Music of *Dick Tracy.*" *American Music* 22 (2004): 50–63.

———. "Sondheim: An American Composer Only a British Musicologist Can Love?" *Indiana Theory Review* 21 (spring–fall 2000): 231–52.

———. "Sondheim's Piano Sonata." *Journal of the Royal Musical Association* 127 (2002): 258–304.

———. "The *Woods* Score: Simple, Yet Enchanting." *Sondheim Review* 8, no. 4 (2002): 14–15.

Teachout, Terry. "Sondheim's Operas." *Commentary,* May 2003, 57–61.

"Thursday in the Park with Georges." *Chicago Tribune,* August 8, 2003, 1.

Tommasini, Anthony. "A Little Classical Music from Sondheim's Youth." *New York Times,* May 17, 2001, E5.

Viertel, Jack. "*St. Louis Woman* and the Harold Arlen Curse." Notes for Harold Arlen, *St. Louis Blues:* 1998 Original New York Cast Recording, Mercury 314 538 148–2, 1998, 12–13.

Walker, Michael. "*The Big Sleep:* Howard Hawks and Film Noir." In *The Movie Book of Film Noir,* ed. Ian Cameron, 191–202. London: Studio Vista, 1992.

———. "Film Noir: Introduction." In *The Movie Book of Film Noir,* ed. Ian Cameron, 8–38. London: Studio Vista, 1992.

Ward, John. *Alain Resnais, or the Theme of Time.* Garden City, N.Y.: Doubleday, 1968.

Weiss, Piero, ed. *Opera: A History in Documents.* New York: Oxford University Press, 2002.

Welles, Orson. *Touch of Evil.* Universal DVD 20470, 2000.

Whitfield, Stephen J. *In Search of American Jewish Culture.* Hanover, N.H.: Brandeis University Press, 1999.

Wilder, Alec. *American Popular Song: The Great Innovators, 1900–1950.* New York: Oxford University Press, 1972.

Williams, Alan. *Republic of Images: A History of French Filmmaking.* Cambridge: Harvard University Press, 1992.

"Williams College. The Class of 1950. Class History." *1950 Gul* (Williams College yearbook), 35–36.

Williams College Bulletin, December 1943, December 1944, March 1948, and March 1949.

Wilson, Steven Blair. "Motivic, Rhythmic, and Harmonic Procedures of Unification in Stephen Sondheim's *Company* and *A Little Night Music.*" D.A. diss., Ball State University, 1983.

Woll, Allen. *Black Musical Theatre: From "Coontown" to "Dreamgirls."* Baton Rouge: Louisiana State University Press, 1989.

Wood, Graham. "The Development of Song Forms in the Broadway and Hollywood Musicals of Richard Rodgers." Ph.D. diss., University of Minnesota, 2000.

"Year History." *1948 Gul* (Williams College yearbook), 122.

"Year History." *1949 Gul* (Williams College yearbook), 73.

"Year History." *1950 Gul* (Williams College yearbook), 90.

Zadan, Craig. *Sondheim & Co.* New York: Macmillan, 1974.

———. *Sondheim & Co.* 2d ed. New York: Harper and Row, 1989.

Zoglin, Richard. "Broadway and Beyond: An Uneven—but Surprisingly Good—*Thou Shalt Not.*" Time.com, October 29, 2001, www.time.com/time/sampler/article/0,85999,181810,00.html, accessed June 28, 2002.

Credits

The author has exercised all due diligence to secure permission to reproduce copyrighted material that is deemed to exceed the terms of fair use.

Music and Lyrics

"Blues in the Night" by Harold Arlen and Johnny Mercer © 1941 (Renewed) WB Music Corp. (ASCAP). All Rights Reserved. Used By Permission. Warner Bros. Publications U.S. Inc., Miami, FL 33014.

Company (all selections within) by Stephen Sondheim © 1971 (Renewed) by Quartet Music, Inc., Range Road Music, Inc., Rilting Music Company, Inc. and Burthen Music Company, Inc. All Rights Reserved. Used By Permission. Warner Bros. Publications U.S. Inc., Miami, FL 33014.

Concerto pour la main gauche by Maurice Ravel © Joint ownership REDFIELD and NORDICE. Exclusive representation by Editions DURAND, Paris, France. Reproduced by permission of Editions DURAND. All rights for the US on behalf of BMG Music Publishing France (SACEM) administered by BMG Songs, Inc (ASCAP).

"The Eagle and Me" by Harold Arlen and E. Y. Harburg © 1944 (Renewed) Chappell & Co., Inc. (ASCAP). All Rights Reserved. Used By Permission. Warner Bros. Publications U.S. Inc., Miami, FL 33014.

"Ev'ry Time We Say Goodbye" by Cole Porter © 1944 (Renewed) Chappell & Co., Inc. (ASCAP). All Rights Reserved. Used By Permission. Warner Bros. Publications U.S. Inc., Miami, FL 33014.

Follies (all selections within) by Stephen Sondheim © 1971 Herald Square Music, Range Road Music, Inc., Quartet Music Inc. and Rilting Music, Inc. All Rights On Behalf Of Herald Square Music, Range Road Music, Inc., Quartet Music Inc. and Rilting Music. Administered by WB Music Corp. All Rights Reserved. Used By Permission. Warner Bros. Publications U.S. Inc., Miami, FL 33014.

Gypsy (all selections within). Lyrics by STEPHEN SONDHEIM. Music by JULE STYNE. © 1959 by Norbeth Productions, Inc., and Stephen Sondheim. Copyright renewed. Publication and Allied Rights Assigned to WILLIAMSON MUSIC CO. and STRATFORD MUSIC CORPORATION and Administered by CHAPPELL & CO. All Rights Reserved including Public Performance for Profit.

"I Am So Eager" by Jerome Kern and Oscar Hammerstein II Copyright © 1932, 1960 by Universal—Polygram Int. Publ., Inc. on behalf of T.B. Harms Co. (ASCAP). Used By Permission. International Copyright Secured. All Rights Reserved.

"I Had Myself a True Love" by Harold Arlen and Johnny Mercer © 1946 (Renewed) The Johnny Mercer Foundation (ASCAP) and S.A. Music Co. (ASCAP). All Rights On Behalf Of The Johnny Mercer Foundation. Administered by WB Music Corp. All Rights Reserved. Used By Permission. Warner Bros. Publications U.S. Inc., Miami, FL 33014.

Into the Woods (all selections within) by Stephen Sondheim © 1988 Rilting Music, Inc. (ASCAP). All Rights Administered by WB Music Corp. All Rights Reserved. Used By Permission. Warner Bros. Publications U.S. Inc., Miami, FL 33014.

A Little Night Music (all selections within) by Stephen Sondheim © 1973 (Renewed) Revelation Music Publishing Corp. and Rilting Music, Inc. All Rights Reserved. Used By Permission. Warner Bros. Publications U.S. Inc., Miami, FL 33014.

"Losing My Mind" by Stephen Sondheim © 1971 (Renewed) by Quartet Music, Inc., Range Road Music, Inc., Rilting Music Company, Inc. and Burthen Music Company, Inc. All Rights Reserved. Used By Permission. Warner Bros. Publications U.S. Inc., Miami, FL 33014.

"The Man I Love" by George Gershwin and Ira Gershwin © 1924 (Renewed) WB Music Corp. (ASCAP). All Rights Reserved. Used By Permission. Warner Bros. Publications U.S. Inc., Miami, FL 33014.

Merrily We Roll Along (all selections within) by Stephen Sondheim © 1981 Rilting Music, Inc. (ASCAP). All Rights On Behalf Of Rilting Music, Inc. (ASCAP). Administered by WB Music Corp. (ASCAP). All Rights Reserved. Used By Permission. Warner Bros. Publications U.S. Inc., Miami, FL 33014.

"My Friends" by Stephen Sondheim © 1979 Rilting Music, Inc. (ASCAP). All Rights On Behalf Of Rilting Music, Inc. (ASCAP). All Rights Administered by WB Music Corp. All Rights Reserved. Used By Permission. Warner Bros. Publications U.S. Inc., Miami, FL 33014.

"My Man's Gone Now" by George Gershwin, Ira Gershwin and DuBose Heyward © 1935 (Renewed) George Gershwin Music, Ira Gershwin Music and DuBose and Dorothy Heyward Memorial Fund Publishing. All Rights On Behalf Of George Gershwin Music, Ira Gershwin Music and DuBose and Dorothy Heyward Memorial Fund Publishing. Administered by WB Music Corp. All Rights Reserved. Used By Permission. Warner Bros. Publications U.S. Inc., Miami, FL 33014.

"Our State Fair" by Richard Rodgers and Oscar Hammerstein II © 1962 (Renewed) Williamson Music, Inc. (ASCAP). Administered by Chappell & Co. (ASCAP). All Rights Reserved. Used by permission. Warner Bros. Publications U.S. Inc., Miami, FL 33014.

Pacific Overtures (all selections within) by Stephen Sondheim © 1976 Rilting Music, Inc. (ASCAP). All Rights On Behalf Of Rilting Music, Inc. (ASCAP). Administered by WB Music Corp. (ASCAP). All Rights Reserved. Used By Permission. Warner Bros. Publications U.S. Inc., Miami, FL 33014.

"Side by Side by Side" by Stephen Sondheim © 1970 (Renewed) by Quartet Music, Inc., Range Road Music, Inc., Rilting Music Company, Inc. and Burthen Music Company, Inc. All Rights Reserved. Used By Permission. Warner Bros. Publications U.S. Inc., Miami, FL 33014.

"Something's Coming" by Leonard Bernstein and Stephen Sondheim © 1956 by Amberson Holdings LLC and Stephen Sondheim. Copyright renewed.

Sweeney Todd (all selections within) by Stephen Sondheim ©1979 Rilting Music, Inc. (ASCAP). All Rights On Behalf Of Rilting Music, Inc. (ASCAP) Administered by WB Music Corp. (ASCAP). All Rights Reserved. Used By Permission. Warner Bros. Publications U.S. Inc., Miami, FL 33014.

Sunday in the Park with George (all selections within) by Stephen Sondheim © 1984 Rilting Music, Inc. (ASCAP). All Rights On Behalf Of Rilting Music, Inc. (ASCAP). Administered by WB Music Corp. (ASCAP). All Rights Reserved. Used By Permission. Warner Bros. Publications U.S. Inc., Miami, FL 33014.

Symphony of Psalms by Igor Stravinsky © Copyright 1931 by Hawkes & Son (London) Ltd. Copyright Renewed. Revised version © Copyright 1948 by Hawkes & Son (London) Ltd. Copyright Renewed. Reprinted by permission of Boosey & Hawkes, Inc.

"What Can You Lose" by Stephen Sondheim © 1984 Rilting Music, Inc. (ASCAP) and Walt Disney Music Company (ASCAP). All Rights On Behalf Of Rilting Music, Inc. (ASCAP). Administered by WB Music Corp. (ASCAP). All Rights Reserved. Used By Permission. Warner Bros. Publications U.S. Inc., Miami, FL 33014

"What's the Use of Wondrin'?" by Richard Rodgers & Oscar Hammerstein II Copyright © 1945 by WILLIAMSON MUSIC. Copyright Renewed. International Copyright Secured. All Rights Reserved. Used by Permission.

Interviews, Correspondence, and Articles

Alain Resnais, Interview with Richard Seaver, from *Stavisky* by Jorge Semprún, translated by Sabine Destrée, copyright © 1974 by Editions Gallimard; English translation Copyright © 1975 by The Viking Press, Inc.; Introduction Copyright © 1975 by Richard Seaver. Used by permission of Viking Penguin, a division of Penguin Group (USA) Inc.

Letter dated October 31, 1949 from David C. Bryant to Barrett H. Clark, Executive Director, Dramatists Play Service. Letter dated November 15, 1949 from David C. Bryant to John F. Wharton, Esq. Letter dated November 23, 1949 from David C. Bryant to Mr. Maxwell Anderson. From the Cap and Bells Correspondence, Box 17, Folder 16. Williams College Archives and Special Collections.

Stephen Sondheim, excerpts from correspondence, interviews, and articles, used by permission from Mr. Sondheim.

Unpublished letter dated August 6, 1953 and undated letter from Oscar Hammerstein II to Stephen Sondheim. Reprinted by special permission from The Rodgers and Hammerstein Organization.

Index

Text design by Mary H. Sexton

Typesetting by Delmastype, Ann Arbor, Michigan

Font: Fournier MT

In 1924, Monotype based this face on types cut by Pierre Simon Fournier circa 1742. These types were some of the most influential designs of the eighteenth century, being among the earliest of the "transitional" style of typeface, and were a stepping stone to the more severe "modern" style made popular by Bodoni later in the century. Fournier has a light, clean look on the page, provides good economy in text and retains an even color.

—Courtesy www.adobe.com